In the Name of El Pueblo

A book in the series
LATIN AMERICA OTHERWISE
Languages, Empires, Nations

Series editors:
WALTER D. MIGNOLO, Duke University
IRENE SILVERBLATT, Duke University
SONIA SALDÍVAR-HULL, University of Texas, San Antonio

IN THE NAME OF EL PUEBLO

*Place, Community,
and the Politics of History
in Yucatán*

PAUL K. EISS

DUKE UNIVERSITY PRESS
Durham & London 2010

© 2010 Duke University Press

All rights reserved
Printed in the United States of America on acid-free paper ∞
Designed by Jennifer Hill
Typeset in Quadraat by Achorn International

Library of Congress Cataloging-in-Publication Data
appear on the last printed page of this book.

Todos los habitantes comentaban la hazaña de los héroes:
U NUC MA (Su respuesta fue NO)
y en honor a ellos, el pueblecito fue bautizado con ese nombre . . .
 ⅋ ANACLETO CETINA AGUILAR, *Cahtal-K'ay: Canto a Mi Pueblo*

All of the inhabitants recounted the heroes' deeds:
U NUC MA (their answer was NO)
and in their honor, the little pueblo was baptized with that name . . .

ᓚ CONTENTS

LATIN AMERICA OTHERWISE: Languages, Empires, Nations is a critical series. It aims to explore the emergence
and consequences of concepts used to define "Latin
America" while at the same time exploring the broad
interplay of political, economic, and cultural practices
that have shaped Latin American worlds. Latin America,
at the crossroads of competing imperial designs and local responses, has been construed as a geocultural and
geopolitical entity since the nineteenth century. This
series provides a starting point to redefine Latin America as a configuration of political, linguistic, cultural,
and economic intersections that demands a continu-
ous reappraisal of the role of the Americas in history,
and of the ongoing process of globalization and the
relocation of people and cultures that have characterized Latin America's experience. *Latin America Otherwise:
Languages, Empires, Nations* is a forum that confronts

established geocultural constructions, rethinks area studies and disciplinary boundaries, assesses convictions of the academy and of public policy, and correspondingly demands that the practices through which we produce knowledge and understanding about and from Latin America be subject to rigorous and critical scrutiny.

"El pueblo" is a concept commonly heard in discussions about Latin America and Latin American history; however, its complex meanings, multiple referents, bumpy transformations—and the distinctive social practices carried out in its name—have not been scrutinized. Paul K. Eiss's exceptional contribution, with its focus on Northern Yucatán, is to show how much we have missed by not taking "el pueblo's" distinctive, disputed, evolving, and interpenetrating meanings into account. To do justice to "el pueblo" requires taking its history seriously as well. Struggles to appropriate its banner incorporated a surprising range of social actors. Indigenous Maya, nonindigenous town dwellers, landowners, priests, merchants, and teachers commandeered "el pueblo" for political, economic, and ideological ends. "El pueblo's" reach extended from village to nation, and from the colonial period into the twenty-first century. *In the Name of El Pueblo* is testimony to its impact and to its importance.

◌ ACKNOWLEDGMENTS

ONE HOT DAY in October 1995 I sat on the ground by a deer carcass, off in the woods somewhere near the Yucatecan pueblo of Tetiz. After a day of tagging along with a hunting party as it pushed through the brush in one-hundred-degree heat, I was covered with dirt, twigs, and small ticks. Another man and I had each been given a trussed deer to carry back to camp in a way working people of the region practice with heavy loads from childhood: hoisted onto the back, with a rope running from the carcass over the forehead and hands. The first couple of times I tried to get the animal on my shoulders, it flopped around and threw me off balance, knocking me over. Finally, I hoisted it up and staggered forward, the coarse, brutal cord abrading my hands and forehead. I made it about one hundred feet before the deer shifted again, snapping my neck back and pulling me down, one last time, atop the carcass. While I struggled to get up, my companion continued on his way. "I'll send help," he said, leaving me to scribble field notes and take a few photographs to distract myself from my embarrassment. About an hour later, help arrived in the form of a short old man who picked up the deer like it was a bag of feathers, strapped it to his head, and trotted off toward camp. Soon we reached the other men as they rested, pouring hot water over themselves to clean off the dirt and dislodge ticks. Even before my ignominious return, the story of my "dance" with the deer carcass had begun to spread. On arrival, I went with it, reenacting my writhing fall several times, to general mirth. Over the days to come, the story of my pathetic dance began to circulate, and when it is retold, seemingly whenever I return to visit Tetiz, it still, more than a decade later, provokes laughter.

I have long struggled under the burden of this book, and if I have succeeded in carrying it or even dancing with it—however clumsily—it is only thanks to the assistance, encouragement, and inspiration of others, most notably the inhabitants of the towns, pueblos, and ex-haciendas of the Hunucmá region. In Tetiz, first the late Don Javiel Sosa Chim and then Doña Dulce María Sosa opened their houses to me. Over the course of my many visits from the early 1990s forward they and their families treated me as a friend and eventually as a family member. Don Alfredo Quintal and Don Alejandro Tzuc invited me to join their *gremios*, or guilds, and taught me much about gremios, hunting, and many other things. On Hacienda Nohuayum, the families of Don Honorio Poot Quintal and Don Leonardo Poot Chuc also welcomed me into their households and, like so many others there and in Tetiz, encouraged my efforts at learning Yucatec Maya by indulging me in impromptu lessons and long hours of conversation. Frequent visits and conversations with Don Dionisio, Pedro, and Julio Chim as well as Don Roque Chuc and Doña Tomasa Chuc also provided a wealth of insights into many things, from labor to hunting to religion and especially to the historical memories of what residents call the times of slavery and the times of liberty. In the town of Hunucmá, the teacher and poet Anacleto Cetina Aguilar shared his expertise on the history of that town in a memorable series of discussions. In too many ways to recount, the people I encountered during my fieldwork in western Yucatán shared their wisdom with me. Even if most cannot be enumerated here—to protect identities, I generally assign them the names of animals and plants similar to those I have heard used as nicknames according to local custom—I thank them for inspiring every stage of the writing of this book, from conception to completion.

While I conducted the bulk of my fieldwork in places like Tetiz, much of my time in Yucatán was spent in the state capital, Mérida, where I conducted archival research. I worked most extensively in the Archivo General del Estado de Yucatán, which has profited immeasurably from the dedicated work of Dr. Piedad Peniche Rivero and of other archival personnel, including Armando Chi, Mauricio Dzul Sánchez, Candy Flota García, and Andrea Vergoda Medina. I also relied heavily on the extensive newspaper and archival holdings of the Centro de Apoyo a la Investigación Histórica de Yucatán and am grateful to its director, Jorge Canto Alcocer, as well as to Patricia Martínez Huchim and other personnel for their assistance. I consulted the invaluable Yucatecan newspaper collection of the Biblioteca Menéndez and the photography archives of the Fototeca Pedro Guerra. I am indebted to Yucatán's office of the Secretaría de la Reforma Agraria for allowing me access to their documents and especially to Angelina Acosta Esquivel for her guidance there. Alejandra García Quintanilla of the Centro de Investigaciones Regionales "Dr. Hideo Noguchi" of the Universidad Autónoma de Yucatán provided assistance, friendship, and stimulating conversations about Yucatecan history and culture. Outside the archives, my friends Mercedes Can Castilla, Edwin Carrillo, Lilí Fernández Souza, Alberto Gamboa, Susy Peniche, Carlos Rendón, and Doña Candita Souza de Fernández made living in Mérida a pleasure, even as they helped me to adapt to living in Yucatán and to understand the complexities of Mexican history and contemporary politics. Above all, from the moment I set foot in Yucatán, Carlos Encalada González proved a friend and teacher without equal. To him I owe my command of the Spanish language, many of my friendships and contacts with other Mérida residents, and sincere gratitude for a decade of hospitality, as he invited me to stay at his home for long periods over the course of repeated visits.

This project would have been impossible to conceive, much less complete, had I not benefited from the scholarship and direct encouragement of several scholars of Yucatán. The work of Gil Joseph and Allen Wells is an indispensable starting point and a continual source of inspiration for any student of modern Yucatán, and both have offered me considerable feedback as this project has taken shape. I had the good fortune of making the acquaintance of Ben Fallaw, Christopher Gill, Matthew Restall, Terry Rugeley, and Paul Sullivan in the archives in Yucatán; all have shared documents and insights with me, and I have profited both from their scholarship and their generosity. Terry Rugeley also provided insightful feedback on an earlier draft of this book. In the library of the University of Texas at Arlington, Maritza

Arrigunaga Coello has done invaluable work in assuring the preservation of Yucatecan newspapers and other sources, and she helped me obtain access to microfilmed sources on innumerable occasions.

I conducted the initial phases of my research in Yucatán as a graduate student in the University of Michigan's Doctoral Program in Anthropology and History and am profoundly indebted to that program and to those who participated in it. I worked closely with Fernando Coronil, who in graduate seminars, as my dissertation supervisor, and over years of conversation then and thereafter has been a perceptive critic, a supportive mentor, and my friend. From our days as undergraduate roommates through travels in Mexico, graduate school, and ever since Aims McGuinness has been a constant and close friend and interlocutor. His intervention at a critical moment to help me carry this project through to completion is especially appreciated. Similarly, David Pedersen has been a comrade in arms since graduate school, and our collaborative work on questions of value has shaped many of the concerns I brought to this book. I am grateful, in ways too diverse to enumerate, to many others, including Jasmine Alinder, Marty Baker, Chandra Bhimull, David William Cohen, John Collins, Val Daniel, Nick Dirks, Laurent Dubois, Elizabeth Ferry, David Frye, Jim Herron, Britta Kallmann, Webb Keane, Oren Kosansky, Mani Limbert, Alf Luedtke, Setrag Manoukian, Steven Pierce, Anu Rao, Bill Rosenberg, Javier Sanjinés, Rebecca Scott, Julie Skurski, Genese Sodikoff, Ann Stoler, Tom Trautmann, Tom Williamson, and Tom Wolfe. I express my gratitude as well to the diverse entities that assumed the burden of funding my research and graduate training: Michigan's Anthropology and History departments as well as the Doctoral Program in Anthropology and History; the Program in Latin American and Caribbean Studies; the Rackham School of Graduate Studies; the Institute for the Humanities; and the Michigan Society of Fellows. The Jacob K. Javits Foundation provided generous support through years of graduate study, and the Fulbright–I.I.E. Dissertation Research Abroad program funded a lengthy period of research in Mexico. Some aspects of this project were supported in later years by postdoctoral grants from the N.A.E.–Spencer Foundation and by an Andrew W. Mellon Foundation "New Directions" Fellowship.

While based in part on research conducted while I was a graduate student in Ann Arbor, I also benefited greatly, as a faculty member, from further support for research and writing from Carnegie Mellon University and particularly from Carnegie Mellon's Department of History. I am especially grateful to Rick Maddox, Roger Rouse, Judith Schacter, and Donald Sutton for their support and for their comments on and engagement with this project. As friends and interlocutors, Albrecht Funk, John Soluri, and Therese Tardio have also shaped this work in more ways than I can convey. I am grateful to many others as well, including but not limited to Sonya Barclay, Raj Dasgupta, Mary Lindemann, Kate Lynch, David Miller, Lisa Tetrault, Joe Trotter, and Patrick Zimmerman as well as Jay Dwyer at Duquesne University. I also thank Reid Andrews, Alejandro de la Fuente, Len Plotnicov, Lara Putnam, and Phil Watts at the University of Pittsburgh, and James Brooks, the director of the School of Advanced Research in Santa Fe, for their engagement with my work. I am grateful to the late Michael Jimenez, who first turned me toward Latin American history when I was an undergraduate and whom I later reencountered upon my move to Pittsburgh. In our last conversation, Mike asked me a pointed question—about whether writing history is necessarily about finding and telling a story—which has haunted me and provoked the writing of this book.

Valerie Milholland, the senior editor at Duke University Press, helped me to carry this project through to publication, offering invaluable insights and encouragement along the way, and making this a much better book. I am also grateful to Associate Editor Miriam Angress, Assistant Managing Editor Mark Mastromarino, and the rest of the staff who assisted me through the processes of revision and production, as well as to the anonymous manuscript reviewers, who provided invaluable feedback and suggestions. David Prout indexed the book, and offered excellent advice in the process. I thank *Ethnology* and *Cultural Anthropology* for permission to include in this book revised and expanded versions of two articles I published in those journals ("Hunting for the Virgin: Meat, Money and Memory in Tetiz, Yucatán," *Cultural Anthropology* 17:3 (August 2002): 291–330; and "The War of the Eggs: Event, Archive and History in Yucatán's Independent Union Movement," *Ethnology*, 42:2 (Spring 2003): 87–108).

Finally, I would like to thank my family, whose support and encouragement over the course of many years made it possible for me to complete this book, despite a few staggers, slips, and falls along the way. My wife, Michal Friedman, has lived with this project almost as long as I have, has contributed innumerable insights and critiques, and has shared the burdens and pleasures of carrying it forward over the course of years of research and writing in Yucatán and in Pittsburgh. My parents, Joseph and Marjorie Eiss, have supported my peregrinations in this and other scholarly pursuits, as have the Eiss and Friedman families generally. Last, I thank my daughter, Elena Eiss, for letting me carry her on my shoulders and thus leading me to realize that my dances with deer were just practice for something else.

FROM ARCHIVE TO ASHES

AT THE CENTER of the small town of Ucú stands a sixteenth-century church and directly adjacent to it a large pile of stones and earth. The mound is probably the remains of an ancient Mayan temple platform—the work, as inhabitants generally say here as elsewhere in rural Yucatán, of *los antiguos*. Some of the stones, when I first saw the mound, had been rearranged in crisscrossing lines and painted red, white, and green, Mexico's national colors. Crosses were planted on top of the pile, which sometimes was used for church ceremonies. Ucú's mound was a presence both ancient and modern, a reformed ruin, its stones and earth subject to multiple claims to the land and its past.

Located just outside Mérida, the capital of the state of Yucatán, Ucú is the gateway to the towns, pueblos, haciendas, and woodlands of what I call the Hunucmá region, after one of its principal towns. Located in the northwestern corner of the Yucatán peninsula, the Hunucmá region, which at the beginning of the twentieth century was classified as one of Yucatán's seventeen administrative districts, is roughly thirteen hundred square kilometers in area. Today, however, the expansion of Mérida has turned the region into a periphery of the capital, one where many Hunucmá residents now work. Brisk car, bus, and taxi traffic join Mérida to Ucú, with its church, taco and meat vendors, cantinas, small shops, and rows of cinderblock houses. To the south, also adjacent to Mérida and part of the expanding zone of urbanization around the capital, is Umán, today a city in its own right ringed by factories, some of them *maquiladoras* owned by transnational companies. Farther west, though, the land opens up into a rural hinterland: scrubby brush, fields enclosed by rocky walls, industrial scale hog- and chicken-raising facilities, occasional piles of trash, and the crumbling remains of haciendas, many of them now uninhabited. A series of pueblos and towns follow, each with a small plaza surrounded by rows of cinderblock and thatched-roof homes. Farther west and north, there are sparsely wooded lands where cattle graze and where some people still scratch out a living cutting down and burning trees and bushes and planting maize, beans, and squash in the thin but ash-enriched soil. Then there is what locals call savannah, a zone of uninhabited woods leading to swamplands and some higher stands of trees. Finally, there are salt pools and the gulf shoreline: a long stretch of uninhabited beaches and mangrove swamps interrupted only by a few fishing villages, like Celestún on the western coast and Sisal directly north of the town of Hunucmá.

The inhabitants of the Hunucmá region, like those of the rest of rural Yucatán, understand many aspects of their lives in relationship to "el pueblo." A portion of the region's population lives in small villages officially denominated pueblos. Those who live on smaller settlements, like ex-haciendas, however, also frequently refer to those places as pueblos or aspire, upon sufficient growth, to assume that title; moreover, those who live in populations classified as towns (*villas*) or even cities (*ciudades*), like Umán, typically refer to them as pueblos despite their larger size. Municipal institutions of governance, public facilities like schools and town squares, and communal possessions like *ejidos*, or collective lands, are often referred to as being of el pueblo (as in *ejidos del pueblo*). Political contests from the local to the national scales are continually waged in el pueblo's name (i.e., as "the people"), one party or another claiming to represent the true interest of el pueblo against its adversaries or against the government. Religious life is oriented around the pueblos and focused on the veneration of local saints

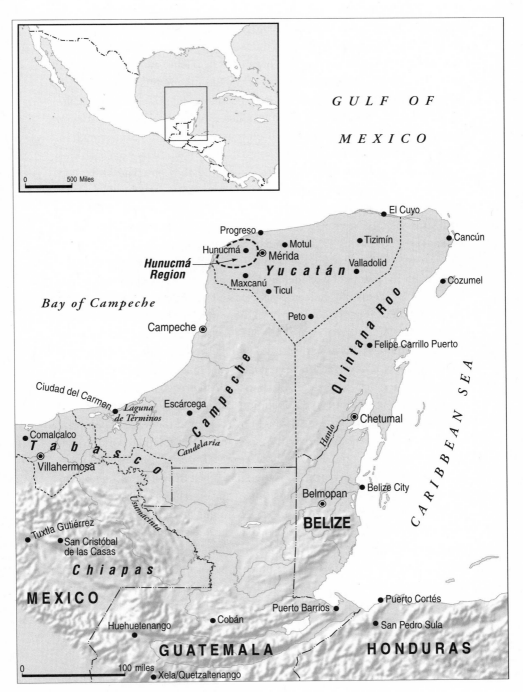

Yucatán and Mexico. Map by Philip Schwartzberg.

and icons, typically described by pueblo residents as possessions of el pueblo (as in *La Virgen del pueblo*). Traditional fiestas, processions, and other festivities, like those of *Carnaval*, are also organized by pueblo and are understood to be fundamental to the way of life of pueblo inhabitants. Where festivities are performed exuberantly and well, residents feel pride in their pueblo; where they fall into disuse or seem lackluster, older residents in particular feel that something has been lost. Even migrants, who in recent years have left the region in search of work in Mérida, Cancún, and Los Angeles, think of themselves as continuing to be part of el pueblo; they associate with fellow migrants from their home communities, send money to their families, watch videos of religious events in their places of origin, and whenever possible return for the largest annual fiestas, both to see family and friends and to renew a sense of having a pueblo and of belonging to one.

El pueblo is ubiquitous in the Hunucmá region, so much so that it seems to be taken for granted by residents as a timeless framework for social, political, and religious life. Indeed, *el pueblo* is a term of exceedingly common usage, not only in that region but throughout much of Latin America, where it is used to refer both to the most intimate forms of communal life and to the broadest mobilizations of partisan and popular politics. The apparent ubiquity of el pueblo, however, masks a complicated historical genealogy. One branch of that genealogy extends back to Spanish precedents, where pueblo refers to rural settlements and populations; such usages reach back at least to the twelfth century and were brought to Yucatán in the wake of conquest and colonization. Another branch reaches across the Atlantic world, to tap into the rhetoric of popular sovereignty, especially that of the late eighteenth century and early nineteenth, with the emergence of collective republican political subjects projected in opposition to ancien régime and colonial rule, whether in the form of *le peuple*, in St. Domingue and France; *the people*, in revolutionary North America; or *el pueblo*, in the movements of national independence throughout Spanish America, including Yucatán. A third branch—highly important in regions like Hunucmá, whose populations are largely descendants of the Maya, many of them Maya speakers themselves—has its roots in indigenous societies, with manifold forms and understandings of community, territory, and sovereignty. Those indigenous concepts endured long after the conquest, even if over time they were eventually translated into pueblo. That act of translation, however, carried with it meanings, practices, and histories that altered the meaning and compass of el pueblo, both within indigenous areas and beyond their boundaries.[1]

Tetiz, Yucatán: Procession of the Virgin of Tetiz. Photo by Paul Eiss.

Because the term *pueblo* has been in use for centuries in various areas and in various ways, the timing of its emergence as a seemingly unified rubric for communal, religious, and political collectivity in places like Hunucmá is open to question. In Yucatán, its consolidation may date only to the early twentieth century, to the years of the Mexican Revolution (1910–20) and its aftermath. In that period, el pueblo became both a political subject and a political object—the primary target of governance and mobilization for indigenous insurgents, capitalist modernizers, reformers, and revolutionary leaders, albeit in the service of markedly different agendas. Far from unifying such disparate causes, el pueblo became a focus of contention and an object of struggle, within which divergent conceptions of community and collectivity came into conflict, sometimes with great violence. In Yucatán and Mexico, and perhaps elsewhere in Latin America, el pueblo provided not only a language of solidarity but also of contention.

In other words, the examples of Latin America in general and of Yucatán in particular suggest both that el pueblo has a complex past and that it is anything but a timeless or unitary subject. Beginning from those observations, this book is an attempt—to paraphrase Bronislaw Malinowski's classic study of the Kula exchange in the Trobriand islands—at understanding the hold el pueblo has in places like Hunucmá as a framework for defining relations among people and between people and things.[2] As such, my text confronts serious analytical and historical challenges. The meaning of el pueblo is a complex matter in Spanish-speaking contexts, where that term commonly is used to refer to small population sites (typically rural villages) as well as communities (whether inhabiting such population sites or wider collectivities). In addition to its use to refer to places and forms of communal life, el pueblo" as "the people" has come to be a predominant mode for organizing collectively and for imagining collectivity in such realms as labor, politics, religion, and cultural production. Taking their cue from such common-sense understandings, anthropological, historical, and political analyses of the concept of el pueblo have tended to focus on one or another of its connotations, diverging into studies of either place (particular villages or towns and their immediate surroundings), community (whether local or broader), or popular politics ("the people").

Regarding the last and most expansive of el pueblo's meanings, namely, as a political abstraction, some consider that entity to be a primordial, or originary, framework for collective legal and political right. For Luis Villoro (1998), for instance, el pueblo is anterior to the nation-state and fundamental, in particular, to indigenous rights to self-determination, or communal sovereignty. Others have followed in the path of Edmund Burke, who in 1791 in a critique of the French Revolution described the idea of the people as "wholly artificial, and made, like all other legal fictions, by common agreement." Recently, in the context of very different analyses, "the people" has been described in ways that, similarly, stress its nature as a political construct characterized by emptiness or artifice: by Michael Hardt and Antonio Negri as a "fallacious unity"; by Ernesto Laclau as an "empty signifier" giving expression to the heterogeneous demands of opposition politics; by Jacques Rancière as a "part that has no part" defined by exclusion from the system; and by Enrique Dussel as a "strictly political" category projected in the process of creating a hegemonic bloc.[3]

Such analyses capture aspects of the workings of "the people," or el pueblo, in terms of political rhetoric and especially in the context of the unfolding of indigenous movements, and popular movements expressing the heterogeneous demands and identities of opposition politics. In projecting el pueblo, as an abstract, purely political subject, however, the philosophers may be purifying that entity of its complex entanglements in the material and social worlds in which it holds meaning and power.[4] For while the diverse meanings of el pueblo might be translated and categorized in distinct ways, in practice these meanings cannot be separated so easily. Consider the following examples: A man hacks away at underbrush, preparing to plant maize in what he has identified, despite the contending claim of a wealthy cattle rancher, as "lands of el pueblo." A rebel in the early nineteenth century declares a revolution against Spanish rule and issues a proclamation of independence decrying the "enslavement of el pueblo" and calling for its liberation. A pilgrim from the pueblo of Tetiz walks in a religious procession under a hot sun, following a religious icon of the Virgin Mary, whom she calls La Virgen del pueblo (The Virgin of El Pueblo). A woman protesting in support of striking egg farm workers throws stones at a police officer, shouting triumphantly, "You see? El pueblo has balls!"

Each of these instances illustrates how variant meanings of el pueblo may be invoked simultaneously. In the first, the cultivator might be referring to a specific town, to the community of people who live in that town, or to a specific set of material possessions, including particular areas of land, attached to that town or community. But he might also be evoking a vision of el pueblo as an impoverished or landless peasantry in contrast to another class of large landholders, or *hacendados*. In like manner the rebel, in his defense of el pueblo, might be seen as referring to a nation of people native to the Americas, as opposed to Spaniards. But el pueblo in this context might be understood by some listeners as a reference to indigenous peasants and peons who suffered exploitation by Spanish-born and native-born elites alike. The pilgrim in Tetiz might be expressing her devotion to the divine patron not just of a particular town, but also of a particular class of Christians who can be understood as differing from other Christians in terms of class, region, language, and ethnicity. The protester's sexualized retort to the police officer can similarly be read both as a defense of a particular town and more broadly of a class of impoverished and exploited workers, whether in that town or elsewhere. As these examples suggest, particular references to el pueblo may not correspond to a neat definition of that term, as *either* place *or* people *or* political abstraction. In some usages el pueblo may lodge neatly into one such domain or another, but in others it transcends such schematic distinctions.

The heterogeneity of the concept of pueblo not only presents a semantic challenge, but also makes it a difficult subject for historical study. This might seem surprising given the richness of the historical and ethnographic scholarship on Latin America. There is an abundance of work—too much to do justice to here—on indigenous history and communal life, on agrarian history, on social mobilizations and political struggle, and on race, class, ethnicity, and nation in indigenous areas of Mexico, Central America, and the Andes.[5] The scholarship on Mexico is notable for its extent and sophistication, encompassing community-level studies, ethnohistories, and close historical analysis of agrarian insurgency and mobilization, state–society relations, and processes of regional, ethnic, nation, and state formation.[6] Within Mexico, Yucatán has been the subject of a most impressive array of studies in every period, with emphasis on the history of the region's indigenous and working mestizo (mixed-race descendants of the region's Spanish, indigenous, and African inhabitants) populations. That historiography and the ethnographic literature connect with many of the questions I raise in this study of communalism and el pueblo, affording firm foundations for a work of this kind and a basis for illuminating comparison.[7]

Despite such points of intersection, a study of el pueblo poses particular challenges to the conventions of historiography. First, there is the problem of scale. El pueblo is a phenomenon that is hemispheric in scope but embedded in locality, making it necessary to transcend the kinds of separation that typically distinguish local or case studies from those broader in compass. Second, there is the problem of periods. The historiography is generally characterized by a tendency to distinguish sharply between colonial and national periods, or even—above all in twentieth-century historiography—to focus on periods of a few years or decades in length, corresponding to political careers or events on the national stage or to important political, economic, and cultural shifts. To study the concept of el pueblo in a way that tracks critical shifts in its use would seem to necessitate, in contrast, a concentration on both the longue durée—reaching back to the colonial period and perhaps even before—and critical political conjunctures, in both the distant and recent past. Third, there is the problem of defining the group or groups under study. Many studies, chiefly social and political histories, tend to focus on specific groups or classes. El pueblo, however, is a concept that both unites particular populations and mediates between, and may even become, an object of contention among, varied groups, for example, inhabitants of certain population sites or communities; distinct class, ethnic, or political groups; municipal, state, and national government officials; and a host of other actors and entities.

In the course of grappling with such difficulties of scale, period, and subject, I have made choices that determined the nature of this book. Most importantly, this is neither a transatlantic historical genealogy of el pueblo, nor a focused study of el pueblo in a single community. Rather, I explore how el pueblo came to have its hold over a fairly large, if delimited, region. In doing so, I have adopted a methodology that is heterogeneous, drawing upon the insights of methods that scholars have labeled "microhistory," "ethnography of history," and the "history of the present." The first of these is a method of resonance in Mexico, building upon a large body of community-level studies produced by anthropologists like Robert Redfield and Alfonso Villa Rojas from the 1920s forward, and by ethnohistorians starting in the 1960s.[8] Perhaps the best known ethnohistorical work, the first to adopt the label microhistory, is Luis González y González's *Pueblo en vilo* (1968) (literally, "pueblo in suspense"), a comprehensive study of the village of San José de Gracia in the state of Michoacán. In subsequent invitations to historians to follow his example, González distinguished microhistory from conventional history written in a national frame, which he termed *historia patria*. González playfully, though problematically, proposed the use of the term *historia matria* to refer to microhistory, to highlight that method's focus upon "the small world, weak, feminine, attached to its mother; that is, the family, the native soil [*terruño*], the so-called little country [*patria chica*]."[9]

For an in-depth study of el pueblo, microhistory seems to offer much. Its intimate scale might capture the multiplicity of social forces and actors involved in constructing and claiming el pueblo, while its temporal depth might reveal important shifts in conceptions and languages of community and collectivity over the long term. Even so, some microhistories and community studies, including *Pueblo en vilo*, are marked by questionable assumptions. First, there has been a general tendency to identify microhistory with the study of particular local communities, typically rural villages or towns (a tendency recently challenged by scholars who conceive of microhistory as a more open-ended exploration of "small worlds").[10] Second, there has been a tendency to identify local community with certain stereotyped characteristics. This is perhaps most starkly expressed in Redfield's classic definition of "folk societies" as "small, isolated, non-literate, and homogeneous, with a strong sense of group solidarity," within which mentality and behavior are "traditional, spontaneous, uncritical and personal." Similar characterizations of local community, however, may be found in more recent works, often as a point of contrast with presumably more expansive forms of national identity, or with global or translocal forms of identification that have emerged in the wake of globalization.[11]

Such assumptions about the nature of certain kinds of communities as local things characterized by homogeneity and solidarity have long been questioned by many anthropologists and historians. Eric Wolf, for instance, famously proposed that while apparently isolated or autonomous, peasant ways of life are largely the product of the ways in which they are articulated to wider polities and economic systems—the "larger integral whole" of which they are a part. Subsequent historical and ethnographic literature from a gamut of areas and periods, ranging from eighteenth-century England to the highlands of contemporary Peru, has offered abundant evidence of the ways in which communities—and the concept and language of community itself— are internally contested and strongly shaped by conflicts with supposed outsiders, whether in the form of landowners, ranchers, or government officials and police. As Gavin Smith's work and E. P. Thompson's *Whigs and Hunters* make clear, communalism, including the versions of it advanced in the name of el pueblo, does not stand outside capital or the state. Its manifestations are rather a product of a centuries-old struggle in defense of community, but also over its very nature as well as that of the forces and entities contending with it and over it.[12]

This book, therefore, is conceived not as a study of community in a specific locale, but as a study of communalism in a defined region. As such, it offers an opportunity to find the large writ small in Hunucmá. It uses a narrow spatial compass, focusing on the pueblos, haciendas, and towns of that region, and an extended temporal reach, from the colonial period to the present, to expose how the terms of community were open to contention, challenge, and change by a variety of actors, from indigenous workers and pueblo dwellers to landowners, merchants, and priests to activists and government officials from the municipal to the national levels. Such a tight focus offers a unique perspective on moments of rebellion and insurgency and it opens a window on what James Scott has called "everyday forms of resistance" that present a constant obstacle to capital and state, even as they help to form a symbolically meaningful and morally charged backdrop to those struggles. Moreover, analysis on an intimate scale reveals several other important factors that bear on communalism. One of these is the place of state formation and violence in conflicts over community and capitalism; another is the importance of *mestizaje*, or race mixing, as an aspect of class and communal transformation for both working-class pueblo residents and gentry of mixed descent.[13]

While portraying the large writ small, microhistory affords an equal opportunity to consider the small writ large: that is, to explore how apparently local issues (for example, struggles over communal resources like lands or salt pools or disputes over work or politics) represent more than generic acts

of resistance and might bear upon, or even shape, expansive entities like capital, state, and nation. In this book I attempt to demonstrate how struggles
of the kind that have unfolded in Hunucmá, both historically and in the present, might have implications far beyond the context of their initial unfolding.
A principal argument of this book is that practices of making or claiming el
pueblo—whether in times of struggle or not—were both internally and externally directed. They were internal in that in the pueblos and towns of the
Hunucmá region, as in other regions, they consolidated el pueblo as a place
of habitation and as a corporate or communal entity. Struggles over community and communal possessions were also, however, externally directed,
elaborated in dialogue with wider political rhetorics and frameworks of governance that also went under the name of el pueblo. My hope is that a close
examination of ground-level struggles over community, capitalism, politics,
and history in Hunucmá might transcend such distinctions between inside
and outside, suggesting some of the ways in which those struggles simultaneously shaped the consolidation of el pueblo as a place of habitation, a form
of community, and a collective social and political subject.

As such a collective entity, el pueblo exists in time and space, thus presuming awareness among pueblo residents of that enduring existence in past,
present, and future—what Ernst Kantorowicz, in his study of medieval political theology, called "sempiternity." Might the claiming or construction of
el pueblo thereby imply a certain kind of shared historical consciousness or,
to use Maurice Halbwachs's term, "collective memory"?[14] Here, I draw on a
second approach, one that the anthropologist Joanne Rappaport has termed
the "ethnography of history." Anthropologists and historians have explored
historical consciousness and historical memory in varied ways and recently
have tended to eschew the assumption of shared collective memory, exploring instead the politics of memory both within and between social groups.[15]
Most recently, some have begun asking about archives themselves: about the
nature and politics of their construction and of contending claims over them
and the documentation they contain. One example of this kind of work is
Rappaport's own study of indigenous communities of the Cumbal region in
the Colombian Andes. In an ethnography of communal archival practices,
Rappaport demonstrates how the reading, writing, and performance of history have been critical not only to the defense and reclamation of communal
lands, but also to the refashioning of indigenous identity and politics.[16]

In a similar vein, throughout this book I argue that documents and histories have played critical roles both in communal struggle and in attempts to

claim or construct el pueblo as a collective entity. These documents take various forms: from records permanently stored in official archives to ephemeral theatrical performances; from community land titles to petitions against land expropriation; from inscribed guns left behind by insurgents to penal files elaborated in an attempt to discover, document, and incarcerate insurgents; from maps to piles of bones; and from community histories to tales of a Virgin's miraculous deeds. Such representations of the past are diverse, and none of them is truly collective, if by that term one means a story, like a creation myth, that is shared and recounted by all members of a community.[17] Even in the absence of shared stories about the past, however, there may exist shared *ways* of telling stories. One of the principal aims of my book, as an ethnography of history, is to explore how aspects of communal experience are given narrative form as history. In doing so, I attempt to demonstrate how, even in the absence of a shared collective memory or an official history of el pueblo, pueblo residents and others nonetheless have arrived at coherent and mutually intelligible ways of relating el pueblo's many pasts.

Here we may consider this book's third aspect, as what Michel Foucault called a "history of the present." In the present context, such an approach involves writing a historical genealogy of el pueblo in the Hunucmá region, featuring the moments and forms of its emergence and transformation. To do so is not to indulge in anachronism—what Foucault called merely "writing the history of the past in terms of the present."[18] Rather, it is to begin by presuming potentially radical difference between present and previous modes of communal and collective identification—whether organized under the name of el pueblo or not. It is to presume as well that those forms of identification have been susceptible to alteration as el pueblo has been appropriated or reappropriated, whether by indigenous communalists, landowners, revolutionaries, government officials, or others.

Moreover, I interpret history of the present to imply a reevaluation of the present, as much as it implies one of the past. Conceived in this way, a history of the present becomes a way to facilitate the deepest possible confrontation of past and present, in a way consonant with Walter Benjamin's challenge to the historian to grasp the "constellation which his own era has formed with a definite earlier one."[19] It may well be that this book, by taking present-day conceptions of el pueblo as its point of departure, begins at the end. Yet it also ends at the beginning. It brings a historical perspective to ethnographic topics—contemporary labor and political mobilizations, the circulation of money and commodities, religious fiestas and processions. Thus, I hope to expose some ways in which present-day references to el pueblo may represent deep and complex engagements with the past, even if the nature of those engagements may not be immediately apparent.

More than just a method, writing strategy, or argument, this aspect of my approach corresponds to my experience in the course of research. While pursuing ethnographic fieldwork, I often felt a jarring sensation as the past seemed to force its way into my perceptions of the landscape and my interactions with those who inhabited it. When conducting archival work, I was equally distracted by my recollection of the words of interlocutors in the field, words that, insofar as I listened to them, guided me and my research in directions sometimes different from those I otherwise might have chosen. The experience of spending part of my life caught between field and archive led me to take interest in and to explore the various ways in which the world is delimited, constructed, and claimed as archive and field. Eventually, it also led me to question what it might mean to divide things, people, and the world in that way. This book is an attempt to ask that question, even if it ultimately leaves the answer, along with el pueblo, *en vilo*, in suspense.

The book is divided into three parts. Part 1 explores the changing terms of community and historical memory from before the conquest through the early twentieth century. Chapter 1 takes a conflict from 1856 between an indigenous cacique and a Maya-speaking mestiza landowner as a point of entry for a discussion of changing paradigms of territorial and political community, from *kah* (the Mayan term for place-based community) to *común* (a term that can refer to both "commons" and "commune") to pueblo. Chapter 2 uses the story of the capture and imprisonment in 1892 of a rebel popularly known as El Rey de los Bosques (King of the Forest) to explore both the rise of a hacienda economy based on the monocultural production of henequen, a large, spiny plant used to produce fiber for rope and cordage, and the transformation of indigenous leaders from legal mediators based in the pueblos into forest-based outlaws and rebels. Chapter 3 begins with the discovery of an inscribed facsimile of a gun found in the aftermath of an insurgent attack on an henequen hacienda in 1913. It reads the gun's inscription as a document offering insights into the visions of pueblo and patria held by Hunucmá's indigenous communalists as they came to understand their struggle as one aimed at achieving el pueblo's collective liberation. Taken together, chapters 1 through 3 trace the consolidation of two incompatible visions of community: one of landholding mestizo gentry and government officials with aspirations to enrich themselves and to rule in the name of el pueblo, and the other of marginalized indigenous communalists who sought to defend communal prerogatives. Moreover, these chapters demonstrate the critical role of historical memory, especially of narratives of communal dispossession and collective liberation, in the elaboration of those visions.

Part 2 consists of three chapters that examine the reshaping of el pueblo as a subject of politics and an object of governance from the revolutionary and postrevolutionary periods through the early 1990s. Chapter 4 begins with attempts by Hunucmá's insurgents and Yucatán's Constitutionalist revolutionary government, in 1915, to end decades of social and political conflict in the region through a novel alliance. Indigenous calls for the recognition and material repossession of el pueblo, however, proved incompatible with government invocations of el pueblo as a passive object of state co-optation and control. The result was the breakdown of the alliance and the onset of renewed repression, which set the stage for intense partisan political conflict in the ensuing years. Chapter 5 focuses on a mass murder in Hunucmá that took place in 1920 amid a bitter statewide political conflict between the Yucatecan Socialist and Liberal parties. An exploration of this gruesome event and of its alleged perpetrator, a man some called General and others called Beast-Man, exposes how acts of rhetorical and physical violence came to reshape the terms of historical memory in the region and to recast el pueblo as a partisan political subject. Chapter 6 discusses the comprehensive agrarian and political reforms instituted by President Lázaro Cárdenas in the late 1930s, reforms that called for the survey, measure, and mapping of the land and provided a framework for el pueblo's tight incorporation within and political subordination to the state. But in the wake of these changes, decades of bureaucratic vacillation and community-level resistance would prevent the complete execution of Cárdenas's will. Finally, in the early 1990s, the collective ejidos would be dismantled by neoliberal reformers who claimed to execute Cárdenas's will by finally mapping the ejidos, even as they embraced a vision of state and pueblo that broke radically with his legacy.

The turn to neoliberal policies and frameworks of governance from the 1970s forward implied a profound attenuation of el pueblo as a framework of collective political mediation and control. Ironically, the way was thus opened for its reappropriation in populist and popular movements throughout the region that have acted in el pueblo's name in ways both old and new. Part 3 explores el pueblo's transformation, in ways reflecting both an awareness of history and its rethinking, in the context of politics, labor, religion, and cultural production. Chapter 7 focuses on an independent union movement that led to a months-long strike and developed into a cooperative movement after the strike was broken. Over the next decade union organizers and advisors, pueblo residents, and a Yucatecan theatrical troupe recounted the history of the strike in variant ways, each reflecting different stakes in its retelling. Chapter 8 is a study of the fiesta and guild system surrounding the most elaborate religious cult of the Hunucmá region, that dedicated to the Virgin of the pueblo of Tetiz. Here I demonstrate the place of the Virgin and her miracles in the elaboration and performance of historical memory and communal identity, both within the Hunucmá region and far beyond its boundaries. Chapter 9 presents the life and works of the Hunucmá resident Don Anacleto Cetina Aguilar, as a poet, educator, historian, Mayanist, and opposition political activist. In this chapter I highlight the central role of the recovery of pueblo history and cultural identity as a response to the dislocating effects of contemporary neoliberalism. Nonetheless, as this chapter and the preceding ones demonstrate, el pueblo has remained salient not only as a framework for political subjectivity, but also as a place of habitation before, beyond, and outside the realm of politics.

POSTSCRIPT

Every year in the pueblos of the Hunucmá region—as elsewhere in Mexico—Carnaval's yearly cycle of festivities reaches its climax and conclusion on Ash Wednesday, with the execution and funeral of the festival's symbolic patron, Juan Carnaval. Mock mourners wail alongside a coffin containing the figure that is placed in the public square of the pueblos, and Juan Carnaval's will is presented and read to the audience. The will refers, in comic fashion, to events that occurred over the course of the preceding year: misdeeds of residents and authorities, squabbles and fights, political conflicts. "I leave my suitcase," Juan's will might read, "to the mayor, so he can pack up all the money he took from el pueblo!"; "I leave a bottle of aspirin to Don Manuel Cuytun, to help with his hangovers!"; "I leave one goat for the police chief, so he doesn't have to steal animals from people's patios!"; and so on. After the final lines of Juan Carnaval's will are read out and the laughter begins to subside, the mourners perform the action that concludes Carnaval. Someone strikes a match and, as the crowd looks on, sets fire to the will, which quickly burns to a crisp to the amusement and applause of all present.[20]

When I heard of this spectacle, my feelings were mixed. If only the wills were not burned but stored away each year after Carnaval—at least photocopies of them!—thus forming a carnivalesque, subaltern, and eminently consultable archive of el pueblo's past. . . . My reaction betrayed problematic assumptions: that is, that the point of documents is to record the past and that the point of archives and historical narrative, whatever their form, is to conserve it. The deliberate destruction of the comical will is, after all, assumed at the time of its drafting and is the condition of its very existence. Like so many other histories of el pueblo, its power derives from performance and witnessing, rather than permanence. Carnival celebrants re-create in this way a meaningful kind of collective organization, communal sensibility, and political claim—one that rises, phoenixlike, from the ashes of its archive. Even if the episodes recounted in the will may soon be forgotten by those who witnessed its reading, the spectacle of the will's destruction suggests that memory sometimes can take its most powerful form in a repertoire of ways of experiencing, telling, feeling, and performing el pueblo and its histories rather than in the documentary, topical, or factual content of any historical narrative.[21]

The same might be said of many of the other forms of history I have encountered, including narratives inscribed in archival documents, which are for the most part stored away in repositories that are unavailable to pueblo residents and seem to be of little interest to most of them. Once politically consequential and profoundly meaningful to the communities that produced them, time has made those documents as ephemeral as Juan Carnaval's will. In their entirety, however, they have played a powerful and pivotal role in the making and remaking of el pueblo: as an object known and a subject that feels and acts; as an entity both material and symbolic; as a subject deeply rooted in the witnessing of this place and this community, yet also the product of so many interactions within and across its unstable boundaries. What follows is one more, perhaps equally transient, invocation of el pueblo, based upon a few of its many stories: from tragedy to redemption; from farce to miracle; from history in the archives to history in ashes.

PART ONE

DISPOSSESSION

CANCION DE AMOR

Cuanto sufro en el mundo tirana.
Cuanto sufro y padesco espor ti
ci algun dia suspiraraz mi desprecio
Sin acer me recuerdo de mi.

Pero haysta un dios que castiga lo injusto
y que premia el cer de los hombres
pero entonces declarar hoy un nombre
a nacer un recuerdo de mi.

Bayo la sombra de un verde naranjo
ahi me puse en terribles penas
y esas campanas que a lo lejos suenan
son las que ponen a mi vida en
    afliccion.

Paso las horas y tambien los cuartos voy
caminando por el viento apriza mi alma
    en el
viento se horroriza
con esos parpados cansados de llorar.

LOVE SONG

How I suffer in this tyrannous world.
How I suffer, and endure, it is for you
if one day you will sigh my disdain
With no memory of me.

But there is a god who punishes the unjust
and who rewards the souls of men so then
declare today a name,
so that a memory of me is born.

Underneath the shade of a green orange
    tree
I landed myself in terrible hardships
and those bells that ring far away
are the ones that afflict my life.

I pass hours and go walking through the
    rooms,
and in the ravages of the swift wind
my soul is horrified,
with these eyes, so tired of crying.

—NEMESIO PÉRES, San Juan de Ulúa Penitentiary
("El Castillo"), 1895

CHAPTER ONE

THE LAST CACIQUE

The Archival Landscapes of *Kah*,
Común, and *Pueblo*

CACIQUE PASCUAL CHAC was "not lacking in guilt." That was the verdict of the criminal court judge José María Rivero Solís, who on 14 January 1857 passed judgment in the case brought by the hacienda owner Juana Peña. Peña had accused Chac of encouraging a group of pueblo dwellers to clear and plant lands on her hacienda, Tacubaya. Even as the trial concluded, the production of a case file went forward. On Rivero's desk was a pile of papers: outraged complaints from the hacendada; Chac's self-defense; the correspondence of courts and government offices; a surveyor's account of a week-long trudge through Tacubaya and a map; a prosecutor's denunciations; receipts. Each was a document in its own right, but all now were stitched together as a single case file under the title "Causa por acusación de Doña Juana Peña contra el casique Pascual Chac."[1]

To read this case file historically is to unbind it: to read each of its elements in its own terms, juxtaposing them with documents outside the file. Unbound in this way, the "Causa" opens a window onto the Hunucmá region of Yucatán in a time of radical changes, among them the decline of the indigenous leaders called caciques and the rise of hacendados. Once fragmented from its apparent unity into a cacophony of voices indigenous and Spanish, communalist and capitalist, the "Causa" offers an opportunity to explore how different ethnic groups, classes, and political entities coexisted uneasily and then came apart in the wake of national independence, the rise of agrarian capitalism, and caste war.

To read the "Causa," is also to rebind the file: to read the sutured text for signs of the political forces that made stories like Chac's end in similar ways and in the process helped to transform the landscape that Chac and Peña inhabited. It is to use the "Causa" as an entrée into an archival landscape in which documents bound people to place and place to people via contrasting historical narratives told by indigenous populations and Spanish and mestizo gentry. Landscapes in the archive, and archives in the landscape—from the first tree felled at Tacubaya to the last stroke of Rivero's pen.

THE HISTORY IN THE LANDSCAPE

Today the Hunucmá region is tightly connected and subordinated to the nearby capital city of Mérida. Five centuries ago, however, it was oriented toward the gulf coast. The shoreline was inhabited by Maya populations that lived in settlements (each called a *kah* in Maya) active in fishing and salt production. The interior was more sparsely populated and more densely forested. Populations there gathered beeswax, hunted and fished, and cultivated maize, beans, squash, chile, and cotton. They did so through swidden agriculture, as Mayan populations did elsewhere in Yucatán and throughout Mexico and central America (where the plots are called *milpas*, a Nahua term). They felled trees and brush in the woods, or *k'ax*, in the dry season, burned the drying refuse as the rainy season approached to create a layer of rich ash over the thin and stony soil, and then planted each forest plot, or *kol*. After two seasons of cultivation, the kol was abandoned to the forest once again, as only a decade or more of regrowth would make the land cultivable once more. Thus the small kahs of the interior—Kinchil and Dzemé, Tetiz, Hunucmá, Sihunchén, Yabucú, Samahil, Umán and Dzibikak and Dzibikal, among others—produced a surplus that they traded with coastal populations, providing maize, beans, and cotton in exchange for salt and fish.

Through overland routes and maritime trade, the people of coast and interior were linked to central Mexico, Guatemala, and Honduras, exporting cotton and slaves and receiving a range of finished goods and precious objects in return.[2]

Centuries had passed since the decline and collapse of the great Mayan city-states of the classic period; the last regional confederation in Yucatán, centered in the city of Mayapán, succumbed to interclan warfare in the 1440s. An era of political fragmentation followed in which noble families, ch'ibal, in Maya, became entrenched as they gained control of the largest kahs. Those kahs were ruled by leaders called batabs, with the batab of a dominant kah, a figure sometimes referred to as the halach winik, exercising dominion over those of neighboring populations. Most lands and other resources like cenotes, or sinkholes, and salt pools were attached to the kahs as communal possessions, but others were held as lineage property of the ch'ibals.[3]

After the Spanish invasion and occupation of the peninsula in the first half of the sixteenth century, Yucatán, where there was no gold or silver to be mined, was spared the heavy influx of European immigration suffered by other regions. Even so, the spread of contagious diseases in areas of dense population, especially along trade routes, decimated coastal areas. In contrast, the kahs of the interior, ranging in population from several hundred to several thousand, survived. To facilitate conversion and tribute collection the Spanish forced survivors to congregate in a few authorized pueblos. Today's pattern of towns and pueblos thereby took shape, with each congregated kah, or indigenous republic (república indígena), based in a core settlement, or pueblo, with a church and plaza and a surrounding street grid.[4]

Despite such changes, the kah remained an entity grounded in communal possession of forests and other resources. While the conquest brought the elimination of the top levels of the Mayan social and political hierarchy, the batabs, whom the Spanish called caciques, a loanword from the Arawak language, retained many of their powers. They adjudicated disputes, regulated communal agriculture, and oversaw the collection of taxes and tributes. In return they won exemptions from tribute and personal service and enjoyed some Spanish prerogatives like ownership of horses and use of Spanish dress and of the honorific title Don.[5] The conquerors imposed some Spanish institutions on their subjects, like the cabildo, or town council, although native elites turned such institutions to their own purposes. Members of leading ch'ibals monopolized positions as officials in the new civil hierarchy (tenientes, alcaldes, alguaciles, regidores), scribes, and gendarmes (tupil, in Maya). Kah officials

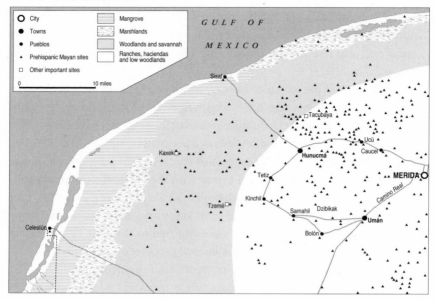

The Hunucmá Region: Prehispanic Structures and Principal Population Sites.
Map by Philip Schwartzberg.

acted as judges, mediating between members of the kah, documenting the
sale or transfer of lands, and representing their kahs in disputes involving
Spanish officials, priests, and neighboring communities. Native elites also
took up positions as assistants to parish clergy and headed religious confraternities (*cofradías*). Those organizations managed extensive ranches and
properties and supported saints' cults and fiestas in which Christianity was
incorporated into native religious practice.[6]

The kah came to play an intermediary role in the workings of the colonial
economy, linking the Hunucmá region to Mérida and to the rest of the Spanish empire. Through the institution of *encomienda* kah members were forced
to pay tributes to their Spanish overlords in labor and kind, from turkeys and
maize to beeswax. Governors, war captains, and other officials also claimed
tributes, as did parish priests. The kahs of the region maintained granaries
for the provision of maize to Spanish populations and also rendered tribute
in salt and fish. One of the most effective forms of extraction was the *repartimiento de mercancías*, or the forced purchase of goods. The kahs in this way
were both subordinated to local Spaniards and articulated to an Atlantic colonial economy through the extraction of products like textiles and wax that
Yucatán exported, principally to silver mining areas elsewhere in Mexico.[7]

Hunucmá's importance to the colonial economy derived from tribute but also from a transport economy. Mérida was connected to Campeche, the region's only major fortified port city, via the *camino real*, or royal road, which passed from Mérida eastward and southward through Umán, giving the region its name in this period: Camino Real Bajo. Merchandise imported to Yucatán from Spain or other areas of the empire passed through the region on its way to Mérida, and exports like wax and cotton traveled the same road back to port. The small pueblo of Sisal, northwest of the kah of Hunucmá, became a secondary transit route, particularly for the trade in cane liquor, or aguardiente. Spanish merchants demanded that the kahs of the region provide muleteers and unpaid transport services. By the 1720s the exploitative nature of this arrangement would trigger a regional crisis, as batabs and kah officials, who complained bitterly to Yucatán's governor in defense of their "tired and skinny" mules, began to withhold transport services and even to blockade merchandise. In response, Spanish officials, merchants, and a local priest denounced Hunucmá's batab as a "notorious" cacique who told "a thousand lies." Facing beatings and imprisonment, the batabs restored the services.[8]

Over time the Hunucmá region came to be important to the Spanish not only for tribute and transport but also for land. Despite protective legislation limiting Spanish acquisition of indigenous lands, ranches, and commercial maize haciendas began expanding west of Mérida over the course of the seventeenth century. From the early 1700s forward, indigenous cabildos sometimes raised funds by selling land to Spaniards, although often with a proviso that the lands in question were unneeded for communal subsistence—in the words of Samahil's cabildo, "because we have enough other lands to maintain ourselves." Even indigenous cofradías began to exploit lands commercially, albeit to communal ends, by raising herds of cattle for sale to raise funds.[9] Nonetheless, colonial forms of exploitation, the rise of a commercial economy, and even the formation of large cattle ranches and haciendas in formerly communal lands implied neither the destruction of the kahs of Hunucmá, nor the elimination of the cabildos and batabs that ruled them. Kah officials in Hunucmá, as elsewhere in Yucatán, made the best of their position as intermediaries. They acted as agents of both Spanish exploitation and communal autonomy, retaining significant autonomy in decision making on matters that affected daily life.

The sovereignty and integrity of the kahs were nowhere more evident than in the usage of written documents and histories composed by batabs and other officials. Before the Spanish conquest, scribes and their writings had been critical to the workings of Mayan society and culture. Historical accounts of the ch'ibals and community titles of the kahs both legitimized lords and their families and endorsed the territory and sovereignty of the kahs they controlled. While Spanish anti-idolatry campaigns destroyed the vast majority of the codices still extant at the time of conquest, under colonial rule indigenous scribes and their archives continued to play a critical role in guaranteeing the territorial integrity of the kahs. From the sixteenth century through the eighteenth, Mayan scribes wrote and compiled Maya-language historical narratives in Latin script, documenting the claims and legitimacy of ch'ibals and the kahs. Moreover, the kahs retained and consulted documents and maps in the context of land sales, inheritance, treaties, and conflicts. Many of those documents were ambulatory texts, narrating walks through forests and fields and noting the presence and location of stone mounds and trees the Maya used as boundary markers. In a document dating from 1735 and relating to the kahs of Umán and Dzibikal, for instance, some fifty-three stone markers are noted. Such walks were rituals of possession that often took several days to complete and led to the production of an extensive body of documentation that legitimated the kahs and the ch'ibals that controlled them.[10] Theirs were histories embedded in the land itself: in stone markers, trees, and other landmarks, in ritual walks of possession, and in Mayan documents that made those features and walks into expressions of community, sovereignty, and history. If Mayan scribes brought representations of landscape into the archives, so, too, did they embed archives in the landscape, transforming stones, trees, and wells into historical traces of the kahs and of their sovereign claims.

This history was still present in 1856, when cacique Pascual Chac led a group of men into the woods near Hacienda Tacubaya. The testimony of several of the men involved indicates that Chac ordered that a breach be opened in the brush, and then he led the men in. Perhaps when the cacique did so he would follow the ancient customs of the kah: walking the lands with his subjects; noting and naming rocks and trees and telling their histories; and leaving landmarks of his own along the way in an attempt to restore and to reclaim an archive in the landscape.

FROM MESTIZO TO TS'UL

Chac, however, found himself in a different landscape from that inhabited by batabs of prior centuries, as it was shared with the likes of Doña Juana Peña. Peña and others of her class were products of the past century of Spanish rule in Yucatán and of a shift away from the Spanish tributary regime toward one based on commercial agriculture and ranching. Partly a result of population growth and commercial development in Yucatán, this change also was fostered by reforms enacted by the Bourbon rulers in Spain. From the 1770s forward, those reforms brought the disentailment of corporate bodies like the kahs, the expropriation of community treasuries, the seizure and sale of properties held by kahs and cofradías, and the centralization of tribute collection and governance in the hands of district-level officials called *subdelegados*. Such measures accelerated the expansion of Yucatán's emergent commercial capitalism at the expense of indigenous communalists. While sugar cane became dominant in southern and eastern Yucatán, in the northwest commercial maize agriculture and ranching prevailed. Moreover, in swampy lands in coastal regions like Hunucmá, gangs of woodcutters cut dyewood (also known as logwood, or *palo de tinte*) to supply merchants involved in the lucrative trade in dye.[11]

These developments fostered the growth of Hunucmá's nonindigenous, or *vecino* (a Spanish term meaning "resident"), population, blurring distinctions between what once, at least in theory, had constituted separate Spanish and indigenous republics. By 1779 the district's total population of 20,899 was roughly 80 percent indigenous and 1 percent Spanish; the remainder was 10 percent *pardo* (African or mixed African and indigenous descent) and 9 percent mestizo (here, mixed Spanish and indigenous descent). Most mestizos and pardos were working people: small farmers, artisans, shopkeepers, and the like. A few, however, like Juana Peña's father, Eduardo Peña, acquired property and capital. They identified with Spanish cultural institutions, and the wealthiest among them wore European clothing, reflected in the appellation *gente de vestido*. While they spoke Spanish, many also spoke Maya or a mixture of Maya and Spanish. To indigenous residents, they were *ts'uls*, a Mayan term originally denoting foreigner that came to have status and ethnic connotations, conveying associations of wealth, privilege, and lightness in skin color.[12]

By the late eighteenth century, kah officials were sharply aware of the threat that the expanding commercial sector posed to kah lands and resources. They lodged petitions with Spanish authorities, claiming the expropriation of communal resources was unjust and a violation of Christian principles. When a cofradía ranch was seized for sale in 1782, Hunucmá's batab and kah officials, identifying themselves as the "old men" of the kah, appealed to the king of Spain for mercy and justice and inquired why cofradía cattle were being slaughtered and other properties "wasted, without any benefit to the Virgin." In 1819 batabs and kah officials from Hunucmá and Tetiz sent Maya-language petitions to Yucatán's governor, complaining of exploitation by a local priest and warning, "Lord, Tetiz kah will be ruined, since there'll be no food to eat. . . . Lord, I shall not abandon [those of] my kah, although they are dying."[13] Kah officials put their maps and documents to use in contending with the expanding claims of Spanish and Yucatecan Creole landowners. Perhaps the most protracted conflict, one that began in the 1730s and continued for almost a century thereafter, pitted batabs and officials of five kahs against the owners of an expanding hacienda. In 1815 the leaders of the indigenous republics involved set off, joined by Spanish officials, on a five-day walk through forest and field to document their contending claims.[14]

Such efforts met the unflagging determination of local ts'uls to expand their holdings. Initially, their success in securing limited concessions to establish cattle ranches on communal lands depended on their ability to negotiate with indigenous authorities. Indigenous scribes prepared documents in Maya signaling the assent of batabs and other kah officials to such concessions but specifying that members of the indigenous republics would retain the right to use wells, cut firewood, hunt, and make milpa in the lands in question. Eduardo Peña, for instance, promising to permit customary usage of the lands in question and to supply the kah with meat, secured a license to pasture twenty-five head of cattle near Hunucmá.[15] Negotiations occasionally became complex. When a wealthy landowner from Mérida attempted to title and purchase a cofradía ranch near Kinchil called Santa María, he confronted what he called the "custom of the Indians to resist every land sale." Colonial government officials enlisted the help of local mestizos, Eduardo Peña and another man named Lorenzo Argaiz, as intermediaries. They were to inspect maps and documents held by the kah, interview old indigenous men on the history of Santa María, and explore the land itself. Once surveyed the land could be titled and transformed from a communal possession into a commodity that might be bought and sold.

The first task, which fell to Argaiz, was to explore the woodlands near Santa María and to describe them in writing. More than just a land survey, his record of the sixteen-day task was a heroic narrative. It began with interviews of indigenous people regarding the history of the lands. Confronting "a great deal of variance, between what some pointed out to me with their fingers, and what others did," Argaiz set off into the woods. There he faced great difficulties, which he described vividly: just how thick the woods were, just how spiny the trees, just how much they resisted his every attempt to struggle

forward, "breaking through the woods" by sheer will. Argaiz repeatedly in-
serted the phrase "with compass in hand" in describing his wanderings, as if
to differentiate himself from the Indians, who were described as confusedly
pointing in all directions. Yet Argaiz did not go alone. While kah officials of
Kinchil refused to help him, indigenous residents of Santa María accompanied and assisted him. On one occasion, as the group neared lands of the kah
of Tetiz, Argaiz summoned officials of that kah with a letter he had written
in Maya, to which they responded in kind, addressing him with the honorific
yum, for "lord." The next day Tetiz's batab, along with cabildo members and
a scribe, met Argaiz in the woods to converse with him and negotiate the
limits of his incursion.[16]

Beyond that encounter, the grindingly difficult process of mapping Santa
María was an ongoing process of collaboration with "Indian experts" (indios
prácticos). They were the ones who laboriously opened holche's, a Maya term
for "breach" that Argaiz, a bilingual mestizo, used more frequently in his
writing than the Spanish equivalent, picado. Day after day, Argaiz's guides
took him deeper into the landscape and its past, teaching him the names
of things. Here was a cenote, or sinkhole, "a subterranean lake . . . called
Chunpich, the Indians assure me." Here were the remnants of a kah forcibly
depopulated by the Spanish: "The old pueblo of Tzemé, of which vestigial
ruins remain." Finally, a much older Mayan site offered mute testimony;
Argaiz called it "a mound of stone, fairly large, built by the ancients, by
hand." More than just a matter of learning the lay of the land, the survey had
become an exploration of the lay of history in the land. In this, the expert
surveyor became the student of his guides.

Once Argaiz's work was complete, the second task, that of producing a
record of indigenous testimony in support of the titling of Santa María, fell
to Peña. First, the kah of Kinchil submitted documents to defend its claims,
which immediately were dismissed by a government official as "confused
maps, made by Indians or unqualified people." It was up to Peña to locate
other witnesses who might supply presumably credible information about
the land's history and then to translate their Mayan words into Spanish testimony favoring the sale. In the end, the titling and sale of Santa María went
forward, even though one official voiced suspicions that Peña and Argaiz had
engaged in "some kind of confabulation" to drive up the price of the property
and perhaps to profit illicitly from its sale.

Similar dramas played out often in the Hunucmá region in the early nineteenth century, as reforms favoring the titling of lands paved the way for

the weakening of the kahs. Government officials now viewed indigenous historical documents, whether ancient maps, treaties, ambulatory land descriptions, or testimony of elders, with contempt, and mestizo gentry, using their intimate local knowledge and expertise in Maya and Spanish, crafted other kinds of documentation. It was their surveys and titles and their transcriptions of indigenous testimony which now held sway. Avid for wealth and power and experienced as middlemen, Hunucmá's mestizo landowners were well positioned to profit from the collapse of the Spanish empire. Taking their cue from Spanish Liberals, who used Napoleon's occupation of Spain in 1808 as an opportunity to refashion the empire as a constitutional monarchy, Creole liberals in Yucatán militated for the abolition of tributes, of religious taxes, and, most importantly, of the indigenous republics.

Such efforts were interrupted for several years by a conservative restoration in Spain. In 1820, however, an army rebellion in Spain forced the reinstatement of the constitution throughout the empire. Hunucmá's gentry joined the cause, led by the influential Peña, who alternately held posts as commanding officer of Hunucmá's militia, town councilman, and mayor (alcalde). Peña joined Hunucmá's town council in denouncing the district's subdelegado for persecuting liberals and blocking their attempts to contribute to the "great task of improving our commerce and agriculture," presumably through the seizure of communal lands and the expansion of cattle ranches and haciendas.[17] The new regime offered unprecedented opportunities to secure such alleged improvements. After Mexico gained independence from Spain in 1821, Creole liberals like Peña, who soon rose to the coveted post of subdelegado, became staunch advocates of untrammeled agrarian capitalist development. Yucatán's new government passed a measure limiting communal lands to ejidos located within a one-league radius around the pueblos, classifying lands outside that radius as wastelands (baldíos) eligible for purchase. In the Hunucmá region, decades-old disputes over communal lands were settled in favor of hacendados and ranchers. Ranchers titled lands they illegally occupied, hacendados and merchants secured lucrative dyewood concessions, and municipal and state officials seized and sold lands still held by cofradías. Ranchers who held concessions expanded them, sometimes transforming ranches into haciendas. On the basis of his license to pasture twenty-five cattle in an area of common lands near Hunucmá, Eduardo Peña enclosed lands and erected buildings on a place he named San Eduardo, which soon grew into an hacienda populated by more than three hundred head of cattle.[18]

The transition to national rule also brought new problems or, rather, aggravated old ones for Creole landowners. With the decline of the kahs in the late colonial period, increasing numbers of indigenous residents fled the pueblos, and thus their tax and tributary obligations, for the woods, a phenomenon Spanish officials called *arranchamiento*. With the abolition of the indigenous republics, the departures increased, as kah residents exercised their right, as supposedly free citizens, to move about at will. Despite their liberal credentials, Yucatecan authorities reacted to such settlements as their colonial predecessors had, namely, by denouncing those who "abused the civil and political liberty of citizens" by living "without restraint outside society, isolated from their priests and judges, dedicating themselves to idolatry, robbery, and carnality."[19] From the 1820s on, the Yucatecan government enacted a series of measures enforcing the payment of rents for use of common lands, disallowed "furtive illegal meetings in the woods," and forced residents of illegal settlements to relocate to haciendas and recognized pueblos. In the Hunucmá region, Subdelegado Peña joined forces with town council officials to destroy unauthorized indigenous settlements and force their residents to move to recognized pueblos and haciendas.[20]

Eventually, in July 1824, the Yucatecan congress reinstituted the indigenous republics, exhorting their leaders to "contain the dispersion of the *indígenas* to the woods, and provide them with an honest occupation, to make them useful for themselves and for society." As envisioned by reformers, however, the restored batabs, or caciques, were much diminished. While empowering the caciques to collect taxes and tribute and to enforce church attendance, the congress made no mention of them defending communal lands. Shortly thereafter, the state constitution of 1825 defined structures of governance in the pueblos, instituting *ayuntamientos* (town councils) in central towns and *juntas municipales* (municipal boards) in smaller settlements. Notwithstanding their race-blind rhetoric of citizenship, the Yucatecan government segregated local governance, concentrating most power in the hands of the local gentry who controlled the town councils; the restored indigenous republics played a subordinate role.[21] Under the new regime, Hunucmá's ts'uls held dominion over the kahs and their leaders. The subdelegado supervised the nomination of caciques. Municipal officials required caciques to supply contingents of men for unpaid labor for public works and road building, and priests called on them to collect religious fees and ensure church attendance. At the orders of indigenous and municipal officials, the tupils, or indigenous police, detained those accused of misconduct and administered corrective whippings and beatings. The caciques thus found themselves in a compromised position. Those who displeased the ts'uls might be deposed or beaten; those who obeyed faced the resentment of their subjects, who sometimes responded to the despotism of their indigenous overlords with insults or even slaps of their own.[22]

Officials of the indigenous republics also played a role in the gentry's acquisition of retinues of indigenous men, women, and children as laborers and personal servants; all were typically brought into service once adult males acquired personal debt, as *sirvientes*. By 1841 in the area of the town of Hunucmá, one quarter of the population resided on haciendas and ranches; near Tetiz it was one third. Officials of the republics compelled indebted workers and their families to obey the will of those who held their debts. In 1845, for instance, a Hunucmá resident named Evarista Chan refused to accompany her husband to a hacienda that was distant from her family, defiantly declaring that town officials would have to "break her into pieces" first. Rising to the challenge, a councilman ordered tupils to bring her to the Peña household, where they shackled her feet and chained her to a rock for three days.[23]

The rising fortunes and growing power of Hunucmá's gentry did not, however, make it a class united. The ts'uls of Hunucmá were a bickering, fractious lot, competing regularly over land, dyewood concessions, and indigenous servants. They unabashedly used political office as a means of enrichment and even came into conflict with the church, sometimes challenging priests' authority over the indigenous population. Parish priests complained, for instance, that Peña told indigenous residents they were exempt from paying church fees and encouraged his followers to sack the convent in Hunucmá. Despite such rivalries, Don Eduardo made the most of the opportunities of a turbulent era. By the time of his death in 1835, his holdings were immense and valued at more than sixty-four thousand pesos: he owned six cattle and maize haciendas, more than fifteen hundred head of cattle, nineteen salt pools, dyewood stands, a fishing operation in Sisal, and houses and other properties scattered through Hunucmá, Tetiz, Samahil, and Sisal. Large retinues of indigenous hacienda workers, muleteers, woodcutters, and cowboys owed him considerable sums of money, which stood as a measure of his power over them as their *amo*, or "master."[24]

Alongside his tenacious campaign for wealth and power, Don Eduardo waged a ruthless domestic struggle aimed at refashioning his family of mestizo origins, one composed of two sons and one daughter, into a dynasty.

When Juana was just twelve years old, her brother Felipe, infamous throughout the region for having an "unbridled tongue," reported a rumor impugn-
ing Juana's virtue to his father. Don Eduardo gave Juana fifty lashes for her
presumed indiscretions and rewarded Felipe with one thousand pesos, with
which he was told to construct a luxurious house on Hunucmá's plaza. Instead, Felipe gambled it away and this time found himself put under the
lash. Afterward Don Eduardo ordered that Felipe's hair and eyebrows be
shaved off in order to shame him publicly for his dishonorable behavior.[25]

The patriarchal violence of the Peña family, as much as Don Eduardo's
ruthless quest for power and privilege, led his children on various paths. One
son, Angel, proved unable to prosper, repeatedly squandering the wealth entrusted to him. Felipe tried to follow in his father's footsteps by establishing
a power base in Hunucmá's militia, serving as mayor of Tetiz, and acquir-
ing properties. He pursued these activities, however, in a style that led one
resident to call him "the most dissolute man, and the most irreligious, pernicious, deceitful, heartless, and disheveled as well." Felipe seems to have
believed that the road to honor, or at least to power, was through the dis-
honoring of others, and he did so with a vengeance: insulting and brawl-
ing with priests, beating and whipping officials of the indigenous republics,
wandering through town in a violent, drunken stupor shouting insults and
death threats at other gentry, even accusing them of incest. Felipe reportedly
insulted every woman he encountered, calling them prostitutes and whores,
and he raped the daughters of several notable families, offenses that once
earned him a clubbing by a group of women from Tetiz. When Don Eduardo
heard of such scandals, he slapped and beat his wayward son, but to no
avail.

Juana Peña took a different path. She married well, joining her wealth to
the rising fortunes of Remigio Novelo, a prosperous landowner, notable, and
municipal official and the owner of several haciendas, including Tacubaya,
a maize, cattle, and dyewood operation a few leagues north of town. Novelo,
who like many other members of the gentry chafed under the Peña yoke,
was no friend of Felipe, and when Don Eduardo died in 1835 the antagonism came to the surface. Felipe, who had lived under Don Eduardo's protection, proved unable to accede to his father's wealth and power. Felipe held
the post of subdelegado as Eduardo's health failed, but after the patriarch's
death it was Juana's husband who rose to that position. Felipe wandered the
streets of Hunucmá screaming that he was the rightful subdelegado and that
he had the power to fire town officials and appoint others at will. He took

to screaming insults at Juana and her husband in public. At night he would get drunk and stand outside Novelo's house, shouting obscenities at him in Maya—still the language of intimacy and insult in the Peña family.

Victory, however, would be Juana's. Juana Peña and Remigio Novelo had political clout and material wealth, the latter significantly augmented after the inheritance from Don Eduardo, as Juana was declared executor of his estate. They also enjoyed social prestige among the region's gentry, wide sectors of which became openly hostile to Felipe upon his father's death. In 1838 the priest in Hunucmá brought charges against Felipe for libel in a case that became a charter for Felipe's social and political demise.[26] The priest detailed his offenses against God, the church, and the clergy; municipal officials and militia officers described his public drunkenness and violence; others told of his sexual crimes and obscenities. They recounted Felipe's "inhumane calumnies" against Doña Juana, hastening to add that her honor was unimpeachable. Even officials of the indigenous republics testified that Felipe had had them publicly whipped. The case file became a compendium of infamy; indeed, as one vecino commented, "To continue relating in detail the excesses and criminal deeds of Peña, one would have to write several volumes." In the end, defenseless before so many accusers, Felipe blamed his downfall on an alliance between the priest and Novelo, both of whom, according to him, were "desirous of putting an end to my interests, and my existence." Given his sister's acumen and power, however, in all likelihood the hands pulling the strings behind that carefully arranged spectacle were Juana's.

By 1856, the year she heard that cacique Pascual Chac had led a group of men into woodlands of Tacubaya, Doña Juana had become the true inheritor of her father's standing and wealth, as the owner of seven haciendas and ranches and other properties valued at about fifty thousand pesos and the creditor, and *ama*, of some two hundred indebted servants.[27] In the "Causa" compiled a year later there is no record of her reaction to that news or of the memories it might have evoked: of Don Eduardo's determined rise to wealth and power; of his domination over the caciques and indigenous republics of Hunucmá and later that of her husband; of the intimate violence and dishonor of her family life; of her success in building her own prestige through the acquisition of property, lawsuits, and marriage: first to Novelo, and then, following Novelo's grisly murder by insurgents in 1847, to another wealthy town resident. Perhaps these memories would guide Doña Juana as she responded to Chac, summoning the cacique to speak with her but also turning to other time-tested strategies that Hunucmá's mestizo gentry used in their dealings with indigenous populations. She would arrange for a land survey, assemble land titles and other documents, and request that the courts begin penal proceedings against Chac and his men. In doing so, she would set in motion the drafting of the "Causa" as one more among the many historical documents with which she and others like her took possession of lands and labor and in the process secured their transformation from mestizos into ts'uls.

FROM KAH TO COMÚN

Doña Juana would not be the only mestizo involved in the "Causa." Although many of the men who followed Chac into the woods near Tacubaya were members of Hunucmá's indigenous republic and had Mayan names like Cool, Pech, and Canché, there would be others as well, with Hispanic names like Cevallos, Castilla, and Maldonado. Like Peña, these men were mestizos, but they were small farmers, artisans, and shopkeepers, not hacendados or ranchers. In Hunucmá, working-class mestizos generally enjoyed a somewhat higher level of income than indigenous residents. Nonetheless, many mestizo men married indigenous women, and their children grew up in Maya-speaking households. When called to give Spanish testimony in court, they often needed translators, which suggests an increasing proximity to indigenous residents in status, occupation, and language.[28]

Under colonial rule, kah officials had distinguished clearly between the *kahnal* (Maya for "person of the kah"), who was entitled to work lands of the kah and was subject to tributary obligations, and the *vecinoil* (a Mayanized version of "vecino"), who was subject only to taxes required of Spaniards and their descendants. In the last years of colonial rule, however, the indigenous republics became more flexible regarding the use of communal lands. In 1815, for instance, when five kahs of the region came to an agreement regarding the "common use of lands," the signatories to that agreement were batabs and officials of the kahs. The document was recorded as having been ratified, however, "with the entire commune of Indians and residents of color present" (*con todo el común de indios y vecinos de color presente*), a formulation that demonstrates *común* was being used as a translation of *kah* into Spanish, but also as a term that referred to a communal entity incorporating working people of mestizo and pardo background who were not members of the republics.[29]

The term *común* had a long history in Spain and the Americas as a way of referring both to communal lands and resources and to the community that claimed those resources. As opposed to the concept of ejido, which was legally delimited to a one-league radius around towns and pueblos, the term *común* referred expansively to all lands historically used by a population, regardless of distance or location. In the Hunucmá region, the term was used to refer to woodlands that residents used for farming or hunting and also to communal wells and to at least twenty-seven named coastal pools where inhabitants harvested salt for their own use or to sell.[30] Moreover, in Spanish law and custom there were precedents for relating the size of the común to population size and subsistence needs, which in theory allowed populations to claim lands not only on the basis of prior possession, as with the kah, but also on the basis of growth or material deprivation. Finally, while the común, like the kah, was a place-based corporate entity, unlike the kah it was not a corporate *ethnic* identity but a corporate *class* entity, capable of embracing both subjects of the indigenous republics and working people of mestizo and pardo descent.

In the wake of independence, the común came to carry political significance as well, a foundation of liberal conceptions of right, popular sovereignty, and commonweal. Even in the face of measures designed to curtail arranchamiento in the early 1820s, residents of some unofficial settlements in the region earned temporary reprieves under the aegis of el común. Yucatán's governor ordered the protection of lands near one such settlement for what he describes as the "common good" of the twenty indigenous families that resided there, opining that while not residing in an official pueblo, they did "live [in] and work lands of the común, forming a true, even if small, pueblo which deserves the same consideration as any other." To sell such lands, he concluded, would be an "unjust and tyrannical act" that would "enslave those who live there by subjecting them to labor obligations and other seigneurial rights, from which they are now free."[31]

Such acts of tolerance were uncommon and became increasingly so in ensuing years. Nonetheless, in land disputes indigenous and working populations in Yucatán increasingly made reference to el común and at least through the 1830s succeeded in slowing the alienation of communal lands through legal action. In 1834 several municipalities in the area of Opichén, directly south of the Hunucmá region, joined forces in a petition against cattle ranches, leading one exasperated prefect (*jefe político*) to denounce the "ancient and ridiculous pretensions" of "malicious and rebellious villains" who claimed lands adjoining the ejidos as communal possessions. In support of their claims, he fumed, they presented "no other title than tradition, and the possession of insubstantial, confused, and legally invalid documents," effectively proposing that "each pueblo should be a small independent nation, whether prosperous or miserable."[32]

Despite such contemptuous reactions, land conflicts in the Hunucmá region in the same period suggest that kah officials' appeals to el común, however ancient in their origins, were contemporary expressions, appropriating liberal political rhetoric to communal purposes. When one landowner claimed alleged wastelands in 1837, Ucú's cacique and kah officials protested that "those woodlands belong to the común of el pueblo . . . and one of our duties is to avoid any harm that may be done to the común . . . those woods cannot be sold . . . since the indígenas don't have any place to make their milpas, and often must rent other lands for that purpose, in addition to the damage that cattle raising will cause to their plots." In the same year the cacique and officials of Kinchil's kah defended their común against an attempt by Felipe Peña to annex an old cofradía hacienda along with its indigenous residents. They denounced the efforts of hacendados to seize areas of the común without citing representatives of the kah to participate in the surveys. In making their claim, the petitioners evoked not only the kah's prior possession, but also the prospect of its dispossession: "If the pueblo of Kinchil has grown large, in its number of inhabitants; if from the ejidos that border it, its vecinos provide themselves with wood, charcoal, and other necessities of life; if its lands are scarcely enough to cultivate the grains upon which they depend—is it not clear that the proposal of a few private landowners to buy or rent those lands is to kill [Kinchil's inhabitants], or at least to enslave them, making them the vassals of the buyer? Is this not clearly opposed to the liberty that the free and philanthropic Government that we enjoy offers, and to the pueblo's possession, since time immemorial, of its lands?"[33] Indigenous residents of Hunucmá made a similar appeal in 1844 in an attempt to prevent a rancher from claiming lands of the común west of Hunucmá, the only lands left for their "subsistence, and that of our poor families" after the purchase of lands to the north, east, and south. They were flatly rejected by a government official, who claimed they had ejidos sufficient to their needs and had been "seduced, or impelled, by ignoble motives" into making the complaint.[34]

While the wording of the appeals probably was drafted by lawyers, the determination of the republics to file such petitions as well as occasional references to the común in trial testimony suggest that the común was a concept of growing currency among indigenous and working populations. That concept had been transformed from its original Spanish meaning through infusion with understandings of territoriality, possession, and history that were particular to the kahs. At the same time, el común widened the kah's compass by incorporating working mestizos and expanded its political compass by incorporating liberal conceptions of liberty and rights. Whereas the kah had been a colonial institution, fully integrated into the workings of Spanish mechanisms of domination and extraction, the común seemed at moments to become an oppositional concept: a hybrid of Spanish, indigenous, and liberal frameworks through which indigenous officials contested dominant Creole visions of progress. As was the case with earlier kah land claims, appeals to the concept of el común often involved strategic reference to history in documents and petitions. Unlike the kah, however, the común shifted toward the evocation of histories not only of prior possession but also of dispossession as a basis for collective claims. For indigenous residents and working vecinos of the Hunucmá region, the landscape was inscribed with histories not only of possession, but increasingly, of loss.

Two decades later, when mestizo workers joined with members of the indigenous republic in following cacique Chac into the woods near Tacubaya, they would do so in the understanding that those lands were part of el común and available for use by all the working people of Hunucmá. In testimony they would give under interrogation, both indigenous and mestizo workers would avow their belief that the woods were lands of el común, a belief that derived partly from their faith in Chac's authority and partly from the proximity of the lands to town. Similarly, when the cacique was brought before Rivero for questioning, he justified his actions in terms of the común. For Chac and his followers it was el común's dispossession, as much as the kah's ancient possession, that was the foundation of their claim.

ENCLOSING TACUBAYA

In 1857 Juana Peña's reaction to the events at Tacubaya was different—harsher and more uncompromising—from what it might have been in the face of a similar event two decades before. Across Yucatán in the intervening decades, land alienations, the decline of the batabs, rural dissatisfaction over taxation, and the arming and mobilization of indigenous soldiers in several regional uprisings had proved to be an explosive mix. What became known as the Yucatán Caste War began in 1847, when indigenous and mestizo rebels joined in an uprising that swept through much of the peninsula, sparing only Mérida and the northwest. Casualties were vast, both in the rebellion itself, and especially during its bloody suppression and in fighting that continued sporadically over ensuing decades. The hacienda economy of the south and east, until then a mainstay of Yucatán's economy, was devastated.[35]

Remigio Novelo was a casualty of the violence, reportedly crucified by indigenous hands in 1847 in what officials called a "horrendous" event.[36] Landowners of the Hunucmá region, however, were spared most of the violence and devastation of the war. Perhaps indigenous populations in the region were too firmly subjected to join the rebellion; perhaps they were too closely supervised or too distant from the contraband networks that supplied others with arms; perhaps they judged joining a bloody rebellion to be against their interests. Overt repression may have played a role as well. In 1847 a town official in Umán, Manuel Correa, claimed to have discovered a rebel conspiracy involving the caciques of Hunucmá, Umán, Oxcum, and Mérida. Though the evidence was scanty at best, the caciques were detained and executed. Then Correa distributed the cattle and maize of Umán's late cacique to vecinos in order, he explained, to "calm their hate." In the main, when members of Hunucmá's republics became involved in the war they did so as allies of landowners, fighting as hidalgo troops and earning tax exemptions as well as cash payments and rations for their families.[37] A few, including caciques like José Tzuc of Kinchil, even acquired small ranches with modest herds of cattles and horses and indebted servants.[38]

Veterans of the battlefield brought the war back with them. From the 1850s on, Hunucmá's mayor, the veteran Eduardo López, dedicated himself to conscripting troops and hunting deserters. Authorities in Umán did the same. Continuing skirmishes with rebels in eastern Yucatán provided a pretext for the surveillance of indigenous residents and for arresting presumed enemy emissaries and sympathizers. Umán's mayor took action against one "disobedient" and "very disorganized" indigenous resident who, upon hearing that a shipment of meat to government forces might be intercepted by indigenous rebels, had said, "Great! Good for them, then!" The mayor sent him off with the next group of conscripts.[39] In 1852 such vigilance bore fruit when several hidalgos from Hunucmá deserted their post in Bacalar, only to be captured by rebel forces. Subsequently, they were invited by the rebel leaders Venancio Tec and Manuel Barrera to take part in a planned invasion of Mérida to "eliminate every kind of tax" and secure the return of "the lands that the government has sold." While several members of the group were retained to serve as scribes, Tec gave the others, who declined to join the rebels, what he called a "passport" in Maya that allowed them to cross rebel territory to return to Hunucmá, where they were detained and interrogated by local authorities.[40]

The ongoing violence fostered a hardened regime of ethnic and class domination. Local judges and municipal officials put tupils to work capturing fugitive debt peons, detaining those suspected of criminal offenses or drunkenness, and administering public whippings. One indigenous resident of Tetiz complained that Anastacio Castilla, Tetiz's justice of the peace, "had the indigenous republic in his personal service, and even working in his house, doing work that he exploits for his own benefit, which should correspond to personal servants, rather than to officials of a republic."[41] Caciques supervised forced labor drafts of indigenous residents for municipal projects and public works, or *fajinas*. Umán's municipal authorities, for instance, drew on the indigenous residents of Umán and Bolón to provide wood and other supplies to the town hall and even to supply contingents of laborers for the ranches and farms of local landowners. When indigenous workers refused such assignments or challenged compensation levels, they were imprisoned and, in the words of one approving jefe político, "punished with whippings, as is their [indigenous] custom." Caciques administered such penalties in the town square, both at the behest of municipal officials and when they sensed their fragile authority challenged. When one of Hunucmá's caciques felt that an itinerant indigenous salesman had "offended his dignity and authority in the presence of his subordinates," he immediately ordered tupils to force the offender to his knees and soundly whip him.[42] The subordination and incorporation of republic officials emerged most graphically in 1864 in a proposal for a new town hall in Hunucmá that included a room for the tupils and an office for Hunucmá's cacique, adjoining a small prison. A crude diagram included in the proposal served as an icon of a political system in which the powers of caciques were lodged not in the land and its histories, but in their disciplinary function within a system of municipal governance managed by landowning gentry.[43]

Working-class mestizos fared little better. When José María Naranjo, a sixty-year-old Cuban immigrant and charcoal maker, failed to make a delivery to a client, Hunucmá's justice of the peace sent tupils to arrest him. Naranjo resisted, and when hauled into court he protested a judge's threat to sell

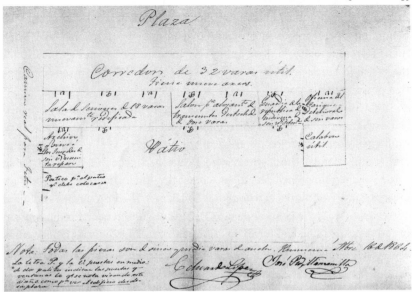

Diagram of proposed town hall for Hunucmá, including rooms for cacique and tupils (1864). Courtesy Archivo General del Estado de Yucatán.

him into a forced labor arrangement: "I am no Indian! You just try and make me!" Naranjo's lawyer later argued that he had resisted because he had been treated "as if he were a thing," not a citizen. In a society heretofore divided into separate ethnic republics but now increasingly characterized by two racialized classes—landowning ts'uls and working indios, or Indians—to be an indio was as much about class as about ethnic background. Working-class mestizos like Naranjo were effectively becoming indigenous mestizos, indistinguishable in condition and predicament from their indigenous peers.[44]

Hunucmá's hardening regime of class and racial domination proved favorable to hacendados and ranchers. To be sure, indigenous and mestizo populations, sometimes led by caciques of the republics, continued to appeal to authorities to prevent the privatization of communal lands. Residents of Kinchil and Umán were still able to secure temporary injunctions against the survey and purchase of some communal lands outside the ejidos, which they claimed as part of the común.[45] Residents of one old indigenous settlement near Umán fended off its survey and purchase by citing their ancestors' possession of the land "from time immemorial" and by appealing for protection as members of a "poor class of indígenas, who deserve . . . protection . . .

due to their ignorance and misfortune."[46] Landowners who sought to expand their operations in the vicinity of communal salt pools—like Doña Juana's second husband, José María Fernándes, a landowner and justice of the peace in Hunucmá—had to promise to "abide by the ancient customs that govern the salt pools."[47]

In the wake of the Caste War, however, landowners increasingly brushed aside whatever impediments the republics and their caciques still presented. Municipal officials carved up areas of the común to facilitate their sale to family and friends. Landowners who earlier had occupied lands for open cattle ranches now enclosed them, converting them into haciendas. They erected stone landmarks in woodlands adjacent to their properties and hired surveyors to walk the lands and map them, now without need for the consent of indigenous officials. They filed criminal complaints against woodcutters and agriculturalists, accusing them of trespassing on their lands and of committing acts of destruction, whether of woodlands chopped down for milpas or of the surveying landmarks that many now recognized as auguries of their dispossession.[48] Increasingly, petitions like that of indigenous residents of Ucú, who attempted to defend lands of el común based on their "constant and long-standing" cultivation of the land, the "customs of [their] ancestors," and their residence in a "poor pueblo, lacking in resources," were disregarded. Government officials determined that the hacendado Manuel Peón was entitled to claim those lands and called for the severe punishment of whomever encouraged what they called an "ignorant" and "audacious" petition for lands located outside the half-league of ejidos that, in their view, rightfully corresponded to Ucú.[49]

It was thus in the confidence of the times that Fernándes worked at expanding Tacubaya. Buildings were erected, and Tacubaya's herds multiplied, reaching eight hundred head by 1856; Fernándes even saw to the planting of a substantial field of henequen.[50] All of this required more land, and so in 1854 Fernándes had landmarks erected in adjoining lands of the común, an action the cacique Pascual Chac reportedly witnessed and authorized. Then Fernándes ordered the clearing of woodlands around a communal well called Yohalal, to the west of the hacienda, or more than two leagues from Hunucmá—well beyond the legally recognized limits of the town's ejidos. Subsequently Fernándes filed paperwork to claim them as wastelands. When Chac went with members of the republic to assign milpas in September 1856, however, he did not walk to Yohalal. He led them to another place, to the east, deep into lands already attached to Tacubaya. As the men opened a breach in the woods, they knocked down the landmarks bordering Tacubaya, walking a path that transected the western third of the land Peña and Fernándes had claimed for the hacienda. The machetes that hacked their way through the brush were thus not merely clearing plots for milpa or even defending against the enclosure of Yohalal: they were leveling a counterclaim on lands already surveyed, marked, and legally annexed to the *finca*.

While Fernándes had arranged the technicalities of expanding Tacubaya, it was Doña Juana who took action upon receiving news of Chac's incursion. She summoned the cacique, who, she later recalled, spoke to her "humbly, but hypocritically," assuring her that he had opened a path only to cross the area, not to stake a claim. Only later did Peña learn that Chac had assigned milpa plots to his subjects, news that led her to file a criminal complaint against him, not only for "destruction" of her property, but for "usurping the prerogatives of public authorities" and for "instigating men of el pueblo to rise up to realize that usurpation." Peña called for the punishment of the "malicious" cacique and the "evildoers" who followed him, "invading Tacubaya with their labor." Implicitly, she evoked the specter of the Caste War, denouncing Chac and his followers as "malevolent" agents of "ruin" who had lost all respect for "things even as sacred as property." Only through the most "terrible" punishment, she argued, could the government protect Tacubaya and "all properties, which would be threatened by such acts of violence."[51]

As the authorities rounded up Chac and his followers, Peña took further measures. While Tacubaya was, according to her, already "well measured, marked, and recognized by the entire world," she arranged a new ritual of possession to seal her ownership and put a presumptuous cacique in his place. A judge and several town residents set out for Tacubaya, bearing compasses and other measuring instruments. Like Lorenzo Argaiz at Santa María thirty years earlier, they walked the lands, opening breaches, exploring milpas, finding old landmarks, and erecting new ones topped with crosses. Unlike Argaiz, however, these surveyors entered into no negotiations with kah officials, took no pause to learn the names and histories of the land, and made no mention of any indigenous assistants. Their survey and the map they produced was more than a map of the landscape of Tacubaya. It was a sanctification of boundaries, with crosses topping the landmarks and etched on the map itself. The map became an icon of possession intended to rewrite the landscape in the archive and reverse the actions of those who, in Peña's view, had transgressed not only against Tacubaya, but also against what she described as the most "sacred" of principles—that of private property.

When hauled before Judge Rivero, those who followed Chac claimed to

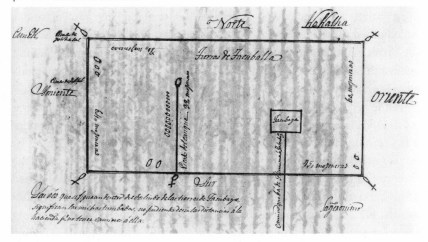

Survey map of Hacienda Tacubaya, showing boundaries and contested *milpas* (1857).
Courtesy Archivo General del Estado de Yucatán.

be unaware that the lands they had cleared were considered the property of Tacubaya. Members of the indigenous republic reported that they had complained to Chac that they had no lands to work and no means of subsistence. The cacique then brought them to the woods north of Hunucmá, assigning them lands he said were of "el común." Mestizo detainees mentioned seeing "many Indians of el pueblo" working in those lands at the cacique's orders. They concluded that the lands were of the común and open for their use as well. When the cacique came before Rivero, he too made reference to el común, but in the context of a more extensive defense. In a letter to the court, he and another kah official described those woods as "lands of the Community, in which people of this Pueblo used to work." Moreover, Chac continued his defense by emphasizing the "impoverished" condition of his subjects and of the común and the history of its dispossession by landlords like Peña. In concluding, he pled for the court to restore the pueblo's "liberty" to cultivate lands of the común, a reference that implicitly cast a struggle over land as a struggle for collective political recognition as well.

Though eloquent, such arguments found no favor. Peña won the case, and at the request of local justices in Hunucmá and with the approval of Yucatán's governor, Chac was deposed for "bad conduct." Finding Chac "not lacking in guilt," Rivero sentenced the ex-cacique to cover court costs and declared him and the other men liable for further criminal prosecution. Weeks after

Rivero's verdict and after the various documents relating to the case traveled to several higher courts for review, ninety-five pages of documents were sewn together into one case file and were committed to the archives. Structured by the verdict and its politics, that case file now seemed to tell a single story: one of an impetuous cacique who attacked private property and suffered due punishment for his actions.

Unbound and rebound, however, the story that file tells is not solely about a conflict over land. It is also about how a cacique revived for a moment the traditional powers of the batab and the possessions of the kah and with them, the histories the kah once had inscribed in that landscape. When called to defend his actions and those of the men who followed him, Chac evoked el común, another beleaguered entity that was inscribed upon the land, albeit as much through a history of dispossession as of possession. Ultimately, the story the "Causa" tells is about the suppression of a communalist vision of the pueblo of Hunucmá by another vision—one founded in communal dispossession, racial subjugation, forced labor, and unbridled exploitation. As such, the "Causa," once archived, joined other case files from Hunucmá and elsewhere in Yucatán, all telling variations of that same story, a story that effaced one kind of history in the landscape to replace it with another.

In this sense, Pascual Chac was Hunucmá's last cacique, even if it would be another twelve years before the remnants of the republics, and with them the caciques, would be abolished for good. But Chac's detractor, Doña Juana Peña, was also last—not the last hacendado, but in a sense the last Peña. She died before Rivero handed down his ruling against Chac. Doña Juana, moreover, had done her best to destroy the career and social prestige of her miscreant brother Felipe and used her control over the execution of Don Eduardo Peña's will to deprive both Felipe and her other brother, Angel, of much of their share of the wealth. In the end, Felipe's wife and two daughters abandoned him, leaving him to plead uselessly before a judge to order the return of his children, lamenting that his "cup of suffering runneth over." Angel was left in what he called a "notorious" state of indigence, living in a dilapidated house, and spending his few remaining resources over the next few decades on futile lawsuits to recover money from Juana and from her estate.[52]

After her death, however, even Juana Peña's children were denied her legacy. Her second husband, José Fernándes, took control of both her estate and that of her first husband, Remigio Novelo, depriving the children from her marriage to Novelo of much of their inheritance and leaving them to lodge decades of fruitless appeals in civil court.[53] From Doña Juana's death forward, the Peña name would no longer be associated in the Hunucmá region with powerful, Maya-speaking mestizo landlords. It became a name of commoners: workers, milperos, and debt peons. As the diverse documents that made up the "Causa" were sewn up into a single file, the fates of cacique and hacendada were bound together and consigned together to the archives.

CHAPTER TWO

KING OF THE FOREST

Civilization, Savagery, and the Annals of History

LIGHT AND SHADOW: that was what the editors
of the newspaper, the *Revista de Mérida*, offered their
readers on 17 May 1892, in an article entitled "The
Crimes of Hunucmá: Light and Shadow." By "Shadow"
they were referring to a series of dastardly acts committed over the preceding decades, culminating in an attack on Xpak, the dyewood operations of the henequen
magnate Rafael Peón, by a man known as the King
of the Forest. Some of those episodes were known to
the public, others were forgotten, but all, declared the
editors, were manifestations of the "laziness, vice, and
crime" that plagued Hunucmá. Their intention was to
bring "light" to Hunucmá, through the collection and
presentation of information about those crimes to public scrutiny and to the Yucatecan government, in the
form of a published chronology.[1]

"The Crimes of Hunucmá" was indeed about light
and shadow, though in a way different from what its

author may have intended. Like light, the annals selected and illuminated those dates and happenings judged important—arson attacks, shootings, killings—and colored the tone of their rendering as episodes of so-called "depravity" and "savagery." Like shadow, they obscured from view that which was judged irrelevant or important to conceal, from the expansion of the haciendas to the enrichment of gentry and oligarchs to indigenous servitude. At the boundary between light and shadow, the annals constructed a border between event and nonevent, in an act of framing that made a series of happenings comprehensible by putting them in sequence, even as it left the connections between those happenings—and between them and what lay in shadow—denied, silenced, or forgotten.

To read "The Crimes of Hunucmá" is to follow the play of both light and shadow, by restoring those dramatic events to their shadowed contexts. It is also, however, to explore the consolidation of the annals themselves, as the Revista, like other regional newspapers, took on the task of documenting Hunucmá over the decades leading up to the attack on Xpak and the years that followed. It is to illuminate the power of those annals as effective history, put to definite uses and to devastating effect. Finally, it is to trace the contours of a landscape divided into opposed social worlds, each of whose inhabitants laid claim to el pueblo, but in ways that had become irreconcilable.

THE PUEBLO'S PROGRESS

In the 1870s the Hunucmá district underwent a dramatic metamorphosis. Milpas and pasturage shrank away, and tall, spiky rows of henequen plants rose in their place. Machine houses, smokestacks, and cramped workers' quarters sprouted on the haciendas, and roads and railways spread throughout the district. New buildings rose in towns and pueblos, and plazas, public markets, and gas lighting came as well; a bell tower rose high over Hunucmá's town plaza, striking the hours with sonorous tones.[2] Not since the era of Spanish colonization had Hunucmá and the rest of northwestern Yucatán been transformed so radically. The metamorphosis was linked to the westward expansion of the United States in the second half of the nineteenth century and to the invention of the binder twine machine in 1872. Demand for cordage and for the henequen fiber from which twine and rope were made increased exponentially. In the same period, General Porfirio Díaz consolidated his power, becoming president of Mexico in 1876 and exercising dictatorial powers for three decades to follow. Díaz aggressively

Haciendas of the Hunucmá District (Haciendas of Neighboring Districts Omitted), ca. 1910.
Map by Philip Schwartzberg.

pursued a policy of modernization based on export-oriented industry and commercial agriculture, often financed by foreign capital. In Yucatán, such policies opened the door to North American cordage companies, which came to control the financing and commercialization of fiber production as well as the manufacture and sale of cordage. At the same time, Díaz consolidated political control over a long-restive peninsula by installing a series of military commanders as state governors.[3]

However stimulated by rising demand in the United States and however encouraged by national political consolidation, the transformation of Hunucmá was owed to decades of effort by local gentry and hacendados. Chief among these were the Peóns, a family of powerful landowners that rose to preeminence in the wake of the Caste War by buying up a series of large cattle ranches in the region. Subsequently they converted those properties to henequen haciendas; Yaxché, for instance, became one of the largest estates in the peninsula. They continued to expand their holdings through the last quarter of the nineteenth century, abetted by national and state government legislation aimed at the parcelization and sale of the ejidos and at the survey and titling of so-called wastelands and national lands. The Peóns also played a leading role in the exploitation of the district's dyewood stands and salt pools and cemented their dominance in the 1880s with the construction of a regional rail network.[4]

Smaller gentry also profited from the opportunities of the era. They took part in the dyewood and salt trades, commerce, and a brisk residential real estate market in towns and pueblos of the area. Despite the rise of the Peóns, Hunucmá's midlevel ts'uls continued to dominate town councils, enjoying the material and social benefits of those positions. Moreover, many local gentry converted small or midsize ranches and haciendas to henequen production beginning in the 1860s and acquired henequen-processing machinery as those enterprises prospered. While land legislation favored their claims—particularly measures meant to speed privatization of communal lands passed by Governor Eligio Ancona in 1876—they did not wait patiently on the application of law. Rather, they seized communal lands in the vicinity of their ranches and haciendas, enclosing them with stone walls called *albarradas* in order to establish de facto possession. Some landowners even seized lands within town or pueblo limits (that is, the *fundo legal*) on the premise, in one claimant's words, that "communal lands no longer exist."[5]

Municipal officials facilitated the enclosure and sale of communal lands. One state government official even censured Kinchil's officials for excessive zeal in selling off such lands, thus reducing that pueblo's "poor class" to a "dissimulated slavery." Local gentry made use of land surveys and lawsuits to ratify and title their claims and sometimes to rename them in Spanish (thus Homhuayum became Buenavista). No longer did surveyors engage in lengthy negotiations with indigenous populations regarding the location and history of communal lands. Instead, engineers quickly surveyed the land and then drew up topographical maps showing the exact location of neighboring haciendas, roads, and buildings. A map of Hacienda San Eduardo, which Eduardo Peña founded, noted the location of recently erected walls—some of which already had been knocked down by pueblo residents—as well as the ruins of a settlement where people once had lived and an old cemetery. Like other hacienda maps, this icon was not innocent of politics. The hacienda boundaries on every side were labeled "lands *said to be* of Hunucmá" (emphasis added), as if laying the groundwork for future expansion, against the claims of that pueblo, now relegated to a questioned orality.[6]

The expansion of henequen agriculture depended on the acquisition not only of land, but also of labor, as ranches were converted into henequen haciendas with much greater, year-round labor needs. Here, the division and sale

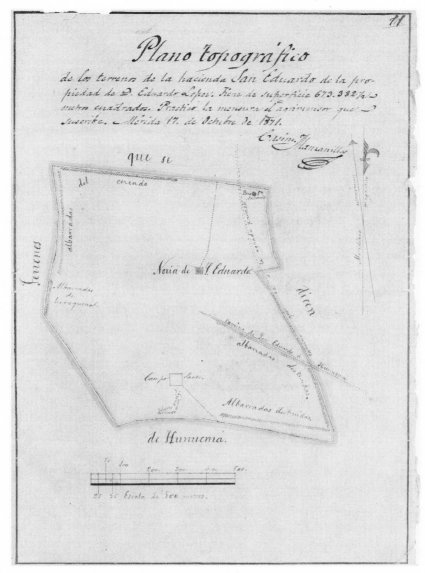

Map of Hacienda San Eduardo, showing boundaries, contested walls, and remains of a settlement (1871). Courtesy Archivo General del Estado de Yucatán.

of communal lands served a dual purpose: it made lands available for exploitation and triggered a severe decline in milpa agriculture, which encouraged pueblo residents to move to the haciendas to gain access to both woodlands and wage labor. Locust plagues, rampant in the 1880s, left agriculturalists in an even more tenuous position. Finally, pueblo residents were subject to military conscription and corvée labor in public works and even on private properties. Men who were drafted were unable to tend to their crops during their two- or three-month terms of service. In contrast, hacienda dwellers, or *acasillados*, were exempt from conscription, were provided with rations and clothing, and had access to water, milpa, firewood, and hunting privileges on hacienda grounds.[7]

Moreover, in an extension of the forms of indigenous indebted servitude already extant in the region, hacendados sought to ensure that workers acquired debts and then secured ownership of those debts in order to oblige the debtors to enter their service. Under the pressures of the time, many pueblo residents became indebted, and hacendados either purchased those debts or used them as a pretext for the seizure of their homes in the pueblos—another way of forcing workers onto the fincas. Hacienda residents tended to acquire mounting debts over time through purchases at the hacienda store, weddings, and other expenses, which generally proved impossible to pay off at the haciendas' exceedingly low levels of compensation. While workers were entitled by law, in theory, to seek another employer to assume their debt, hacendados often refused to accept money offered to them in payment of debts.[8]

Once bound to the hacienda, workers found themselves subject to a regime of systematic brutality. *Encargados* (overseers or supervisors) regularly administered whippings to groups of workers as exemplary punishments, or so-called "cleansings" (*limpias*), intended to improve work discipline. Testimony regarding the practice entered the record only rarely, as for instance when a worker of Hotzuc was found dead near the hacienda, with lash marks covering his chest, belly, and testicles.[9] Escapees were rounded up by police and bounty hunters and were punished with conscription or stints of forced labor; when they could not be found, hacendados joined forces with local authorities to interrogate, harass, and detain their family members. The wife of one escaped worker scoffed at such intimidation, suggesting under interrogation that "perhaps [her husband] was hiding up her ass, and she could pull him out for them." She suffered three weeks of detention for her insolence.[10]

As such testimony suggests, landowners sought to turn the intimate bonds of family life to their advantage. They ordered the marriage of female residents to chosen employees; those who abandoned husband or hacienda were captured and whipped. Unpaid female labor—from the preparation of tortillas to some tasks in henequen fields to domestic work—was critical to the daily functioning of the haciendas. Moreover, the hacendados seized and claimed legal custody over the children of working families, whom they then put to work as hacienda laborers or domestic servants despite the tenacious resistance of their relatives. In a statement before a civil court, Felipa Tzuc denounced the Hunucmá notable Pedro Magaña for claiming her orphaned grandchildren, exclaiming, "I never thought there existed, in society, people capable of trying to tear my little grandchildren away from me." Another woman, Atanacia Canché, recovered her daughter only after physically seizing her. Then they left the district as fugitives.[11]

By the end of the nineteenth century, the effect of such strategies was clear. Roughly 50 percent of the district's population—in some areas, like the vicinity of Umán, 60 percent or more—resided on henequen haciendas (see appendix).[12] For landowning elites, such changes were auguries of Yucatán's imminent metamorphosis from a provincial backwater into a vanguard of progress. From the 1870s forward, regional elites timed the inaugurations of public works projects like railway and telegraph lines, markets, and public buildings to coincide with national holidays like Cinco de Mayo (a commemoration of a Mexican victory over French forces in the Battle of Puebla of 1862), making such material constructions into manifestations of the political refashioning of pueblo and patria. In 1880 the governor of Yucatán noted the appropriateness of such timing, explaining that "pueblos that are able to advance through material improvements show that they are deserving of the glories they have achieved." At the inauguration of a railway line during national independence celebrations in the town of Acanceh, one speaker called on his listeners to "look at the face of el pueblo, and the hope of progress and happiness reflected there. . . . ! It sees these celebrations, frenetically applauds the triumph of civilization, and envisions, with its excited imagination, the indecipherable mysteries of the future, of the vertiginous rapidity with which the way has been opened to the great, majestic, train car of Progress! Who does not feel the stirrings of love of country, even if barely awakening, in the depths of his soul?"[13]

Such events transformed the pueblos into staging grounds for the remaking of state and nation. After an official visit to the Hunucmá district

Studio photograph of a "field servant," meant to illustrate dress and labor practices typical of male hacienda workers in rural Yucatán. Courtesy Fototeca Pedro Guerra, Universidad Autónoma de Yucatán.

Studio photograph of woman grinding maize, meant to illustrate dress and labor practices typical of females in rural Yucatán. Courtesy Fototeca Pedro Guerra, Universidad Autónoma de Yucatán.

Hacendado with wife, encargado, and peons. Date and location unknown.
Courtesy Fototeca Pedro Guerra, Universidad Autónoma de Yucatán.

in 1876, one governor referred to its pueblos as being mired in "decadence"
and enjoined its inhabitants to "dedicate themselves with enthusiasm to
their labors, convinced that the prosperity and well-being of individuals and
of the entire country depend on peace and work." During a visit by Governor
Ancona five years later, state officials again decried "ruinous" and "deplorable" pueblos like Samahil and Ucú. Tetiz's main road, on the other hand,
seemed to epitomize modernity. "What a beautiful road!" one commentator reported. "Straight as an arrow, without the slightest bend: not a single
loose stone on it, from the main plaza of Hunucmá all the way to the plaza of
Tetiz!" In the town of Hunucmá, which seemed just like a "piece of Mérida,"
the governor was received with what news commentators called a "beautiful spectacle": fireworks, music, and parades by both of the town's militia,
including a still-extant pardo regiment. All in all, the event presented a "great
example of the effects of a democratic government, in which the governor
has talked with the leaders of el pueblo so sensibly about the most important
interests of their community."[14]

At the time of Díaz's advent to power in 1876, the Hunucmá district seemed an unlikely stage for such performances. The majority of pueblo and town residents were poor and indigenous; churches and public buildings dating from the colonial era were decrepit. Buoyed by henequen, however, Hunucmá's ts'uls changed the image of the region through a sustained effort to materially transform its towns and villages into modern pueblos. At the inauguration of a railroad running from Umán to Mérida a poet passionately declared, "Today the West / covers itself in splendor / the spirit of progress / visits its mansion." Soon the railroad would bring "glory to the country" and fortune to el pueblo, allowing "radiant Yucatán / to glimpse its future." Local efforts to build schools in the district were saluted by the Yucatecan press as heralding the "awakening" of el pueblo. One urged the residents of Hunucmá to "Sell your jewels like the queen of Castile. . . . Do everything—everything!—for work, morality, education. Thus you will conquer the Future."[15]

In Hispanic civic and cultural institutions Hunucmá's gentry found a way to set themselves apart from the region's indigenous working populations, even as they linked themselves to elites in the capital. A group of residents led by local notable Pedro Magaña organized a nonprofit theatre company to perform short works and Spanish zarzuelas. Merchants and shop owners in Hunucmá, Tetiz, and Umán financed the publication of a newspaper entitled "The Voice of the District," also under Magaña's direction. On the occasion of the newspaper's inauguration, the Yucatecan poet and man of letters Rodolfo Menéndez wrote a paean to the honor of Hunucmá in which he hailed the town as "queen of the West / of heroic Yucatán" and a "beautiful pearl, set / in the road to Sisal." In a series of florid stanzas, Menéndez saluted the town for its moment of "sublime awakening / in which they suddenly shout / Progress!" and commended residents on their movement in that direction: "With the printing press, and with the school / you go toward the future / with work and science / with goodness and truth. . . . Forward, Hunucmá!"[16]

Even as they strove to make Hunucmá modern, regional elites, state government officials, and local gentry collaborated in the celebration of traditional Hunucmá. The region was known for several cults venerating saints and The Virgin, and the scale of processions and other religious events increased through the late nineteenth century. The Virgin of Tetiz attracted visitors from far and wide, and Hunucmá sponsored important religious festivals. Local hacendados donated icons and funds to the church, taking up collections from the wealthy to pay for improvements to church facilities. In 1878, when the state government called upon town councils to append the names of famous personages to town and pueblo names, Hunucmá's councilmen chose to rebaptize the town Hunucmá de Caldera, in honor of a famous local clergyman; Lorenzo Caldera was credited with acting on his "civilizing instincts" toward indigenous populations by writing "dramatic and comical theaters pieces" intended to "inculcate good manners" in indigenous children. Ucú and Sisal, by contrast, adopted the names of local merchants who had been active in transport and the dyewood trade.[17]

The place of tradition was nowhere more evident, however, than in fiestas, which featured public performances of traditional music and dances known as *jaranas* and *vaquerías*, respectively. So much is clear from a theater play originally performed in Mérida in 1875. Entitled *El rábano por las hojas: una fiesta en Hunucmá* (The Radish by the Leaves: A Fiesta in Hunucmá), the musical farce recounts the attempts of the son of an elite family in Mérida to seduce a pious and betrothed working-class mestiza at a fiesta in Hunucmá. The young man resolves with a friend to "lower ourselves to her level, by adopting her [traditional mestiza] dress and dancing in the jaranita" at the fiesta. After some rustic dances and a series of songs in Maya and Spanish, the young woman's betrothed—a man who "serves the Government" and is committed to "order, religion, and peace"—uncovers the plot. Outraged, pueblo residents denounce the "little gentlemen." "Not content with mixing up el pueblo in the farces called elections," they cry, "They come here . . . joining in [pueblo residents'] dances and even wearing their clothes, in order to insinuate themselves more easily among the mestizas." In opposition to those who "under the pretext of civilizing el pueblo, corrupt it iniquitously," *El rábano* offers the traditional culture of el pueblo and the honor of mestiza women as correctives to the corrosive effects of modern commerce and as a supplement to good government.[18]

Viewed from the capital, Hunucmá's fiesta thus offered a stage for the display of authentic popular virtues and for the disclosure of the nature of government, whether as moral undertaking or insidious masquerade. Viewed from Hunucmá, the fiesta del pueblo was a political ritual, a theater of state formation meant to cement the local hegemony of rural gentry even as it reshaped pueblo–state relations. From the 1880s on, official government visits to the district of Hunucmá were accompanied by abundant public festivities and traditional dances. Fiestas also marked inaugural events, as for instance at the opening of a bazaar market in 1884, a celebration that one commentator called a "fiesta of progress" in which the population "succumbed to a joy as intense as it was legitimate." Yucatán's governor attended the festivities, witnessing public dances that reportedly featured the "grace and beauty" of daughters of the town's principal families.[19]

These performances of tradition, like the performances of modernity they often accompanied, were illuminated in copious press coverage, seeming to constitute the history of the Hunucmá region. Left in the shadows was the brutal regime of forced labor that made such performances possible. The annals of Hunucmá, as performed and documented in the pages of the newspapers read throughout the peninsula, were all light: progress, civilization, joy, virtue, festivity. Hunucmá's regional culture came to occupy a special place statewide, embodying the harmonious synthesis of modernity and tradition in pueblo life. This vision of Hunucmá was both utopian and nostalgic; it offered auguries of imminent redemption by capital and patria, even as it claimed to sink taproots into country virtues, traditions, and religiosity. Against this backdrop—one of railroads and jaranas, telegraph lines, bell towers, and pilgrimages—oligarchs and ts'uls staged el pueblo's progress.

IN THE SHADOWS

Although henequen reigned supreme in northwestern Yucatán, there were limits to its realm. While haciendas expanded throughout the center, south, and east of Hunucmá, a hinterland consisting of shoreline, swampy woodlands, and savanna lay along the coast and inland. While maize agriculture was sharply reduced in the core henequen areas, subsistence agriculturalists and hunters still worked marginal lands at a greater distance from the town of Hunucmá, five to ten miles to the north and west. In those old lands of the común residents continued to hunt deer and plant their crops, to cut wood and *huano* (a kind of palm used as a roofing material), and produce charcoal. Even when locust plagues or adverse weather devastated milpas, demand for wood and charcoal kept the prices for those products high.

The most valuable sylvan commodity was dyewood, which remained an important export in the late nineteenth century. Dyewood was cut by small gangs, often under the leadership of an overseer; middlemen then sold the wood to merchants. Cutters faced enormous physical hardship in the course of their work, which took them to distant swampy areas like the woodlands near a small settlement called Kaxek (Maya for dyewood, literally "black wood") and exposed them, according to one observer, to "misfortunes and

Woods and a cenote, or sinkhole,
near Kaxek. Photo by Paul Eiss.

diseases that decimate the dyewood cutters, year after year." By the 1880s
the exploitation of dyewood stands in the Hunucmá region had left behind
only old stumps and roots in some areas, which cutters struggled to extract
with their axes. Small cutters faced competition from hacendados like the
Peóns, who acquired vast tracts of forestland in order to mount large-scale
dyewood-cutting operations with contract laborers and debt peons.[20]

Even though many hunters, subsistence agriculturalists, and their families spent long stretches of time out in old woodlands of the común like
Kaxek, they retained homes and social bonds in the pueblos and returned pe-
riodically and seasonally to buy provisions, to sell their crops, and to attend
church. Working residents participated in gremios, or guilds, dedicated to
patron saints or became patrons of one of the crosses or shrines that ringed
the pueblo, donating whatever profits might be gained from milpa, hunting,
and woodcutting to those purposes. They appealed to the Virgin and other
saints in time of trouble and traveled both within and outside the district

to take part in fiestas and processions. When hauled into court, they often could not testify to calendrical dates but were able to situate events in relation to religious festivals or to the masses, rosaries, novenas, and other rites that structured their lives.[21]

For other indigenous and mestizo residents, the woodlands offered a sylvan refuge on a semipermanent basis. During the Caste War and in the decades afterward, military conscripts fled their postings across the state to return to the region; unable to live in pueblos and towns, where they faced detention, they lived in sparsely inhabited woodlands like Kaxek. There they joined others who had fled conscription or tax or forced labor obligations in towns and pueblos as well as fugitive indebted servants from the haciendas. By the late 1850s local officials complained that such men were "wandering around in armed groups, doing as much damage as they can," through cattle rustling and banditry. Facing the complaints of local ranchers and landowners and confronting increasing difficulty in raising enough troops to satisfy the demands of military campaigns, local officials tried in vain, with the assistance of soldiers, to apprehend the roving deserters.[22] In 1864 Hunucmá's mayor, the Caste War veteran Eduardo López, wrote to the governor suggesting a new way to apprehend what he termed "bad citizens." "There is one measure," he wrote, "that gave us good results in the past, which is to apprehend their families, imprisoning them until those men return. While this is against the laws that are currently in effect, since this is an exceptional case, I think that these extraordinary measures should be taken."[23]

Neither pueblo residents nor Hunucmá's itinerant sylvan population remained passive in the face of the expansion of the haciendas. Beginning in the 1860s residents began to express their discontent in acts of resistance. They shot cattle, often claiming, when hauled into court, that they had mistaken them for deer; they toppled walls enclosing contested woodlands, stole henequen leaves, and destroyed landmarks.[24] The violence only increased in the 1870s in the wake of Governor Ancona's attempts to encourage the division and sale of communal lands. In 1873, after a local ts'ul claimed lands near Hunucmá, a group of men shot up the main building of his hacienda and knocked down the stone walls enclosing those lands. When a judge arrived on the scene, an angry crowd turned against him, lifting up his carriage and carrying him off. Three years later, when another judge set out, accompanied by troops, to survey dyewood stands on lands called Xluch, an armed group said to number in the hundreds emerged from nearby woods. The rebels, who reportedly wore red sashes, easily routed the soldiers and then proceeded to town, where they burned down several houses and killed five local notables.[25]

Governor Ancona sent large contingents of national guard units to the area with orders to engage the alleged revolutionaries, confiscate their guns, and arrest those responsible for the attacks in order to demonstrate the "respect that must be shown to property." When the soldiers headed out into the woods they met determined resistance from pueblo residents, who had built stone defensive walls and trenches there. The troops struggled to make their way through swampy woods, the water sometimes reaching the bellies of their horses; occasionally they engaged in firefights with the elusive enemy. In the end, their successes were limited: a few arms caches discovered in places like Kaxek; a handful of arrests. Interrogations yielded names, both Mayan and Spanish, of suspects from Hunucmá and Tetiz. Efforts to search houses and detain suspects, however, proved fruitless, as many men took off for the woods; one officer's proposal to surround the church in Tetiz during Sunday Mass in order to carry out detentions was sensibly vetoed by a superior. In the end, the soldiers simply withdrew, leaving what one newspaper termed the "evildoers of Hunucmá" still "infesting" the region.[26]

In coming years the attacks escalated, typically targeting not older haciendas, but smaller, more recently established fincas and ranches. Conflict erupted again at Xluch, after a ranch was established there. Milpa growers, enraged at the owner for not fencing in his cattle, chased off cowboys, shooting and slashing cattle. Assailants assassinated Hunucmá's mayor, subsequently desecrating his grave. Groups of men from Kinchil and Tetiz assaulted and torched fincas and the home of a dyewood trader. A group of men assaulted Hacienda Bella Flor near Kinchil, destroying telephone poles and lines and toppling corrals before leaving behind a note threatening to kill the hacienda's owner in punishment for his seizure of communal lands. From the 1880s forward, the attacks followed in quick succession: arson, wall toppling, bombings, cattle killing, robbery, homicide. In Tetiz, even the local authorities were implicated in the violence; in 1880 Hunucmá's prefect (*jefe político*) secured the dismissal of the municipal council, whose members he called "delinquents" guilty of fostering "disorder" and "anarchy."[27]

There were rebellions and other outbreaks of violence in late nineteenth-century Yucatán, typically in areas outside the henequen zone on the southern periphery of the state. In the southern reaches of the districts of Maxcanú, Peto, and Ticul, smallholding farmers resisted the encroachment of surveyors from the 1880s through the early 1900s.[28] Hunucmá was unusual, however, for the intensity of its violence and for its proximity to both a major henequen-producing zone and the state capital. Some of the most intense conflicts erupted over communal salt pools on the coast north of the town of Hunucmá, where residents extracted salt for personal consumption and for sale to merchants. From the 1870s, however, hacendados and local gentry began to survey and stake exclusive claims over the pools. When Doña Loreto Peón, matriarch of the Peón clan, claimed a salt pool in the area, town residents rioted and were immediately arrested. When Joaquín Peón and local officials suggested to residents that they contribute to a fund for the purchase of one or more pools for their own use, so-called "dissidents" reportedly refused, stating that "they would continue exploiting the pools as they always have, and . . . nobody could stop them."[29] Tensions came to a head in 1889, when the hacendado Tomás Aguilar ordered the surveying of a salt pool near his coastal finca, Xtul. As one of Aguilar's servants placed marks around the pool, six Hunucmá residents paid a visit, warning that if the survey continued "they would see what would happen." It did continue, and two weeks later, near midnight, a group of twenty-five men marched silently to the main house of the finca, where the Aguilars lay sleeping in their hammocks. The men fired their shotguns in unison, killing Aguilar's young son, Ricardo. They left—as a servant recalled, "without saying a single word"—and returned to the salt pool to remove the landmarks and close the breaches opened by the surveyors. Then they disappeared into the woods, although three days later three men with guns returned to visit the pool, reportedly "guarding, or patrolling it."[30]

Some landowners and local officials perceived episodes of violence in Hunucmá as foreshadowing a new Caste War. In 1882 Hunucmá's jefe político reported rumors that thirty rebel emissaries had established contact with indigenous residents and that an "indigenous uprising" was imminent. On 31 October the rebellion seemed to arrive, as vecinos of Umán reported hearing "scandalous cries" and sighting mysterious groups of men on the outskirts of town. Within a few hours, the story went, there would be an "invasion of rebel Indians" and a "terrible slaughter" in Umán. Eighty vecinos armed themselves and gathered in Umán's plaza, and Hunucmá's jefe político rushed twenty-five soldiers to their defense. On their way there, however, they met a town official who assuaged their fears. Three or four drunks had started yelling, he explained; the rest was hysteria.[31]

In contrast, officials of the state government rejected the notion that Indian rebels might stalk a place of civilization and progress just a stone's throw from the state capital. In a speech to the state congress in 1876, Governor Ancona attributed the actions of Hunucmá's "bad citizens" to conflicts over common lands, which he called a "fecund source of discord." His government, he declared, would resolve such disputes by enforcing land legislation and by explaining to rural dwellers that such "modern laws" were intended not to "despoil them of their land, but rather to divide the large areas of land that they used to hold in common into small properties." His words did not reassure Hunucmá's communalists, and the attacks continued. By the late 1880s many officials had come to see the population of the Hunucmá district as characterized by generalized and intractable tendencies toward criminality and delinquency. In 1889 the state Commission of Justice and Public Education objected to a proposal to eliminate Hunucmá's district court, stating, "Nobody is unaware of the fact that for quite some time, that part of the state has been the theater of prodigious crimes, which unfortunately have disrupted the tranquility and order of Hunucmá's society: a society that is essentially oriented towards progress, and is deserving of better fortune."[32]

Even though public officials characterized the region as being threatened by criminality rather than race war, when state courts investigated the attacks they demonstrated a persistent interest in the race of suspects. Whether suspects' surnames were Spanish or Mayan, the investigators characterized them as indios or indígenas. Suspected rebel leaders, however, as well as informers against the rebels often were identified as light skinned or "wearing pants," a qualification that differentiated them from indigenous men with their skirt-like garb. After the killing of Ricardo Aguilar near Xtul in 1889, for instance, a Hunucmá resident came to Mérida to give Aguilar's brother the names of the men who had taken part in the attack. While the mysterious figure refused to identify himself, Aguilar's description of him—"dressed as a mestizo, with a shirt of striped ticking, and breeches, with somewhat colored skin [coloradito], of medium stature, and thin"—identified him as neither a barbarous indígena nor a civilized mestizo, but as a working mestizo of unclear loyalties.[33]

After violence intensified in Hunucmá and the neighboring district of Maxcanú in the late 1880s, the governor of Yucatán, Daniel Traconis, felt impelled to take a public stand on the region. While Traconis had won office as a decorated hero of the Caste War, when he spoke to the state legislature in January 1892 he did not connect events in Hunucmá to that conflagration but declared them "light disturbances, of no political significance, purely socioeconomic in nature." According to Traconis, the idea of a "traditional right" to common lands was "deeply rooted to this day in the indigenous class," which remained "tenaciously opposed" to the survey and division of the ejidos. His government had been working to surmount such difficulties "with a great deal of prudence and practical knowledge of the character and customs of our aborigenes."[34]

As the expansion of the henequen haciendas transformed the public image of Hunucmá from that of a provincial backwater into that of a heartland of civilization and progress, it also generated sporadic glimpses of a shadowy region mired in poverty, disorder, and violence. Local gentry and state government officials had collaborated in staging performances of el pueblo's modernity and of its virtuous mestizo "traditions," all recorded in newspapers as annals of progress and enlightenment. Hunucmá's indigenous and working-class mestizo residents, on the other hand, were dismissed as primitives whose dangerous traditions were worthy only of extirpation, through division of communal lands, policing, and careful governance by state officials. Even as Hunucmá's gentry showcased the region in celebratory modern and traditional performances demonstrating their allegiance to the government, however, Hunucmá's pueblo communalists were forging alliances of their own. For many of them, the común had gone from a customary right to a rallying cry: a call to arms against landowning ts'uls. Hunucmá was no longer one pueblo but two, and the two could no longer coexist. This conflict was understated in newspaper coverage and official reportage, but on the night of 22 April 1892, that would change.

A SCOURGE OF DEPRAVED MEN

As night fell over the dyewood operations at Xpak, a group of servants belonging to the hacendado Rafael Peón finished their labors, hauling the dyewood they had cut and stacking it in piles. Two overseers, Hilario Sosa and Marcelino Molina, barked orders, while an administrator, Adolfo Rosado Vega, supervised the operation, riding back and forth on horseback. After a quick dinner, the men pitched their hammocks, Rosado, Sosa, and Molina tying theirs at a distance from those of the cutters. Meanwhile, another group of men lay in wait in the woods nearby. Once darkness fell, they walked silently toward the sleeping men and fired their guns in unison, spraying the hammocks with shot. Rosado and Molina managed to make it to their horses and fled. Sosa, however, was too slow, and the attackers finished him off with their machetes. Then, leaving the astonished woodcutters unmolested, they slipped back into the woods.[35]

News of the attack soon reached Governor Traconis, who immediately dispatched fifty troops and police in pursuit. Peón brought a posse of his own men, one of whom accidentally fired his rifle, killing the mayordomo of Peón's hacienda. Despite the mishap, the police arrested some twenty men, mostly in Tetiz, as they returned home from the woods. Reporters identified them as indigenous and celebrated their arrest as "disturbers of the peace, bandits and assassins." They blamed them for other attacks in recent years, conjecturing that "some sort of alliance existed among various men for the commission of such crimes, and that the center of their plans and combinations was the jungle or forest called Kaxek, where they lived, constantly outside the action of the authorities." The leader of that "alliance," now arrested along with the others for the Xpak incident, was a man named Isidro Tzuc, also known as the King of the Forest.[36]

Though described in newspapers as being indigenous, the men bore a mix of Mayan and Spanish surnames; even those with Spanish names had spouses, relatives, and friends with Mayan names. While characterized as living "constantly" off in the jungle, they were working residents of Tetiz and Hunucmá. Letters they sent and received while in prison, which subsequently were confiscated, contained well wishes for and from their families and friends, offers of assistance with clothes, food, and money, and in some cases information about the difficulties faced by their families. The wives of several of the prisoners complained of becoming indebted to local gentry and described their futile efforts to fight off their demands. Exiquia Mex, for instance, a resident of Tetiz, implored one landowner "in the name of God, to leave me the horses, so that I can care for our little ones. I told him not to do it for me, but for the poor little children, but it was all useless, until he finally took the horses from me. Now he is suing me, to take away our house plot." Ever since her husband's arrest, Mex's creditor had shown his determination to "take even the bread away from the mouths of our children." The letters also demonstrate the religiosity of the prisoners and their families. One wife assured her husband, "I never cease to pray to the Holy Virgin of our pueblo that you stay healthy and take care of yourself and can return to us one day"; another wrote that she had paid for two Masses to fulfill a *promesa* (promise) her husband had made to the Virgin.[37]

Far from backwoods reprobates removed from family, religion and society, the prisoners were working-class pueblo residents who were tightly integrated into family and religious life in their pueblos and subject, like other residents, to the despotism of landowners. The same was not true, however, of the King of the Forest. Under interrogation, Tzuc testified he had "no relatives at all, or any close friends." He didn't even own a gun, having borrowed one to use on the day of the attack. The prisoner Benito Péres, who gained his release by testifying against Tzuc, called him a "bad man" and a prison escapee. He related that after Tzuc's recapture, he had been sent to work as a forced laborer on a ranch called El Cuyo, on Yucatán's eastern frontier. Tzuc surely had faced privations there, among gangs of indigenous, Chinese, and central Mexican laborers, who worked at tapping rubber and cutting dyewood, suffering from disease and exhaustion. Eventually Tzuc escaped from El Cuyo as well and made his way to the other side of the peninsula to Hunucmá's woodlands, where, according to Péres, he now "wandered around . . . working, without recognizing any master, and with no fixed residence." Tzuc's experiences of imprisonment and forced labor and of survival and escape had given him intimate knowledge both of servitude and of what it meant to reject all masters.[38]

Most intriguing of all was Tzuc's nom de guerre, El Rey de los Bosques, surely a translation of the Maya words Yum K'ax or Yumil K'ax. Yum K'ax was an ancient Mayan god who protected woodlands and milpas; the Yumil K'ax was a kind of vengeful forest spirit that protected forests and their denizens from excessive hunting and woodcutting by inflicting punishments on transgressors. Perhaps in response to previous incidences of violence relating to common lands or salt pools, unknowing police had asked who was responsible, only to be told, Yumil K'ax, a mocking reference to the lords of the forest. Somehow the nickname had stuck to Tzuc; perhaps he had chosen it himself. In any case, the use of the term rey, rather than dueño (lord), seemed to accord him, or to accord the forest itself, a kind of power superseding that of Yucatán's secular authorities.

It is difficult, especially given that the Xpak case file has not survived in the archives, to know with certainty what happened that night in the shadows of Xpak. It is clear, however, that the event was an outgrowth of decades of struggle over the común. The Peón family had been in the business of exploiting dyewood from the early nineteenth century, especially near the pueblo of Maxcanú, to the southwest of the Hunucmá district. By midcentury, as stands there dwindled, Simón Peón's servants pushed ever deeper into the woods in their search for dyewood; by the 1890s workers, now at the command of Simón's son Rafael, began to intrude into communal lands of

Tetiz and Kinchil, now classified as baldíos by the government. In 1892, one month before the attack on Xpak, Peón carried out a deft legal maneuver: a servant of one his fincas claimed a vast area of land, almost twenty-five hundred hectares, and once the claim was approved by none other than President Díaz, the servant sold it over to Peón for a paltry one hundred pesos. The formalities were arranged by Adolfo Rosado Vega, a notable of Hunucmá who had occupied various public offices, ranging from school director to president of the town council of Hunucmá to a stint as jefe político, before taking a job as hacienda administrator for Peón. Soon he was charged with supervising the woodcutter operations at Xpak.[39]

Perhaps the King and his men were aware of Peón's acquisition of the woodlands. They all worked on communal ranches in the area—Chenchic, Chihabal, Xquintinché—that could have easily been the next lands surveyed and claimed by Peón. Perhaps on the night of 22 April they raised a group of armed men on the pretext of the hunt, eventually turning toward a different quarry and marching silently toward their target. Such things had happened before in Hunucmá. What was novel about Xpak was less the attack than the swiftness and severity of the response to it. Previous episodes in the district had gone unpunished, the penal investigations dissolving into chaos, in part because of what one official called the "complete disorder" of Hunucmá's court of first instance. Just a few months earlier, however, a large-scale rebellion in the nearby town of Maxcanú had sapped the credibility of Governor Traconis's administration, confounding his efforts to convince congress of his aptitude at mediating with indigenous communalists. Traconis's reaction to the attack on Xpak was a measure of just how sensitive he had become to the prospect of further agrarian violence in the western districts.[40]

The response of newspaper editors and commentators to Xpak was equally dramatic. The official newspaper of the state government, *Razón del Pueblo*, represented the attack as an affront to public order and morality, albeit of a kind "inevitable in every human society." The state government, an editor opined, had taken prudent and opportune measures in response, acting in a "swift and efficacious manner, always vigilant in maintaining the good morality, and proverbially good customs, of this State." Others, while approving of the government's response, argued that the event suggested the advisability of the creation of a permanent rural militia as a "solid foundation for the morality of the pueblos."[41] Critics of Traconis—most notably the newspaper *Revista de Mérida*, which was closely associated with the prominent Caste War veteran and gubernatorial aspirant (and eventual governor) Francisco Cantón—took the event as an opportunity to level a much harsher indictment. A lengthy editorial published by the *Revista de Mérida*, presumably written by its editor, Delio Moreno Cantón, moved the discussion of Xpak from one focused on public order to one focused on civilization and savagery. He distinguished between "civilized pueblos," in which property was treated as a "sacred thing," and "savage tribes," like the pueblos of Hunucmá, where crimes against property went unpunished. Hunucmá, he claimed, was plagued by "true incarnations of evil and vice"; "monsters [lived in its] immense and dark forests . . . isolated from public power and freed of all restrictions" and perpetrating an "uninterrupted series of evil deeds" against landowners. "Public opinion," he declared, "accused Hunucmá" of those crimes and demanded that Governor Traconis send men to become the "scourge of those depraved men . . . treating them with full military rigor, like the true savages they are, enemies of civilization and of progress itself."[42]

The *Revista* editorial triggered criticism from more liberal commentators, who claimed the newspaper was reacting "as if individual rights and guarantees had been suspended, and the government were at the orders of the army."[43] In response, the *Revista* fired another salvo: a history of Hunucmá in the form of annals whose self-declared purpose was to pressure the state government into pursuing a vigorous repression of "laziness, vice, and crime," and especially into "moralizing . . . the lower classes, from which such criminal monsters generally emerge," to the benefit of the "culture and civilization of the State in general." While consisting of a list of a series of twenty crimes perpetrated by "savages" and "evil-doers" from 1873 to 1892, "The Crimes of Hunucmá: Light and Shadow" did not begin with 1873 but reached back a quarter of a century earlier, to the "cowardly and miserable crucifixion" of Doña Juana Peña's husband, Remigio Novelo, in 1847. By situating the origins of Hunucmá's history in a crucifixion, the *Revista* represented subsequent events as a religiously charged saga of struggle between good and evil, beginning with a martyr's sacrifice. Moreover, the year 1847 would have immediately associated that death and subsequent history with the Caste War, deliberately leaving in shadow the communalist motivations of violence. The *Revista* thereby also cast into darkness the region's image as a vanguard of rural modernity, progress, and civilization, one so amply documented in newspapers like the *Revista* in preceding decades.[44]

With so much at stake, judgment against the King and his men was swift and severe. Based on confessions they later denied making, the men were convicted of homicide and attempted homicide and received twenty-year sentences, the maximum penalty allowed under law. Those sentences were to be served far away in Veracruz, in the prison of San Juan Ulúa, widely known as El Castillo ("the Castle"), an infamous colonial-era fort whose dungeons were reserved for the confinement and torture of the most dangerous criminals and political prisoners. Even a lawyer for the defendants declared the sentences to be just, and Yucatán's supreme court confirmed them, adding that Xpak had "caused deep alarm among all of the inhabitants of this State, making it necessary to issue an exemplary punishment."[45]

Moreover, Governor Traconis found the desired scourge for Hunucmá: Alfredo Tamayo, a military officer who had taken part in counterinsurgency operations in Hunucmá as far back as 1876 and had captained the suppression of the Maxcanú revolt in 1891. Immediately upon being appointed as jefe político, Tamayo set about conducting house searches, mass arrests, and interrogations. Local authorities drew encouragement from Tamayo's unwavering support of their own abuses. Kinchil's mayor, Saturnino Solís, reportedly called up large groups of indigenous men to perform what he called "government service"; they were then sent to work on haciendas, whose owners paid Solís for the service. At the same time, Hunucmá's scourge also lent his direct assistance to the region's hacendados, notably, the Peón clan. When indebted laborers fled an hacienda of Joaquin Peón, Tamayo sent forces to capture them and then had them soundly whipped and put to work in the salt pools. He crushed a rebellion in the small pueblo of Bolón and immediately launched crackdowns to respond to cattle rustling and assaults on haciendas and ranches. Rafael Peón did not hesitate to call on Tamayo when he came into conflict with thirty indigenous men from Kinchil and Tetiz who, he complained, had "invaded" his dyewood stands with "violence and threats." Tamayo sent forty soldiers to join a posse Peón raised, and together they scoured the woods. For Tamayo, such collaboration was fruitful. With a two-thousand-peso loan from Augusto L. Peón, he purchased Xkumak, a henequen hacienda near town. Later, he annexed an area of Hunucmá's ejidos to the finca and put conscripts and prisoners to work there as unpaid laborers.[46]

Such developments were made possible, in part, by "The Crimes of Hunucmá," whose publication shifted the place of the Hunucmá region in the perceptions of government officials and the Yucatecan reading public. It did so by shadowing the spectacles of modernity long performed in the region and bringing to light a different history, one that recast Hunucmá as a new front in the Caste War, a place of ineffable evil and sin. More than a representational shift, "The Crimes of Hunucmá" was a charter for a campaign of violent military repression in the region, one waged not only as a drive to reestablish law and order in the Hunucmá district, but also as a war for the future of Yucatán and for civilization itself. That war required that Hunucmá be put under the light of a certain kind of history, one that lent itself to the efforts of the government, the military, and the courts. All joined in documenting the sources of Hunucmá's evil in order to unleash a scourge against its depraved men.

REVISING THE ANNALS

Less than a year after the incident at Xpak, Governor Traconis made a highly publicized trip to the district, one reportedly undertaken "without arms, and without escort, because [Traconis] knows that he governs the safest state in Mexico." The governor was met outside Hunucmá by a mounted escort of twenty of the principal vecinos of Hunucmá as well as the jefe político Alfredo Tamayo. After a tour of the area, the governor returned to town for one of its famed traditional dances, in which the "angelic beauties of [Hunucmá] showed off their graces." This was no den of evil, but a town "called to progress, by a thousand of its qualities," a "fine place for relaxation and for passing the summer," a place whose residents had the "frank character of a coastal people, and the unaffected amiability of people of good upbringing."[47]

To all appearances, Hunucmá had returned to the path of progress. In his yearly address, Traconis claimed that the "energy and commitment" of the government's executive and judicial branches had returned "confidence and tranquility" to a district of "unfortunate celebrity." As Traconis finished his term, his publicists once again ascribed the violence in Hunucmá and the "vandalism" at Xpak to a communalist "tradition" that remained "tenaciously rooted in the indigenous class" and was an "insuperable obstacle to defining the rights of communities, in accord with constitutional principles." Nonetheless, guided by his "practical knowledge of the character of our indígenas," Traconis reportedly had ensured the equitable division of ejidal lands and moved the "most irritable spirits" to "conciliation."[48]

In Hunucmá, however, conciliation was hard to find. To be sure, when some indigenous and mestizo workers petitioned government officials, they

distanced themselves from the King and his men; in the course of a protest
against forced labor in Kinchil, for instance, the petitioners asserted, "We
have never had the reckless idea of imitating the execrable deeds of the
wicked men who, drunk on vengeance . . . treacherously attacked Xpak on
that ill-starred night." For many working residents, however, the King and
his men were heroes, not vandals. Several Tetiz residents led by Florentino
Poot, the brother of one of the prisoners, took up a collection in support of
the prisoners' families. Poot reportedly asked residents to contribute "because the men had defended the lands of el pueblo, and for that reason had
been imprisoned in the castle of Ulúa." When one man was reluctant to contribute, Poot warned him, "The roof of your house is made of huano [palm
leaves], not grass. You will see what happens." The words were cryptic but
meaningful. A debt was owed to those who had defended the woodlands,
where huano grew; those who did not honor that debt might regret it if they
dared set foot in the woods again (that is, to cut huano).[49]

While Xpak's alleged vandals had become heroes of el pueblo, those who
betrayed them became its villains. Chief among these was Benito Péres,
who was rewarded for informing against the King with a job as caretaker of
Kopté, a ranch owned by the hacendado Diego María Solís. When Péres returned to Hunucmá for the fiesta of the Virgin of Tetiz, Poot told him that he
had done a "very bad thing." Later, at the Corpus Christi fiesta, another man
approached Péres to tell him "he was bad, for having [informed], and that
various times he had seen that informers got hurt." It was not long before
Péres awoke to find his house on Kopté burning; as he ran out the front door,
five men opened fire on him. The next day Tamayo arrested and searched the
houses of Poot and other relatives of the prisoners at Ulúa, while Péres, mor-
tally wounded, insisted that Poot and others had told him he would "pay" for
informing and that they had shot him out of "vengeance . . . as is customary
for them."[50]

Military forces, penal court judges, government officials, and Hunucmá's
landowners again joined forces in an investigation which quickly turned into
something like a military occupation. The circle of arrests and detentions
grew ever wider: first, close family and friends of the prisoners at Ulúa; then
people who had the same last names as the prisoners in Ulúa; then anyone
who worked on or near the Poots' milpa plots; then anyone who worked
in the vast extension of woodlands that stretched north and west of Tetiz
and Hunucmá, especially near Kaxek. Tetiz's justice of the peace received
orders to arrest "everyone who lives in those places, whether men, women,

or children, for presumed involvement in arson and homicide," and he did so, assisted by troops, who immediately arrested twenty-two men, women, and children. Those arrested were detained for lengthy periods of interrogation. By mid-February, the number of prisoners being held in Hunucmá had become so great that the governor ordered additional troops to the town, "for the security of the prisoners, and to support the efforts of the judicial authorities."[51]

The residents of Hunucmá and Tetiz were far from intimidated by such measures. When a judge and gendarmes found Fabian Caamal out in his milpa, Caamal refused to take off his hat, turned his back, and began whistling while peeling a pile of beans, gestures of disrespect that got him arrested. When Dámaso Poot was told that a footprint found at Kopté matched his foot, he answered with pique: "Well, there are lots of guys in the pueblo who have the same kind of foot." Later, Hunucmá's justice of the peace noticed that Dámaso and his brother Ricardo were taking turns hanging around near his office in an effort to spy on the investigations and to intimidate potential informers. As the investigation foundered, the mass arrests succeeded only, it seemed, in providing a pretext for detaining suspects for up to nine months.

Traconis's successor as governor, the liberal leader Carlos Peón, continued the approach of his predecessor. On one hand, he proposed to "civilize" Hunucmá's "indigenous element" through the building of new schools; on the other, he kept Hunucmá's scourge, Tamayo, in place as jefe político. Official reports from Tamayo and other district officials and school inspectors suggested that law and order had returned to Hunucmá. Tamayo earned accolades in the press for the construction of a new public market in Umán, which was inaugurated on Cinco de Mayo, and for vaccination campaigns, school construction, and other public works. In his final report, in June 1895, the jefe noted with satisfaction that "nothing to date has disturbed tranquility and public order in all the pueblos that make up this district."[52]

By the time Tamayo's report was published in the press, however, the imperious jefe lay dying. As he rode on a carriage toward his finca, Xcumac, men concealed behind screens constructed out of tree branches had ambushed and shot him. Police and soldiers detained every indigenous and working man they encountered in the area north and northwest of town: some fifty farmers, hunters, and dyewood cutters. Soon they descended into another quagmire of speculation and rumor. From his deathbed, Tamayo blamed Hunucmá's priest and local populations, who he claimed were angered by his enforcement of a law prohibiting processions at Corpus Christi celebrations. Just before firing, Tamayo claimed, the attackers had shouted, "¡Viva Corpus!" Other town residents attributed the ambush to "jealousy and envy for the expansion of [Tamayo's] finca near town, and his use of the influence and prerogatives of his position to that end." Then there were the death threats Tamayo had received over the preceding years: from men whom he had whipped; from a drunk he had imprisoned; from escaped peons he had beaten and returned to their masters; even from the former district jefe político and Xpak survivor Angel Rosado, who later claimed his threat was a joke. Even the King haunted the investigation, in the form of José Angel Chuc, the brother of one of the prisoners in Ulúa. Though "never, or rarely ever seen in town," Chuc was sighted near Tamayo's house following the shooting. Several residents suggested he had attacked Tamayo in vengeance over the King's imprisonment and was rallying indigenous rebels somewhere out in the woods.[53]

Once again indigenous and working pueblo residents presented concerted resistance to the investigation. Those detained repeatedly changed their stories, frustrating interrogators. Town residents buried their guns or hid them in wells. One witness, himself detained as a suspect, admitted he was reluctant to identify the attackers "because he was, and is, seized with fear, because the inhabitants of Hunucmá are a vengeful people." Another suspect, who shared his cell, reinforced those fears by intoning repeatedly, "Jail doesn't eat you, and so I am not afraid of it." Two cousins of Chuc were detained, one of whom was heard bragging that he had "screwed Tamayo, killing him." Just as investigators seemed to be closing their case, however, a sergeant of the national guard reported that soldiers had been involved in the killing and that the local hacendado Pedro Telmo Puerto had compensated them with liquor and money. Finally, the case dissolved, bringing freedom to twenty-nine men who had languished in prison for much of the preceding year.

Horrified news commentators interpreted Tamayo's killing and the investigation's denouement as events of dire implications. Despite its own previous call for a scourge, the *Revista de Mérida* faulted Tamayo's abuses for "perverting the organization of pueblos, infesting their wounds with gangrene, and producing explosions." Only by "increasing the number of honorable men" and "expanding the patria" through education might such problems be solved in the pueblos. There was little hope, however, for Hunucmá, a town of "vengeful instincts" that had become a "theater of horrific scenes of butchery." "Like the man-eating tigers of South America," the *Revista* editorial concluded, "Hunucmá has tasted human blood and has grown to like its flavor."[54]

Despite such ominous predictions and a few sporadic episodes of violence in ensuing years, progress would have its way in the end. The largest hacendados continued to expand their estates, snapping up those of smaller growers. While small and mid-sized landowners faced difficult years during downturns in the henequen market, many continued to acquire lands, especially following the measurement, parceling, and breakup of the ejidos, which accelerated at the turn of the century. They increased their retinues of indebted servants, vigorously using intimidation, physical punishment, debts, and seizure of children as means to that end. They controlled local government positions, using their monopoly over pueblo-level governance to support the enforcement of indebted servitude and the expropriation of land.[55]

The apparent restoration of Porfirian order and progress convinced many that Hunucmá's notorious thirst for blood had been slaked at last. A new jefe político enlisted the support of "patriotic" town gentry to secure the "material, moral and intellectual prosperity of our pueblo" and even noted the ease of militia recruiting, given the "docility of [Hunucmá's] citizens."[56] Newspaper reporting again became annals of progress, tracking the opening of schools, the construction of town squares and parks, and the inauguration of public markets and slaughterhouses. Local officials repeatedly attested to a state of complete tranquility in the region, and their bland reports were republished by the press.[57]

As in the years before the attack on Xpak, national holidays became occasions for press commentators to salute "enlightened vecinos who have always given proof of their love for Education and Progress."[58] On Cinco de Mayo of 1899, the inauguration of a telegraph line in Tetiz provided an occasion for the hacendado-turned-mayor, Diego María Solís, to praise the "advances and progress of our beloved State" and for Governor Francisco Cantón to salute Hunucmá's jefe político, the Xpak survivor Angel Rosado, for "realizing the ideals of Progress" by inaugurating a telegraph line that was "the most eloquent commemoration of this day of the patria." Local notables exuberantly publicized the festive attractions of pueblos that were as traditional as they were modern. At one lavish fiesta in Hunucmá in 1898, for instance, a local enthusiast proclaimed, "The high price of henequen fiber and the high spirits of Yucatecans and Campechanos, to whom we are now linked by the

Henequen cutters with typical garb and hand tools. The shadow of the photographer and camera can be seen at lower left. Courtesy Fototeca Pedro Guerra, Universidad Autónoma de Yucatán.

railroad, lead us to offer to all Tyreans and Trojans these agreeable diversions, which will surely enter into the annals of history!"[59]

The annals of history, as performed and documented by Hunucmá's gentry, charted the culmination of a victorious struggle for the construction of a modern state and civilized pueblos in the region. Excluded from those imagined annals were counterimages of the Caste War and indigenous barbarism featured so prominently in the press just a few years earlier. Neither was there any place in those annals for the story of the King of the Forest or for the intense repression that had relegated him, like so many others, to prison cells. Hunucmá's hacendados and ts'uls had refashioned el pueblo, as an entity defined through its possession both of modern infrastructure— railroads, telegraphs, schools, bell towers—and traditional culture. History, for them, had become a story of possession. For working indigenous and mestizo pueblo residents, however, that history was predicated on the eradication of the claims of kah and común and thus had become a record of dispossession.

Shotguns and provision bags
used on a hunting trip.
Photo by Paul Eiss.

A few weeks before the beginning of the twentieth century, Isidro Tzuc,
having served seven years of his twenty-year sentence, sent a parole request
to the Yucatecan government. Ulúa's warden seconded it, noting that Tzuc
had "behaved well, and willingly fulfilled all of the diverse tasks he was assigned, thus demonstrating that he has acquired habits of order and morality." Seven other men imprisoned with Tzuc sent similar requests, accompanied by testimony of their rehabilitation. Governor Cantón and Yucatán's
supreme court rejected the requests, urging the state of Veracruz to keep
the men where they were for the remainder of their sentences.[60] It would be
many years before Tzuc gained his release from Ulúa. When he did, he made
his way back to Yucatán, back to Hunucmá, and, finally, back to the woods
of Kaxek. There he grew old, making milpa and hunting. Despite so many
losses and so many defeats, the landscape remained, and with it the ways
of working and living that linked people like Tzuc to forest and field. Even
after the passage of so many years, Tzuc was recognized by the inhabitants
of the region. They dignified him with a variation on his old title, reported

in newspapers as El Rey de los Campos—though in Maya it must have remained the same: Yum K'ax.[61]

A century after the attack on Xpak, a flatbed truck lumbers onto a rough dirt
road that leads into the woods, not far from Kaxek. I am standing with a
group of hunters from Tetiz, all of us crammed into the back and clinging
to ropes tied along the sides of the swaying vehicle. Suddenly, one of the
hunters, a man called Rabbit, seizes his shotgun and perches at the side
of the truck. He lowers the gun to point at a cow standing by the roadside
and shouts with fake bravado, "I'll shoot that deer!" There are guffaws of
laughter—and then silence.

It is a joke that has been told many times and is an echo of many things: of
the seizure of communal lands by cattle ranchers in the mid- and late nineteenth century; of the actions taken by the communalists of Hunucmá and
Tetiz in defense of their lands; of the wiles of residents as they faced police,
courts, and soldiers, under indictment for cattle rustling, and offered up a
transparent defense for their actions. That defense earned them no reprieve
from jail time but at least seemed to color their actions as unintentional, thus
excusing the court, if only for a time, from having to investigate yet another
budding insurgency, with so many cattle killed, so many walls knocked
down, so many presumably accidental fires in field and pasture.

Rabbit's joke also played upon the ambiguities of that history, in the
figure of the cow, "mistaken" for a deer. A symbol of the expropriation of
communal lands—and hence of Tetiz's dispossession—the cow, for a moment, is perceived as a deer, the sylvan creature that for pueblo residents is
a consummate symbol of el pueblo's continued claims of possession over
the communal woodlands and their denizens. Here, the joke plays upon a
comical ambiguity. The shot, if it had come, would have left us all suspended
somewhere between a hunter's myopia and el pueblo's repossession.

CHAPTER THREE

HUNUCMÁ'S ZAPATA

Objects of Insurgency and Auguries of Liberation

"MAY 4, 1913. They have made Yucatán's great Mauser and its great iron sword. For liberty, long live liberty, boys, *que viva*, long live the valiant ones, *que viva*. We swear we will not give up. We swear, as long as there is no liberty." These words were inscribed on a gun, or rather on the surface of a piece of wood carved into the shape of a rifle. Adjacent to it was a sword, fashioned out of an old barrel hoop. Cristino Concha, a justice of the peace from nearby Tetiz, found the two objects when he went to the Hacienda Chicché. They lay next to a large water tank whose walls were smeared with blood, and the imprints of bloodied hands. Spent cartridges littered the staircases and halls of the main house of the hacienda, where minutes earlier the judge had found an employee of the place lying motionless in a blood-soaked hammock. He counted twenty bullet holes in the man's back. The judge hurried to collect the gun and the sword; he later sent them to state officials in Mérida, along with a written report of what he had seen.[1]

Meanwhile, police and soldiers hunted for the rebels who had attacked Chicché the night before. They did so with a sense of urgency derived less from what the attackers had done than from the words they had left behind. Two years earlier, Mexico's aging dictator, Porfirio Díaz, had been overthrown in a rebellion led by Francisco Madero, in alliance with regional insurgencies led by Pancho Villa in the north and Emiliano Zapata in the southern state of Morelos. In Yucatán the Revolution had not brought the civil war that raged elsewhere, but it did trigger two years of partisan conflict, political violence, and rebellion as rival parties contended over the spoils of Díaz's fall. Before the violence could escalate into all-out war, however, regional elites had settled their differences, restoring order by late 1912. In early 1913, after a military coup overthrew Madero's government, Yucatecan authorities consolidated their control, cracking down on all expressions of dissidence.[2]

By attaching such a provocative caption to the attack on Chicché a few months later, the attackers blindsided the regime. That is why police and soldiers raced to the Hunucmá district, followed by newspaper reporters, who presented their findings the following day under the headline, "The Horrors of Zapatismo in Hunucmá." Chilling accounts evoked the prospect of violence in Yucatán on the scale of that experienced in Zapata's Morelos. "Macabre hordes" of "Yucatecan Zapatistas," one reporter wrote, now stood at the very "gates of the beautiful city of Mérida." As evidence of the impending menace, the newspapers reprinted the words inscribed on the gun.[3]

As material documents, the gun and the sword became embedded in two emerging inquiries. In the first, a judicial investigation, they were evidence: objects whose significance lay in the role they might play in the arrest and conviction of those who attacked Chicché. In the second, a discussion in the press, the objects were significant for the inscription, which transformed them into frightening omens of Yucatán's future and fate. For those who had created them, however, the objects had other meanings. They were icons of a long-standing struggle, indications of its transformation into an insurgency, and auguries of the history that movement might make. Despite radical differences in the perspectives and purposes of their creators, the penal files, newspaper coverage, and the facsimile gun were alike in one respect: they documented the emergence of an insurgent political subject, one that took el pueblo as its name and liberation as its cause.

THE GOOD AND TRUE LIBERTY

In Yucatán, the fall of Díaz came as the coda to years of crisis. Owing to the monopolistic consolidation of North American harvesting machine companies and secret fiber purchasing agreements with the henequen magnate and Díaz ally Governor Olegario Molina, fiber prices dropped from over twenty-one cents per kilogram in 1902 to less than ten cents by 1908. By 1907, declining prices had triggered a general economic malaise, as hacendados reduced wages to meet the bottom line and protests and rebellions erupted on some fincas.[4] To the economic crisis was added a political one: Yucatecan liberals, along with foreign critics such as John Kenneth Turner, whose exposé *Barbarous Mexico* (1910) denounced the plight of Yucatecan debt peons, launched a series of public demands aimed at bringing an end to oligarchy and debt servitude. Chief among such critics was Tomás Pérez Ponce, a lawyer, journalist, and political organizer who drew on the testimony of escaped laborers to publicize the forced labor and beatings taking place on the haciendas.[5]

Even in the face of repressive measures, critics intensified their efforts as Díaz's hold on power loosened. In 1909, as the reformer Madero launched a national political campaign and then an insurgent movement against Díaz, the Porfirian regime cracked in Yucatán as well. Two rival reformist parties called the Central Electoral Independiente and the Partido Antireeleccionista (known as *morenistas* and *pinistas*, respectively, after their gubernatorial candidates, Delio Moreno Cantón and José María Pino Suárez) allied themselves with Madero and challenged Molina's handpicked candidate for governor. Those electoral challenges, along with a series of related plots and uprisings in the countryside, failed.[6] In 1911, however, a host of new uprisings erupted as hacienda laborers joined the rebels, attracted by vague promises of land distribution and the abolition of debt servitude. Despite a general amnesty offered by the governor in mid-April, the rebellions continued for as long as Díaz remained in office.[7]

The Hunucmá district was no exception to these trends. In May 1911, morenistas organized large pro-Madero demonstrations in Umán, drawing hundreds of hacienda workers to protest wages and working conditions. In the vicinity of the town of Hunucmá and in the pueblos of Tetiz and Kinchil, pinistas were predominant, and they unleashed a campaign of shootings, bombings, and arson attacks against the persons and properties of their morenista rivals.[8] In response, state troops arrested the protesters and carried out their own campaign of thefts, beatings, and sexual assaults. Yucatán's governor ordered the jefe político of Hunucmá to "awaken the patriotic sentiments" of "citizens" of the district through conscription, a weapon the jefe used to target both escapees from the haciendas and political activists—in one case, a man who merely had shouted, "¡Viva Madero!"[9]

Immediately following Díaz's resignation and Pino Suárez's appointment by Madero as acting governor of Yucatán, leaders of both parties instructed their supporters to demobilize; nonetheless, the clashes continued. Conditions might have seemed propitious for ending partisan violence. The rhetoric of pinistas and morenistas, after all, was similar, combining effusive appeals for the redemption of indigenous workers with a cautious gradualism regarding abolition. In a manifesto to "el pueblo yucateco" regarding what he called the "indigenous question," for instance, Pino warned against the "uncontrolled liberation" of populations that, once freed, might behave like "tribes of savages." Instead, he proposed a "patriotic" liberation, through the gradual reduction of debts, improvement of working conditions, and the "regeneration" of indigenous workers through the "consolidation of Mexican nationality" in their hearts. In a manifesto of his own, Moreno Cantón declared it "imperative that the Indian be redeemed and rehabilitated through a well-directed and carefully controlled process of evolution, so that social order might not be shattered."[10]

Despite the cautious rhetoric of political leaders, the Yucatecan countryside could not be restored to order, especially with the approach of gubernatorial elections scheduled for September 1911. Workers fled the fincas or stopped working, demanded pay increases, threatened encargados and hacienda administrators, and even sacked hacienda stores. In some cases, they joined workplace grievances with political demands, chanting, "¡Viva Madero!," "¡Viva Moreno!," and even "¡Viva la Libertad!"—these last words shouted by workers of Chimay as they threatened to cook their encargado into a salpicón (a kind of meat stew). Police and soldiers responded to such incidents with mass arrests and occasionally shootings. Both criminal courts and the press, however, typically downplayed the political content of workers' mobilizations, ascribing them to drunkenness or presumed indigenous deficits in intelligence and self-control. A lawyer defending Chimay's workers, for instance, described them as "beasts of burden . . . [who are] incapable of distinguishing good from evil."[11]

In Hunucmá, attempts to impose order and restore hacienda production were particularly ineffective. One encargado reported that "on practically all of the haciendas, many servants have abandoned their homes and their families in order to take part in electoral clubs."[12] Large-scale raids, bombings, and arson attacks targeted the haciendas as well. Desperate to renew fiber production, representatives of the district's landowners met with the governor and with Yucatán's Chamber of Commerce to stress that such attacks were "not political" in nature. At their urging, morenista and pinista leaders in Mérida issued a joint statement under the heading "Bombers do not belong to any political party," in which they declared that the violent episodes in Hunucmá had "neither revolutionary content, nor political cause, but were merely acts of personal vengeance, undertaken to satisfy old hates and rancor."[13] Such entreaties failed to stop the violence, and even military force—100 federal and state troops supported by an armed militia of townspeople—proved ineffectual.[14] On 7 August 250 men reportedly stormed Hacienda San Pedro, where they killed cattle, knocked down stone walls, and decapitated an overseer. The next week at Hacienda San Román walls were knocked down, nine houses put to the torch, and once again an employee was slain.[15]

In response, Hunucmá's landowners called on the government to "crush . . . the head of this baneful hydra," seconded by the pinista and morenista press. Reporters viewed toppled walls, smoking ruins, and homicides as material evidence that a "wanton mob" was "sowing anarchy" with acts of "savagery" and "vandalism."[16] The pinistas and the *Diario Yucateco* continued to characterize the violence as "nonpolitical" in nature. In contrast, the *Revista de Mérida*, whose editors favored the morenistas, blamed the violence on pinista militants who riled up "inebriated masses" of indigenous workers, transforming them from "honorable and humble workers" into "terrible instruments for the commission of every kind of crime."[17] Writers for the *Revista* mockingly condemned local pinistas like Feliciano Canul Reyes of Hunucmá, even publishing letters he had written that were riddled with spelling errors they called "expressive" and "picturesque."[18] Hunucmá's pinista organizers, they alleged, were "libertarians who behave like complete libertines," carrying out attacks in order to make themselves the "absolute masters of el pueblo."[19] Those who had "strayed" into the movement, they declared, had to "return to their old ways, as honorable workers and family men who respect the authorities."[20] Finally goaded into action, Yucatán's governor sent eighty-five troops to Hunucmá to scour back roads and woodlands for alleged vagrants and anarchists.[21]

Soon an electoral tour of Hunucmá by Pino Suárez provided an occasion for his celebration, or denunciation, as either the candidate of el pueblo or its enemy. As represented by the pinista press, Pino was welcomed by adoring throngs who danced vaquerías in his honor and praised him in speeches in Spanish and Maya.[22] Reporters for the *Revista de Mérida*, on the other hand, depicted a region divided between upstanding vecinos who supported the candidacy of Moreno Cantón, thus representing el pueblo, and Pino's "illiterate" Indian supporters. Residents of Tetiz reportedly affixed black mourning ribbons to the fronts of their houses, and "the entire aware pueblo" left town before Pino's visit. "Not one of the people that we would call 'vecinos,'" a reporter for the *Revista* wrote, "went to receive Señor Pino, who was surrounded only by poor workers of the haciendas, who have been stirred up and deceived by unscrupulous people." Similarly, in Kinchil only indigenous workers feted Pino, while "el pueblo was conspicuous by its absence."[23]

In his last speeches before the November elections, Pino Suárez sought to distance himself from the violence. In a manifesto to "el pueblo yucateco," he declared that he had ordered all of his organizers in the countryside to deliver speeches in Maya advocating for the gradual "evolution" of indigenous workers toward full civil rights free of the "dangerous perturbations" of those "blinded by the immense brightness of liberty." His supporters, he claimed, had denounced the "false, dangerous, and criminal promises" of those who raised hopes for immediate abolition and instead worked through their "preachings" to lead "the indigenous race" on a "shining path toward the truth"—what Pino called the "good, and true, liberty." Amid escalating political violence, however, the nature and implications of that liberty would remain open to contention.[24]

THE TASTE OF BLOOD

Before sunrise on 25 November 1911 Marcos Ek knocked at Herminio Balam's door, to pick him up for a hunt, he said. The two walked silently on a narrow path leading out of Hunucmá to the northeast, and a few hours later they met five other men, including Federico Tzab and José Pío Chuc, in the henequen fields of Ulilá. The band ducked into the brush onto another path the men knew well. Reaching a railway that ran toward Hacienda Hobonyá, they took up positions, some staking out hiding places and others preparing to charge. Ek and Tzab went out to pile rocks on the rail and then returned to the woods.

It was not long before there were sounds of a rail car approaching and then stopping as it reached the rocks. The men fired in unison and rushed out to grab a passenger, the administrator of Hobonyá, Miguel Negrón. Negrón handed them the money he was carrying to pay workers and pleaded for his life, in Maya: "Please don't kill me! If it is money you want, take it!" Pío Chuc rebuked him, "What you say shall not be, for you have done many things to us!" and struck him in the face with the butt of his gun. Then he slammed his machete into the back of Negron's neck, just behind the skull. Ek slashed Negrón's throat and cupped his hand to collect blood from the wounds. He drank some and called Balam over: "Come! Drink some too, to cure your fear!" Balam cupped his hand and drank.[25]

Negrón's body was found by the police later that day. His friends recalled that the week before, Negrón was about to drink water from a jug when an "odious reptile" jumped out of it—an augury of impending doom.[26] Reptiles aside, there had been many other signs that the region's violence might not abate. On winning the gubernatorial elections, Pino had announced the dawning of what he called a "new era of progress" for Yucatán. All, he declared, would now lay down their arms, return to their labors, and collaborate in the task of "carrying the patria . . . down the path of well-being and greatness."[27] Unrest continued after the elections, however, leading Governor Pino to blame morenista agitators for continuing to "provoke uprisings and push . . . ignorant country dwellers . . . who have no political opinions or desires into rebellion."[28] Even in pinista Hunucmá, though, there was violence. A group of men sporting Pino Suárez buttons, for instance, reportedly shouted, "Death to morenistas!" as they disemboweled a man in view of his terrified family.[29] The *Revista de Mérida*, which denounced the killing as a "new black page" in Hunucmá's history, declared the name of Hunucmá to be "bloodied by political hate" and called for justice in the name of "society" and the "public conscience."[30] The worst, however, was yet to come. A series of robberies and assaults on haciendas culminated in an attack on New Year's Eve on San Eduardo in which a large group of marauders robbed houses and workers of the finca, knocked down walls enclosing fields, slashed henequen plants with their machetes, and blew up processing machinery.[31]

Most newspaper commentators attributed the violence either to political rivalry or to latent indigenous tendencies toward savagery. One anonymous writer for the *Diario Yucateco*, however, argued that Hunucmá's "rebellious attitude" originated neither in politics nor a penchant for villainy, but in the enclosure and purchase of communal lands. Although residents still considered those lands "rightfully theirs," now they were charged by the hacendados for their use; harsh treatment of wood poachers and conscription campaigns further aggravated the situation. The result was that "el pueblo has been very discontent," leading residents to kill cattle, destroy walls and enclosures, and commit "every kind of depredation." "History has shown us," he concluded, "that every time they have tried to rise up in arms, that has been the only cause. . . . left only the swampiest of lands, with the hacendados charging them two pesos for every cartload of charcoal they produce, and rent for the right to make their milpas, finally, *¡paf!*, things blew up, and the same depredations that they committed, once upon a time, and that our fathers and grandfathers saw, began once again."[32]

There was indeed much to suggest that the violence of 1911 and 1912 was linked to earlier communalist struggles. Attackers targeted not the largest and oldest estates, but small and midsized fincas more recently carved out of common lands. Moreover, the suspects, who ranged in age from fifteen to sixty-nine, were tightly integrated into the working communities where they lived. Some, like the herbalist and healer José Sabino Canul, had arrest records dating back to the communalist violence of the 1890s, while others, like the leader of the attack, José Pío Chuc, the son of José Angel Chuc, were the children of earlier rebels. Often those involved in attacks were close kin, and the surnames of more than 120 suspects show the preponderance of certain family names: Canul, Balam, Chan, Uc. While men were the primary suspects, brief references to women in investigations indicate that they took part behind the scenes by helping to organize clandestine meetings, hiding weapons and loot, misleading police, and aiding suspects in their attempts to escape capture by fleeing to the neighboring state of Campeche.

While the movement's social base was broad, it was not bereft of hierarchy. Most of the attackers blacked or masked their faces, but a few wore clothing that resembled military uniforms, setting them apart as organizers. Canul Reyes was rumored to be their leader, but there were commanders beneath him as well, like Canul's second in command and so-called "secretary," Federico Tzab (nicknamed Perico, or "Parakeet"). Even these hierarchies, however, were shaped by communal practices. Attacks were planned and organized much like communal hunts; indeed, under interrogation, participants sometimes referred to them as hunts and used Mayan terms to describe techniques of communicating, hiding (*pa'atlil*), stalking, flushing out (*p'uh*), and attacking clearly derived from team hunting.[33] As in communal hunts, days or weeks before the attacks the organizers issued invitations to men to participate, typically extended "in the name of" Feliciano Canul. Balam, for instance, was first invited by Ek to take part in the killing of Negrón; in a later episode, however, Balam invited others to participate, indicating that he had risen in the hierarchy. Canul and other organizers held meetings, called *juntas*, in their homes. Those attending, according to one informer, were told that "when asked to give money, [they] should give whatever they had," in order to pay for the acquisition of weapons, dynamite, and even disguises and flags. The attacks were planned as well. As one resident observed, "Every time they hold a junta, the next day there is news of bombs exploding someplace."[34]

The insurgents' tactics, too, were drawn from an old communalist repertoire. They looted and stole from the fincas, carrying off maize, beans, livestock, clothing, and work tools, whether for personal use or to barter for liquor to share with their friends. Loot in cash or kind was divided in roughly equal proportions. They killed landowners' cattle, eating their fill and leaving the rest of the carcasses behind to rot. The acquisition of personal wealth for the sake of prestige could be seen as a violation of this ethic, as el Perico discovered when he showed up at a fiesta in Hunucmá dressed in fine clothes and carrying a fancy parasol. Another town resident, himself reportedly involved in some attacks, confronted Tzab, accusing him of earning his money "at the expense of the inhabitants of el pueblo by deceiving them and encouraging them to commit crimes."[35] The most dramatic attacks, like those of the late nineteenth century, included bombings of hacienda equipment, arson and machete attacks against henequen fields, and, most frequently, the toppling of walls enclosing henequen fields and woodlands. In the attack on San Pedro in which the overseer Bonifacio Yam was beheaded, for instance, the assailants knocked down stone walls and placed Yam's corpse next to piles of sticks that were arranged in the outline of two graves. Then they stuck an envelope in Yam's armpit, with "Buenos Días" written on it. Inside was a letter ordering the finca's owner not to rebuild the walls. If he did, the letter warned, his own grave was ready.[36]

As much as the attacks were of a piece with preceding struggles in defense of the común, by 1911 there was clear evidence they were also part of a different kind of movement—a revolutionary struggle, waged under the banner of emancipation. A baker and rancher, of higher station than indigenous hacienda peons, Canul Reyes embraced the cause of liberty years before the attacks began. He was a member of the Libertarian Circle, a group formed in Mérida in January 1909 under the leadership of Pérez Ponce. The *Círculo* espoused its aims to be those of "proclaiming and defending the Rights of Man" and "working to achieve complete Human Liberty." In

March 1911, its members sent a petition to the governor denouncing abuses that had transformed Yucatán into a "modern Bastille."[37]

In the Hunucmá district, like much of the hacienda zone, that Bastille was most manifest in the haciendas themselves, with their stone walls and armed guards. Unlike the communalist mobilizations of decades before, indebted servants were protagonists in some of the attacks, which thus became acts of liberation from bondage. Eight of the men accused in the New Year's attack on San Eduardo, for instance, including its organizer, worked for its owner and were indebted to him. Fugitive peons of Chel and San Gerónimo returned by night to rob and intimidate workers on those haciendas, and twenty masked assailants destroyed papers stored in the main house of Xkumak—presumably records of worker debts—before proceeding to rob the hacienda store and resident workers. Assailants often tried to persuade resident workers to abandon the haciendas; on San Gerónimo, attackers urged workers to leave and "not to be fool[s], since they [that is, the attackers] earn good wages and have their liberty."[38]

Most strikingly, during the attack on San Eduardo the attackers called to other Hunucmá residents to join them in a "revolution" in which they would "kill the demons," the "sons of the devil" who ruled the hacienda. The attack, like others, had multiple aims: to liberate servants of their debts; to liberate lands stolen from el pueblo; perhaps to liberate working people of Hunucmá from the ts'uls, who had oppressed them for so long. Fittingly, it was all planned to fall on New Year's day. For a moment, San Eduardo might become Hunucmá's Bastille, a place and time for a revolution that might destroy old hierarchies even as it inaugurated a new era of emancipation.[39]

Some of these associations may have been in the thoughts of Herminio Balam as he drank Negrón's blood. That act may have been what marked his promotion in the group's ranks, transforming him from a follower into an organizer. Later, he would confide to his twelve-year-old fiancée—in words uttered in Maya but translated into Spanish in trial testimony— "Christian blood is bittersweet." Balam's words suggest he may have perceived the vampiric slaying as a sacred act, with Negrón's bittersweet, Christian blood, seeming to evoke sacramental wine and the state of spiritual communion the Eucharist brought. This was neither the reflexive response of a community long subjected to violence, nor an action meant to subject others to use violence for political ends. Rather, it may have been a rite of passage: an emancipatory communion, consecrated in the taste of blood.[40]

FROM PUEBLO TO PATRIA

Shortly after his election as governor, José María Pino Suárez was selected by Francisco Madero to serve as his vice president. Just before resigning as governor to take that position in late 1911, Pino sent a contingent of heavily armed troops to occupy Hunucmá, a measure celebrated in the press as presaging the end of that district's "reign of terror." In December Pino's successor, Nicolás Cámara Vales, widened the crackdown throughout Yucatán, sending soldiers and police to track down rebels and quell discontent on the haciendas. At the same time, he levied a hefty so-called public security tax on working men who did not reside on the haciendas, a measure intended to encourage workers to return to the fincas. The governor dedicated special attention to the Hunucmá district, ordering the state's second penal court to base itself there temporarily to investigate crimes and reestablish "public tranquility."[41]

State congressional representatives enthusiastically seconded such measures, calling for the establishment of a permanent mounted police force to "exterminate" the "bandits" who had "alarmed society, eroded family bonds, and destroyed the principle of authority" in Hunucmá.[42] Local merchants and landowners, large and small, appealed to the government to remove pinista municipal officials, and a purge soon began throughout the district, continuing over the year to follow. When denouncing such officials, petitioners from Umán, including the mestizo notable Bartolomé García Correa, did so in racially charged ways, calling them "illiterates . . . from the fincas" and "automatons controlled by malicious hands." "Just as it is never advisable to put a gun in a child's hands," they declared, "unaware people should not be allowed to govern." Abelardo Correa Franco, also a resident of Umán, publicly slandered the police commissioner, José Julio Pech, calling him a "shameless bastard, and a wretched Indian."[43]

When Yucatán's second criminal court opened in Hunucmá, hacendados and merchants rushed in to bring their complaints. San Eduardo's owner, Secundino Maldonado, visited repeatedly to share the rumors he had heard: of how before the attack some people in Hunucmá had said he would be "covered with machete slashes"; of local pinistas selling objects stolen from the hacienda; of forty-seven men who, he suggested, were "up to no good" and whom he suspected of being involved.[44] Soldiers and police ransacked houses and dragged suspects off for questioning. They trafficked avidly in disturbing rumors: of clandestine nighttime meetings; of Maya-speaking bandits roving the area with their faces blacked; of death threats against informers; of unspeakably violent acts, including beheadings; of men who "don't do any work at all, but always seem to have money to waste."[45] Articles of clothing and work tools were confiscated and carried back to the court, where hacendados claimed to recognize them—a pair of pants, even a bit of rope—as objects stolen from their fincas. Onetime pinistas were interrogated, among them Canul Reyes, whose testimony that Hunucmá pinistas were "honorable and hard-working men" who had disbanded as a political grouping left court officials unconvinced.[46]

Over the weeks, hints of something more disturbing than banditry began to emerge. Maldonado reported that Guillermo Canul, the leader of the attack on San Eduardo, had "formed evil ideas" and had invited a worker named Ignacio Koyoc to join in "exterminating all of the gentlemen [caballeros] of Hunucmá, so that they might become the lords of the population." Koyoc corroborated the story, claiming that Canul pressured him to join what he called a "club" to that end and noting that "many Indians from here say the same thing, when they are liquored up." Koyoc said he had refused, telling Canul "not to think of such a thing, because it is said that the Indians did that once upon a time, but back then today's civilization did not exist." Then there was the tale of Negrón. Under interrogation, Balam, who had been turned in by his fiancée, admitted his involvement and implicated others as well, including the erstwhile pinista leaders Canul Reyes, Pío Chuc, and Tzab. Moreover, Balam described the blood-drinking rite in detail, while claiming his own participation was forced.[47]

Along with the testimony of Maldonado and Koyoc, Balam's words seemed to lead court officials out of the realm of judicial investigation and into that of history. They began to interpret events in Hunucmá as manifestations neither of banditry nor partisan strife, but as atavistic revivals of Caste War violence or even of ancient Mayan practices. A prosecutor argued that Negrón's killing exemplified an "intense phenomenon of regression" that manifested the " 'blood instinct' of bygone eras of barbarous sacrifices, which has reawakened, bringing mourning and terror to our homes and families." In "sucking the hot blood of [their] victim," he declared, Hunucmá's "savages" had returned to "their old ways, as related in the stories of the terrible crimes of our Indians in historical epochs." The prosecutor suggested the men had used magical objects—"antiquated" and "stupid . . . fetishes and amulets"—to evade justice by supernatural means. "But against those amulets," he declared triumphantly, "there stood the conscience of other poor people, who rushed to report the crime to the authorities."[48]

Soon, however, court and soldiers left Hunucmá, and the violence returned with a vengeance. In April 1912 the *Revista* reported a "new link" in Hunucmá's "long chain of atrocities" after a large group of men from Hunucmá, Tetiz, and Kinchil ransacked and set fire to the house and store of Elías Xcaer, a Lebanese trader in Kinchil. Later, police collected his three-year-old daughter's charred remains.[49] Suspicions again fell on former pinistas, including Kinchil's mayor, who was arrested, leading news commentators to express outrage that such "villainous acts" were now committed by pueblo authorities rather than by "bandits hiding off in the woods."[50] Again, haciendas were targeted; attackers killed a worker on Hacienda Abal, leaving his body to roast on a pile of coals, and "evildoers" reportedly "fell like an avalanche" on several other places, all the while emitting "savage screams."[51] In Tetiz, plunderers sacked and set fire to La Bancarrota, a general store owned by Rafael Larrache, a prosperous former morenista. As in Kinchil, the suspects were erstwhile pinistas, including the mayor of Tetiz Catarino Tinal, justice of the peace Federico Solís, and Pastor Balam, who was found sleeping off a hangover in the woods with Larrache's wallet in his hands and surrounded by boxes of cigarettes, soap, and Nestlé powdered milk. Investigators did not explore the possibility that political rivalries might have motivated the attack; instead, fueled by suspicions of a brewing race war, they focused on the suspects' "influence" over and relations with those they termed "the indígenas" of Tetiz. Chicché's owner, Don Diego María Solís, testified on the basis of his long residence in Tetiz ("he knows the residents of that pueblo," court officials noted) that Tinal and Solís exercised "influence and control over the indígenas." Other merchants noted that so-called "indígenas" often gathered at night in Solís's store to get drunk and then committed acts of mischief.[52]

Despite dozens of arrests, however, the investigators found themselves frustrated by the refusal of most residents to testify, by the flight of suspects, and by the limited legal value of the testimony they collected. Only a handful of men like Balam—none of them attack leaders—were convicted. All the incriminating objects and tantalizing rumors had stoked an endless series of questions but provided few answers. A defense lawyer in the Negrón case remarked that while "sensational public rumors" had implicated his clients, the investigation soon fell to pieces, clouded by contradictory testimony and unfounded speculation. "The shadows of doubt cleared for a few moments," he concluded, "but then darkness fell. In the search to get to the bottom of things, we stirred up the mud, and found ourselves lost in turbulence once again."[53]

Eventually, Yucatán's penal court justices admitted defeat. One attributed the collapse of the Xcaer case to "stupor, mixed with strong fear, which then became terror," among the inhabitants of Kinchil. Convinced that the government would take "terrible measures" against them because of the attack, the population had been seized by a "contagious" fear that subverted the investigation. The judge absolved those accused of the crime and even argued in their favor when the prosecutors appealed to Yucatán's Supreme Court. The case against the men, he declared, was built not on hard evidence but on an "immense collection of presuppositions" concocted by prosecutors who had "woven a fabric" out of the "threads of popular imagination."[54] Similarly, Judge Ernesto Patrón Villamil absolved those accused of involvement in the sacking of La Bancarrota, noting he was "well aware of the damage and shock caused by the many attacks committed in the western pueblos, whose causes are not understood, and whose authors remain unknown." Patrón fulminated against the "baneful league of evildoers that has been hiding in Hunucmá since time immemorial, spreading terror among the inhabitants of the pueblos there." As in Kinchil, that fear had left the judge with witnesses who would only testify to "knowing nothing, and seeing nothing." In frustration, Patrón declared, "I can cite many [similar] cases, but it would be useless to list them. They may be found in the files of the three penal courts, dealing with the crimes committed in the district of Hunucmá."[55] Initially intended to serve as documentary weapons in a war without quarter against Hunucmá's evildoers, the files had become something else entirely: testimony to the power of terror to stymie the state's will to know and ability to punish. They became a record, in the end, only of that impotence and of human blood's bittersweet flavor.

Yet even as the investigations foundered, an end to years of upheaval seemed to draw nigh. In his yearly address before congress in January 1913, Governor Cámara Vales trumpeted the success of his administration in exterminating what he called the "insalubrious germs" of banditry and rebellion, which according to him inevitably grew in the aftermath of revolution, like Zapatismo in Morelos. His government, however, unlike that of Morelos, had succeeded in "injecting vitality into the State," thus leaving it "satisfied, as it contemplates the tranquility, order, and even happiness that reign in el pueblo."[56] Shortly thereafter, events at the national level seemed to further the consolidation of law and order. In February 1913, President Madero and Vice President Pino Suárez were overthrown and executed by General Victoriano Huerta, who imposed a national military dictatorship aimed at reversing Madero's Revolution. Within a month, the northern *caudillo* Venustiano

Carranza proclaimed a new revolutionary movement, in alliance with Villa and Zapata, to unseat Huerta and restore constitutional rule. In Yucatán, however, as the government imposed military rule and meted out harsh penalties for continued rebellion and dissidence, pinista and morenista leaders came to terms with the government, and the remaining rebel leaders demobilized.[57]

But once again, Hunucmá begged to differ. To be sure, in late 1912 and early 1913 the frequency and scale of attacks there diminished markedly. Hunucmá's jefe politico judged the moment propitious for a revival of henequen production and invited hacendados to give him lists of fugitive workers, whom his forces tracked down and returned to the fincas. He also ordered the confiscation of shotguns and other weapons, hoping to cut off the supply of arms to rebels.[58] Rather than stemming the region's volatility, however, such measures seemed only to worsen it. Residents of Tetiz reportedly said that "if the Government wanted to confiscate their weapons, then they would just bury one gun for each one they gave in, and that if they were required to turn in all their guns, then they would use matches to burn down houses, unless the sale of matches were also prohibited."[59] As if to demonstrate that point, in late April 1913 as many as one hundred men joined in an assault on Hacienda San Ramón, where they killed cattle, burned down twelve houses, and blew up the hacienda's machinery. Newspaper reporters declared that Hunucmá's "evil" had become a "chronic" condition, with its residents "converted into true Zapatistas . . . hordes that burn, plunder and murder."[60]

By May 1913 the stage was set both for the attack on Chicché and for a perception of it as the work of so-called "Zapatistas." Situated just outside Tetiz, where it had been carved out of communal lands, Chicché straddled the road to large areas of national lands to the north and west, a route traveled by residents as they transported wood, charcoal, and the products of milpas back to the pueblo. While serving as mayor of Tetiz in 1899, the owner of Chicché, Diego María Solís, had compelled residents of the pueblo to widen and improve the road. Subsequently, however, he had closed it to the public, charging fees for its use. Directly adjacent to the road, Solís built Chicché's main house; he once described it as "a kind of fortress, since it has two floors," making it easier to surveil the area. Over the years, Don Diego came into repeated conflict with the residents of Tetiz, dozens of whom he denounced for wood poaching and cattle rustling. From 1911 forward, he and Chicché had been targeted by assailants several times. On one occasion he was shot in an ambush and survived by playing dead.[61]

The remains of Hacienda Chicché, near Tetiz, 1998. Photo by Paul Eiss.

Late in the afternoon of 4 May rumors of another impending attack reached the ears of Solís and his nephew Camilo. The men prepared to defend Chicché, distributing guns to a few trusted servants and mounting a guard on the second floor of the main house. During Camilo's watch, just before midnight, a dog began barking, and Camilo grabbed his gun and ran outside, peering into the darkness. He asked who was there, and when there was no response he shouted, "Answer, you bastard!" Then he saw them: dozens of men, their faces blacked, emerging from the darkness and bearing guns and machetes. Someone yelled, "We are not bastards!" and then the firefight began. Ten minutes later, having killed a Chicché defender named Magdaleno Mendoza, the attackers fled, leaving Don Diego and his men to mount a tense watch from the roof. First, they watched the glow of fires the attackers had set on Chicché. Then, off in the direction of San Rafael and San Luis, there were more fires and an explosion.[62]

Solís's running conflict with Tetiz's communalists initially made the attack seem like one more installment in that struggle. Thus, when investigators arrived at Chicché, Don Diego named forty pueblo residents whom he suspected of attacking his property out of anger over his efforts to halt wood poaching. The investigators took down their names and then inspected the detritus on the fincas: spent cartridges; burned storehouses and fields;

Mendoza's corpse, riddled with shot. It was a familiar scene, until Tetiz's justice of the peace found the facsimile weapons. The objects, identified in their inscription as a "great sword" and "great Mauser of Yucatán," demanded a different reading. Unlike the shotguns and machetes proper to rural uprisings, sword and Mauser were military weapons. Moreover, in referring to them as weapons "of Yucatán"—rather than of Tetiz—the authors of the inscription made clear that the attack was meant to have peninsular implications. In declaring their war to be one waged in the name of liberty, they distinguished themselves from partisan political groupings. By stating that "they," in the third-person, not "we," had made the weapons of war, they seemed to be anticipating how their words might be received by a wider audience, making the artifacts stand both as an oath and as a declaration of war. Perhaps the bloody handprints Concha found on the walls and water tank of the hacienda were part of it all, as the attackers sealed the oath with their own blood.

The most important part of the inscription, however, may have been its date. The assault on Chicché took place at midnight on 4 May, making the attack the inaugural event of Cinco de Mayo. The timing of the attack was far from coincidental. On several occasions previously, Hunucmá's insurgents were reported to have voiced patriotic sentiments. Witnesses reported hearing cries of *¡Viva México!* during attacks on the haciendas, including the one on Chicché. A flag—probably a Mexican flag, reportedly with an inscription of some kind—was a prized possession of the rebels, gracing meetings and battles with its presence.[63] Indeed, two weeks before the attack of 5 May, organizers used the upcoming national holiday to rally participants, declaring that "whoever rose up in revolution against the government on Cinco de Mayo would win." The route the men planned was almost like a parade, with a march to Chicché for a midnight assault, then to San Luis and San Rafael, and finally passing through the main plaza of Tetiz on their triumphant return. All of this, one informer claimed, was planned "to celebrate Cinco de Mayo." By scheduling the coordinated attacks for that date, the insurgents drew an equivalence between national struggle against foreign imperialists in the 1860s and their own battle with ts'uls like Don Diego. At the same time, they declared that theirs was a war not only for land and liberation, but also for a patria over which elites had long claimed exclusive ownership.[64]

Gun and sword, with their inscribed date, were meant to stand as a battle cry, yet they simultaneously made a material claim on history. They were both a tribute to the attack on Chicché in the moment it became history and a commemoration of a future liberation war, a war in which the insurgents might one day be victorious. These were landmarks, meant to mark many passages: from rebellion to revolution, from slavery to liberation, and from pueblo to patria.[65]

THE LIBERATION WAR

According to the Revista de Mérida, the morning after the attack on Chicché, Hunucmá's Cinco de Mayo celebrations were "somewhat subdued."[66] It was no wonder. The sword and the gun were eloquent refutations of the presumptions of the gentry presiding over Hunucmá's festivities. Yet even as they transcribed the inscription left by the attackers, commentators failed to take notice of the attack's obvious timing or of the insurgents' avowed patriotism. Instead, they offered the inscription as evidence that the "macabre hordes" of "Yucatecan Zapatismo" stood at the "gates of the beautiful city of Mérida" as a "stain on our civilization." In a lengthy editorial, the editor of the Revista, Carlos Menéndez, compared the "parallel Zapatismos" of Morelos and Hunucmá: whereas in Morelos the rebels protected the haciendas, in Hunucmá they had declared a "war to the death" against them; whereas Zapatistas in Morelos were brave enough to fight by day, those in Hunucmá were cowards who attacked "under the shadows of the night." Far from recognizing the patriotism of the insurgents, Menéndez declared that unless Hunucmá's Zapatistas were defeated, "there can be neither patria, nor family, nor society."[67] That, for him, was the message of sword and gun.

Yucatán's governor momentarily entertained the possibility of negotiation, charging none other than Feliciano Canul Reyes with contacting the rebels in a "mission of pacification." That option was closed by an open letter from Hunucmá's landowners denouncing Canul's "libertarianism" and lack of patriotism and by demands in the press for an "implacable" war to "exterminate" Hunucmá's "Zapatismo."[68] Two hundred soldiers set off for Tetiz, where they clashed with rebels and carried out a campaign of beatings, thefts, shootings, and sexual assaults.[69] Meanwhile, the penal investigation into the Chicché attack proceeded. While Diego Solís and his henchmen initially told investigators they were unable to identify their assailants, over the days to come their memories seem to have improved. All returned to speak with investigators, claiming they could now identify their attackers. The accused, most of them former pinistas, were taken away in shackles.[70]

In the months following the attack of 5 May, Hunucmá's jefe politico undertook a broad campaign of repression, largely through the arrest and conscription of fugitives from the fincas, political activists, and criminal suspects. When many suspects in the Chicché attack, for instance, were released in October 1913, they were immediately drafted into the federal army. Hunucmá's residents were disproportionately represented among Yucatecan draftees, and Chicché suspects appeared on draft lists in especially high numbers.[71] In one list of eighty-eight Yucatecan draftees for the federal army, supposedly chosen at random, at least twenty-six were residents of Hunucmá or Tetiz, including eleven whom Solís had named as suspects in the attacks, as well as several former pinista leaders. In November, of the first group of sixty-five Yucatecans sent off to join federal forces, fifty were from the Hunucmá district.[72]

The repression intensified in February 1914, following Huerta's appointment of General Prisciliano Cortés as governor of Yucatán. On assuming power, Cortés called for Yucatecans to "listen to the call, for peace, truth and concord . . . for the good of the State," sentiments seconded by the editor of the *Revista*, who exhorted readers to join Cortés in working for truth, justice, and the patria.[73] Cortés appointed a new, even more despotic jefe político for Hunucmá: Felipe Molina Villamil. Molina patrolled the woods in the area, restricted the movements of pueblo residents and hunters, conscripted draftees immediately on their return from prior terms of service, and avidly tracked down fugitive hacienda workers. The new jefe became infamous for issuing arbitrary fines to pueblo residents and then selling the debts and thus the labor of those who could not pay to hacendados.[74] The starkest abuses were reserved for the Canul Reyes family. Molina threatened Feliciano Canul with conscription and had police kidnap his daughters; eighteen of his soldiers then sacked his house, beat his elderly mother, Isabel Reyes, and sexually molested his wife, Agustina Poot.[75]

In the wake of the Chicché attack, Hunucmá became emblematic of the abuses of the Huertista regime in Yucatán. Even the editor of the *Revista* denounced the conscriptions, which he believed encouraged what he called the region's "Mayan Indians" to flee to the woods, where they would give themselves over to "laziness, disorder, pillage, and revolution."[76] For stauncher critics, the situation demonstrated the persistence of slavery in the Yucatecan countryside. Pérez Ponce took on the defense of the Chicché suspects and appealed the conscriptions, which had only deepened a "profound state of ill-feeling among the *hunucmenses*." Such abuses had led "citizens formerly dedicated to work" to "head for the woods, where they are disposed to commit the greatest misdeeds."[77] Later, Pérez dispatched a telegram to President Huerta, accusing state and district officials of persecuting Hunucmá's "peaceful citizens" and of conspiring with "hacendado slavers" to preserve the forced labor system. Although ninety-nine of Hunucmá's gentry sent a telegram of their own to Huerta denouncing Pérez Ponce as an "anarchist" and a "supporter of bandits,"[78] federal officials took note of the situation in Hunucmá. When an agent of the Department of Labor visited Yucatán in March 1914, charged with assessing the situation on the haciendas, he was favorably impressed by several of the haciendas he visited in the state. In Hunucmá, however, he met with Aurelio Chablé, an escaped debt peon from Nohuayum, who described beatings on the hacienda and the collusion of local authorities and hacendados in hunting down and punishing escaped workers. Chablé's testimony cast a dark shadow over his report.[79]

It was working-class residents of the region, however, rather than political activists or government officials, who denounced slavery most vociferously. Complaining that Molina had detained their husbands and then handed them over to a hacendado to work as servants, Nicolasa Pech and María Ana Mex declared that Molina "considers the inhabitants [of Hunucmá] to be truly slaves."[80] After being assaulted by soldiers, Isabel Reyes and Agustina Poot went to Hunucmá's military garrison to berate them as "sons of whores" and "chicken thieves" and to declare that they "shit on the jefe político, the governor and all of the authorities." "Soon Yum Carranza will come," they shouted, to "take care of all the big shots."[81] When indicted for defamation, the women provided a detailed indictment of Molina as a "slaver" and a defense of Canul Reyes as the leader of a group of "citizens" who according to them had only taken to the woods to "escape the claws of the slavers."[82]

As in the past, repression only spurred more violence. Assailants killed the encargado of Hacienda San Miguel, and workers of Chel reportedly carried an administrator off the hacienda "in procession, with disconcerting screams and hostile gestures." Arsonists destroyed henequen fields near Hunucmá, Kinchil, Samahil, and Tetiz. Policemen were ambushed.[83] Woodcutters and charcoal makers, long locked in a land dispute over lands adjoining San Román, waylaid and shot that finca's owner. The evildoers responsible, he later alleged, were men who followed Canul Reyes "blindly" and were conspiring to assassinate all of Hunucmá's landowners.[84] In the wake of the Chicché attack, Canul Reyes's fighters had vacated their homes, setting up armed camps hidden in woodland refuges like Kaxek, that old haunt of rebels and fugitives. Knowing the forest and marsh well, they evaded all attempts at capture. They raided haciendas for cattle and sabotaged telegraph lines, sending men out on covert missions for supplies and recruits in nearby pueblos. Increasingly fearful of the insurgents, Molina posted armed guards on the roof of his house, kept lights burning all night long, and conscripted residents desperately, determined, as Pérez Ponce alleged, to "expel from his domain any man or woman who might be involved in an imaginary plot against him."[85]

Written sources do not tell much about the experiences of the insurgents. They left no additional inscribed weapons, or if they did the police and soldiers did not record their messages. A few stories about the final phase of Canul's movement have survived. One is the tale of a young man who boasted of his bravery but blanched in fear during battles. When the insurgents captured a soldier who had been sent to track them, Canul took the young man and gave him a knife. Gripping his hand, Canul forced him to stab the soldier in the chest. As the soldier died, Canul bathed the young man's face with his blood, saying, "This is to cure your fear." As in the Negrón killing three years earlier, the anointment was a rite of passage in which an elder initiated a young man into the ranks, converting him into a hardened insurgent. The enemy whose blood sanctified the ritual, however, was now a soldier of the government rather than an overseer or encargado, making the story one that highlights the transformation of the struggle from a rebellion against the haciendas into a revolutionary war.[86]

That war prospered as the fortunes of Mexico's dictator declined. By spring 1914, Huerta faced an uprising by Carranza's Constitutionalist army as well as forces of Villa and Zapata. The U.S. occupation of the port city of Veracruz in April 1914 brought the crisis to a breaking point. To jefe Molina, such events seemed to offer an opportunity for reconciliation. He organized a large demonstration against the United States, citing the danger to "our beloved patria" and calling on Canul Reyes and his insurgents to "forget old grudges, to unite fraternally, so that when the moment comes, they may fulfill the sacred duty of joining the struggle to defend our national integrity and sovereignty." More than two hundred men emerged from the woods for the event, in which the national anthem was sung and local notables gave speeches in Maya, interspersed with *vivas* for Mexico and *mueras* ("death to") for the Yankees. A group composed of landowners and former pinistas was commissioned to contact other men who were still "off in the woods, outside the control of the government" to offer them amnesty in return for their "defense of the patria."[87] By 2 May, however, an armistice was reached with the United States, and Canul Reyes and his men melted back into the woods. By June, Hunucmá's insurgents had joined ranks with forces under the command of Lino Muñoz, another onetime pinista from the port city of Progreso. Muñoz's men were in rebellion against not only the Huertista regime, but also the jefe político of Progreso, José María Ceballos, who had earned infamy for his despotism, corruption, and other abuses, including what one U.S. consul called a "questionable attitude toward the young girls of Progreso." In late July the attacks on haciendas began once again. Rebels took part in several assassination attempts against Ceballos and sabotaged the railway from Mérida to Progreso as well as telephone, telegraph, and electrical lines. Police and soldiers searched the woods and caves of the district, engaging in occasional firefights with the rebels but capturing few of them.[88]

With the fall of the Huerta regime in July and Carranza's rise to power, Yucatán's Huertista governor grasped at other solutions to the conflict in Hunucmá. He replaced Molina, ordering the new jefe to resolve the longstanding conflicts over the road through Chicché. Soon the jefe declared that Don Diego had committed an "odious" act by closing the road and ordered that pueblo residents be allowed free passage.[89] It was as if opening the road might turn back the clock in Hunucmá, to the day before the attack on Chicché, the day before so many oaths were struck in blood, the day before sword and gun, and before the insurgency. Newspaper reporters perceived the reopened road as signifying a return to complete tranquility. One, observing the annual fiestas of the Virgin of Tetiz, rejoiced at the sight of "inhabitants of that pueblo, so full of happiness before the prospect of a new era of peace which is drawing near for our beloved patria."[90]

Despite such public statements of optimism, preparations were underway for harder times. Seventy-five soldiers were stationed in Hunucmá to guard against the insurgents. In Tetiz, secret police agents acting on direct orders from the governor prowled the pueblo to collect information on the insurgency. Agent Luis Sánchez reported using a family carriage to "simulate a recreational trip to the countryside"; he had his men, disguised as personal servants, make casual conversation with anyone they met "hanging out on the street corners" of Tetiz. Residents responded evasively, however, leading Sánchez to concede failure. "Everybody here," he exclaimed in frustration, "is of the same caliber."[91] Soon, the caliber of the insurgency would become only too clear. At the stroke of midnight on 18 August insurgents under the command of Canul Reyes and Lino Muñoz attacked government buildings and a military garrison in Progreso. After a forty-minute gun battle, the garrison surrendered, but only after Canul Reyes and his brother, José Cirilo Canul, died in combat. Afterward, the rebels tied Progreso's jefe político to a tree, and then, ignoring his entreaties that "those defeated should be spared," shot him and slashed his throat. Later, they dragged him off to a public slaughterhouse, where they hitched him up on a meat hook, like a pig.[92] Newspapers published detailed accounts of the "bloody and terrible tragedy" in Progreso along with photographs of the ground where the bodies of the Canul brothers had lain. Their bodies were gone, but blotches of blood were visible, along with a cross etched on the spot where Hunucmá's Zapata ended his days.[93]

The next day Lino Muñoz issued a manifesto allying himself with the Constitutionalists and proclaiming a movement under the "redemptive banner of the Revolution" to "reclaim the rights . . . of the humble classes." Now swelled to about five hundred in number with the addition of Canul Reyes's men, his forces set off toward Hunucmá. They occupied Tacubaya and prepared to take Hunucmá by force, to honor what Lino called a promise he had made to Feliciano Canul.[94] While Carranza sent a telegram declaring an end to hostilities and newspapers called, "in the name of the patria," for Lino to avoid "once again soaking our beloved Yucatecan soil with the blood of brothers," on 25 August rebels attacked the central plaza of Hunucmá in force. Soldiers took up positions atop the church, the municipal government building, and houses nearby. As both the rebels and the troops garrisoned in Hunucmá were now under Constitutionalist authority, both sides, oddly, shouted, "¡Viva Carranza!" at each other during fifty minutes of fierce fighting. In the end the rebels were unable to prevail and withdrew.[95]

Even as Lino's attack stalled in Hunucmá, other mobilizations swept the district. Rebels near Kinchil, fortified by workers recruited from nearby fincas, occupied Kinchil's plaza and seized its garrison. In Tetiz, a headless body was found in the middle of the pueblo. Reporters announced that in Tetiz the "indigenous population has risen up, with no recognized leader or cause" and warned of the possibility of "bloodier events, in the imminent future." Desperate landowners and their families fled the region in droves.[96] In the end, though, after a federal decree dictating the death penalty for any who "disturbed public order," a commission from the state government convinced Lino to stand down. A cease-fire agreement was signed by Feliciano Canul's brother Saturnino as well as by other insurgents, including Pío Chuc and Tzab.[97] While there was some violence in the days to follow—three killings in Tetiz, one of them of the encargado of Chicché—Lino ordered his forces to police towns and pueblos, guard fincas, and arrest suspected bandits. The commander reportedly lectured his troops, urging them, in the name of the patria, to forget the "old personal hates" that had led them to take up arms.[98]

Soon Carranza's appointee as governor of Yucatán, Coronel Eleuterio Avila, arrived in Mérida to take up his position. In a bid to build support for the Constitutionalists and to end rebellion, Carranza had ordered him to promulgate a decree ending debt servitude, which he did shortly after his arrival in Yucatán. At the invitation of the new governor, Lino Muñoz and his forces boarded a special train sent to carry them through the gates of Mérida, as if to fulfill the Revista's terrified prophecies in the wake of the Cinco de Mayo attacks. On 11 September 1914 they assembled in Mérida's central plaza, where they were addressed by a government official who praised them in words seemingly intended to efface years of violence: "You have not robbed, you have not committed arson, you have not attacked any homes, you have not violated the inviolable rights of civilized society." In protecting the pueblos and haciendas from attack, he added, they had become "true soldiers of order." Then Governor Avila appeared, to announce that the Revolution had come at last to transform Yucatán's "pariahs" into "citizens" of the patria. Avila read the liberation decree which he had just signed, declaring it an act of "redemption" that abolished the debts of indigenous servants, freeing them to reside and work wherever they chose.[99]

After a chorus of vivas to Avila, Carranza, and the martyrs Madero and Pino Suárez, the troops left Mérida for Progreso. As many as two thousand people walked to the cemetery in Progreso, where a ceremony was held for Feliciano Canul Reyes and other insurgents who had died during the fighting there. Lino Muñóz saluted them as "worthy men: patriots and citizens." If sword and gun once had marked the beginning of a path to liberation and patria, now the body of Hunucmá's Zapata marked its ending. With the ceremonies of 11 September the insurgents had been transformed from evildoers without home, pueblo, or patria into liberation's heroes and the nation's martyrs. Long scorned and repressed, they were now absolved by executive order and recognized as citizens. Thus, it might have seemed, the war had been won, Hunucmá's "slaves" were redeemed, and the inscribed oath of 5 May 1913 was, at last, discharged.[100]

More than thirty years after the end of indebted servitude, Eleuterio Avila's onetime secretary, Albino Acereto, wrote a political history of Yucatán. In a discussion of the liberation, Acereto made only the briefest of mentions of Hunucmá's insurgents—a reference to "ragtag conscripts from Hunucmá"

Ruins of Chicché.
Photo by Paul Eiss.

attending the promulgation of the decree in Mérida.[101] There was no other reference to them, as Yucatecan historians like Acereto focused their attentions on leaders like Avila and their legislation and debated whether the liberation decree truly freed indigenous workers or not, and whether the title of liberator rightly fell to Avila or to other leaders who followed.

In the Hunucmá region, however, neither the liberation decree of 11 September 1914 nor Avila is celebrated or recalled. If older residents tell stories about those times at all, they do so to recall not how liberty was given by the government, but how it was won, in places like Progreso. Some still tell stories about the man named Feliciano Canul Reyes, and if asked they can point out his grave in the center of Hunucmá's cemetery, even though it carries no engraved dedication and no mention of his name or date of birth or death. Canul had many enemies, they explain, and had to be buried secretly, in clandestinity. The battle at Chicché on 5 May 1913, and the sword and the gun, however, seem to be recalled by no one.

For the son of Teodosio Cuytún, who lived in Tetiz, the most important souvenir of the liberation was an object he inherited from his father: an old, beat-up shotgun. Don Teodosio, who once feuded with Don Diego over Chicché's woodlands and was a suspect in the 5 de mayo attack, told his son he had carried and used the weapon on the day liberty was won. If Cuytún indeed took part in the insurgency and witnessed the inscribed devices that the rebels used to dedicate their cause on 5 May 1913, it may be that his weapon carried special significance. Perhaps the old weapon reminded him of that other gun and was something in which he took pride. Although the facsimile sword and gun of 5 May 1913, were long ago lost and forgotten, perhaps their message survived, for a time, in that object.

∂ PART TWO

REPOSSESSION

Solo Ud. Señor, podria remediar
tan grabe mal y como práticamente
que los ejidos de otros pueblos que
lograron tenerlos y fueron distribuidos
á los padres de familias estan hoy en
manos de ricos propietarios, quienes
persiguen a cuantos vean o sepan
que pasan por aquellos lugares con
el fin de sembrarles temor para hacer
respetar a sus derechos. . . .
A Ud. Exelentismo Señor: supli-
camos, que al mandar la mensura de
los ejidos dejen un perímetro ó fundo
legal suficiente para el ensanche de
la poblacion y mensurados, quede
á veneficio del pueblo sin que nadie
pudiera alegarle propiedad para poder
conjurar el mal que tanto perjuicio ha
causado á la propiedad del pueblo.

Only you, Sir, can remedy this great
evil, as the ejidos of other pueblos,
which were distributed to heads of
family, are now in the hands of the
rich landowners, who chase whoever
they see or hear pass through those
lands, in order to plant fear in them,
so that they respect their rights. . . .
To you, most Excellent Sir,
we request, that when the ejidos
are measured, they leave, and
measure, a perimeter sufficient for
the growth of the population, and
once measured, it remain for the
benefit of el pueblo, so that no one
might claim it as property, in order
to conjure the evil that has caused
so much damage to the property of
el pueblo.

—JOSÉ PÍO CHUC et al., Hunucmá, 1915

CHAPTER FOUR

THE REDEMPTION

Subjects of Revolution and Objects
of Governance

"MOST EXCELLENT GOVERNOR." These words
were meant to signal deference and attract attention.
They appeared, written in large letters, at the top of a
sheaf of ledger paper whose pages were covered by a
single stream of uneven, choppy, and compact writing.
The message, nonetheless, was eloquent: a plea in the
name of el pueblo for Governor Salvador Alvarado to
bring "justice" and "liberty" to Hunucmá. A rambling
history followed, recounting the despoliation of communal lands and appealing for the restoration of those
lands to el pueblo, to free it from "opprobrium and misery." Finally, there was a date—2 May 1915—and more
than three hundred names. Most of the names were Mayan and signed by the same hand, as if the signatories
could not sign on their own behalf. The first on the list
was that of José Pío Chuc.[1]

The petition was written as an entreaty and was
saturated by images of abjection and expressions of

adulation. It did more, however, than just convey a request. The authors of the petition presented its signatories as a collective—el pueblo de Hunucmá—while identifying that entity as "the needy class." They addressed their intended audience as a collective entity as well: more than simply the man named Salvador Alvarado, the petition's addressee was *el gobierno*, the government. In their remarkable document, presented to Governor Alvarado during a festive and highly publicized visit he made to Hunucmá, the petitioners called for the restoration of Hunucmá's communal lands and for its recognition as a collective political subject, one whose legitimacy was founded in its historic insurgency. But in addition they evoked the possibility of a new relationship between government and pueblo. The petition, with its entreaties for salvation from above, was an act of statecraft from below.

The petitioners were not alone in their desire to reshape pueblo and government. From the moment of his arrival in Yucatán, Salvador Alvarado, a leading figure in Venustiano Carranza's Constitutionalist Revolution, had declared his intention to reinvent the workings of government in Yucatán and to modernize Yucatecan society through a series of social and political reforms. Alvarado presented his mission as one of liberating, uplifting, and redeeming el pueblo in ways that inspired hope among Hunucmá's communalists. Alvarado's pueblo, however, was different from theirs. The general evoked el pueblo not as a subject of insurgency, but as an object of governance and a framework for state-directed social reform and modernization.

Amid the swirls of confetti, Alvarado and his petitioners alike seem to have imagined that his encounter with el pueblo in Hunucmá might lead to a historic alliance of pueblo and gobierno. Yet the exuberant festivities masked fundamental differences between the general and his petitioners that led them to hold variant visions of pueblo, government, and the relation between the two. To read the Hunucmá petition is to discover the nature and extent of those differences. Above all, it is to explore the distinct understandings of history held by Alvarado and his petitioners, understandings that soon would lead their alliance to unravel.

THE LEXICON OF LIBERATION

On 20 December 1914, when Governor Eleuterio Avila paid an official visit to Hunucmá, droves of residents welcomed him. He received a chorus of *vivas* as the foundation stone for a new school was laid in his honor. Then local notables looked on as the schoolteacher Candelaria Ojeda first lauded

Carranza's "revolutionary work, for the good of the Patria" and then praised Avila's efforts on behalf of indigenous workers. "You have laid the foundations for the redemption of the Indian," she declared, "so that the indigenous race might enter into full possession of its usurped rights, and might intone a song of glory in your name with tears of gratitude in its eyes." In a speech of his own, Avila lectured his audience on the history of the Mexican Revolution, from Madero's Revolution through Huerta's usurpation and Carranza's Constitutionalist movement. Then he discussed plans to return ejido lands to Hunucmá's working poor. Fortunately, he announced, lands already had been "graciously donated" for that purpose by the wealthy hacendado Augusto L. Peón.[2]

Avila's visit to Hunucmá represented the culmination of a series of events that began on 11 September 1914 with the promulgation of a liberation decree that annulled workers' debts, outlawed physical punishments, and established freedom of movement and marriage for hacienda workers. Couched in the language of universal rights and sweeping political change, Avila's decree had announced the advent of a new era of liberty, characterized by the reclamation of what he called the "sacred and inalienable rights" of citizens. The government commissioned the Hunucmá resident, schoolteacher, and Mayanist Santiago Pacheco Cruz to translate the decree into Yucatec Maya and dispatched agents and officials to the Yucatecan countryside to read it to pueblo and hacienda residents.[3] In Hunucmá, the task fell to José Dolores Concepción Ceballos, an ally of Lino Muñoz and Canul Reyes whom Avila had appointed jefe político, an appointment that, according to a letter signed by hundreds of area residents, was "congenial to all." Concepción set about commissioning agents from the ranks of former pinistas and morenistas, among them Pacheco Cruz, to disseminate the liberation decree.[4]

This liberation, however, had limits. First, the decree did not address the status or restoration of communal lands. Moreover, two circulars published as addenda to the decree mandated a two-week period of notice for departing hacienda workers, restricted their freedom of movement, and made *cohecho*, or "incitement," a crime punishable by imprisonment. Such penalties were applied broadly by officials like Concepción. Workers who merely mentioned the liberation decree to other workers were subject to arrest if those words were thought to have incited them to leave the fincas. Military officials and police patrolled the woodlands in search of former hacienda workers who attempted to settle there and forced them to move back to recognized population sites—often, to the haciendas. By the time Avila visited Hunucmá and Umán in December, it must have seemed—to the chagrin of indigenous workers but to the reassurance of hacendados like Peón—that the new era of liberty was not so different from what had preceded it.[5]

Just a few weeks later, however, Governor Avila would be out of office, dismissed by Carranza after he refused to levy hefty new federal taxes on henequen fiber. His replacement, General Toribio de los Santos, lasted even less time: in mid-February 1915 he was toppled by a coup led by Coronel Abel Ortíz Argumedo with the support of many Yucatecan hacendados. In response, Carranza dispatched an army led by General Salvador Alvarado, a native of the state of Sonora, to retake the peninsula by force, with orders to enforce Constitutionalist social reforms and capture a larger share of henequen revenues for the federal government. By late March the general had succeeded in that task, establishing a new civil and military government throughout the interior of the state.[6] Upon taking power, Alvarado empowered the state's henequen regulatory commission, the Comisión Reguladora, to establish a state monopoly over the purchase of henequen fiber from planters and over its sale to foreign buyers. Given the high demand for fiber in world markets during the First World War, the commission profited from a sustained rise in henequen prices. The resulting expansion of government revenues provided financing for a bold series of state initiatives aimed at fostering Yucatán's agricultural, industrial, and social modernization.[7]

Alvarado undertook such reforms in the name of el pueblo and of its liberation. Several weeks before arriving in Yucatán, he had issued a manifesto declaring that "true revolutionaries" were on their way, determined to "liberate el pueblo" from its oppressors.[8] On taking power, Alvarado declared that as Avila's liberation had not been enforced, the charge of emancipating indigenous hacienda workers had fallen to him. Beginning in April 1915, military commanders and government agents visited haciendas to liberate indigenous workers, typically by firing abusive encargados, informing workers of their rights, and ordering wage raises. The first such actions—as publicized in *La voz de la Revolución*, the newspaper that became the regime's official press organ—were taken in Hunucmá, where a visit to a hacienda by the district military commander, Enrique Sánchez, reportedly inspired "astonishment and joy among the workers, who saw that the times of slavery had ended, that their rights are respected, and that their labors now will be compensated fairly." Two days later, there were more reports of the "breaking of slaves' chains" on the haciendas as Sánchez demonstrated that the "benevolent principles that the Constitutionalist Revolution carried as its banner are not just sonorous rhetoric, but are made reality, wherever men who are revolutionaries at heart, like General Alvarado, set foot."⁹

Notwithstanding such emancipatory rhetoric, in the new regime el pueblo featured most significantly as an object of governance: that is, as a framework for social and political control. Upon taking power, Alvarado issued a circular calling for the "moralization" of government and the instruction of public officials in what he termed their "obligations toward el pueblo." "It is time," he declared, "for the pueblos to no longer see their authorities as a scourge, but rather as men guided by the spirit of justice."¹⁰ In a similar spirit, commentators reported exuberantly on Alvarado's tours of Yucatán's pueblos and haciendas, one declaring that "for the very first time, rural workers and indígenas are sitting down at the same table to talk with the Head of the State, who chats affectionately with everyone."¹¹ For Alvarado, however, the abolition of servitude had left unchanged an underlying backwardness and moral degradation he attributed to Yucatecan populations, conditions he proposed to remedy through measures aimed at "destroying corrupt customs which, perverting the condition of man, convert him into a true slave." "Whatever form slavery takes," he declared, "will be fiercely battled by Public Power. . . . The hand of the Revolution . . . will cut these abuses at their root."¹² Indigenous hacienda workers, in Alvarado's view, were the most degraded, owing both to the "slavery" that had left them "brutelike," and isolated from the patria and to the influence of the Church, which had left them mired in "fanaticism." Alvarado considered reforms, especially indigenous education, as "powerful weapons" to be used against "masses who have let themselves be exploited, who have lived deceived and dispossessed for so long, who have lived unaware, like wretched slaves [and live like] simple organisms, leaving behind detritus as their only trace . . . as in prehistoric times."¹³

It was around the question of land that the Alvarado regime would face the greatest difficulties in its drive to realize a sweeping, but tightly controlled, emancipation of indigenous populations. Here, Alvarado seemed to promise the most radical departure from prior regimes. Within weeks of taking power, he established an Agrarian and Public Works Office, and agrarian engineers began to prepare for land distribution by touring the countryside, mapping ejidos, and measuring hacienda lands.¹⁴ Land reform, to Alvarado, was not simply a question of land, but one of race, involving the education and uplift of presumably primitive indigenous populations. Hence when Alvarado, soon after his arrival in Yucatán, published a call for suggestions on how to carry out land reform he also solicited opinions on how to make what he called "Indian" lands—and thus indigenous workers—more productive through the introduction of modern crops and agricultural techniques.[15]

The most significant response to Alvarado's query came from the hacendado Joaquín Peón, who a year earlier had argued against Avila's liberation decree, citing Mayan "racial idiosyncrasies" and "lethargy."[16] Now Peón argued against agrarian reform, offering the example of Hunucmá in support of his views. That region's "Mayan and mestizo inhabitants," Peón informed Alvarado, "resist the division of land, and would rather hold the nearby forests in common." As "refractory" primitives, he wrote, they were out of step with "the present epoch"; their communalism was immovably opposed to the spirit of private property, an institution that, as much as family and religion, was a foundation of modern society. Peón's letter was published in *La voz* on 3 May, the very day of Alvarado's visit to Hunucmá; the timing was likely no coincidence. Alvarado's reception there served as the clearest rebuke to Peón's racist argument.[17]

Yet in some respects Alvarado's views on land and race may have been closer to Peón's than to those of Hunucmá's communalists. As an unpublished government proposal for agrarian regulations from early April makes clear, Alvarado perceived communal ejidos as an atavistic phenomenon, at best a temporary means of providing for the subsistence needs of indigenous populations. He did not intend to abolish private property but viewed the ejido as a transitional institution that would pave the way for a movement away from feudalistic landed estates to midsized agricultural enterprises and small farms. Indigenous "proletarians," in his view, were to be transformed into a class of small landowners: holders of small plots and gardens where they might cultivate crops that were not labor intensive, thus leaving them "free to go to work on large properties as well," as wage laborers. In the future, Alvarado imagined, traditional hacendados, peons, and indigenous communalists would disappear, evolving into entrepreneurial capitalists, modern agricultural workers, and smallholding farmers.[18]

By early May, however, the finer points of Alvarado's approach to land reform had not yet been widely publicized. In the Hunucmá region, as elsewhere in the state, residents from across the social spectrum, from landed gentry to indigenous workers, attempted to link themselves to the general, claiming allegiance to his expansive, if still somewhat ambiguous, project of liberation. A few weeks after Alvarado's advent to power, for instance, when former governor Toribio de los Santos toured the district to "inform el pueblo of its rights," he received universal acclaim from its "long-suffering" inhabitants, who made a collective declaration of loyalty to the Constitutionalist Revolution.[19] But such gestures of unity quickly dissolved as local factions sought to turn Alvarado against their adversaries. A group of former pinistas in Umán now grouped in a "Círculo Libertario" wrote to the governor to denounce the mayor of Umán, Bartolomé García Correa, as a "slaver" who had returned escaped workers to the fincas, collaborated with the Huerta regime, conscripted town residents into the military, and generally worked for "evil."[20] Several months later, after Alvarado had assumed power, Sánchez went about appointing and overseeing elections of new authorities in the towns and pueblos of the district. After García and his ally, the hacendado Atilano González, returned to power in April in elections, Umán's *Círculo* again sought their deposal as "so-called benefactors of el pueblo" who blocked poor workers and artisans from gaining access to land and food.[21] Unless Alvarado took their side, they concluded, their only prospect was "martyrdom [and] death."[22] Such appeals were not peculiar to Umán. Another large group of former pinistas from Tetiz sent a petition saluting Alvarado's "glorious army" and requesting supplies and assistance so that "our children will not perish of hunger."[23] From Hunucmá, a commission of several former allies of Feliciano Canul Reyes, led by Pío Chuc, traveled to Mérida on 6 April to speak with Alvarado. Their efforts, to judge by Sánchez's subsequent appointment of their adversary, the hacendado and onetime morenista Esteban Larrache, as mayor, may not have borne fruit.[24]

On the eve of Alvarado's visit to Hunucmá the stage was set for the general's trip to be perceived as a historic opportunity to reshape the relationship between gobierno and pueblo. For Alvarado, the encounter must have seemed an ideal opportunity to demonstrate how his Revolution, founded both in military force and a commitment to social reform, could finally restore the pueblo of Hunucmá and its rebellious indigenous populations to peace. If government and pueblo could unite even in Hunucmá, what couldn't the Revolution achieve? Hunucmá's small and medium landowners, for their part, may have felt ambivalent: threatened by the new government's as-yet-undefined labor and land reforms yet reassured by the general's obvious interest in preserving the henequen economy and breaking the monopoly of oligarchs like Augusto L. Peón. For the working and indigenous residents of the region, the general's commitment to the distribution of lands may have suggested he could become a new ally in an old struggle in defense of communal lands, one waged in the name of pueblo and patria. As gentry, workers, and communalists prepared for Alvarado's visit on the eve of Cinco de Mayo celebrations, some may have imagined, for a moment, that despite their differences peace might have finally arrived, brokered by the revolutionary government and inscribed in a lexicon of liberation shared by all.

VISIONS OF EL PUEBLO

On 3 May 1915 Governor Alvarado arrived in Hunucmá by train, accompanied by a large retinue of civil, judicial, and military authorities. As he arrived, according to reporters from *La voz*, a multitude of residents thronged outside, desperate to demonstrate its "loyalty to and respect for the Constitutionalist government." A procession followed the governor and his entourage as they walked to the center of town. There, Hunucmá honored the general with a series of speeches in Spanish and Maya, followed by a banquet and a traditional vaquería to the strains of music provided by the town's orchestra. In honor of the Sonoran general the musicians added central Mexican favorites like "La cucaracha" to their Yucatecan repertoire.[25]

Although a report in *La voz* presented Alvarado's welcome as unanimous and unequivocal, a closer reading hints that the visit was a complex event shaped by contending expectations. When Alvarado arrived in Hunucmá's train station, legions of "beautiful señoritas" in traditional festive regional dress—women whose surnames were those of prominent local landholding families—reportedly boarded the train to welcome him; on his arrival in the center of town, female schoolteachers, also daughters of notable local families, offered speeches in Alvarado's honor. One welcomed the governor as a "valiant soldier of liberty" who defended the "noble cause of el pueblo." Another saluted him for "bringing redemptions [sic] to those who have suffered the chains of humiliation and servitude." Long oppressed by hacienda "slavery," she declared, "el pueblo" called upon Alvarado to "redeem" it by "building a solid bridge between labor and capital." Another emphasized the importance of educating "the Indian" in order to secure the "enlightenment and growth" of "el pueblo." One schoolteacher evoked Hunucmá's loyalty by gesturing toward the assembled crowds: "Do you see, sir? With happy and smiling faces, el pueblo presents itself to you. All have come to meet the man who has come to see the peace that now reigns among us—to see the illustrious and valiant Jefe whom they identify with their happiness and their future."

While the daughters of local landholding families donned their mestiza finery, offering themselves to the government as mediators with el pueblo,

Salvador Alvarado received by women in mestiza finery. Date and location unknown.
Courtesy Fototeca Pedro Guerra, Universidad Autónoma de Yucatán.

indigenous workers made appeals of their own. According to news coverage, when Alvarado exited his train there were cheers from "hundreds of mouths, especially those of Hunucmá's Indians." Houses were adorned with "all kinds of rustic ornaments, with which the Indians celebrated the arrival of the governor." Alvarado's entourage reportedly was met by a large procession of "Indians" and workers, who marched along bearing banners and Mexican flags, led by representatives of Hunucmá's Círculo Libertario. Not to be outdone by the señoritas of landowning families, two "Indian women" reportedly marched at the head of the procession, carrying the Círculo's banner; on catching sight of the general, indigenous women were "visibly moved, displaying the greatest happiness." In several speeches at the events in Hunucmá, indigenous communalists like the aging José Angel Chuc, a communalist leader from the 1870s whom La voz called an "estimable Indian," requested the freedom of Tomás Pérez Ponce, Herminio Balam, and several other "fighters of oppression" who still languished in prison as "victims of the landed bossism [caciquismo] of prior times." Most striking of all was the presence of Feliciano Canul Reyes. Alongside the dais where Alvarado was received, according to one reporter from La voz, a portrait of

the "unforgettable" Canul was displayed "ostentatiously." "Indians of the region," he explained, had ordered that a portrait of the martyr be hung there.

Government officials brought their own agenda to Alvarado's visit.
Alvarado's general secretary reportedly "spoke directly to el pueblo," deliver-
ing a forty-minute speech in which he explained the "noble" policies of the
new government regarding the responsibilities of citizens, the agrarian problem, and the "uplift of the Indian [race]." He proclaimed Alvarado to be a
"symbol of the Mexican Revolution, with its mission of liberty, equality, and
justice." Government officials took pains to engage in dialogue with their
indigenous interlocutors and to feature those exchanges, in press coverage,
as performances that vividly demonstrated the changed nature of the relation
between gobierno and pueblo. Agents reportedly "made good propaganda
among the Indians," and the former pinista leader Alfonso Alonzo engaged
in an "animated" discussion with "the indígenas," demonstrating to them
"through reasoning and example, the government's attitude, as the savior
of [their] race." General Alvarado, who typically appeared in public in his
military uniform, made a statement of his own by wearing a white suit, traditional Yucatecan festive dress. In a brief speech, Alvarado announced that
he had ordered Pérez Ponce freed and would provide government stipends to
the Canul Reyes family, acts of pardon and recognition that reportedly made
a "magnificent impression" on his listeners.

Such gestures were the capstone of a carefully scripted performance that
dramatized both Hunucmá's redemption and Yucatán's passage from an epoch of slavery to a dawning era of liberty, peace, and unity. The spectacle
of virtuous and traditional, yet modern, mestizas, of onetime insurgents
become humble petitioners, and of state officials lecturing Hunucmá's residents on their responsibilities seemed to suggest that Alvarado's Revolution
finally might end social conflict in the district, replacing it with a new spirit of
order and civic responsibility. To make that point more graphically, a series
of photographs in La voz documented the day's events, with captions framing them as orderly collective encounters: "El Pueblo, waiting for General
Alvarado"; "El Pueblo says goodbye to the Governor"; and so on.

Despite the copious detail of newspaper accounts, however, one thing escaped coverage: the presentation of a lengthy petition to Alvarado, signed
by three hundred residents. La voz did mention that several "Indians" approached Alonzo to request the return of lands taken "iniquitously, to exploit
for the planting of henequen"; perhaps they handed him the sheaf of paper at
that moment. The document must have seemed odd. It was a petition in the

form of a history: a rambling story of el pueblo's oppression by local hacendados and an account of the expropriation of its lands and an appeal for their
restoration. It must have seemed a hodgepodge of themes and styles, with
some sections written in formally correct, even florid, Spanish and others
filled with spelling errors and tangled syntax.[26]

Rather than a hodgepodge, however, the petition was a composite of
phrases and themes that had long characterized political rhetoric and historical narratives in the region. The petitioners framed their narrative as one
of possession, referring to woodlands far to the northwest that they had held
for "centuries" and that still were "known by the name of El Común." The
theme of dispossession loomed as well, in repeated references to the alienation of common lands as haciendas expanded and their owners became
"absolute lords." As a result, the petitioners wrote, their "Liberty" had been
"unjustly lost and submerged for centuries," a situation that continued even
after the liberation as hacendados, assisted by police and forestry officials,
chased and "planted fear in the hearts" of all who dared to enter the old
woodlands. "Freedmen"—presumably, onetime insurgents—who had fled
the haciendas "eager to lend their services to the patria as free Citizens" were
forced, because of the lack of land, to place themselves once again "under
the yoke" of the hacendados. They were returned to so-called "slavery" by the
owners, who made "immense fortunes out of [their] sweat and badly paid
labor." But while the petitioners cast their history as a story of possession
and dispossession, they did so to plead for el pueblo's future repossession.
They called for common lands to be returned for the "benefit of el pueblo, allowing no one to claim them as property, in order to conjure the evil that has
caused so much harm to the property of el pueblo." Thus the petitioners put
history to use in a bold attempt to bring about el pueblo's repossession—not
by renouncing their long insurgent struggle, but by continuing it, through
an unprecedented alliance with a revolutionary government, in the name of
justice, liberation, and patria.

The history in the petition to Alvarado would go unrepresented in official
photographs and news coverage. Nonetheless, José Pío Chuc and the others
who had set their names to that document had participated in a consummate
act of statecraft, as dramatic as those staged by local gentry and government
officials during the amply, if partially, documented festivities of 3 May. Government officials, gentry, and indigenous workers all declared their determination to break with times of slavery and inaugurate future times of liberty.
They all avowed a desire to repossess el pueblo and thereby to reshape the

relationship between pueblo and government. The Hunucmá petition, however, suggests that the apparently seamless and exuberant joining of government and pueblo was actually a tenuous production, as the festive ensemble gathered under the title of el pueblo—what one reporter called an "immense wave of humanity"—threatened to split into its component factions. Events soon would show that their factious visions of el pueblo and of its future were not only distinct but incompatible.

IN THE NAME OF THE REVOLUTION

By the time of Alvarado's visit to Hunucmá, his government had already issued detailed regulations governing the process of agrarian reform. Those measures implied intervention into land tenure on a scale unprecedented in Yucatán. By October 1915, engineers had surveyed some four hundred haciendas, laying the basis both for definitive agrarian reform and for provisional distribution of subsistence lands to residents of fifty-three pueblos, pending definitive grants.[27] Documentation and historical narrative played critical roles in this process. The new regulations made the written and oral documentation of the past and the formation of narratives about it central to the procedure of agrarian reform. Such narratives bore little resemblance either to the lineage histories of the kahs, or to the stories of dispossession recounted in the name of el común. They were unlike the history presented in the Hunucmá petition, with its references to the insurgent struggle of el pueblo for liberation. These were accounts rendered by bureaucrats, who collected and scrutinized land titles and cadastral documentation dating back to colonial times and walked through field and forest unearthing old landmarks and hearing the testimony of elders on the boundaries between ejidos and haciendas. On that basis, agrarian officials elaborated narrative accounts of the history of land acquisition and the fragmentation of communal lands in the peninsula, in some cases ratifying the antiquity and legitimacy of hacendados' claims over the land and in others denouncing illicit land expropriations. Throughout Yucatán, pueblo dwellers sought out the engineers in order to press their claims, and the agrarian engineers found themselves drawn into complicated conflicts over land and history, with outcomes at times favoring landowners and at times pueblo residents.[28]

After Alvarado's visit to Hunucmá, provisional agrarian reform there initially seemed to proceed in an orderly fashion. One week after Alvarado's visit, there was a response to the petitioners. It was brief: a few lines typed on a single, unsigned sheet of paper, explaining that the government had established an Agrarian Cómmission, which would resolve the land issue in due course. The terse response seemed intended to communicate that agrarian matters could be addressed only through impersonal governmental procedures. Impassioned renderings of history and appeals for el pueblo's redemption, it seemed, would hold no sway.[29] Within a week of the government's brusque reply to the Hunucmá petition, however, the government appointed Petronilo Chuc, an ally and perhaps a relative of Pío Chuc—to become forest inspector for the district. According to Hunucmá's military commander, Chuc was a "true friend of el pueblo" whose naming would be well received; perhaps, he might have thought, it also would mitigate the petitioners' disappointment at the response to their petition. Moreover, an agrarian engineer who had accompanied Alvarado on his visit to Hunucmá immediately got to work reviewing titles and surveying lands. While the government's legal department upheld the legality of the land titles of most of the largest haciendas in the area, several smaller fincas that had formed more recently were found to be composed of communal lands illegally expropriated starting in the 1870s. Pending definitive reform, the officials helped to make arrangements for pueblo residents to gain temporary access to privately owned lands thought to be located within the boundaries of the old ejidos.[30]

Despite such apparent progress, however, dramatic conflicts over wood and woodlands soon erupted in Hunucmá. The issue of wood was fraught with conflict throughout rural Yucatán. Agrarian officials often found their efforts at provisional distribution of subsistence lands stymied by woodcutters and charcoal makers, who expanded their operations in lands communal, public and private, whether ceded to their use or not. While subsistence agriculturalists found such activities beneficial—profits from the sale of charcoal might finance the cost of renting additional lands for milpa or the purchase of livestock or seed for the next year's crop—hacendados and government officials perceived them as a serious threat. Large-scale woodcutting undermined henequen fiber production and hence state revenues, both by threatening a fuel source vital to processing fiber and by decreasing workers' dependence on hacienda labor for cash. Moreover, commercial woodcutting seemed to represent a threat to the emergence of Alvarado's much-desired class of small-owning farmers. Government warnings were issued to pueblo residents who cut down trees with "aims distinct from those of agriculture," and officials denounced woodcutters for committing actions "prejudicial to el pueblo."[31]

Hunucmá's woodlands, more than those of any other part of Yucatán, became scenes of struggle not only over land, but also over the meaning of the Revolution. Near Umán, for instance, a group of men occupied woodlands of Santa Cruz, forcibly ejecting several of its workers. After the hacendado Atilano González and his ally, Umán's mayor Bartolomé García, denounced the men as "rebels" who "maliciously distorted the agrarian law of January 6," Alvarado authorized their removal. The men, however, refused to move, responding that "the Revolution protected them" and that if any hacienda workers returned they would "chase them off with bullets."[32] Even when Alvarado castigated the men for "retarding the development of the ideals of the Constitutionalist Revolution" they refused to leave. González continued to rage against "Indians" who were "wandering around armed with shotguns, threatening to kill anyone that approaches [their] lands" and enforcing a "horrible tyranny" by blocking his access to fuel wood. "If, *señor gobernador*," he wrote, "you have won universal acclaim for ending tyranny from above, then you are obligated to put an end as well to tyranny from below."[33] Similar conflicts arose as residents of Tetiz, Kinchil, and Hunucmá, also in defiance of direct orders from Governor Alvarado, occupied and cut wood on lands of Haciendas Tumpech and Chel.[34]

Agrarian officials eventually worked out compromises in those conflicts. In the town of Hunucmá, though, their efforts foundered. The engineer José Polanco found that when he inquired into the boundaries of Hunucmá's ejidos, residents insistently directed him to "some old landmarks, in spite of the fact that they were located completely outside the area provided in the Agrarian law." "Insatiable in their petitions," he complained, "they ask for more and more. Now they claim that the borders of Hunucmá extend a distance of two leagues, or double what corresponds to them by law, invading neighboring properties to the detriment of their owners." Worst of all, they were converting those lands into what he described as a "wasteland" by cutting wood for sale to the railway companies and to fuel merchants in Mérida. Such behavior, Polanco declared, was "contrary to the ideal which is pursued by the Revolution, which is to create small independent farmers, not to authorize the despoliation of landowners to nobody's benefit." The engineer—himself denounced for accepting work on the side from several hacendados—soon resigned in frustration, recommending punitive measures to protect landowners and put an end to the "anarchical proceedings" in Hunucmá.[35]

By September 1915, government officials came to see the conflicts in the Hunucmá district as the advance front of a crisis that might threaten henequen production and social order throughout the state. In response, Ramón

García Núñez, the director of the state's Agrarian Commission, decided to intervene. He began by reversing his subordinates' findings on the questionable legality of many land titles and criticized Hunucmá's inhabitants for believing "they should be given all the lands which once were inside the ejidos, in spite of their legal titles." Even more erroneous was their claim over distant national lands, which he considered to be the cause of the "frequent attacks against private and national property" in the district. García's haughty dismissal of Hunucmá's communalists, however, in no way helped him to resolve the conflicts. His every attempt at mediation between communalists and landowners failed, eventually leading him to recognize that events had escaped his control. Declaring that "we must legalize the way people are laboring in Hunucmá," García ceded ten thousand hectares of public lands to them "as definitive property, to possess in common."[36]

The concession, effectively fulfilling the request made by the petitioners a few months before, was a humiliating personal defeat for the director. In its wake he denounced Hunucmá's residents to Alvarado, accusing them of sullying the "prestige of the Constitutionalist Revolution." "Perverse people," he fumed, had taken advantage of the "wounds of our unhappy proletarian classes" in order to "sow anarchical sentiments" in Hunucmá. García proposed a twofold strategy in response. First, government propaganda agents should work intensely in order to "make el pueblo understand" that "the Revolution is democratic, socialistic and just, both restoring despoiled property and respecting acquired rights, guaranteeing the safety of both rich and poor and preventing the attacks which one or the other might commit." At the same time, he argued, punitive measures should be undertaken to prevent the growth of the "morbid germs" that infected Hunucmá.[37]

García Núñez's advocacy of propaganda accorded well with measures already taken by Governor Alvarado, measures that aimed at realizing a union of interest between government and pueblo, based upon the tutelage of the government over the pueblo. In one circular, the general urged military commanders to "assimilate themselves into el pueblo in order to better understand its misfortunes and to remedy them." Above all, they were to "convince el pueblo of the idea that they are now governed by [leaders who] desire the social betterment of this country, and that the men of the Revolution are merely men of el pueblo, like them." In another, Alvarado instructed public officials to "educate el pueblo" and to extirpate its "fanaticism" and vices as a means to "liberate the children of the Maya from their brutish state."[38] Alvarado created an Office of Information and Propaganda, charging it with sending Maya-speaking propaganda agents throughout the countryside to act as "heralds of progress" and to teach the "great mass of el pueblo to know its rights and how to deduce them without vacillation, without fear, [and] without intermediaries."[39] In extensive instructions for the propaganda agents, Alvarado directed them to be "living examples" of the "teachings" they were to "impart to el pueblo" and to work at "redeeming the Indian" by countering the effects of "slavery and the whips of the old masters." Above all, the agents were to teach indigenous Yucatecans that they were "part of the same great National family; that we are all Mexicans." Only thus, he hoped, might indigenous workers be made to understand their duty to "make [the Patria] strong and great," presumably through the continued production of henequen.[40]

Alvarado appointed Pacheco Cruz, the translator of Avila's liberation decree, to serve as propaganda agent for the Hunucmá district. Pacheco Cruz, moreover, was a school director and resident of Hunucmá who, in Alvarado's words, "knew those lands well."[41] In reports filed during his tour of duty, Pacheco Cruz provided Alvarado with a roseate vision of the district. According to him, the workers on the fifty haciendas he visited lived in "complete tranquility," were satisfied with working conditions and wages, and voiced their "infinite gratitude" to Alvarado.[42] "More than a finca," he wrote, Hacienda Tebec was a "republic," where workers were the "absolute masters of themselves and of the finca" and demonstrated a "strict sense of order and morality." Noting the sobriety of Tebec's workers, Pacheco Cruz also opined that "in that place hygiene is not unknown." In sum, even as officials like García Núñez denounced the "infection" of Hunucmá's proletarian "wounds," Pacheco Cruz's communications depicted an orderly liberation as achieved fact on the region's haciendas.[43]

Notwithstanding Pacheco Cruz's reports, by late 1915 conflict and violence were on the increase on Hunucmá's haciendas and in its pueblos and towns. First Hacienda Chicché and then nearby Nohuayum were attacked, the latter by a group of twenty-five men led by a figure who identified himself only as El General—a nickname borne by Hunucmá's notorious former insurgent leader and first signatory of the petition to Alvarado, José Pío Chuc.[44] Badly paid hacienda workers rustled and slaughtered cattle and set fire to henequen fields; onetime indebted servants returned to the fincas they had served before liberation, torching henequen fields and coming into conflict with encargados over woodlands and milpas. As optimistic as Pacheco Cruz was about the situation in the district, he was not exempt from its violence: he became the target of an assassination attempt during one of his hacienda visits.[45]

It was in light of such events that Alvarado enforced the second part of García Núñez's recipe for Hunucmá, supplementing tepid propaganda with vigorous punishment. The district military commander Sánchez had arrested several dozen town and pueblo residents, but his efforts paled next to those of his successor, Comandante Alonso Villanueva. The new commander formed what he called the Villanueva Brigade, a group of ten rural police who patrolled roads, fincas, and forests.[46] With Alvarado's approval, Villanueva, who was criticized by one landowner in Hunucmá for acting "just like they did back in Porfirian times," bypassed the formalities of court trial by summarily sentencing suspects to six-month periods of forced labor.[47] In Umán, such measures reportedly fostered an "atmosphere of hate" as residents informed against enemies and political opponents in the hopes of triggering their detention.[48]

Villanueva reserved the harshest treatment for the infamous Tetiz, where he unleashed a campaign to "eliminate noxious elements." Shortly after assuming his charge in September, Villanueva occupied Tetiz with his troops, exhorting residents to disclose information on the identities and misdeeds of that pueblo's "evildoers." While most refused, Villanueva reported that a few "honorable and hard-working people," all of them merchants and landowners, were willing to talk. They informed against a gang of men with nicknames like Negro Oro ("Black Gold"), and Bokol ("Bug"), whom they blamed for crimes ranging from the killing of the encargado of Chicché to other murders and beheadings and innumerable episodes of cattle rustling, wood poaching, robbery, and assault. Villanueva jailed one man on rumors that he had beheaded a man and forced his victim's widow to marry him, and another merely on a report that he "wasted money and made frequent trips to Mérida."[49] Later, Villanueva's troops headed off to Kinchil, where they arrested sixteen men as suspected cattle rustlers and then beat and starved robbery suspects, threatening them with execution until they finally confessed. Of Villanueva's repressive measures, the most dramatic were public executions. In Hunucmá and Umán suspected murderers were sentenced and executed without the benefit of a court trial in public spectacles Villanueva described as a "means of social moralization." During such events, he reported, "el pueblo" felt "tranquility" as it contemplated the prospect of an end to the "robberies and crimes that have gone unpunished in the region for some time."[50] A writer for La voz concurred, calling one execution in Hunucmá a severe, but necessary warning to bandits and a salubrious example of "the Revolution's inexorable justice."[51]

Facing a new crackdown under the auspices of the Revolution, residents of the region tried to defend themselves by appealing to their own revolutionary credentials. Wives of the men arrested in Tetiz petitioned Alvarado for their release. They claimed their husbands, onetime pinistas, had been falsely accused because of their struggles for "electoral and social freedoms,"[52] and demanded justice "in the name of the Revolution."[53] The detainees also protested, claiming they had been targeted because they had fought under the "revolutionary banner" of Lino Muñoz and Canul Reyes. They urged Alvarado to verify their claim by consulting with "people of el pueblo" rather than with the "intellectual bosses" who had incriminated them.[54] Even a criminal court judge from Mérida ordered the convictions from Tetiz thrown out, as they were based on rumor rather than evidence; the office of the state attorney general concurred, recommending that the charges against the men from Kinchil be dropped, and opining that "someone, in his desire to appear a capable discoverer of criminals, might have sacrificed, for the sake of vanity . . . the dignity that he should have maintained in the dispassionate investigation of the truth."[55] Governor Alvarado, however, dismissed both the petitions and the judge's ruling, sentencing the men from Tetiz and Kinchil to six-month sentences of hard labor in a state penal colony.[56]

Just a few months after the historic encounter between government and pueblo in Hunucmá, many signatories of the Hunucmá petition, including Pío Chuc and his closest allies, found themselves in jail or at hard labor. In the name of the Revolution, the government had dismissed their petition and discounted communalist claims of deep historical precedent as anarchical and erroneous. After staking their dramatic claim as representatives of el pueblo, Hunucmá's communalists found themselves pushed to the margins by a regime that defined el pueblo as an object of control and governance rather than as an insurgent political subject. Just a few months earlier, history had seemed to offer itself as a medium of statecraft, suggesting the possibility of a revolutionary transformation of the relationship between government and pueblo. Like the communalists themselves, however, that history had been pushed to the margins.

DESTROYING TO REBUILD

By late 1915, Alvarado had issued several laws relating to land tenure, labor, education, and taxation that were meant to fulfill his promises of decisive social and institutional reform. The laws, he announced, were a means of realizing the "well-being of el pueblo" by making it "economically free." The centerpiece of the new legislation was Alvarado's agrarian law. In a long preface to the law, Alvarado blamed speculators and landlords for land theft and for "indirectly enslaving" indigenous populations. Only through the breakup of the large estates, Alvarado argued, could the "future [and] happiness of el pueblo" be secured. Rather than reconstituting communal holdings, Alvarado declared that land reform would foster the formation of small properties, thus providing incentives for "the Indian[s] . . . to increase [their] production and form independent homes." Such a smallholding peasantry would "strengthen our pueblo, rescuing it from the clutches of the proletariat, which weakens every pueblo that does not have strong and deep roots in the land."[57]

According to the director of the Information and Propaganda Office, the promulgation of the agrarian law on 7 December 1915 was welcomed as the "crystallization of the ideals of el pueblo,"[58] and as an occasion that in his view seemed to realize a mystical union of gobierno and pueblo. "El pueblo, en masse," he noted, filled the streets of Mérida, which became a "great clamorous sea, a great insane asylum in which everyone suffered a happy delirium. Everywhere there were acclaim, shouts, blessings." Throughout the countryside, according to Avila, an "infinite cry of joy sprang from the popular soul," as "el pueblo" saluted the "immortal" revolutionaries.[59] The articles of the law, he recalled, were read publicly to thunderous applause for the revolutionary leaders, who "embodied Constitutionalist ideals, in the benefit of el pueblo." When the law was published in La voz the next day, readers tore out that page, to "keep, like a relic."[60]

The fanfare surrounding the new law, however, did not help the decree win recognition at the federal level. Carranza prohibited its enforcement, for treading on federal prerogatives, and Alvarado's pleas that the measure was necessary to cement the allegiance of rural indigenous populations by "binding them to the nation, and to the revolutionary undertaking" fell on deaf ears.[61] Yucatecan hacendados were quick to herald the defeat of agrarian reform, based on federal opposition and on the difficulties in Hunucmá; one hacendado, who would be fined heavily for his words, declared that Alvarado was a "perfect lunatic" and that land reform was a "failure, as the events in Hunucmá demonstrate."[62] Despite such setbacks, Yucatán's agrarian officials enforced other portions of the law relating to the provisional distribution of uncultivated lands. Such arrangements, which typically provided small areas of uncultivated land to each petitioner for clearing and cultivation over a one- or two-year period, also allowed the state to expand its involvement in regulating land tenure.[63] In Hunucmá, military commanders, local government officials, and newly installed agrarian committees composed of local residents routinely arranged the temporary cession of privately owned woodlands to pueblo residents, using such grants as a way to defuse brewing conflicts over woodlands.[64]

Even as they used provisional distribution to allay agrarian conflicts and aggressively searched out and imprisoned suspected cattle rustlers and bandits, government officials intensified their revolutionary propaganda in Hunucmá. One propaganda agent reported that when he spoke to hacienda workers about "all of the good things that the Constitutionalist Revolution . . . has done to fulfill the aspirations of the working class," they listened "religiously" to the his words, which "had the same effect on their hearts, as a clear stream of water, on a plant." According to him, they responded with a "thunderous and spontaneous hurrah for the Revolution, which had given them things of which they had never dreamed."[65] Schools for indigenous children were opened in towns and pueblos and on haciendas, often in buildings confiscated from churches and convents; they were inaugurated, as per tradition, on national holidays, with feasting and vaquerías. Government officials traveled the pueblos and towns of the district, giving a range of speeches on a variety of topics, including one on the "advantages that gardening would bring to El Pueblo," at the end of which audience members reportedly "left the place, in the most orderly fashion, all quite happy and enthusiastic, and taking with them pamphlets and samples of seed."[66]

Such activities were consistent with Alvarado's redoubled efforts to publicize his utopian vision of Yucatán's future. In a "Letter to El Pueblo," published on the occasion of Cinco de Mayo in 1916, Alvarado argued that the best way to honor the fallen heroes of Mexico's wars of independence was to pursue policies that might secure the "growth of the Patria," and the uplift of "el pueblo." The conversion of hacienda machinery to petroleum fuel, he went on to say, would "free" fifteen thousand "miserable" woodcutters, like those who had troubled the agrarian reform in Hunucmá and elsewhere, to become a "great contingent of laborers for agriculture and industry in the State." In rural schools, the government would convert backward indigenous paupers into "true agriculturalists . . . [by] introducing the habit of rational agriculture into popular customs." Indigenous children would be taught the duties of citizens, thus "awakening love of Patria in el pueblo." For those who could not be redeemed, Alvarado envisioned the creation of an agricultural Penal Colony that might purge vagrants and criminals who were a "venomous pestilence infecting the national organism."[67]

This was the backdrop for Alvarado's visit to Umán in June 1916. Scarcely a year after his visit to Hunucmá, Alvarado arrived with his entourage at the place where the very first definitive restitution of ejidal lands under Carranza's law was carried out: the first not only in the Hunucmá district or in Yucatán but reportedly in all of Mexico. According to an account in La voz, as Alvarado arrived in the town square, he encountered "el pueblo," which "waited to hear from his lips something that had burned in its heart as a hope, and which it had feared would never be realized." After Alvarado allocated the first plots of land, the propagandist Rafael Gamboa harangued the audience in Maya, charging it to "demonstrate to the world that the land has not been given to lowly whores but to men who know how to defend their rights to the death." Gamboa urged them to "crush the head of the viper called Reaction" by dedicating themselves to their agricultural labors, by obeying the Agrarian Commission, and by resisting the "seductions" of those who tried to coax them into committing crimes, in order to later denounce them and secure their hanging as bandits. "Ask for lands, cultivate and work them," he advised, "and you will be with the Government, which wants you to be honorable working men."[68]

Commenting on the occasion, a reporter noted that in Umán, "the sweetest fruit of Constitutionalism, now ripened, was plucked by el pueblo." This was so, he continued, even though unlike other areas of Mexico, "el pueblo de Yucatán" had never had to "offer its blood" for the Revolution, "felt the hunger and misery of war," or "seen executed men hanging from telephone poles." "Thus," he emphasized, "el pueblo does not yet realize the full significance of what General Alvarado did in Umán." Scarcely a year after Alvarado's initial visit to Hunucmá the history that had formed the heart of Pío Chuc's petition—a history of insurgent struggle, sacrifice, deprivation, and indeed of war—had been effaced. The pueblo Alvarado and Gamboa evoked in their speeches in Umán was an entity that owed its liberation, its land, its allegiance, and its future to Alvarado and his government.[69]

This vision of el pueblo was not simply imposed from above and without, but also embraced from below and from within, as local factions sought to consolidate their power by making allegiances with Alvarado's regime. In Umán rival factions led by Bartolomé García and Pedro A. Canul headed contending agrarian committees, alternating in power and contending for the favors of Alvarado's government. In the town of Hunucmá, even as some former insurgents slaved away in labor corvées, others rose to power in municipal government. Hunucmá's town council was a coalition of former pinistas and morenistas, including both onetime communalist insurgents and gentry like Mayor Epitacio Bojórquez, an hacendado who had been involved in town government since the 1880s.

The town council's attempt to consolidate its position as a mediator between government and pueblo was evident in the Boletín municipal, published in Hunucmá. While largely dedicated to mundane issues of municipal governance, the bulletin was a vehicle for local power brokers to identify themselves publicly with government plans to control, construct, and transform el pueblo. In its pages, the district military commander was commended for his "correct and fair proceedings" and for his work on behalf of Hunucmá's "progress and prosperity." Local hacendados who had not paid an education tax were scolded for "opposing the efforts of the Revolution's Government to educate and instruct el pueblo." Above all, readers were instructed in the importance of the "free municipality" as a keystone of Alvarado's struggle to "liberate el pueblo from all of its old yokes." Only through reformed municipal governance, the authors of the Boletín declared, might the abuses and corruption of the past disappear forever and the interests of pueblo, state, and nation prosper. "El pueblo must understand," they declared, "the importance of the free municipality. One only arrives at Liberty by degrees, and it is only by reaching the most local entities, that Liberty will reach all of Mexico."⁷⁰

A similar account of liberation by degrees was made by Villanueva's successor as military commander, Isaac Centeno. According to Centeno, as one of the areas where henequen agriculture first expanded, Hunucmá had suffered the "uncontrolled ambitions of capitalists" to acquire lands for their fincas. Their "reprehensible" efforts left indigenous residents in "rags, misery, and anguish," forcing them to join the ranks of "pariahs, Helots, and illiterates" on the haciendas. Therein, in Centeno's view, lay the origins of the "natural antagonism" of Hunucmá's "proletarian class" and of the district's "extremely unfortunate reputation for criminality." Therein as well lay the reason why its "great, ignorant majority"—especially, he noted, residents of Tetiz—committed "acts of vandalism, sometimes toppling walls, sometimes destroying private property, sometimes killing cattle . . . assaulting, and killing, and taking justice into their own hands." All of that had changed with Alvarado's arrival in the state. In Hunucmá, the government had taken measures aimed at "destroying bad elements" and "fostering a climate that was favorable to the ideals of the Revolution" by substituting local municipal authorities with "people who were committed to the cause." The Revolution had uprooted corrupted customs, spread morality, truth and justice, reclaimed long subverted rights, and, most importantly, "brought those [who were] guilty, whether rich or poor, to justice." Since "vandalism" and "banditry" had continued thereafter, only one remedy remained: punishment. In Centeno's view, mass arrests, imprisonment, and especially public executions finally halted the misdeeds of Hunucmá's criminal proletarians.[71]

Thus, as Centeno explained, Hunucmá was a perfect example of how the Constitutionalist Revolution, in its "great and patriotic work of social transformation . . . in certain cases, must destroy, in order to build upon solid foundations." With law and order assured, the Revolution's constructive program was able to proceed, despite the "refractory character" of pueblo residents. Liberty dawned on the haciendas, as the government ensured that workers were paid fairly and that labor law was enforced. Provisional lands were made available to local farmers. Health officials conducted an ambitious vaccination program. Religious icons were removed from churches, which were then used to house schools where teachers worked at "defanaticizing el pueblo" by eradicating the "illiteracy and [religious] fanaticism" that were "so strong among the indigenous class."[72]

History, it would seem, had borne out Alvarado's vision, transforming Hunucmá from a place of slavery and savagery into one of liberty, order, and civilization. So much was suggested by a report Alvarado sent to Carranza the next month, summing up the achievements of his government in its first twenty months. It consisted mainly of a series of triumphant claims: Alvarado's revolutionary government had resolved all strikes justly; it had rescued rural workers from slavery and transformed them into citizens; it had distributed lands to the needy, brought justice to workers and the poor, and established rural schools through the state. Alvarado made such claims in general terms, but in only one case did he cite a region of Yucatán as exemplary of the successes of his Revolution: Hunucmá. Even though at the time he took power "every day the most lamentable episodes occurred" there, the "active work of Constitutionalist authorities, in providing justice, protection, and education [had] finally brought peace and order." "I have given," the general triumphantly declared, "lands, security, and support to all." On concluding his report, Alvarado claimed that his presentation of the results in Hunucmá and elsewhere in Yucatán was a "clear and truthful demonstration of the work of Constitutionalism" and of the fulfillment of Carranza's philosophical and revolutionary principles.[73]

Just eighteen months before, Alvarado had stood in Hunucmá beneath a portrait of Feliciano Canul Reyes, taking part in a spectacle whose participants, from gentry to communalists to government officials, seemed to form a revolutionary alliance in the name of pueblo and patria. Each made its own vision of history a central part of the spectacle, and each evoked gobierno and pueblo and the relation between the two in different ways. The gentry offered their services as intermediaries between government and pueblo, joining a new rhetoric of revolution to an older one of tradition and modernity. Indigenous communalists used an account of el pueblo's enslavement and of its heroic struggles for liberation as a petition for their redemption through the restoration of communal lands. Government officials had proposed to liberate el pueblo, but to do so in a way that—despite a few gestures to Hunucmá's martyrs—ultimately recognized no history and no power but their own.

Over the course of the ensuing months the pact contracted in Hunucmá in May 1915 fell apart, and each party to it found they could not write the history of el pueblo exactly as they pleased. Communalists like Pío Chuc found their petitions and history disregarded, as they suffered a new wave of repression; landowners were caught between the threat posed to their property and position by government social reforms and a sense that their powers could be maintained only through the favors granted by that same government. For government officials, Hunucmá initially seemed to symbolize the failings of the government and the fragility of its policies. By late 1916, however, that had changed. A combination of punishment and propaganda and a tenuous alliance between the state government and a few members of the local gentry and of the indigenous working population seemed to remake Hunucmá as a place where pueblo and gobierno might at last unite in common purpose. El pueblo, it must have seemed, had been destroyed to be rebuilt, with a history and a destiny now inextricably linked to Alvarado's own.

In 1953, almost four decades after working as a propaganda agent, Santiago Pacheco Cruz published memoirs that recounted his services to Alvarado's government. The compendious tome, composed largely of missives and reports Pacheco Cruz wrote during his work in various rural districts, includes a chapter dedicated to his time in Hunucmá. The old man's recollections of his work in the region differed starkly in tone from the nostalgic tone of the rest of his memoirs and from that of his cheery official reports to Alvarado in 1915. From the moment he arrived in Hunucmá to begin his work as a propaganda agent, he wrote, he felt disillusionment and was wracked by "concerns and premonitions." Hearing of his mission, the residents of the town reacted with "hostility and repulsion," seeming not to appreciate the "principles and achievements of the Revolution." Moreover, they showed excessive curiosity about his movements, leading him to fear for his life. "I knew those people well," he recalled, "and I knew that among them were killers who laughed at the sight of human blood." Above all, he suspected that Pío Chuc—"one of the notable murderers of that place"—was conspiring against him.[74]

One day, as he traveled on horseback to visit a nearby hacienda, Pacheco Cruz was surprised to see a man who was carrying a shotgun emerge suddenly from the woods by the side of the road. "On seeing him," he wrote, "I felt a terrible dread, which made my blood run cold. I didn't know whether to attribute it to the man, who might have been a sign of some great danger, or else to all of the questions that people had asked me before I left, which echoed in my brain. I was shocked, and lost the power of speech for a few minutes." Nothing came of the encounter at that moment, but later, disabled by fear and by the "terrible incertitude" that tormented him, the agent decided to ride a rail car on his return trip, sending a boy from the finca to ride his horse back to town. Soon, the agent's premonitions were confirmed, when ambushers fired on the boy and the horse from the side of the road.

After the agent informed Alvarado of the attack and of his suspicions of Pío Chuc's involvement, the general issued orders to execute the communalist leader and his principal allies. Pacheco Cruz did not carry out the order, but instead, with the assistance of a contingent of soldiers sent by Alvarado, he arrested Pío Chuc and his allies, sending them off to the state penitentiary. Subsequently, that military entourage seems to have enabled him to recover composure. Accompanied by the troops, he recalled, he continued his visits "tranquilly"—visiting even Tetiz and Kinchil, which he considered to be the most dangerous pueblos of the region. Pacheco Cruz's power of speech returned as did his ability to write sanguine descriptions of the situation in Hunucmá. He made no mention of his fears, the assassination attempt, or the military escort in those official reports.

Decades after his days as a propagandist, however, Pacheco Cruz reflected, in writing, on the experiences he had excluded from his official reports. Yet these memoirs were no less selective than his missives of decades before. Even though he had lived in Hunucmá for years preceding Alvarado's arrival in the peninsula, in his memoirs Pacheco Cruz made no mention either of Hunucmá's liberation war or of the struggles and demise of Canul Reyes.

He described neither Alvarado's warm reception in Hunucmá in May 1915, nor Pío Chuc's role in that celebration and in the presentation of a petition that day in the name of el pueblo. Neither the detailed account of the past offered by Pío Chuc and the other petitioners nor the hopes and possibilities represented in their claims on the Revolution found any place or echo in the memoirs of the onetime propaganda agent.

The petitioners' rendering of history was not the only casualty of the violence. Another was the official story—of Hunucmá redeemed—scripted and publicized by General Alvarado and other government officials. Whereas Pacheco Cruz's memoirs of his work in other parts of Yucatán were laden with triumphal accounts of Alvarado's Revolution and its achievements, the chapter on Hunucmá stands in terrifying counterpoint as a tale that forced even the most voluble propagandist to fall silent. If both ways of representing Hunucmá's history had become inconceivable for Pacheco Cruz by 1953, that was at least in part the product of events that took place years after he concluded his work in Hunucmá. For Pacheco Cruz , those events once again would make tales of senseless violence and of killers who laughed at the sight of human blood the only conceivable way of remembering Hunucmá.

CHAPTER FIVE

THE GENERAL AND THE BEAST

Murder, Martyrdom, and the Bones of el Pueblo

FROM A DISTANCE the men saw vultures wheeling, and so they walked toward them through the brush. Soon they smelled the unmistakable, overwhelming odor of rotting flesh. When the group of Hunucmá residents escorted by soldiers reached an old dry well called Cacab Dzul, startled vultures took flight, revealing human remains. The birds had plucked the eyes out of the faces and stripped off their musculature. Chunks of flesh littered the area. There were four skeletons near the well and some scraps of clothing. Those, rather than the bits of flesh and bone, were what they recognized; one man saw his father-in-law's pants and another his little brother's handkerchief.[1]

Then they approached the well. Several meters down they saw more bodies, jumbled one on top of the other. One man, desperate to find his father, descended into the pit. Struggling to maintain his footing atop the slippery heap, he found what he sought, but as he tried to lift the cadaver pieces of it separated, falling back onto the pile. After collecting them, along with parts of what seemed to be a boy, he collapsed, gagging. Another took over, removing the corpse of his little brother and a few other bodies. When he too succumbed, the captain of Hunucmá's garrison ordered others to continue, but they refused. The townspeople examined the bodies they had recovered, matching names to some remains. Then they threw the rest back into the pit and covered them with earth and stones. One man fashioned a cross out of two sticks and planted it in the pile, offering an impromptu prayer. Finally, those who had retrieved the remains of their sons, fathers, and friends hoisted them for the walk back to town. They shouldered their burden alone, for others in the group refused. It was on account of the stench, they said. When they arrived in Hunucmá, the captain learned of another reason for their reluctance. Among those who had walked to the well were six men rumored to have taken part in the slaughter at Cacab Dzul.

Divided against itself and shrouded by suspicion and fear, the search party as much as the macabre well was a product of partisan political violence that had turned working residents of Hunucmá against each other. As the police and investigators interviewed those who returned from the well, they joined their efforts to those of journalists, government officials, and pueblo residents. All of them alternately disinterred and reinterred the fragmented remains found at Cacab Dzul, interrogating them as documents, of a kind, and seeking to recover—or to silence—their message. In the process, some of the victims of the violence were recognized as martys. Others were left unclaimed and unrecognized and went unredeemed. To read the significance of the human remains at Cacab Dzul is to explore how political violence played a role in shaping el pueblo as a collective corporeal subject, through both the remembrance and the dismemberment of those who killed and died in its name.[2]

BOUNDS OF EL PUEBLO

On 27 January 1917 Bernardino Mena Brito disembarked in the port of Progreso to inaugurate his gubernatorial campaign. As the candidate of the Yucatecan Liberal Party, he faced a formidable Socialist Party opponent: General Salvador Alvarado. Clashes erupted immediately on Mena's arrival. When Mena attempted, he later recalled, to "speak to el pueblo" in Progreso, he was drowned out by jeering Alvaradistas. Alvarado's supporters, however, later complained that Mena had insulted them, calling them "contemptible plebes." The confrontations escalated when Mena arrived in Mérida, planning to give a speech to "rouse el pueblo," and to "teach [it] what liberty really means." He was interrupted first by shouts and then by gunshots. While Mena claimed that Alvarado's "rabble" had fired the shots that killed one Socialist, state police arrested Mena, accusing him of "shooting on el pueblo."[3]

Such events were the product of the return to constitutional rule in 1917. With the era of military government drawing to a close, Alvarado launched a campaign for a second term, this time as an elected official. In June 1916 he founded the Partido Socialista Obrero, which became the Partido Socialista de Yucatán in 1917. The party sponsored the formation of "resistance leagues" (*ligas de resistencia*) throughout the countryside, coordinated by a Liga Central in Mérida. While helping to further Alvarado's electoral aspirations, under the leadership of firebrands like Felipe Carrillo Puerto and Rafael Gamboa the leagues became aggressive advocates for indigenous workers. Such activities deepened the opposition of wealthy Yucatecans to Alvarado's regime and drew the ire of President Venustiano Carranza. With Carranza's encouragement, Yucatecan hacendados organized their own political party, the Partido Liberal Yucateco. While opposing Alvarado and the Socialists, Liberals like Mena presented themselves as reformists, calling for the "socialization of resources and means of production," and the elevation of the masses through education and "racial improvement."[4]

Leaders of both parties addressed themselves to el pueblo, both as a framework for governance and as a political constituency. Alvarado made a series of well-publicized tours of Yucatán, determined to "learn the needs of el pueblo, in order to address them."[5] He and his panegyrists published futuristic and messianic texts presenting Alvarado as a redeemer whose words and laws were founded, according to one admirer, in "el pueblo's soul."[6] Government officials and Socialist activists frequently evoked el pueblo as an object of reform—an entity to be instructed and uplifted through schooling and through measures against alcohol, bullfights, religious fiestas, and other forms of "social gangrene" that "corrupted the good name and health of el pueblo."[7] For their part, Liberals also addressed their party platform to El Pueblo, declaring they would "teach el pueblo the obligations [of citizens,] and make it fulfill them strictly"—in part, by rolling back government-run rural school programs and restoring the "broadest liberties" to hacendados.[8]

As Socialists and Liberals clashed, activists of both parties represented themselves as heroes of el pueblo, and their opponents as its enemies. One Yucatecan Socialist manifesto, published under the heading "The Reactionaries Murder el Pueblo," accused Liberals of seeking to "bring back the epochs of terror in which moneyed tyrants seized power to extort el pueblo, first stealing its sweat, and then its honor, by violating its daughters and sisters." Its authors called on Alvarado to "decapitate his detractors, and give us their heads to burn"; thus the "liberators of el pueblo" would assure the Revolution's triumph. Another manifesto warned Liberals to "fear the rage of el pueblo" and threatened to transform Yucatán into a "new Sahara covered with blood and ruins" if the Liberals took power.[9] Liberals, for their part, accused Alvarado of "oppressing el pueblo" through authoritarianism and of violating "el pueblo's rights," most notably, what they referred to as the sacred right of property. They leveled a torrent of complaints in the name of "the true pueblo," condemning Socialists as "enemies and corrupters of el pueblo" who awakened the "dormant hates of the indigenous race" with "subversive and antipatriotic harangues."[10]

Eventually both Alvarado and Mena Brito were disqualified from participating in the gubernatorial elections for, respectively, failing to meet residency requirements and a criminal indictment on charges of rebellion. Their parties, however, found other candidates. Given Alvarado's control over the state government and the strength of the Socialists on the ground, the Socialist Carlos Castro Morales easily won election as governor. The Socialists also swept most elections for state and local positions, repeating their victory the next year in state congressional elections. Afterward, Castro Morales declared that the party's redemptive reforms and its electoral victories had demonstrated that "we have served . . . the noble cause of EL PUEBLO."[11] Liberal leaders like Mena Brito, on the other hand, viewed the elections as a fraud perpetrated by what he termed Yucatán's "illiterates" against the "best of Yucatecan culture and society." One Liberal critic decried Socialist evocations of el pueblo as a "pretext for . . . crimes that dishonor society," an "idol, before which every greedy orator kneels," and a means to "excite the multitudes" and the "wild plebeians," moving them to "invade streets and plazas like an overflowing torrent." In contrast, the "true pueblo," in his view, consisted of people who were "peaceful and tranquil, industrious and useful," whether artisans, doctors, jurists, or agricultural workers. This "heterogeneous mass," constituted society's "potent arm," and its "soul and life."[12]

With Castro Morales as governor, Felipe Carrillo Puerto as president of the Liga Central, and Alvarado commanding the federal military in Yucatán, the Socialists seemed well positioned to push forward with their social and political agenda. Their ability to do so, however, was hampered by external developments. The end of the First World War brought a precipitous decline in henequen prices, undermining the negotiating power of Alvarado's Regulatory Commission. Carranza took the opportunity to dissolve the commission and transfer Alvarado out of the state. His replacement, General Luis Hernández, came with orders to suppress the leagues. Troops confiscated the weapons of league members and ejected pueblo residents from woodlands they had been assigned for provisional use. Hacendados seized contested lands and fired workers who had joined the leagues. In response, Carrillo Puerto accused soldiers and hacendados of joining forces to "enslave Indians" on their fincas; Alvarado, from afar, lamented that the "work of el Pueblo" was being "destroyed."[13] By late 1919 the situation worsened. Determined to engineer the electoral defeat of the Socialists, Carranza replaced Hernández with an infamously brutal general Isaías Zamarripa. Troops arrested and beat Socialists, attacked league offices, and ejected pueblo residents from ejido lands, threatening to kill those who returned. Soldiers destroyed ballot boxes and altered electoral tallies. Governor Castro Morales was allowed to remain in power on condition that he withdraw support for the resistance leagues and back Ignacio Bonillas, Carranza's handpicked candidate for the presidency; Carrillo Puerto fled the state, declaring from exile his support for Bonilla's opponent, Alvaro Obregón.[14]

By April 1920 the winds of politics had shifted yet again, as Obregón launched a military rebellion against Carranza. By May, Carranza had been executed and Obregonist troops arrived in Yucatán. Carrillo Puerto and other Socialists returned to the state to take power, liberated of federal opposition and poised, it seemed, to defeat the Liberals once and for all. It was in this time of political upheaval that the search party in Hunucmá made its way to its macabre destination. It was searching for more than thirty town residents who had disappeared over the previous week, reportedly kidnapped by followers of the fearsome José Pío Chuc. Stories about the find at Cacab Dzul quickly spread, crowding the newspaper headlines. For the Liberals, the bodies were compelling evidence of the worst crime ever committed by Yucatán's Socialists; for the Socialists, they threatened to undermine the legitimacy of the renascent Socialist regime. For all, questions remained to be asked and answered: How might the victims of the violence at Cacab

Dzul be reclaimed, whether as heroes of el pueblo or its martyrs? Or had the victims, along with their killers, been cast outside el pueblo's bounds?

THE ROAD TO CACAB DZUL

In June 1917, a government inspector reported to Governor Alvarado on the situation in Hunucmá. He wrote that fair wages were being paid and working conditions were acceptable on the district's haciendas, crediting those changes to the Constitutionalist Revolution's "unwavering protection" of workers. "Now," he declared, "[Hunucmá's] workers are not like those of former times. Now, they understand their own actions, and even if the reactionary elements wanted to, they will never return to a state of abandonment and slavery." To further the region's progress, he proposed to establish libraries in the pueblos, so that residents might read books that would "transform them from ignorant citizens into enlightened citizens."[15]

By mid-1917, such a vision of Hunucmá was naive. Agrarian tensions simmered, and hacienda workers were anything but satisfied with working conditions.[16] In late 1916, for instance, workers at Oxcum reacted to decreasing wages and increasing maize prices by organizing work stoppages and by beating and imprisoning the hacienda's administrator. Alvarado ordered the military commander Guillermo Mangas to defend the "interests of the finca, and of the State"[17] by correcting workers' "false interpretations" and explaining that the "intent of this Government, in liberating the rural laborer, was neither to allow him to impose his whims, nor to obstruct the labor necessary for the haciendas to survive."[18] Mangas scolded the workers for their "ingratitude," but they continued to rebel, even after he sent policemen with orders to "stamp out their insolence." Thereafter, Mangas busied himself expelling those he called "troublemakers" from fincas throughout the district and lecturing workers on the "benefits of the Constitutionalist Revolution, which . . . imparts strict justice to proletarian people by ensuring that they are paid fairly."[19] At the same time, Mangas clashed with Hunucmá's town council, which he denounced for apathy and incompetence, and with the town's mayor, Epitacio Bojórquez, whom he accused of antagonizing the "cultivated part" of Hunucmá. He clashed with Umán's authorities as well, breaking up one meeting by riding into Umán's town hall on horseback with pistol drawn. As much as the imperious Mangas tried to impose his will, however, the changing politics of the times would frustrate him. Here it was not Mangas, but Bojórquez, who won out, by joining the Socialist Party and cobbling together a ruling coalition composed of small landowners and merchants, pueblo residents, and some of the men who once had fought alongside Canul Reyes, like Andrés Lizama, now head of Hunucmá's resistance league.[20]

State officials antagonized the residents of Umán as well by ordering a government crackdown on the regional trade in bootleg liquor, a mainstay of strongmen like Bartolomé García Correa. When undercover agents arrested four local traffickers, a wealthy town resident declared, "These men you are taking are of my pueblo, of my very own pueblo." After the agents refused a bribe for their release, he warned, "You are only three in number, but we are many."[21] Moreover, in Umán—where, according to one observer, long-standing political rancor dating from the early years of the Revolution had "left an indelible mark"—factional conflict reached the point of crisis.[22] One side was led by García Correa, who after years of clashing with woodcutters and so-called libertarians as Umán's mayor subsequently underwent a political metamorphosis, founding a workers' union and becoming president of the town's Socialist league. The other was led by Pedro A. Canul and former members of Umán's pinista Libertarian Circle. Canul, who led his own union, rose to power following his election as mayor. While both groups supported Alvarado's candidacy, their enmity came to the fore in early 1917 when García Correa's group accused Canul and his faction of being "incapable of serving el pueblo."[23] Sent to mediate the dispute, a state government official blamed both groups for Umán's "shameful state of backwardness." Then he deposed Canul, appealing to the "patriotic sentiments of this pueblo" and to the leaders of both factions, as "cultured sons of Mexico," to forgo political office for the good of el pueblo.[24]

In the eastern towns of Hunucmá and Umán, the Socialist Party consolidated its power despite internal rivalries and tense relations between local and state government officials. The Socialist presence was more tentative in the western pueblos of Tetiz and Kinchil. There, the Liberal Party established chapters, enlisting municipal officials and even former pinista insurgents like Eleno Canché and Camilo Tinal in its ranks. Throughout the district, partisans of both parties contended as bitterly as state Party leaders. In Hunucmá and Umán, league organizers denounced the Liberals as "slavers" and reportedly urged their followers, in the event of Liberal electoral victory, to "sharpen their machetes," kill as many Liberals as possible, and then escape to the woods to mobilize an insurgency.[25] In Hunucmá, Liberals complained that Socialist patrols—ostensibly formed to "care for and conserve public order"—were used to intimidate Liberals; Socialists, they claimed, took action against those who refused to join the leagues, preventing them from harvesting their milpas and threatening and harassing them into leaving town.[26] In the western pueblos, where Liberals formed their own patrols, Socialists faced similar reprisals. Socialists in Tetiz requested assistance from state troops "so that our enemies will not continue to ridicule us." In Kinchil Socialists complained that local authorities opposed the league, thus "refusing to recognize the rights of el pueblo."[27]

From the moment of their creation the resistance leagues became deeply involved in local labor and agrarian disputes. Umán's league, under the leadership of García Correa, was the region's largest. A sizable number of workers on the large haciendas were members, along with artisans, small merchants, and some landowners. The league actively registered members, pressured employers, and occasionally—in accord with state labor law and directives of the Liga Central—organized work stoppages, including a synchronized strike on at least six large haciendas in October 1918. Working conditions, the hiring of replacement workers, and especially wages were its primary concerns.[28] A league newspaper published in Umán, called "The Voice of the Indian: Organ of Combat and Politics of the Hunucmá District," alternated between denunciations of capitalism and adulation of the Socialist Party and Carrillo Puerto. The editors shared the paternalistic indigenism of government officials and thereby evoked the greatness of ancient Mayan clans and colonial-era resistance figures but referred to those they termed "slaves"—perhaps indigenous workers who refused to join the league—as "disgusting." They urged them to forgo sex in order to "spare women the shame of being the mothers of your children" and called on them to "redeem yourselves, or kill yourselves" rather than continuing to "infect the world."[29]

Hunucmá's league also organized work stoppages and drafted petitions against managers and encargados of haciendas like Yaxché and Texán whom they denounced as "tyrants" who "believe[d] that slavery still exists, as in former times."[30] In contrast with Umán's league, Hunucmá's was distinguished by its focus on agrarian issues. That emphasis was apparent in the league's seal, which pictured a man carrying a gun and farming utensils and accompanied by a hunting dog, as if on his way to the woods. The league counted onetime communalist insurgents among its members and organizers, and its treasury depended heavily on the sale of wood and charcoal produced in communal lands. But support was not universal. Pío Chuc and his closest allies seem to have refused affiliation, at least initially, a split that became manifest in January 1917 in a conflict over a flag that Feliciano Canul Reyes had carried during the liberation war of 1914 and that Pío Chuc had inherited. A group of 116 league members led by the league president, Andrés Lizama, unsuccessfully petitioned the government for it, on the grounds that during the insurgency it had been purchased with "monies of el pueblo."[31]

Despite such conflicts, the league's communalist and insurgent origins strongly affected its character, and members retained their libertarian edge. When league leaders, following the dictates of the Liga Central, attempted to institute by-laws, the members rebelled, declaring that "by-laws are not necessary in Socialist organizations, in which liberty alone should reign."[32] Responding to the concerns of communal agriculturalists, league leaders in Hunucmá encouraged residents to occupy contested woodlands and became aggressive advocates in conflicts over communal lands that, as the head of Yucatán's Agrarian Commission conceded in a case relating to Hunucmá, "el pueblo demands as its own."[33] They pressured state officials to expedite agrarian reform, leading a commentator for La voz to observe that Hunucmá "wants to begin, at last, to enjoy the promises of the Revolution, which offered lands to the pueblos." In communications with Yucatán's governor, league leaders cited the "despoliation of communal lands" and the "iniquitous exploitation" of the "indigenous class" from the mid-nineteenth century forward as the origin of "el pueblo's discontent" and the best argument for the restoration of communal lands.[34]

The league's independent streak led to frequent conflicts with government officials. When Oxcum again erupted into rebellion over wages in July 1917, a Labor Department agent quelled the revolt, leading one worker to fume, "If politics was what was being played here, then [we can] play as well."[35] Another agent clashed with workers of San Antonio Tamay, who, when he asked why they had pastured cattle in a newly planted henequen field, reportedly replied "Because it is [ours]." The agent scolded them for "thoughtlessly destroying henequen, which is what sustains the State," and inveighed against workers who "call[ed] themselves lords of the finca."[36] The local Socialist leader Isidro Poot denounced such agents, accusing them of "working against our cause."[37] He faced increasing difficulties with government officials, however, following the Socialist Party's electoral victory. Immediately thereafter, the director of the Labor Department sent a letter to Poot in which, after acknowledging the triumph of "our cause" and Poot's valiant service to it, he ordered Poot to cease "unjust" work stoppages and ensure the "continued triumph of our cause by helping us secure the prosperity and growth of our State." "Now that we have triumphed," he concluded, workers should "get back to work."[38]

The issue of land access presented even greater frustrations, as legal challenges by hacendados and federal officials slowed agrarian reform to a standstill, and Hunucmá's woodlands again became a hotbed of conflict. The hacendado José Palomeque complained that pueblo residents "badly influenced by Socialist propagandists" considered themselves "absolute lords of the finca[s];" another hacendado blamed the Socialists' "malevolent preachings" for pueblo residents' disrespect for private property. League officials, for their part, complained that landowners continued to exploit ejidal lands illegally.[39] Government officials intervened in such disputes erratically, alternately championing pueblo residents, in the words of one agrarian official, as rightful "masters of the ejidos of el pueblo" and denouncing them, in the words of the same agent on another occasion, for cutting down woodlands "shamelessly."[40] The head of the Agrarian Commission forbade acts of "destruction" by Hunucmá residents, leading Isidro Poot, now as head of Hunucmá's town council, to protest that land recipients were not "CUT- TING" the woods, but "CULTIVATING" them in accord with the dictates of agrarian law.[41]

By fall 1918 tensions reached a breaking point. Andrés Lizama addressed a letter to the governor in the name of the "immense majority of el pueblo," demanding access to ejidal lands adjoining Hacienda Texán. While government officials prevented pueblo residents from working those lands, the owner, Palomeque, had his workers cut wood there with such rapidity that soon "there [would] not even be stones left." Lizama's appeal in defense of what he called the "rights of el pueblo" was dismissed. In a protest meeting thereafter, onetime insurgent Anastacio Canul rose to denounce government officials. "Among the main promises of the Revolution," he raged, "was land for the pueblos. Now, even as the . . . Revolution fulfills its promises . . . the poor here find themselves every day in greater difficulties." As government officials contemplated the prospect of renewed insurgency in Hunucmá, only a hastily arranged visit by Canul Reyes's old ally Lino Muñoz calmed league members.[42]

Frustrations would only intensify with the occupation of the state by federal troops under General Hernández in late 1918. Soldiers forcibly ejected residents from their milpas in contested lands like woodlands adjoining Augusto Peón's Hacienda Chac, leading Hunucmá's resistance league, now led by Juan Bautista Pech Balam, to threaten Peón that "el pueblo [would] know how to punish him" for the expulsions. After Carrillo Puerto publicly denounced events on Chac as evidence of Hernández's alliance with workers' "enemies," the general made a visit to Hunucmá, where he gave a speech denying he was beholden to the hacendados and avowing his determination to "impart justice to both rich and poor."[43] Then he headed off to a banquet hosted by a prominent local Liberal, where he rubbed elbows with Hunucmá's principal hacendados. For appearance' sake, it began with a toast offered "in the name of el pueblo of Hunucmá" and concluded with a traditional vaquería performed in Hernández's honor.[44]

In the wake of Hernández's visit, however, troops continued ejecting workers from contested woodlands, leading the Socialist García Correa of Umán, now a member of the state legislature, to appeal to the governor to expedite agrarian reform for the "noble and long-suffering pueblo" of Hunucmá. In García's view the expulsions, which coincided with declining wages and price inflation, conjured the specter of that pueblo's historic penchant for communalist insurgency: "You well know," he wrote the governor, "that if Hunucmá has always fought, it has especially been for its lands. . . . As long as they have lands to work, they are happy and live peacefully. When not, difficulties emerge at every instant, and in their desperation to reclaim the land, which is the basis of their liberty, they are ready for any sacrifice."[45] The crackdown, however, would only intensify in 1919 following the arrival of General Zamarripa and the flight of state Socialist leaders and Obregón supporters like Carrillo Puerto. Liberals attacked the office of Tetiz's resistance league, where they killed two young Socialist organizers, throwing their bodies into a pit. During municipal elections, Liberals and troops intimidated Socialist voters and seized ballot boxes, securing the victory of the Liberal candidates in Tetiz, Kinchil, Ucú, and Hunucmá. Liberals organized armed patrols in order, they claimed, to "impose order"; one such group reportedly sacked stores, burned down houses, and raped the daughters of known Socialists. Victory was sealed with the election of a Liberal as the district's representative to the state legislature, leaving the Socialists in power only in Umán.[46]

As Liberals assumed municipal office they triumphantly donned the mantle of el pueblo. The district's new congressional representative, the Maya speaker Luciano Noh Novelo, was welcomed, according to news reports, by "el pueblo en masse" as he toured the district giving speeches "in favor of the indigenous Mayas." Before a vaquería celebrating his own victory, Tetiz's mayor, Eleno Canché, "spoke passionately to el pueblo, promising to provide protection to all citizens, regardless of their political affiliation." In Kinchil, a Liberal vaquería was described by Liberals as a "show of unity," but only "since now the 'socialists' no longer exist"; on that very day, to emphasize the point, arsonists burned down the house of a leading Socialist. Carnival celebrants in Tetiz made a comedy of it all, enacting the pursuit, capture, and execution of Juan Carnaval, the symbolic patron of Carnival, by mock cavalry; for the occasion, they renamed Juan Carnaval Perico Boxtorón, perhaps a veiled reference to the regional Socialist leader García Correa, who was widely known by his nickname, Box Pato ("Black Duck").[47] Such performances accompanied the systematic repression of Socialists, as Liberals dispersed their meetings and torched their houses.[48]

These measures fragmented the resistance leagues, leading some Socialists to flee the region. They also unleashed forces the leagues previously had helped to contain. Masked attackers again bombed and torched stores and homes and raided haciendas. One hacendado was shot dead, his corpse stabbed repeatedly afterward. Several dozen men killed the owner of a store in Bolón along with his son; they reportedly left their remains in the street as a "pile of bloody meat" and then sexually assaulted female relatives of the men. In early April, arsonists simultaneously attacked seven haciendas near Hunucmá and torched others in ensuing weeks, twenty thousand pesos in damages resulting at Chel alone. Some blamed Hunucmá's beleaguered Socialists for the attacks; one witness claimed to have overheard the league leader Juan Bautista Pech covertly ordering his comrades to torch the fields, warning them that "what had been agreed on, had to be fulfilled, and that whoever didn't do his duty would be killed."[49]

It was amid this crisis that Hunucmá's police chief, Nemesio Suárez, accompanied by the head of the town's federal garrison, visited the house of Pío Chuc on 29 April 1920. They entered and walked toward the back patio. Perhaps they had heard there was a meeting going on in his house and planned to break it up. On entering, they may have glimpsed the large pile of weapons and ammunition by one wall and dozens of packs and provisions piled against another. This was no political meetinghouse; it was an insurgents' cache. There was no time, however, for further investigation. Shots rang out, and the two men fell. Theirs were the first steps on the road to Cacab Dzul.

THE TALION LAW

Even as Liberals celebrated their victories, there were rumors of mysterious assemblies out in the woods, late at night. Men like Lizama, who had left Pío Chuc to join the resistance leagues, again recognized him, as El General.

Second in command was Chuc's wife, Dolores Chuil, called La Capitana, a woman known for carrying a rifle and wearing ammunition belts. There was a second so-called captain, Chuc's son Isidoro, and below him nineteen chiefs (jefes) like Lizama, most of them liberation war veterans. At their command were as many as two hundred soldiers (soldados). By late April, Chuc's people clearly were preparing a rebellion, though it is unclear whether they intended to do so in concert with the general Obregonist movement or in demand of land and liberty or both. Perhaps they planned the movement to coincide with Cinco de Mayo.[50] In any event, the unexpected arrival of Hunucmá's police chief forced the rebels to act prematurely. They killed the intruders, and then split into two groups. Lizama led one group to a hideout north of town, while Pío Chuc took another group west to Kaxek. As they neared their destination, they met and detained an old man, Isidro Tzuc, the King of the Forest, who had been an ally of Chuc's father, José Angel Chuc, in the communalist struggles three decades earlier. Perhaps that old alliance explains why Pío Chuc allowed the old man to continue on his way, on the condition that he keep their presence in Kaxek a secret.[51]

Meanwhile, a military train packed with troops arrived in the town of Hunucmá, transforming it into an armed camp. Soldiers raped Chuc's daughter and seized his young son Saturnino, along with two of Chuc's close allies. Later, the soldiers released them and told the three to run, upon which they shot them dead as fugitive prisoners.[52] Such actions, added to rumors that hundreds of armed men had taken to the woods, triggered a panic among the town's residents. While the new commander of federal forces in Yucatán, General Pablo De la Garza, dismissed such stories as "popular fantasy," soon the King—rebel no more—walked into the office of Kinchil's mayor to report that he had seen as many as two hundred men at Kaxek. As wealthy families fled Hunucmá, soldiers, joined by armed Liberals, began mounting watches and digging defensive trenches in the center of town.[53]

By the time reports of their presence at Kaxek emerged, Chuc and his men had moved again, to woodlands north of town. Two contingents of rebels, Lizama's group to the east of the road to Sisal and Chuc's group to the west, sealed off the entire zone. Then came the disappearances. Two rail cars that had set out from Hunucmá returned without the woodcutters who had manned them. A rail car that left Hacienda San Joaquín carrying the sons of its owner also rolled into town empty. An automobile was emptied of its passengers outside Sisal. Others vanished while walking to their milpas. The captives—as many as forty men, including some boys as young as twelve—were told they had been taken prisoner "by orders of General Pío." They were bound, beaten, and kicked; a few had their arms broken. Then Chuc's men led them to Hacienda Concepción, which Chuc had seized for use as a base, and forced them into an empty water tank, which served as a holding cell. Soon El General and La Capitana appeared, scrutinizing the captives and walking off to confer with their jefes.[54] After night fell, Chuc's men tied the prisoners together in pairs and led them back into the woods. One prisoner overheard his captors whispering, "They are going to be killed—every one of them." He yelled and a dozen of the captives twisted free, running off into the darkness to the sounds of gunshots, screaming, and moans. One man hid underneath some bushes, waiting for dawn before running home through the brush. Others wandered through marshes and salt flats until reaching the coast, where they found some canoes and paddled to Progreso. A few lost their way in the brush, searching desperately for water to slake their thirst.

Despite the kidnappings, the troops dared not venture into the woods in pursuit of Chuc and his men. The stalemate would not last long. By late May, the national political situation suddenly changed, with the victory of the Obregonist rebellion. As Obregonist forces arrived in Yucatán, and Socialists like Carrillo Puerto returned to power in Yucatán, Lizama emerged from the woods with twenty of his men. He declared that they were not in rebellion against the government but had fled persecution by the previous government. Even Pío Chuc, Lizama explained, would happily lay down his arms if his life and those of his men were guaranteed. Soon the rebels returned home. By late May, the local Socialists José Dolores Bojórquez, Andrés Lizama, and Juan Bautista Pech Balam had returned to Hunucmá to form a new town council.[55]

Amid these developments, a few escapees made it back to town, to share tales of horror. Young boys, some said, had been whipped and tormented; poor farmers had been tied to trees near their milpas, left to die of thirst and exposure. One of the missing, an elderly man, reportedly reappeared in Hunucmá in a state of agony, his lips "completely sewn together with string."[56] Nonetheless, Bojórquez, the newly appointed head of Hunucmá's town council, wrote the editors of the *Revista* to declare that events had been "blown out of proportion." "Everyone in el pueblo," he announced, knew that such tales were part of an ongoing Liberal "conspiracy" against the Socialists.[57] On May 20, however, a former police chief named Eusebio Borges set out for the woods, vowing his determination to "arrive at an understanding of the truth." On his return, he brought more grisly stories: of bodies piled by a well, and of bits of human hair, flesh, and bloodied clothes scattered in the woods. Borges then led a second group back to Cacab Dzul, one composed of soldiers, relatives of the missing, and twenty resistance league members, including some of Chuc's men. They found the well and extracted a few bodies, leaving fifteen or twenty behind. Back in Hunucmá's cemetery, the recovered bodies were carefully reassembled and then interred in consecrated ground. Soon there was news of yet more remains, these found near Chicché, which news reporters called "fragments": the remains of at least three men who had escaped from Cacab Dzul only to stray into the woods and eventually succumb to thirst and exhaustion.[58]

People demanded explanations. The killers hadn't done much to conceal their actions, leaving the well uncovered and the remains where they would easily be found. They had dismembered and even decapitated some of the corpses, perhaps intending those actions to send a message. Neither Chuc, Lizama, nor anyone else claimed responsibility for the killings, and the nature of the victims—not political figures but for the most part common working men—left the motives of the slaughter obscure. Relatives of the disappeared filed a complaint before a penal court judge, demanding the opening of an investigation; reporters interviewed survivors of Cacab Dzul and published gory descriptions of bodies left behind in the woods to the ravages of bird and beast.[59]

Neither local nor state authorities, however, returned to collect the remains, and by late May a penal investigation still had not been opened. When reporters asked the attorney general why not, he responded that he "wasn't going to bother with those 'little pants' "—a reference to short pants found near the well and perhaps to the victims, reduced to scraps. When a judge finally instructed the local authorities to retrieve the bodies, they refused; state forensic doctors also refused to recover and autopsy them, citing their advanced state of decomposition.[60] Only in mid-July, almost two months after the killings, did a penal judge finally issue orders to Hunucmá's justice of the peace to open an investigation based on interviews, in lieu of formal autopsies. Strangely, the list of prospective interviewees included many who had perished in the violence and who thus could not be located; moreover, the justice of the peace inexplicably declined to interview several survivors. One of the few who did testify, Pablo Choch, was particularly distressed that the killers not only murdered his adolescent son, but also had decapitated him. Then, however, Choch refused to say more, stating that he "feared that they will take vengeance against me." In the end, the judge found no grounds for arresting anyone, leaving the identities of killers and victims alike in obscurity.[61]

Even in the absence of recovery of the bodies, residents, politicians, government officials, and newspaper commentators pondered their significance. For Socialists from the local to the state level the killings were inconvenient. While Pío Chuc was not a prominent Socialist, some of his allies were. The bodies thus threatened to tarnish the resistance leagues as well as the Socialist Party and the government. In another respect, however, the timing of the killings was fortunate. Committed during a time of national rebellion, they could be classified as political in nature and, if so, would fall under the provisions of political amnesty. Even if those responsible were discovered, they would be exonerated, making any investigation an exercise in futility. For Liberals, on the other hand, an investigation had much to offer: an exposé of a horrific massacre associated with the Socialist regime. Writers for the *Revista* denounced the state government's refusal to document the killings, publishing a front-page manifesto declaring the crimes to be the work of Obregonists. Somewhat contradictorily, the article called for the prosecution of those responsible under the normal penal code rather than under provisions for political crimes.[62] When the criminal investigation went nowhere, relatives of the victims wrote to President Obregón, denouncing the "political aspect" Socialists attributed to the killings and the immunity conferred on the killers. Obregón flatly dismissed their appeal.[63]

For some, the macabre well held not only political, but also historical significance. In mid-June, the author F. Pérez Alcalá published "José Pío Chuc: A Beast-Man," a discussion of prevailing explanations of the violence. Some, he wrote, credited the killings to an "ancient rivalry" between indigenous populations and whites and mestizos; that "hereditary racial hate," they believed, made indigenous residents determined to "exterminate or expel the whites, in order to become the lords of the populations and lands of that region." Others, whom Pérez found more credible, attributed the violence to the "innate and traditional attachment" of the "Yucatecan proletarian, and especially the Maya," to the land. According to Pérez, in Hunucmá the loss of ancestral lands engendered a "never-extinguished hate" toward landowners, hatred the resistance leagues had encouraged in order to win "absolute authoritarian power" over indigenous workers. Once triggered, that "thirst for blood" could be slaked only at Cacab Dzul.[64] Remarkably, Pérez's article drew a letter of protest from Pío Chuc, who declared his innocence and decried the persecution he and his family had suffered for his "political ideas." In response, the Revista's editors claimed they presumed no one's guilt, "whether he be named Puc or Pérez." Despite the Revista's coy gesture toward impartiality, Chuc's letter exposed the characteristic underlying all of the theories entertained by Pérez: a racism that ascribed a tendency toward savagery to Hunucmá's indigenous population, whether attributing that tendency to ethnic or agrarian origins.[65]

Such discussions took place against a backdrop of resurgent political violence. With the restoration of the resistance leagues, Liberals complained of attacks on their persons and property. Some league leaders organized attacks against haciendas, in one case triggered by rumors that the hacendado Augusto Peón was deliberately sowing locust eggs on Hacienda Tedzidz in order to hatch swarms to attack ejidal milpas.[66] In Kinchil, Socialists went on a shooting spree, shouting, "¡Viva José Pío Chuc!" as they killed several residents. While Liberals protested such attacks, with one Revista commentator declaring that "el pueblo demanded justice" for them,[67] Socialists leveled complaints of their own over the imposition of Liberal interim officials pending municipal elections. In Samahil, "el pueblo," according to a news report, protested against an imposed mayor, saying that "they were not inhabitants of a hacienda, to be assembled and informed of their new boss."[68] Lizama and hundreds of petitioners complained that Hunucmá's Liberal interim mayor had "confronted el pueblo, saying that it had neither voice nor vote." In response, the head of the federal military toured Hunucmá, holding meetings, he said, to "speak to el pueblo" and arranging plebiscites to "satisfy el pueblo" by replacing unpopular officials. Such measures did not, however, address long-brewing agrarian discontent. In October, conflicts over ejidal lands led the Socialist Party president, Miguel Cantón, to send an urgent communiqué to the governor warning that if Hunucmá's land scarcity went unaddressed, it might take a "mistaken path, forming an army of the hungry, an army of the poor, that in throwing itself into a desperate and crazed struggle for bread, might disturb what peace and well-being still exist, and which are so necessary to maintain in order to transform the promises of the triumphant Revolution into a beautiful reality."[69]

Political violence reached a climax on the eve of the elections of 4 November as partisan gangs clashed throughout the peninsula in what came to be known as the Terrible Week (la semana espantosa). Even Carrillo Puerto was targeted, as Guillermo Poot, a Liberal strongman from Kinchil nicknamed El Oscuro ("the Dark One"), squeezed off three shots at him, all of which missed.[70] In Hunucmá, the violence claimed a prominent victim. On

4 November José Pío Chuc and his father, Angel Chuc, went out woodcutting in their milpas, not far from Cacab Dzul. After a few hours, Don Angel heard screams and shots. He rushed in the direction of the screams and found his son's body, riddled with ten bullet holes, one through his right eye. A machete blow to the back of his neck had nearly decapitated him. Finally, to complete Chuc's bodily desecration, the killers had severed his penis, shoving it into his mouth.

Even as the Socialists routed the Liberals throughout the state, news of Pío Chuc's death spread. Upon receiving word of it from Hunucmá's mayor, the governor did not seem excessively distressed, penciling, atop the communication, "Sensational event. José Pío Chuc died. . . ."[71] In an eerie replay of Cacab Dzul, state forensic doctors refused to travel to Hunucmá to carry out an autopsy. Pío Chuc's cadaver, like those in the well, remained unexamined by the state, with even the cause of death left undetermined. Timed to take place during elections, Chuc's killing, like the slaughter at Cacab Dzul, could be categorized conveniently as political, leaving the killers protected by the ensuing amnesty and making an investigation seem pointless.

While government officials quietly shelved the case, commentators in the press celebrated the death of the man who had been a "living affront to Justice and law in Yucatán." Though never laid to rest, Chuc's victims were at least avenged, and peace might return to Hunucmá.[72] For Pérez Alcalá, however, who had dubbed Pío Chuc a "beast-man," the circumstances of his death were cause for concern. Pérez criticized other journalists for omitting mention of how Chuc's body had been "profaned" and "horribly mutilated, with a cruel and savage mockery" that demonstrated a "satanic" vengeance. Nor, in their optimistic predictions of the return of peace, had they shared with their readers what had happened when Dolores Chuil, La Capitana, viewed her husband's remains. She raged against those who had "exploited her husband for political purposes," declaring that their turn would come. Then she swore an oath over Chuc's dismembered body, promising to hunt down his killers and punish them by the "talion law": an eye for an eye and a tooth for a tooth.[73]

At best, Pérez concluded, the gruesome episode might serve as a cautionary tale for Socialists and Liberals alike, so that the "calvary of the Yucatecan pueblo . . . might cease." At worst, it was an augury of new links on Hunucmá's "unending chain of hate, vengeance, and retribution," a chain, it would seem, ungoverned by the laws of the Revolution or of the nation.[74] The violence had exceeded partisan animosity and ancient rivalries of race and land, to the point of the invocation of talion, a law before and beyond both.

SPECTERS OF REVOLUTION

In the aftermath of Pío Chuc's killing, the mayor of Hunucmá told the governor that "complete tranquility reigned." If that was the case, it would not be so for long. As word of Chuc's death spread, the panic began. Landowners fled to Mérida, armed bands of Socialists and Liberals stalked the outskirts of settlements, and merchants funded a night patrol to protect their businesses. Then came the violence. Bandits in the western woods assaulted and killed passersby; arsonists burned henequen fields across the region; masked men attacked the haciendas, shooting employees and encargados and bombing machinery. Attackers sacked Chel, urging the workers, reportedly in the name of the Socialist Party, to help them and threatening those who refused that "they would be their enemies, and would come back later in greater numbers to track them down." Another group ambushed a car carrying the encargado of Tedzidz, killing the driver and then reportedly "profaning" his body; they forced the workers of Tedzidz to join in, threatening to "barbecue" those who resisted.[75] Bandits raided Tacubaya and Tanchen, assaulting and robbing residents and carrying off hacienda property.[76] One band raided Tucichen, brandishing guns and machetes. Seizing the shopkeeper of the hacienda store, one of the attackers slammed a machete into the front of his throat. According to the victim's widow, the attacker—in a revival of the blood rituals of insurgency—"collected the blood that spouted out in his hands, and drank."[77]

To hacendados and merchants across the state, Hunucmá again became emblematic of violence that they claimed had transformed rural Yucatán into something like a lawless frontier; one journalist called Hunucmá a "land inferior even to that of the Hottentots."[78] While violence in Hunucmá had triggered such perceptions in the past, now the specters of Pío Chuc and of those killed at Cacab Dzul seemed to lurk behind events. In April 1921 the editors of the *Revista* surmised that the violence of late 1920 and 1921 was the work of supporters of Pío Chuc who continued "sowing terror and alarm in the region." Now, supposedly, they planned to celebrate the anniversary of Cacab Dzul by "finishing off the rest of the vecinos and destroying the properties of their enemies." With "Chuc's men," according to the *Revista*, occupying positions on Hunucmá's town council, local authorities took no action against criminals, claiming that the "evil" could not be "cured." While Hunucmá's Socialist mayor and town council denounced the *Revista* for slander, Yucatán's attorney general took such charges seriously. He sent secret agents to Hunucmá to investigate, later informing the governor that the rumors were accurate.[79]

In the end, however, with the redoubled vigilance of police and troops, that dreaded anniversary came and went without the predicted orgy of violence. The revival of the resistance leagues may have helped contain the violence, as the leagues helped channel labor and agrarian discontent, especially after the passage of a federal law of December 1920 mandating the provisional distribution of presumed idle lands to needy populations. Hunucmá's woodlands again became politicized as terrains of dispute. Hacendados denounced league organizers as well as what some called the "poor illiterate Indians" who followed them; pueblo residents lodged complaints of their own, like that of a man who wrote to President Obregón accusing hacendados of "attacking the ideals of the Revolution for which you have struggled, and of whose triumph we dream."[80] Socialist officials pursued a series of educational and cultural initiatives, from literacy campaigns to efforts to "defanaticize" indigenous populations by countering Catholicism and the "bacchanals" of Mayan shamanism and animal sacrifice to the formation of pueblo baseball teams with names like Soviet and Third International. The party further consolidated its position in elections of November 1921, establishing a monopoly on political office from the municipal level to the office of governor, now assumed by Carrillo Puerto. Local Socialists like Kinchil's league president heralded Carrillo Puerto's advent to power, saluting his "government of the poor" and declaring him to be "of el pueblo, and for el pueblo."[81]

These developments opened the door to renewed government efforts to enact definitive agrarian reform. By early 1922, the Agrarian Commission began sending engineers throughout Yucatán to collect land titles and oral testimony and map the landscape. As in the Alvarado years, they elaborated official histories of the pueblos—narratives specific in factual content but generic in form, recounting the pueblos' original possession of communal lands, subsequent loss of them, and the formal steps taken by residents to petition the state to have the land returned. They excluded any mention, in the case of Hunucmá, of the history of communalist insurgency. These official histories were intended for legal use in court, against the documents which hacendados assembled to defend their henequen haciendas against indigenous claimants, whom they dismissed in their legal arguments as "primitive" and "barbarous."[82] They were also meant for public enactment. With much fanfare Governor Carrillo Puerto attended mass meetings in Umán and Hunucmá in which el pueblo was summoned to witness the ceremonious reading of agrarian resolutions and the official assignment of lots of land to local representatives.[83]

Confronting the consolidation of the Socialist regime and the prospect of definitive agrarian reform, Liberals despaired. They filed repeated complaints with the federal government, blaming Socialist activists for political violence and banditry and denouncing government-issued amnesties that created a climate of impunity in Yucatán.[84] While President Obregón was unsympathetic to their protests, for a moment some took solace in a federal anti-Bolshevik measure prohibiting the "incitation of the masses to rebellion" and forbidding "el pueblo" to "fly revolutionary banners" or foment "anarchy." Attempts to invoke such measures against what the detractors called the "subversive propaganda" of Socialists in the Hunucmá region proved fruitless.[85] For the most part, Liberals and other critics of the Socialists raged impotently against them. Luis Rosado Vega, for instance, denounced partisan political conflict under Socialist rule, and the resulting "war of brother against brother." "The devil has us by the hair," he lamented, urging the government to reconcile all factions in order to bring about the "salvation of our homeland."[86]

In no place so much as in Hunucmá did prospects of salvation seem more distant. Socialists attacked and jailed Liberal organizers and reportedly coerced hacienda laborers and town residents into joining the leagues. Factionalism brought violence within Socialist Party lines as well. When Mayor Bojórquez of Hunucmá challenged Umán's García Correa in state congressional elections, attackers waylaid a car bearing propagandists for Bojórquez, killing one man and killing and dismembering an eight-year-old boy accompanying them. Not long after, Bojórquez's brother, Adolfo, was stabbed to death.[87] In 1922, Liberal leaders complained that Socialist violence and government misconduct in Hunucmá and elsewhere in the state seemed to them to be returning Yucatán to "Porfirian times," threatening to convert the entire region into a "lake of blood."[88] But in the Hunucmá region, the Liberals were equally disposed to violence. In Kinchil, the decapitation and disfigurement of a Socialist left residents "tired, by now, of so much 'democracy.'" Moreover, the Liberal strongman Guillermo Poot, known as El Oscuro, made a public oath that, in the event of Liberal electoral defeat, he would bring fifty men from Tetiz—still a Liberal stronghold: the onetime gubernatorial candidate Mena Brito received a hero's welcome when he visited there in October 1921—to "settle everything with bullets and blood." When defeat came, Poot and his men took to the woods, carrying out a series of ambushes, shootings, and killings.[89] Bandits continued to raid haciendas like San Lorenzo and Santa María near Kinchil and to assault and rob railway passengers in the region.[90]

In mid-1922, Governor Carrillo Puerto attempted to crack down on banditry in the region. Municipal police were ordered to hand over their weapons to the resistance leagues, and troops and federal police broke into houses in Kinchil and Tetiz in search of suspects. While El Oscuro evaded capture, fleeing to safe haven in Tetiz whenever chased, several members of his band were tracked down, one by one, and summarily executed. In another case, police agents dragged seven men out of their houses, driving them away on a bus. Two months later their bodies were found, piled into an old well off in the woods. Some suggested that high police officials or even officials in the state government had ordered the executions. As in the killings at Cacab Dzul and Pío Chuc's killing, however, too much time had passed to identify the bodies formally or determine the cause of death, and so they joined the expanding ranks of what one reporter called Hunucmá's disappeared (desaparecidos).[91]

Newspaper commentators and state government officials took such events as presaging the return of Hunucmá's troubled past. For residents of the district, however, that violence had never been relegated to the past but was constantly recollected in commemorative rituals honoring the dead. In 1919, on the fifth anniversary of Feliciano Canul Reyes's death, Hunucmá's resistance league organized a procession and candlelit vigil at his tomb, in the first of what would become yearly commemorations of his passing. The tomb of Canul's brother Cirilo, who also died at Progreso, was adorned with the Socialist Party's triangular emblem, making him a retroactive Socialist martyr, though he, like Feliciano, died years before the party's formation.[92] Similarly, in May 1920 an event was held in the cemetery at Hunucmá to honor those the Socialists referred to as the "victims of Hunucmá"—not the dozens slain at Cacab Dzul but those executed by soldiers in late April, including Pío Chuc's son Saturnino. Six months later, and on the first anniversary of their deaths, there would be similar ceremonies. The next year local Socialists appealed for state recognition and publicly subsidized tombs, for the martyrs, including Saturnino and another boy, invoking the martyrs' "love for public liberties" and the "gratitude that we should feel toward those who have sacrificed themselves for our cause."[93]

Many others were not commemorated in Socialist rituals, most notably those who had been slaughtered at Cacab Dzul. Special church masses—religious events, in contrast with secular Socialist ritual—were offered in Mérida

JOSE CIRILO CANUL
MUERTO EL 17 DE ACOSTO DE 1914 ·
EN EL PUERTO DE PROGRESO POR ·
LAS HUESTES DEL USURPADOR VIC-
TORIANO HUERTA.

José Cirilo Canul's grave in Hunucmá cemetery. It is inscribed with the triangular emblem of the Socialist Party. Photo by Paul Eiss.

and Hunucmá on behalf of those whose bodies had been recovered. Floral wreaths were laid at their graves, and survivors and relatives hosted events to offer prayers for the "suffrage of their souls." While many relatives and survivors of the violence, like some of its victims, were not members of the Liberal Party, Liberals embraced the dead of Cacab Dzul as martyrs in their cause, using funerary commemorations as occasions to denounce the Socialist government.[94] In the wake of further political violence and continued electoral defeats, Yucatecan Liberals adopted Cacab Dzul as a metaphor for their continuing persecution across the state. In mid-1921, for instance, Anastacio Manzanilla Domínguez published a political treatise cataloguing violence against Liberals, describing it as an act of homage before the "tomb of so many heroic and humble citizens sacrificed by the red barbarians." Manzanilla gave Cacab Dzul pride of place in his narrative, as the center-piece of a chapter entitled "The Bolshevik Thirst for Blood." While denouncing the Socialist Party and government officials for covering up the killings, Manzanilla studiously avoided any mention of Liberal and military violence preceding Cacab Dzul and left unmentioned the martyrs whom Socialists honored in their rituals.[95]

Such recognition, however, was only for those whose remains had been identified and returned to town, for burial in hallowed ground. Theirs were the souls of martyrs, named and honored in church and home. The bodies, or body parts, that remained in the pit, however, were simply referred to as "the disappeared." Uncollected and unnamed, they remained out in the woods, their deaths unsanctified and undecorated. José Pío Chuc was not admitted to the ranks of Socialist martyrs either. Perhaps he was judged unfit or too dangerous or even too dishonored by dismemberment. All were victims of a violence whose origins may have been political, but whose extremity had banished its victims from any possibility of collective political or spiritual reclamation. They were consigned to a shadowy existence out in the woods, in the places where they had been killed, dismembered, unmanned, and unnamed. Thus, the woodlands, so saturated with historic claims and struggles, became burdened with new layers of meaning as places of fear.

For agrarian engineers and Socialist government officials, however, those lands—as well as uncultivated and abandoned hacienda lands, of which there were many in the district—occupied the center of plans to reconstitute el pueblo as a collective entity. In November 1923, Carrillo Puerto issued a decree "in the name of el pueblo" calling for the expropriation of all uncultivated haciendas, for the formation of agricultural collectives. While Socialists celebrated Carrillo Puerto's plan, others denounced him for populist despotism. As a comment on such developments, the *Revista* published an article by the sociologist and jurist Ricardo de Zayas Enríquez, who argued that "el pueblo" had thrown off the rule of Porfirio Díaz to fall under a worse dictatorship, that of the "multitudes." While "el pueblo" was, "if not entirely civilized, then at least not barbarous," the "horde" was "savage"; whereas el pueblo had a patria, the horde had "neither patria nor home." Zayas called for a new leader to protect el pueblo, by "conquering the hordes" who had usurped power in places like Yucatán.[96]

Such a figure, it seemed to some, soon emerged in the person of General Adolfo de la Huerta, the leader of a military rebellion against President Obregón and Obregón's candidate for the presidency, General Plutarco Elías Calles. Delahuertista forces invaded Yucatán; their commander, General Ricardez Broca, declared himself governor and decreed the closure of all so-called "popular groups," including the leagues. In Hunucmá, many fled to the woods; a few organized bombing raids against the Delahuertistas. The troops made short work of them, however, using captive Socialists as human shields and killing those who refused to assist in the task. Within a few days,

Carrillo Puerto and his companions were captured and executed by Ricardez Broca's forces, convincing Socialists throughout Yucatán that all was lost.[97]

Hunucmá's officials, whether Liberal or Socialist, made their peace with the new regime. El Oscuro emerged from the woods to seize control of Kinchil in the name of the Liberals. Umán's mayor was not far behind, urging wealthy town residents to make contributions to a fund he planned to offer the new governor. Even Hunucmá's longtime league leader, Juan Bautista Pech Balam, turned coat. He provided Ricardez Broca with the names of local Socialists and was appointed mayor in return. After Carrillo Puerto's execution, Pech informed Broca that "people who belonged to the late José Pío Chuc intend[ed] to repeat their deeds" out of vengeance, "sowing pain, among people who live in the center of this town, and among the authorities." Pech suggested that Ricardez Broca have his soldiers "get in touch with [Pío Chuc's] jefes, whose names I have."[98]

While the anticipated threat from Pío Chuc's old chiefs did not materialize, Pech's about-face bought him power for a few months, until Obregón and Calles put down the rebellion and Obregon's forces retook Yucatán, enforcing the dismissal of all those who had served under Ricardez Broca. Yucatecan Socialists immediately began the recuperation of Carrillo Puerto's legacy, publishing accounts likening his persecution by De la Huerta's forces to the calvary of Jesus. Carrillo Puerto's last words to his killers, they said, were, "Don't abandon my Indians!" Such selfless martyrdom seemed to confirm the redemptive mission of the Socialist state in relation to its indigenous subjects, even after it became clear that the reforms Carrillo Puerto had contemplated had not survived his demise.[99]

The implications of Ricardez Broca's downfall were, however, unclear to the onetime insurgent and onetime Socialist Juan Bautista Pech. Even after he was removed from office in April, Pech continued to persecute former members of Hunucmá's league. He even insinuated to one, Dimas Novelo, that "there were only two days left, before [Pech] would burn the few socialists" remaining in Hunucmá. Novelo turned toward Pech and pulled out a knife; shouting, "Long live liberty! And long live General Calles," he plunged it into Pech's heart. The blow was aimed at Pech, and the shout evoked liberty. The deed, however, was committed not in the name of el pueblo, but of Calles, and through him, of a state that made some into martyrs of the Revolution but many others into its specters.[100]

Marcelino Avila's son, fourteen-year-old Tomás, had been missing for five months. The only trace of him was his hat, which was found among other scraps of clothes and body parts at Cacab Dzul. Searchers saw a body—or pieces of one—they suspected was his, but Don Marcelino was unconvinced. That was why he visited a psychic in Mérida. Perhaps that woman's conjurations would confirm Tomás's final resting place in the accursed well. The psychic, however, had other news: the boy was alive, lost out in the woods near the seaside pueblo of Celestún. Avila immediately drove out to the port with a few relatives. After searching awhile on old paths through the woods, they met a few people who reported seeing an unknown person wandering there. One woman described the strange figure as a young man with long hair and torn clothes who was in a "deplorable state" and unable even to speak. The description seemed to fit Tomás, and the Avilas rushed back to Celestún to raise a search party. For days they roamed the woods, swamps, and savannah, searching desperately but without success. Five months after the killings at Cacab Dzul, it seemed, its ghosts had begun haunting the woodlands and dark places of Hunucmá. After his traumatic death, Tomás had been doomed to tormented, speechless wanderings. Like the others who moldered in Cacab Dzul, his mortal remains had been left embedded in unhallowed ground, and out in the woods he would remain.[101]

More than a half century later, the ruins of Hacienda Concepción and the nearby woods of Cacab Dzul were purchased by a commercial poultry company. While excavating an old dry well, workers found a pile of human bones mixed in among the rocks and dirt. Hearing of the findings, older town residents told of the Revolution, of a man called José Pío Chuc, and of those some still call the "warriors" (guerreros) of el pueblo. Some recalled tales of the fateful words Chuc had uttered on hearing of his own son's death—"They have killed the innocent, and now the innocent will die"—words that offered motives for the slaughter only in the depths of a father's grief. Others talked of Chuc's own killing and dismemberment. Most, however, associated Chuc's name only with fragments of stories: of killers stalking the woods who cut off tongues and ears, flayed the skin off feet, and drank human blood.[102]

Perhaps the bones of Tomás Avila were there, in the pile. The names of the disappeared, however, had been lost to memory, and neither he nor any of the other victims was identified. In the end, the bones seemed as bleached of their past and of politics as the rocks surrounding them in the well. They bore no name and no history besides that of el pueblo. In this, Cacab Dzul and its infernal well are not alone. For, as hunters in Hunucmá and Tetiz know, there are many wells out in the woodlands that contain the bones of the dead. Who knows their histories? or their names? If you stay near the wells as night falls, you may meet their spirits. They come out to whistle at you and chase you away from their resting places. By day, though, when you are out hunting, you must drink from those wells filled with bones, for the sun is hot and water scarce. What can you do? You must drink.[103]

CHAPTER SIX

THE PRESIDENT'S DEAD HAND

Surveys, Maps, and the Measure of el Pueblo

ON OCTOBER 15, 1937, a group of agrarian engineers and municipal and ejidal officials assembled at Hunucmá's town hall and set off for the outskirts of town. There, they began the *deslinde*—a survey demarcating the *linderos*, or boundaries, between areas of land. They noted the location of each hacienda and of lands that would become part of Hunucmá's definitive ejidal grant. Then they continued walking in straight lines, measuring the distance they traveled: 1,150 meters southwest, 120 meters to the east, and so on. They walked by haciendas like Santa Cruz, Abal, Nohuayum, and Yaxché, always finding the borders between them and separating ejidal lands from those that the hacendados would retain. At day's end they erected a landmark on the last point they had reached, returning the next morning to continue their work. For eight days they traced a series of polygons that separated ejidal lands from private property, distinguished Hunucmá's ejidos from those of neighboring pueblos, and set off planted fields from woodlands and coastal marshes.[1]

On 21 October the group assembled again in the town hall to elaborate the official document, or *acta*, that described the route they had walked. They had done so, the acta stated, at the direct orders of President Lázaro Cárdenas, in fulfillment of a Resolución Presidencial mandating the immediate definitive ejidal grant to Hunucmá. The acta was the penultimate step in a process that would end a few days later, when ejidal workers, or *ejidatarios*, of Hunucmá took possession of those lands in a public ceremony. The drafting of the acta was itself a deslinde, and of more than the land. It also registered the points of connection between federal, state, and municipal authorities, distinguishing between the power of the state in designating ejidal boundaries and that of el pueblo in assenting to them. In addition, the acta marked a subtler border, that between the textual description of the deslinde and the material, social, and political world it purported to define and delimit. In a sense, it was a deslinde of time as well, which set apart the land's complicated history of claims and struggles from its future as a collective ejido titled by the state. Thus the deslinde and the land ceremony that followed might make history irrelevant, supplanting it with an act of sovereign executive will.

All that remained, it seemed, was to carry out a detailed survey and to draft a map, making a fine-grained icon of the land and its boundaries. Yet it would take more than half a century to do so. Hence to understand the acta's significance, it is not enough to place it within the context of the Cardenista state's efforts toward the establishment of ejidos in places like Hunucmá. One must follow the acta over the decades that came after, as engineers, officials, and residents of the pueblos struggled to lay claim to the Resolución of 1937—or to circumvent it. It is to explore how the relations between state and pueblo came to be governed not only by such surveys, but also by the inability to survey: not by the making of maps, so much as by the lack of maps.[2] It is to read the acta to its final reiteration, in the moment when the president's dead hand would be summoned to conclude the long struggle over ejidal survey. When the acta finally was inscribed on the landscape in the form of a map, it would trace the route to a future radically different from the one Cárdenas or Hunucmá's communalists might have imagined fifty years earlier.

UNMAPPING HUNUCMÁ

In April 1924, in the wake of the overthrow of Ricardez Broca, President Alvaro Obregón appointed José Iturralde interim governor of Yucatán. The new governor made gestures toward the reactivation of agrarian reform and the restoration of the Socialist Party and its leagues.[3] The restored Partido Socialista del Sureste (PSS), however, was much changed. Its offices and positions were taken over by local bosses and regional power brokers who ensconced themselves in power through the co-optation of the leagues and the adept use of electoral fraud and intimidation.[4] Moreover, just a few months after Iturralde took office, Yucatán's state congress replaced him, voting to invalidate several provisional ejidal grants he had approved. Officials of the Agrarian Commission in Yucatán protested unsuccessfully—"not as politicians, but as committed agrarians [agraristas]," they emphasized—against measures that would compromise agrarian reform and "sow mistrust" in the region's rural populations.[5] Such changes, however, were in keeping with the policies of Obregón's successor, President Plutarco Elías Calles (1924–28) and those of two of his handpicked successors (1928–34), under whose rule the federal government took a conservative, anti-agrarian turn.

In 1924 the Hunucmá region seemed to return to its former restiveness, with groups of masked bandits, in some cases their faces or bodies painted blue or black, assaulting travelers. Armed groups of workers from Ucú and Tetiz blockaded railway lines and denounced abusive practices on haciendas like Nohuayum; residents of Samahil came into conflict with the hacendado José Palomeque, both for his seizure of woodlands near Texán and for enforcing conditions of alleged slavery on Texán, in denial of the "great benefits that the glorious revolution has brought us."[6] Such attempts to rekindle emancipatory struggles foundered, however, under the new regime. While still named after Feliciano Canul Reyes, Hunucmá's restored resistance league was now controlled by landowners and merchants, some of them onetime Liberals, who lectured members on the "obligation all comrades have" to vote for official candidates. They expelled, intimidated, and beat those who dared to voice opposition, calling them traitors—such as a group that named itself the José Cirilo Canul Committee and dared to break ranks over the presidential elections of 1927.[7] Bartolomé García Correa used his control over Umán's league, his political connections, and a Maya-inflected populist style to continue his rise to power, vaulting into the governorship by 1930; subsequently, he established a Revolutionary Defense corps to intimidate and spy upon his opponents. García's father, moreover, ran a monopoly over the wood and charcoal trade in the Hunucmá region, purchasing those commodities from indigenous workers and league members at what some critics called "slavery prices" and reselling them at exorbitant rates.[8] Umán's hacendados came to terms with local PSS leaders and offered their support and the votes of their estate workers in exchange for assistance in labor discipline and recruiting. In Kinchil, a clique of merchants, ranchers, and planters led by the Solís family, who had held sway as caciques since the late nineteenth century, remained ensconced in power. Kinchil's bosses enriched themselves and enforced their political dominion through assassinations, beatings, and intimidation by a much-feared gang of thugs.[9]

Declining henequen prices in international markets, in combination with the low productivity of western soils, further darkened the prospects of Hunucmá's working populations. One Socialist leader denounced hacendados throughout Yucatán for reducing the workweek to two or three days, "thus reducing the Indians to hunger, and making them work once again as slaves on the haciendas, forced to accept whatever wages are offered to them."[10] In the Hunucmá region, some hacendados, in a drive to realize short-term profits, ordered workers to overcut the plants. Plants were denuded of the minimum number of leaves they needed to survive, leaving many fincas on a path to decline. Numerous haciendas in the region reduced their operations, first temporarily and then, by the 1930s, permanently, their aging henequen fields reverting to weeds and brush. As a result, workers were hard put to stay in the good graces of the few hacendados who still offered employment, often at wages as low as seventy-five cents a day, a rate that according to one observer made the minimum wage a "true utopia" in Hunucmá.[11] Some workers cut wood and made charcoal on abandoned estates or paid rent for milpa lands. Others worked for hacendados in large-scale commercial firewood and charcoal operations, often conducted illegally in ejidal lands. The resident hacienda population continued declining, as many emigrated from Hunucmá to the eastern districts of the henequen zone, where more work was available (see appendix).

In 1924 and 1925 the Agrarian Commission authorized provisional grants in various places in Yucatán, including the Hunucmá region. Land distribution, however, was stymied by the reluctance of federal and state officials to enforce agrarian rulings. As a result, one federal agrarian engineer complained, Hunucmá's hacendados "didn't pay the slightest attention to . . . the National Agrarian Commission."[12] Even many agrarian officials showed little interest in benefiting Hunucmá's working-class residents, but instead helped hacendados and landowners to evade agrarian rulings or used their offices to favor them. In Ucú, an agrarian official advocated in support of an offer by the powerful Peón family to substitute distant, poor-quality lands for an area of Yaxché located inside the provisional ejidos. The residents reacted with outrage, reportedly lodging a "clamor of protests" outside town hall.[13] One engineer faulted agrarian officials for never conducting precise land surveys in Samahil but merely "giving el pueblo a map made in our office" along with "a few other documents." Since recipients "never knew exactly which were the lands materially affected," the old landowners retained control over ejidal lands. Another engineer blamed officials for Samahil residents' "lack of faith in true agrarianism [agrarismo]." "There is a belief," he wrote, "that nothing will be effective, since the few commissioners and engineers who have set foot in that region have begun a multitude of projects, without resolving anything in benefit of the population." While well-intentioned engineers advocated for "true agrarian work" and a "definitive deslinde" of the ejidos,[14] their efforts were undermined by lackadaisical supervisors, one of whom they criticized for never leaving his office and working with a "laconicism that was beyond the pale."[15]

Even when agrarian officials attempted to carry out deslindes, they often found their efforts stymied by the opposition of working populations. One engineer blamed de la Huerta–era repression and the concurrent suspension of agrarian activities for the distrust of agrarian authorities shown by the residents of Ucú. Experience, he claimed, had taught them to resist performing arduous, unpaid labor for the clearing and measurement of ejidal lands they might never receive.[16] As time passed, resistance only seemed to intensify. In 1928 an agrarian engineer who attempted to carry out a deslinde in Hunucmá suspended his work after residents made an attempt on his life. Three years later another attempted deslinde triggered more violence. A group of sixty men, led by the onetime insurgents Andrés Lizama, Anastasio Canul, and Buenaventura Quintal, marched to the town hall, where Hunucmá's mayor was holed up with resistance league officials and police. The protesters reportedly "shouted subversively against local authorities and the state government," including Governor García and the PSS, and threatened to kill an agrarian engineer and sack stores in town. After some protesters began throwing stones, the besieged men fired a hail of bullets into the crowd, leaving one protester dead and several wounded. Eighteen men were arrested in the aftermath, while others escaped to the woods.[17]

As the dust settled, a state government official arrived on the scene, determined to convince town residents to cooperate in the survey of local wood-lands. Within a few months, a police crackdown on cattle rustling and dis-satisfaction among woodcutters regarding the miserable prices paid by García's charcoal monopoly brought such efforts to naught. Newspaper re-porters claimed that anywhere from one hundred to an improbable one thou-sand "Indians" stormed Hunucmá's town plaza, overwhelmed police and troops, and seized five members of García's Revolutionary Defense force be-fore heading off for the woods. As in the times of Pío Chuc, the men formed into insurgent ranks, reportedly led by a new general and a colonel. In what must have recalled memories of Cacab Dzul, they shot the captives and cut them up with machetes, piling their bodies into a cave north of town.[18]

The governor immediately sent a large force of soldiers and Revolutionary Defense gunmen in pursuit of the rebels. And he put new technology to use, lending his personal airplane to the cause. After a couple of flights the rebels were located: one small group was north of town near San Joaquín, and a few bands were in that venerable western communalist haunt, Kaxek. Declaring that "events in Hunucmá are of no importance, except for the local—overly local—interests of that population," Governor García dismissed the reb-els as "people without any sense" who were "idle in the worst way that one can be idle." At the same time, the governor declared his intention to visit Hunucmá's workers to "learn personally of their problems and needs." A few days later he did so, welcomed by local authorities and speeches pledging to defend the PSS and to realize the "true and noble ideas of the emancipa-tory Revolution, incarnated in the figure of Bartolomé García." The governor then reportedly reasoned with several of the detained rebels and gave orders to "give to each his due: liberty to the innocent and guarantees to honorable and hard-working citizens." Behind the scenes, García promised to improve the remuneration of woodcutters.[19]

Yet these were short-term measures, and in ensuing years labor disputes, political violence, and agrarian discontent continued to dog the region. In 1933, members of a cattle cooperative complained to the national Agrarian Commission that the agrarian question had not been resolved in Hunucmá, leaving them in what they called a "dubious situation." Their request for a deslinde was rebuffed, as was one from a woodcutting cooperative that hoped a survey might facilitate the exploitation of wood and charcoal, which they called the "only patrimony of this pueblo." The director of Yucatán's Agrarian Commission tersely responded that in the past, engineers attempt-ing deslindes in Hunucmá had been attacked, and in the absence of a proper survey no permits would be issued.[20] Such responses left tensions between local populations and the government unabated. At a public meeting of the Feliciano Canul Reyes resistance league in 1934 Basilio Chac—a former insurgent reportedly "distanced, for quite a long time" from Hunucmá's resistance league though reputed to have "great influence" over the membership—voiced "incendiary words" with a "clearly communistic bent." He attacked "not just the state government, but the federal government as well . . . declaring that all governments are bad, and that the only popular solution would be a new revolution." Chac reportedly "recognized his error" when chided by a government official who thought his words threatened to "undermine el pueblo's confidence in state institutions."[21] Tensions in Hunucmá soon boiled over again, however, when workers, enraged at the lack of employment on the fincas and declining purchases of wood by the railroad, rebelled, threatening to kill all who opposed them. Only the arrival of federal forces and the governor's agreement to put the unemployed to work cutting wood and to remove local officials who "occupied themselves in harassing el pueblo" put an end to the rebellion.[22]

In short, ten years after Felipe Carrillo Puerto's dramatic agrarian decrees, the agrarian reform had come to nothing. This was evident to the engineer Vicente Guanche, who toured the pueblos of the region in early 1934. Tetiz's ejidatarios had been awarded a provisonal ejido in January 1925, but in the absence of a deslinde they were unsure of its boundaries and still paid rent to the hacendados for those lands. Similarly, residents of Samahil complained that the boundaries of their ejido were not "well defined" and that the provisional ejido improperly encompassed some small plots rightfully owned by working-class residents.[23] When he moved on to the town of Hunucmá, Guanche learned of the dissatisfaction of the residents with their provisional ejido. Hunucmá's population had grown, making the original grant insufficient; besides, ejidal woodlands had already been largely cut down, diminishing their potential for maize agriculture. A detailed deslinde had never been done, and Hunucmá's ejidal map, like Samahil's, consisted merely of a bricolage of hacienda maps. As a result of "el pueblo's refusal to provide any assistance" to surveys, Guanche concluded, Hunucmá's provisional ejido was not "perfectly delimited," frustrating inhabitants' desires for access to land.[24]

From the early years of the Revolution forward, land surveys had figured centrally in reformers' attempts at repossessing el pueblo of communal resources, even as they incorporated el pueblo into a dependent relationship to the state. By 1934, however, it was the absence of deslindes that had become definitive of the relationship between government and pueblo, with pueblo residents both dispossessed of land and alienated from the government and its agrarian agencies. For so many reasons—from political shifts at the state and national levels, to the incompetence and corruption of agrarian officials, to the evolving complexities of land tenure, to the opposition of pueblo residents—Hunucmá had remained unmapped.

BY THE PRESIDENT'S HAND

In March 1934 General Cárdenas arrived in Yucatán on a campaign visit. As the presidential candidate of the official party, the Partido Nacional Revolucionario (PNR), he declared his intention to restore the greatness and dignity of the descendants of the ancient Maya, principally through the distribution of privately owned henequen land to impoverished villagers. In so doing, Cárdenas not only evoked the legacy of Carrillo Puerto; he also foreshadowed the populist reformism that would become a hallmark of his government and the foundation of an enduring corporatist regime in Mexico. Soon after assuming power, Cárdenas had broken with Calles, advocating for worker rights, land distribution, and other social reforms. At the same time, he launched a project of nationalistic cultural transformation through the expansion of the federal rural school system and of agencies relating to indigenous affairs: what he called a "Plan for the Reincorporation of the Indigenous Classes into Civilization." In Yucatán, Cárdenas charged agrarian and government officials with encouraging the formation of agricultural and ranching cooperatives and with moving toward the definitive expropriation of henequen fields and the establishment of collective henequen ejidos. At the same time, he courted the support of a variety of other groups—cordage, port, and railway workers, women, students, teachers, Communists—in the hope of building a popular coalition to challenge Yucatán's entrenched ruling cliques.[25]

Cárdenas's utopian plans for Yucatán soon foundered. Federal financial assistance was limited, and the few henequen ejidos established in 1935 quickly entered into crisis. There was strong opposition to the ejidos, most notably among indigenous workers. Rural populations generally preferred access to woodlands over henequen fields, and hacienda residents opposed agrarian policies that seemed to privilege town and pueblo residents at their expense. Many ejidal officials and community leaders, moreover, immediately turned the ejidos into opportunities for graft and political gain. Clashes soon erupted between federal troops and local populations; opponents of the Cárdenas reform, from hacendados to peons and from Socialists to

Communists, joined ranks with the anarchosyndicalist General Confederation of Workers (CGT) to block the formation of the ejidos. By 1936, Cárdenas's agrarian project was a shambles.[26]

Early on, Cardenista officials and agrarian engineers perceived Hunucmá—with its blighted haciendas, powerful landowners and strongmen, and seemingly intransigent indigenous population—more as a region of obstacles than of opportunity. The agrarian engineer Enrique Gamboa blamed what he called the "politics of deception" of previous governments for Samahil residents' "indifference and even hostility" to land surveys. He undertook to win over pueblo residents by supplying them with medical and financial assistance to "rescue them from the claws of ruin." In addition, Gamboa delivered a series of historical lectures meant to "provide the people with a synthetic history of our revolution: its origin, causes, and goals; its triumphs and aspirations; with special emphasis on its agrarian accomplishments and the plans of the government for the future."[27]

Other officials were less sanguine. The agrarian engineer Manuel Prieto held an assembly with Hunucmá's workers, listening to their complaints about unemployment and about their difficulties in securing permits for the exploitation of wood and charcoal in ejidal woodlands. When he responded by advising them of the desirability of forming agricultural cooperatives in order to reap the "benefits and promise of the Revolution," workers inquired whether the federal government would be obliged to help them financially if they did so. After Prieto responded negatively, advising workers instead to "help themselves," his disgruntled interlocutors declared, much to his dismay, that in that case they refused to form an organization of any kind. Moving on to Sisal, Prieto found that the inhabitants requested repairs to the main road to Sisal but balked at his proposition that they do the work themselves. "Since they are people of little character," Prieto fumed, "they refused, saying that they wanted the Government to do it for them." What was more, what he referred to as Sisal's "indolent" inhabitants, refused, like those of Hunucmá, to form cattle and agricultural cooperatives. "They say," he wrote, "that 'one shouldn't get involved in such things,' and resign themselves to their lives of eating, fishing, getting drunk, and sleeping, day after day with no thought for the future." To Prieto, Sisal's inhabitants seemed to be mired in a state of "promiscuity, in which parents, children, and animals are all mixed up together, as if they were inhabitants of a desert island far from civilization." Only if they embraced cooperativism might they "awaken from their state of stagnation, and feel that the Revolution finally has come to them."[28]

Any attempts at inculcating such sentiments played against a backdrop of entrenched struggles over land, labor, and political power. In the area of Umán, hacendados joined forces with PSS politicians to detain and imprison Cardenista labor organizers, fire workers who called for wage increases, and block the formation of cooperative stores. At the same time, they encouraged hacienda workers to resist the formation of the ejidos, typically by refusing to assist ejidal surveys.[29] In the town of Hunucmá, some workers appealed to federal officials to end the fiefdom (*cacicazgo*) of hacendados who exploited ejidal woodlands, while others formed a charcoal cooperative named Revolution.[30] But federal forestry officials continued to dismiss Hunucmá's woodcutters and charcoal makers as contrabandists and scofflaws, whose difficulties originated "exclusively in their own ignorance" and refusal to assist in surveys. One exasperated official even suggested that agrarian officials refer Hunucmá to the Department of Indigenous Affairs, whose agents might convince Hunucmá's indigenous population of the urgent necessity of ejidal surveys.[31]

Only the pueblo of Kinchil seemed to offer hope to federal officials, mainly owing to the efforts of the federal teacher Bartolomé Cervera Alcocer. Cervera, a Communist, organized a peasants' union and charcoal-producing cooperative. He encouraged residents to register their complaints against Kinchil's overlords, the Solís clan, both for exploitation that left workers living a "life worse than the lowest animals, in miserable, dark, dirty huts" and for acts of violence he described as a "stupid bacchanal" intended to "drown the aspirations, and liberty, of el pueblo, in blood."[32] Hundreds of pueblo residents seconded Cervera's pleas in a petition of December 1935 denouncing the Solíses for "martyring us ever since the odious Porfirian Dictatorship." Calling themselves the "slaves of this little ranch (pueblo)," the petitioners called for the authorities to bring the Revolution to Kinchil by deposing local officials, in accord with President Cárdenas's "pro-labor stance [*obrerismo*], morality, and justice."[33]

While initially Cervera and pueblo residents focused their complaints on abuses and violence committed by local authorities—notably the killing of the popular local Cardenista Felipa Poot—agrarian issues soon came to the fore as well. In September 1936 Cervera contacted agrarian authorities to demand the expansion and definitive distribution of Kinchil's ejidos to what he called the *campesino* masses. Kinchil's ejidatarios also sent several letters to Cárdenas, requesting the reversal of land losses el pueblo had suffered since the "Porfirian dictatorship."[34] Cervera even named a pueblo orchestra he established Agrarian Sound (*Son Agrarista*), calling it a "diversion for el pueblo, and a basis for the economic emancipation for the masses, removing them from vice, establishing solidarity among the youth, and marshalling the struggle against el pueblo's enemies." It was no wonder that by 1937 President Cárdenas referred to Kinchil as a "revolutionary pueblo" that kept the "flame of socialism burning" in Yucatán.[35]

Throughout the rest of Yucatán, on the other hand, the Cardenista agrarian program had come to a standstill by mid-1937, leaving Cárdenas determined to wrest control over agrarian reform from the state government officials. In early August he visited the state again to announce his "Solución Salvadora": a plan to resolve all pending ejidal petitions by executive fiat. Cárdenas ordered agrarian engineers to finalize 272 ejidos throughout the henequen zone, expropriating all privately held hacienda lands in excess of 150 hectares and incorporating both resident workers and pueblo residents in collective ejidos.[36] By early September, agrarian officials had arrived at decisions regarding the size of the ejidal grants to be definitively awarded to Hunucmá's populations, including resident hacienda workers, who were in some cases incorporated into the ejidal grants of nearby towns and pueblos and in others assigned to ejidos specially created for them. Based on these findings, Cárdenas issued Resoluciones Presidenciales: detailed, lengthy documents that set out the total amount of land to be assigned as ejidos, the amount to be taken from each hacienda, and measures relating to the use and conservation of ejidal resources.

After Cárdenas signed the Resolución for the town of Hunucmá on 16 September 1937, a group composed of three agrarian engineers, Hunucmá's mayor, and twelve officials of the town's ejido formed to carry out the deslinde. They walked along the borders of the ejido, simultaneously drafting an acta de deslinde that traced their route in writing. Once it was finished, an acta de posesión sealed the process, awarding "el pueblo de Hunucmá" formal possession of its definitive ejido. Similar events transpired in all of the towns and pueblos of the district and on its haciendas. The deslindes, however, had implications far beyond land tenure. As officials walked the bounds of what would become the ejido, they also took part in the deslinde of their own roles and powers and of the territorial and political limits of those powers. Beyond their technical role, the agrarian engineers stood for the power and prerogatives of the national government, specifically of the president. Thus, the deslindes were acts that illuminated the border between federal and local powers, as both collaborated in leveling claims to the land in the name of el pueblo.

Finally, the deslinde set the stage for federal officials to expand the second major front of the Cardenista crusade in Yucatán: education. Inspectors toured the pueblos and haciendas, conducting censuses of the school-age population and taking careful note of literacy rates and the supposed race of working populations (whom different inspectors classified variously as Maya, indigenous, "aboriginal," or mestizo). By early 1938 schools had opened their doors on haciendas throughout the region, and educational officials held public assemblies in which they exhorted workers, often hacienda residents, to support the schools in the name of el pueblo. "All of us," Hacienda Tedzidz's representatives declared in enthusiastic response, "form a humble and hard-working pueblo, raising with pride its red banner of equality, and defending it, heroically, as if we were one man." The schools, in their view, would fulfill Mexico's "struggles for the complete liberation of campesinos and workers" and build support for agrarian reform and inculcate the principles of cooperativism to create a new society in which producers and consumers would collaborate as "class brothers, rather than irreconcilable enemies."[37] Teachers declared their intention to introduce children to what they termed revolutionary literature to "arrest the nefarious influence of bourgeois rituals, with their Mystified and Reactionary Ideology"; history classes would give children an "orientation regarding the men of the Revolution, who in prior epochs were the ones to show the way to the benefits that their parents are now receiving" and explain "who General Cárdenas is, and what he has done for el pueblo in Mexico."[38]

Here, the deslindes of 1937 found their counterpoint, in another kind of deslinde, one that demarcated appropriate routes of political conduct and sentiment, set off the path of Revolution from that of reaction, and put history to use in etching the features of the new citizen and new state that might emerge in Hunucmá's schools. Like the acta de deslinde of 1937, the public declarations of Hunucmá's teachers and ejidal assemblies traced points of connection between Mexico's corporatist state and el pueblo, demonstrating the power of the president's hand not only to designate and distinguish the lay of the land and the functions and powers of local officials, but also to survey el pueblo's mind and spirit. All that remained was for the engineers to work out the finer points of the survey and draw up final maps of the ejidos. All that remained for Hunucmá's future citizenry was to take those maps as guides not only through space but through time, with the contours of an emancipated future emerging along the routes envisioned by President Cárdenas and sketched by his hand.

LORDS OF ALL THEY DID NOT SURVEY

The ceremonious *deslindes*, however, appeared to be Cardenismo's last gasp in Yucatán. The fledgling ejidos entered into difficulties, given the haphazard distribution of henequen fields of varying ages and productivity, the lack of administrative expertise, the resistance of hacendados who controlled processing equipment, and insufficient federal financial support. Furthermore, impending presidential elections left Cárdenas increasingly concerned with the victory of his party's candidate and less willing to expend political capital on a costly agrarian experiment.[39] The solution proposed by Governor Canto Echeverría and accepted by Cárdenas was to transfer the financing and administration of Yucatán's ejidos from the federal to the state government, under a statewide cooperative called Henequeneros de Yucatán. The collectives would be organized into a single Great Ejido (Gran Ejido), which Canto claimed would combine the collectivist spirit of ancient Mayan working practices with centralized management by Yucatecan engineers. Through the plan, many of the ejidos were restored to operation, largely by securing the compliance of hacendados through payment of large fees for use of their processing machinery (52 percent of the ejidal fiber they processed). To critics, however, the measures inaugurated a system of so-called neopeonage, in which ejidatarios were paid poverty wages and hacendados garnered handsome profits and from which officials of the government and of Henequeneros de Yucatán skimmed off vast amounts of wealth through graft.[40]

Such developments did not go unprotested. In 1939 the Ejidal Defense Committee (CDE) mobilized workers in Hunucmá and elsewhere in demand of wage increases and in protest against the Great Ejido as a system that, in their view, subjugated the true owners of the ejidos to those who were technically their employees (that is, agrarian engineers and bank officials). In response, Yucatán's governor enlisted police and local strongmen in the repression of the movement. CDE members in Samahil, for instance, suffered arson attacks, threats, beatings, and three assassinations, leading many to flee with their families to Mérida by September 1940. Their complaint to Cárdenas—against "authorities who sully the revolutionary ideology that has cost so much workers' blood"—went unattended.[41]

Other residents of the region opposed the ejidos as proponents of "synarchism," a Catholic movement hostile to the PNR that denounced class conflict and socialism in favor of a system in which society would be governed by "legitimate authority, derived from the free democratic activity of el pueblo."

In May 1940, according to one hostile account, as many as eighty synarchists from Tetiz and Hunucmá stormed an ejidal assembly in Kinchil, demanding that the haciendas be returned to the old owners and, as stated by one witness, "insulting the state government, the President of the Republic, and local authorities." In the ensuing fight, Andrés Valencia, a prominent Maya-speaking synarchist known for his work in indigenous populations throughout Yucatán, was killed. Afterward, Kinchil's ejidatarios denounced the synarchists as "foreign elements that came here to cause disorder, to stir us up and divide us" and as "bad elements that came to violate the sovereignty and tranquility of a hard-working pueblo."[42]

Despite such dramatic acts of resistance, most workers eventually came to terms with the new system. Ejidal authorities mediated between indigenous working populations and the government, translating circulars and decrees into Maya and explaining them at ejidal assemblies. They became advocates for their constituents, drafting petitions for ejidal expansion, submitting requests for the admission of workers to the ejidal rolls, and encouraging ejidatarios to occupy lands of abandoned fincas. They lodged complaints with agrarian authorities over illegal wood- or henequen-cutting by hacendados and over the exploitation of ejidal woodlands by residents of neighboring pueblos. They requested the punishment of unruly ejidatarios and occasionally accused agrarian officials of making mistakes and committing misdeeds. They applied to the Agrarian Bank for loans and assistance and relayed requests for radios, public lighting, work tools, cheap maize, and even baseballs, bats, and mitts for ejidal teams.[43]

Unlike officials of the indigenous republics and insurgents of the revolutionary years, ejidal officials no longer made reference to histories of communal possession and dispossession in staking their claims to land. Rather, they took a new point of origin and source of historical legitimacy: Cárdenas's Resoluciones Presidenciales of 1937 and the actas de deslinde. Whereas their predecessors had struck out against the hacienda system, aiming at the repossession of communal woodlands, now Hunucmá's ejidos were focused on the production of henequen. Pueblo residents were thus brought more firmly than ever before under the relations of exploitation characteristic of henequen production, albeit under the tutelage of a different master. Bureaucratic applications for conclusive deslindes and their associated maps replaced the open-ended struggle of earlier years; ejidatarios still invoked the name of el pueblo in communications with government officials but now did so in a dependent, petitionary mode.[44]

In the wake of the withdrawal of the federal government from the ejidal sector, however, neither deslindes nor maps were forthcoming. Ejidatarios and their leaders were left in the position of being unable to demonstrate the correspondence between particular lands and the executive fiat that had marked them out as ejidos. Decades-old conflicts with landowners festered without resolution in the 1940s and 1950s, as agrarian engineers complained that the incompleteness of ejidal files and the lack of precise deslindes made the Resoluciones impossible to fulfill.[45] By the 1950s, moreover, the henequen sector had entered a deep crisis because of pervasive corruption and falling demand and prices after the end of the Second World War. In 1954, with the industry near the point of collapse, President Adolfo Ruíz Cortines ordered the dissolution of Henequeneros de Yucatán, mandating the return of the henequen ejidos to the control of the federal government. From now on, funds would be directed not to state officials or ejidal leaders, but to local ejidal credit societies and smaller so-called "solidarity groups" that would be subject to the supervision of officials called checkers. Workers were enjoined to become more productive by behaving as owners of the henequen fields rather than as peons or wage laborers. By 1964 a new phase began when the government nationalized the state's cordage mills, creating a new state-owned cordage company, Cordemex, to control fiber production and commercialization.

In the Hunucmá region, these developments spurred the expansion of the ejidal rolls. In groups of a dozen or more, ejidatarios in all the pueblos of the region submitted formal requests to ejidal assemblies and officials for access to woodlands and credits for agriculture, apiculture, and ranching. In arrangements brokered by agrarian officials—sometimes consensual, sometimes conflicted—ejidatarios split into multiple solidarity groups, dividing up lands and henequen fields among their constituents.[46] In communications with government officials, Hunucmá's ejidatarios, most of them educated from childhood in federal schools established in the Cárdenas years, cited neither their historic possession of the woodlands of el común nor their long history of struggle and insurgency to bolster their claims. Rather, they appealed to laws that, in the words of one group of petitioners, "emanated from the glorious Mexican Social Revolution," and to party leaders like President Adolfo López Mateos, whom they saluted as a "paladin" whose "hands brought the benefits of the Revolution to the economy of our Beloved State." They declared their intention to "entrust our future destinies to your generous hands" and concluded with the salutation, "The peasantry [campesinado] of Hunucmá salutes you affectionately, with its heart in its hand."[47] Although the ejidatarios pled their cause as el pueblo, typically they posed their claims as matters of general interest, citing the benefits their lands and labor might yield for the "economy of our beloved state" or for the growth of "our national economy" or of "our patria."[48]

Finally, the hand of Cárdenas seemed to draw nigh. Copies of the Resoluciones Presidenciales and actas de deslinde were typed up and carried through the Hunucmá region by engineers, who examined them as they mapped and marked areas of land for new henequen fields. They consulted the records of the walks of 1937, when they were called on to locate ejidal lands or to adjudicate disputes between pueblos like Kinchil and Tetiz.[49] In 1956, Hunucmá's ejidal assembly demanded a definitive deslinde of the 1937 ejido, hoping to "learn, in a legal and official way, where it extends." When their requests went unanswered they protested that lands that rightly belonged to Hunucmá were still held by hacendados and reiterated their demand for a new deslinde so that they might "know the exact borders . . . of Hunucmá's ejido."[50] Ejidal leaders in Tetiz drafted similar petitions for deslindes and an ejidal map, hoping to "alleviate the penury in which the Ejidatarios live"; when engineers visited, however, most ejidatarios refused to cooperate, leading the president of Tetiz's ejido to convene new assemblies in hopes of "sounding out [ejidatarios'] point of view."[51]

Whatever that point of view, it was surely shaped by the deepening crisis. The expansion of Yucatán's ejidal rolls—from forty-five thousand in 1955 to fifty-nine thousand by 1965 to seventy-four thousand by 1970—fostered a labor surplus. As a result, most ejidatarios were limited to two or three days of work per week. And, moreover, measures ostensibly meant to free ejidatarios from middlemen had left them subject to new masters: Agrarian Bank officials who took over all decision making and brought nepotism and graft to the ground level. Such corruption and the mounting frustration of henequen workers tended to lead to the neglect of the henequen fields, contributing to declining productivity and fiber quality. Fiber production, which reached its height in 1961, declined steadily thereafter; federal subsidies, that is, unrecovered credit outlays, increased just as steadily, rising from 28 percent in 1956 to 43 percent by 1964. For leaders of the official party, now called the Partido Revolucionario Institucional (PRI), and of the state-controlled national peasant union, the Confederación Nacional Campesina (CNC), such money was well spent, facilitating the incorporation of henequen workers into the official party.[52]

By the late 1950s, some of Hunucmá's ejidatarios began to mobilize in protest. A group that identified itself as that town's "authentic working ejidatarios" petitioned Yucatán's governor, denouncing the theft of henequen seedlings by an Agrarian Bank supervisor, the overcutting of henequen plants, the theft of communal funds, and a series of other abuses committed by the ejido's president to the detriment, in their view, of "Society and the General Economy of the State." Local officials and state police responded to the complaints by detaining and beating those who had made them. "El pueblo, in its entirety," a sympathetic local schoolteacher wrote, called on President López Mateos to order the imprisonment of the local functionaries involved.[53] No such measures were taken, and by 1961 a group identifying itself as the "authentic ejidatarios" of Hunucmá protested the takeover of the ejido by a group of shoemakers, masons, and local merchants—men who were "almost in their entirety outsiders to the ejido" but used it for political gain. For their part, ejidatarios of Ucú denounced the "vandals who [were] destroying [our ejido], without consideration for the fact that it represents the PATRIMONY of el pueblo." The only way to protect some ejidal henequen fields from negligence and corruption, they argued, was to divide the ejido in two, allowing the petitioners, in their words, to "save our revolution through our honest work."[54]

Cárdenas's as-yet-unfulfilled Resoluciones seemed to some to offer a way out of such conflicts. In March 1966 the mayor of Hunucmá joined forces with officials of the ejido, the resistance league, and the CNC to convoke a mass meeting of "el Pueblo" in the town square. There, the men delivered a series of speeches on the desirability of carrying out a new deslinde to determine the exact location of Hunucmá's ejido. Hunucmá's ejidal president argued that a deslinde would allow for more intense agricultural development, thus benefiting workers. A vote was called, reportedly resulting in unanimous acclaim for the idea. Similar requests were filed in Kinchil and Tetiz, the president of Tetiz's ejido calling a deslinde the only way to avoid "spillage of blood" over persistent boundary conflicts with neighboring ejidos.[55]

Such plans foundered yet again. With the henequen economy deteriorating, federal officials attempted redressive measures, targeting not bloat and corruption in the henequen bureaucracy but the ejidatarios themselves. In 1966 the Agrarian Bank broke with precedents for uniform wage rates by linking pay to productivity. Ejidatarios mounted protests in Mérida, denouncing bank functionaries for corruption and demanding pay increases, debt forgiveness, and the revocation of the incentive scheme. The arrest of the movement's organizers, including the rising student leader Víctor

Cervera Pacheco, only spurred larger demonstrations. Finally, the bank and the government relented: the incentives were revoked, pay was increased, and restrictions on ejidal membership were loosened for the children of ejidatarios.[56]

In this effervescent political climate, agrarian engineers sent to survey Hunucmá's ejido found their efforts frustrated from the moment they began, in April 1967, until the moment they gave up trying, in August. The population had grown far beyond the territorial limits set in 1937, and occupants of far-flung sites wanted their plots and houses recognized and incorporated within it, so as to be immune from expropriation. When the engineers refused, the residents withdrew their assistance from clearing and surveying work. Other residents, believing they would be billed for the surveying work, despite the engineers' strenuous arguments to the contrary, refused to cooperate as well. Even those who agreed to help disappeared without warning or failed to complete the tasks they were assigned. One engineer faulted residents for an "absolute lack of cooperation"; another wrote that "everybody knows that the population of Hunucmá is one of the most difficult ones, since the campesinos there are extremely divided"; yet another blamed the broader ejidal movement. Whatever the causes of resistance, its consequences were evident. After four months of work the chief engineer suspended the deslinde, which he called extremely unproductive.[57] Perhaps this was why agrarian officials declined a deslinde request from Kinchil the next month, alleging that every time they had sent engineers, "you people have refused to provide help."[58]

Thirty years after the actas de deslinde of 1937 had traced out a new landscape of power, Yucatán's collective henequen ejidos had become something quite different from what President Cárdenas had envisioned. A system founded in a determination to survey and map el pueblo and its lands seemed to have transformed into its opposite—one in which the lack of survey had become a governing principle. This deferral was a sign not of power's failure, but of the mode of its conflicted exercise, as government and el pueblo contended for mastery of all they could not, or would not, survey.

LIBERALIZING CÁRDENAS

In January 1975 the engineer Ermilo Guëmes Lara received orders from his superiors at the Secretariat of Agrarian Reform to carry out a general deslinde of Tetiz's ejido and to draft a map of the ejido based on Cárdenas's Resolución Presidencial. Guëmes sought out pueblo residents to assist him, applying for one thousand days' worth of rations and wages to compensate them. Month after month, however, the engineer confronted the resistance of pueblo residents, who, faced with repeated difficulties securing the promised compensation, worked for him by fits and starts, requiring him to interrupt his labors frequently to engage in what he called the "work of persuasion."[59]

Then there was the land. Almost forty years had passed since Cárdenas's engineers had placed landmarks to mark their acta de deslinde, and brush and trees had grown thickly over them. Local agriculturalists had carried off many stone markers for use in marking their milpas or in constructing charcoal-burning pits. This lent an improvisatory character to Guëmes's work, as he planted new landmarks where he thought the old ones might have stood. Residents of Hacienda Nohuayum interrupted the survey to correct a boundary, and woodcutters who considered certain areas of the ejidos to be national lands and exploited them on that basis intervened even more directly, by opening false breaches in order to mislead and confuse the engineer and his assistants. By November the engineer reported that the deslinde was almost complete, but he made no final report, leaving it unclear whether he had completed the survey or, by reviving some of its indeterminate marks, had only reinscribed the earlier deslinde a bit more deeply into the land.[60]

In the 1970s agrarian engineers remained active in the Hunucmá region despite the failed general deslindes of previous years. Partial deslindes were conducted as government officials attempted to mediate contending claims to the land, whether between ejidatarios and private landowners or between ejidos of neighboring pueblos like Tetiz and Kinchil, whose ranchers, woodcutters, and agriculturalists habitually, in official parlance, "invaded" the ejidal lands of their neighbors. Such situations became more frequent with population growth and the expansion of both henequen cultivation and ranching—herds of fifty head or more—in ejidal lands.[61] Surely the most intractable conflict was a decades-long dispute between Tetiz and Kinchil over an area of land known as Los Huanales, so named because of the presence of palm groves. Agrarian officials intervened frequently in the dispute, holding meetings to respond to complaints and confiscating illegally cut wood and huano. Throughout their work, the engineers consulted the acta de deslinde from 1937 as they attempted to settle rival claims. The acta seemed to offer, in one official's words, the prospect of "knowing reality" and thus of bringing the invisible hand of Cárdenas to bear in settling festering conflicts.[62]

The continuance of such conflicts despite their presumed settlement encouraged agrarian authorities to again attempt conclusive general deslindes aimed at the production of detailed maps. Hunucmá was first. Engineers worked over the course of much of 1971, with their ration request—1,920 days of rations—indicating the extent of local collaboration they anticipated. Tetiz came a few years later as well as Kinchil, whose inhabitants had demanded a copy of what engineers called the "nonexistent map of 1937" in the course of a conflict with ejidatarios of Tedzidz.[63] Yet those attempted deslindes met the same fate as the earlier ones: residents refused to assist survey teams, or, if they did help, refused to participate in areas where they felt the deslinde might be prejudicial to their interests; woodcutters removed or destroyed landmarks; work brigades never appeared or petered away gradually, absenteeism bleeding time and resources. Eventually the engineers gave up, leaving it to their successors to execute the Resolución Presidencial.[64]

By the mid-1970s the prospects and purpose of such deslindes were called into question by the henequen sector's ever-deepening crisis. Fiber prices and demand continued to decline in international markets, largely owing to the competition of synthetic fibers. The henequen economy also eroded from within, productivity and fiber production continuing their steady decline even as state subsidies continued to increase. In the mid-1970s these trends coincided with a national economic and political crisis. Following the brutal repression of several opposition movements in the late 1960s, Presidents Luis Echeverría (1970–76) and José López Portillo (1976–82), seeking to mitigate continued unrest, dramatically expanded social aid and public spending. Soon, however, speculation by international finance capitalists, combined with increasingly volatile fiscal conditions in Mexico, triggered widespread capital flight. The government was forced to devalue the peso by 58 percent in 1976, a measure that stabilized capital markets but triggered skyrocketing inflation.[65]

Amid this financial, political, and social crisis, Mexico's national government undertook a shift toward neoliberal policies. In return for a package of International Monetary Fund loans, the Mexican government pledged to cut public spending and institute austerity measures. Yucatán's state-run henequen industry became an ideal target for such reform. In a visit to the state in 1977, President López Portillo announced a new set of goals for the industry, focusing on reducing federal subsidies and making fiber production and commercialization more efficient. In translating the president's directives into policy, the Agrarian Bank proposed to increase the industry's profitability through the purge of about thirty thousand of the eighty-one thousand people on ejidal rolls. Agents of the CNC traveled the henequen zone on a campaign of what they called "consciousness-raising" intended to convince workers of the desirability of the new reforms. Notwithstanding such efforts, ejidatarios mounted a series of protests, marches, and demonstrations in Mérida, some targeting even the CNC, which previously had controlled such actions. The protesters eventually won an increase in pay to help offset the devaluation and the restoration of around twenty thousand purged ejidatarios. Such successes, however, were qualified; the Agrarian Bank still reaped substantial savings and workers either were removed from the ejidal system or were left in a more precarious position within it.

While shortly thereafter the discovery of oil reserves in Mexico—what became known as the Mexican miracle—briefly appeared to resolve the country's economic problems, a fall in oil prices in 1981 brought the boom to an abrupt end. As López Portillo concluded his term as president, he suspended payments on Mexico's foreign debt and ordered another devaluation of the peso. His successor, President Miguel de la Madrid (1982–88), embraced a thoroughgoing platform of reforms aimed at reestablishing stability through the radical reduction of deficits and public spending. In the agricultural sector, such measures meant opening domestic markets to international competition, directing government expenditures away from programs that provided price supports and subsidies, and dismantling or privatizing large public sector companies like Cordemex.

The national crisis and the government's neoliberal response to it could not have come at a worse time for Yucatán's henequen industry. Fiber prices on the international market had continued to decline, leading many ejidatarios as well as increasingly indifferent managers to forgo the costs and effort associated with planting new fields. As fields aged, their productivity declined and the costs of production increased. On top of that, the surface area planted in henequen declined drastically, by 60 percent, over the course of the 1980s. By the late 1980s, fiber production fell so far that Cordemex began importing fiber from Brazil in order to meet the company's commitments to its international buyers. Ejidatarios' real wages continued declining, and there were more purges of ejidal rolls as well as protests in response. In 1984 the federal and state governments (the latter under the interim governorship of the former student and Yucatecan CNC leader Cervera Pacheco) began to push a new "reorganization" program, ostensibly as an attempt to rescue Yucatán's henequen ejidos. That plan, however, merely extended the logic of the earlier reform, by reducing government investment in the henequen sector, promoting market-based incentives, restricting credits to the ejidatarios, and redirecting state resources out of henequen into the growing maquiladora (duty-free factories owned by foreign transnational companies) and tourism sectors. Such measures were couched in a neoliberal language of individual responsibility. According to Cervera Pacheco, the policies were aimed at fostering a new relationship between the state and the ejidos, one based on the "effort, equity and responsibility of the ejidatarios."[66]

The measures yielded results satisfactory neither to neoliberal reformers nor to Yucatán's ejidatarios, paving the way for more drastic reforms with the advent to the presidency of President Carlos Salinas de Gortari (1988–94), in concert with a like-minded government in Yucatán led by Governor Víctor Manzanilla Schaffer (1988–92). Salinas, assisted by Víctor Cervera, now his appointee as head of the national Secretariat of Agrarian Reform, embarked on an ambitious program of what was called structural adjustment, focused on trade liberalization, the privatization of public sector businesses, and economic deregulation. Salinas identified Mexico's ejido as the source of many of the country's economic problems, characterizing it as an unproductive and antiquated institution that stifled individual initiative through excessive government involvement. The way forward, he announced, was through the reduction of state involvement and subsidies in the agricultural sector, the opening of the ejidal sector to private capital, and the revocation of revolutionary-era restrictions on the use and sale of ejidal lands. At the same time, in 1988 Salinas established a new program, called the National Solidarity Program (PRONASOL), through which he proposed to improve living conditions and create employment through the distribution of public financing to local projects and public works. Salinas described the program, which critics perceived as an attempt to contain growing domestic discontent and political opposition, as a "new State–pueblo relationship." In the eyes of neoliberal reformers like Salinas, the relationship between pueblo and gobierno no longer would be defined by the communal possession of land or other resources. Rather, it would be predicated upon individual private appropriation of such resources, supported by acts of state monetary largesse undertaken in el pueblo's name.[67]

In tandem with national reforms, the Yucatecan state government moved to eliminate state involvement in the henequen industry and in the ejidos, announcing plans for the phased shutdown of henequen-processing plants and the privatization of Cordemex, which stopped operations in April 1991 and was then sold off to private investors. Government credits to ejidatarios were to be phased out, and most remaining ejidatarios were to be, in one official's words, "liberalized": purged from the ejidal rolls. Central to the new policy was the breakup of the henequen ejidos into two-hectare parcels, to be assigned to individual ejidatarios who would cultivate them on the basis of their own resources rather than government subsidies. In 1990 an agrarian reform official declared that "the future of the ejido is individualization . . . since it is already clear that collective agriculture doesn't work." It was imagined the ejidatarios might work more productively as individuals drawing on their own resources to engage in citriculture, ranching, or pig raising. "Individualization" was doomed from the start, however, since the average family needed six hectares of land to subsist; most received plots of one-half hectare or less. Moreover, such plots were of widely varying age and quality, and the recipients generally lacked access to the resources necessary to replant or maintain them. As a result, most were forced to take short-term profits, at the expense of long-term productivity, by overcutting the existing henequen plants. Officials touted higher production figures in 1990 as evidence of the beginnings of henequen's recovery, but that increase was really a symptom of the fields' destruction and a harbinger of henequen's demise.[68]

Developments in Yucatán fit well with the legal reform of the ejido at the national level, which was the centerpiece of Salinas's plans. The reform of Article 27 of the Mexican Constitution in February 1992 ended the distribution of land, revoked the inalienable character of ejidal lands and resources, established the basis of ejidatarios' claims to those lands as individual rather than communal in nature, and transformed the ejidos into civil associations on a legal par with other civil and commercial organizations. In Yucatán, the measure afforded a retroactive legal framework for the policy of individualization, which could now proceed unimpeded. On 6 May 1992 the state government, now under the leadership of Governor Dulce María Sauri, formally dismissed all of Yucatán's remaining ejidatarios, subject to compensation. In the same month, the government issued a Program of Regional Development announcing a complete withdrawal of the state from any involvement in henequen agriculture.

In the Hunucmá region, such measures merely confirmed the effects of two decades of crisis. A few residents expanded their herds of cattle, raised pigs, or profited from commerce, while many more were pauperized. Most families relied on collaborative strategies for survival. Older males continued harvesting henequen and taking part in milpa agriculture—itself in crisis owing to the elimination of price supports for maize—and older females remained involved in household work, artisanship, and petty commerce. Most young males, however, left the agricultural sector, finding wage labor

Cattle grazing at Hacienda Nohuayum, near Tetiz, 1995. Photo by Paul Eiss.

in large-scale commercial chicken and pig raising. Other young men and women migrated—to Mérida, Cancún, Seattle, Los Angeles—in search of work.[69]

It was in this context that the Secretariat of Agrarian Reform, in September 1990, ordered the execution of Cárdenas's will. Engineers returned to Hunucmá bearing copies of the Resolución. Unlike their predecessors, they made short work of the deslindes, eschewing the arduous work of searching woodlands and fields for landmarks. Instead, they visually checked the large polygons traced out in the original acta de deslinde and confirmed that the areas of land traced by those walks conformed, approximately, to the total acreage of land Cárdenas had granted. Then they posted signs convoking ejidatarios to a mass meeting. When a majority failed to attend that meeting, precluding a quorum, they issued a second convocation announcing that that meeting would have legal force regardless of how many people attended.[70]

At that meeting, held on 12 November and attended, signatures suggest, by some thirty residents, the engineer in charge announced that the deslinde had been completed. He went on to propose that since a map of the ejido did not exist, the deslinde of 1937, with slight corrections, would be used to elaborate such an ejidal map, in accord with Cárdenas's Resolución Presidencial. The president of Hunucmá's ejido then spoke: he recognized the "measurements that have always been recognized as the boundaries of our ejido," confirmed "our agreement to those boundaries," and requested the execution of the Resolución as an action of "vital importance to our ejido." Representatives of the ejidos of neighboring ex-haciendas affixed their seals and signatures to a new acta. Shortly thereafter, agrarian engineers—fifty-three years after their predecessors had created the original acta de deslinde—at last drew up a large, definitive map of Hunucmá's ejido.

From 1990 through 1992 similar deslindes, meetings, formulaic statements of approval, and requests for execution took place in other towns and pueblos of the region, and the abbreviated deslindes went forward despite the refusal of some residents to ratify them. Thus the Resoluciones were reinscribed, for the last time, on the landscape and, for the first time, in the form of definitive heliographic maps.[71] Now it was the existence and presence of those maps, rather than their absence, that would define what Salinas had called the "new State–pueblo relationship." In some sense, the deslindes and maps of the early 1990s seemed to have fulfilled the promise of Cárdenas's Resoluciones Presidenciales in that they ended half a century of struggles over the ejidos and of failed surveys. Yet the definitive execution of the deceased president's will came at the very moment that his legacy and that of the Revolution were being systematically dismantled. Ironically, the actas de deslinde of 1937 now served not as a means of collective and communal repossession of the ejidos, but as the means to their privatization by landowners, cattle ranchers, maquiladoras, and industrial-scale chicken- and pig-raising companies. So long absent, the president's hand had returned, but it was a dead hand. Its gestures now inaugurated neither a new era of repossession, nor even one of collective dispossession. That dead hand now traced the contours of a world in which el pueblo, so long defined by communal territorial dispossession, seemed to be literally displaced.

Old Guillermo Chuc, whose father fought alongside Feliciano Canul Reyes in the liberation war, told his own story about the events of 1937, one that differed from those rendered by agrarian engineers. Though Cárdenas, he recalled, had ordered the hacendados to give up their lands for the creation of the ejido, they refused to do so. So Hunucmá's workers organized armed brigades, led by old insurgents and their families, to seize the lands themselves. Anastacio Canul led a group that seized control of the woodlands of Texán, until then controlled by the powerful and arrogant Palomeque clan. Nazario Chablé and his five sons led another group to occupy Tacubaya, where Canul Reyes had once had his base; Andrés Lizama, Benjamín Chay, and Feliciano

Ventura led another group, which occupied the woodlands of Chac, Ulilá, Chunhuás, and Chunchén. This was how the land that would become the ejido was retaken.[72]

For old-time insurgents and their descendants it was these acts of occupation, not the actas de deslinde, that created the ejidos. In many respects, Chuc's account could not differ more from those of Cárdenas's engineers. Chuc's version located the ejidos' origins in acts of armed force rather than in executive decrees or the scribblings of topographers. Cárdenas's Resolución was intended as a zero-point of history, one that would make the president's will the origin of the ejido and hence might make the lands' many pasts irrelevant. The story recounted by Chuc, however, suggests that for former insurgents the occupation of those woodlands was not so much the point of origin as the coda of a much longer history. In forming brigades to take the haciendas, they recalled and reenacted insurgent struggles from the nineteenth century forward, an association further strengthened by the placement of old insurgent leaders and their families at the head of each brigade. By occupying not the henequen fields that would be the focus of the new collective ejidos, but the woodlands of those haciendas, they signaled the centrality, for them, of the historic struggles over Hunucmá's forests. This was not so much a new beginning, as projected by the actas, as an ending.

Yet in other ways the two versions of 1937 may not have been so different. Taken together, the actas and the land occupations signaled the end of warfare in Hunucmá and the decisive incorporation of Hunucmá's rebellious communalists and of their vision of el pueblo within the institutional forms of the postrevolutionary state. In this, the occupations might also have been a symbolic laying down of arms, as the legal framework of the collective ejido and agrarian bureaucracy came to replace organized insurgent violence, and thus surveys and maps came to replace the expansive liberation that had been the horizon of communalist mobilizations in Hunucmá for a century or more. It is possible even that these two "documents"—the acta of 1937 and the story of the occupation of the haciendas—are two refractions of the same event, one in which brigades were formed to accompany the agrarian engineers as they did the deslinde, or preparatory to the actas de posesión that formally announced the creation of the ejidos.

For contemporary residents outside of some older men and women, however, neither account of 1937 has much purchase. A few men, it is true, are still involved in making milpa and cutting henequen in ejidal lands. When conflicts arise with private landowners or with neighboring ejidos—or, in recent years, with the state government, as it seeks to expropriate lands for sale to real estate developers and for the expansion of Mérida's airport and water facilities—they do lay claim to them as lands of el pueblo. When some ejidatarios from Tetiz learned that I was doing research in the archives of the Secretariat of Land Reform, some even appealed to the possibility that the ejidal map, if located and consulted, might resolve such conflicts in their favor. Most, however, continued to express skepticism regarding the accuracy of the maps and the impartiality of the agrarian officials who mediate such disputes. Indeed, for most younger residents, who now make their living working as wage laborers in local maquiladoras or in stints of labor in distant cities in Mexico and abroad, such conflicts over land and the long histories of which they are part have little relevance. It is not that the land is unimportant; it is that for most contemporary pueblo inhabitants the land and its many histories no longer play as significant a role in conceptions of el pueblo: neither as a communal possession, nor as something of which el pueblo has been dispossessed and might someday repossess. In this sense Cárdenas's Resolución Presidencial did what the president intended, but not in the way he intended. It relegated the history that preceded it to the shadows but seems to have replaced it, in the end, with nothing.

The hunt that day, in the scrubby woods near ex-Hacienda Nohuayum, was luckless. There was nary a glimpse of deer or peccary, and so eventually Bull and Bug, the two young men I had accompanied, gave up. We started back, noisily joking in Maya about the movie Highlander, which had been on television the night before. Suddenly, Bull stopped and pointed into the brush, asking if I wanted to see a mul, or mound, nearby. They waited while I found my way to the ancient Mayan structure, clambering over the stones and threading my way up through bushes and small trees. At the top, I saw a large hole—a sure sign of looters—and made my way over to take a look inside. Before I could do so, however, I heard a low, sonorous, humming sound; to my ears, it sounded like a large, buzzing swarm of bees. I immediately abandoned my tour, turning and stumbling down the mound toward my companions. When I mentioned the noise, they nodded matter of factly but dismissed my suspicions of bees. "That's just the way that mul is," Bull said; "Yan u yik' ti,'" it has its own wind. They explained: the ik'—wind, spirit, breath—that inhabited that place was its guardian, watching over the mound and afflicting all who did not respect it.

Nohuayum's mul stands on land that has been inscribed with the marks of multiple possessions, from the ancient claims of kah and común, to the regime of private ownership instituted by the hacendados and the Porfirian regime, to the collective ejido system enacted through agrarian reform in the 1930s. Now, with the ejido in decline and amid a new round of reforms under neoliberal auspices, the land is exposed to yet another regime, one that raises the prospect of its transformation back into private property, as a commodity to be bought and sold. The mound bears the traces of all these regimes and their histories. Through it all, the ik' has remained, as a fleeting memory of those histories but also as a reminder and a warning: that our possession will be neither the first, nor the last.

PART THREE

RECOGNITION

REFUGIO

Amasado con lágrimas,
suavizado con sonrisas,
hilvané la pétrea constelación
de mis muros amigos.
. . .
Ignoro cuántas estrellas
ocultan sus noches;
no sé cuántos soles
sus tibios amaneceres,
pero si buscas reposo a tu
    cansancio . . . ,

ven a este pueblo, caminante,
y acepta el fraternal abrazo
de rocas y estrellas consteladas
que serán la dulce prisión
de tus lágrimas y pesares.

REFUGE

Covered in tears,
Softened with smiles,
I built the stony constellation
Of my friendly walls.
. . .
I know not how many stars
Are hidden in your nights;
I know not how many suns
Are in your cool dawns,
But if you search for rest for your
    weariness . . . ,

Come to this pueblo, wayfarer,
And accept the fraternal embrace
Of constellations of rocks and stars
That will be the sweet prison
Of your tears and afflictions.

—ANACLETO CETINA AGUILAR,
Cahtal-K'ay: Canto a Mi Pueblo, 1983

CHAPTER SEVEN

THE WAR OF THE EGGS

Tragedy, Redemption, and the Carnivalesque

IT WAS A BITTER ENDING to a long struggle. For five months, beginning in January 1990, the workers of the Fernández avicultural farms in Hunucmá and Tetiz had fought to form a union independent of what they called a phantom union established at the owner's request by the Confederación de Trabajadores de México (CTM). Women and men from the pueblo of Tetiz stood alongside the strikers, providing food and support, barricading roads, and even battling strikebreakers and state police. Facing imprisonment and beatings of the leaders and advisors of their union, severe ultimatums from the farm owner, Jorge Fernández, and the governor, Víctor Manzanilla Schaffer, and warnings of imminent repression by federal forces, the independent union finally admitted defeat. On 25 May 1990 the workers voted to disband the union and quit en masse, abandoning the farms they had occupied.

While the outcome of the events popularly known as the "war of the eggs" was unambiguous, the meaning of those events remained open to question. During the conflict, workers, pueblo residents, union organizers, company spokesmen, party and government officials, political activists, and a host of journalists transformed it into a matter of public debate. Newspaper articles, television and radio broadcasts, and pamphlets and broadsides offered contending representations of the origins and nature of the conflict and of the prospects for its resolution. From the moment the movement began, union activists took pains to document the happenings in Tetiz by clipping newspaper articles, copying documents and press releases, and filing photographs, leaflets, and correspondence. Even before the fate of the independent union was resolved, organizers worked at assembling its archive, guided by a keen awareness of the movement as history in the making.

Despite the defeat of the independent union—perhaps in some sense because of it—union organizers and advisors thus found a way to continue their struggle in the domain of history. Initially, that history took the form of a one-hundred-page compilation of anonymously written narrative, anecdotes, and firsthand testimony entitled *La batalla de Tetiz y Hunucmá: los 140 días que commovieron a Yucatán* (The Battle of Tetiz and Hunucmá: The One Hundred Forty Days that Shook Yucatán). More than a chronological record of the happenings of preceding months, the history was meant to cast those happenings as a single, comprehensible event: namely, a battle in a wider and longer class war. While framed by that narrative, however, *La batalla de Tetiz y Hunucmá* was not tightly subordinated to a single story line. It was permeated by many other stories, becoming a composite of the varied perspectives and testimonies of union organizers and workers, men and women, poets, politicians, priests, and even regional theater artists.

To peruse *La batalla de Tetiz y Hunucmá* is to enter the fray of events, reading the text against the backdrop of Yucatán's transition to social and political conditions characteristic of contemporary neoliberalism.[1] That transition had brought the decline of henequen and of the ejido system; it had brought the decline of Mexico's corporatist political system, and the advent of one directly subject to the imperatives of capitalist accumulation. To read *La batalla de Tetiz y Hunucmá* is to consider a union's simultaneous attempt to mobilize workers and organize a broad popular movement amid the novel challenges posed by those changes. At the same time, it is to explore how the struggle changed as it moved beyond contemporary workplace and political issues to connect with older, historical struggles over capitalism and community in Hunucmá and beyond. Like their predecessors in earlier periods, the union's supporters and opponents, pueblo residents and company owners, government officials and politicians came to see the conflict as one focused not so much on the union, but on el pueblo, in ways that both invoked that entity's past and evoked the possibilities of its future transformation.

As the authors of La batalla de Tetiz y Hunucmá undertook to commit the conflict over egg work to historical memory, they began to write a chapter in the history not only of class struggle, but also of el pueblo. As such, La batalla de Tetiz y Hunucmá became a tale of multiple voices and varied stories, from tragedy to farce to redemption. Though compendious, this history would not achieve finality as a definitive account of the events. Subsequent events, from national economic crisis to the waxing and waning of the Zapatista movement in Chiapas, led the union activists who had written and compiled La batalla de Tetiz y Hunucmá to confront, assimilate, and recast their earlier accounts of a battle that refused to end long after the union had ceased to exist.

A HISTORY OF INFAMY

Hacienda Nohuayum is an hour's walk from Tetiz—about five kilometers, reckoned from Tetiz's church. A road heads straight to the northwest, passing large cinder-block dwellings near the center of the pueblo and then smaller, thatched-roof houses. From the outskirts of Tetiz, the road heads into the brush, flanked by tall grass and shrubs. There are few trees along the way, offering scant shade for anyone making the trip on foot. Eventually, there are citrus groves and henequen fields, a few well tended, with tall spiky plants, others choked with weeds. Last of all, there are the beginnings of Nohuayum: small thatched houses, a few streets transited by straying turkeys and pigs, and walls and old structures of the hacienda, now fallen into ruin.

The geography the road traverses—notably its termini, in church and hacienda—is an old one, and it is structured by histories of settlement that date to the colonial period. In the middle of the route, however, lies a relatively novel feature: a series of large, hangar-like structures, nine of them directly adjoining the road and many others off side roads on either side. These are the granjas (farms) of Avícolas Fernández. From the road, the bobbing heads and flapping wings of untold thousands of chickens are visible, massed into the open-walled structures. Following the rhythm of shift changes, groups of men bicycle back and forth between the buildings and their homes on Nohuayum, shouting the traditional Maya greeting to passersby: Tu'x ka bin? ("Where are you going?").

Like other commercial chicken and pork farms in the region, the gran-jas near Nohuayum are the product of the decline of the henequen ejidos, which brought new opportunities for companies seeking cheap land and la-bor. Companies like Campi, Sanjor, Kaki, and Avícolas Fernández expanded, supplying not just the state-level demand for eggs and chicken but national markets as well. More than two hundred farms employing some two thou-sand workers were established in the vicinity of Mérida. By 1990, Avícolas, owned by the Yucatecan entrepreneur Jorge Enrique Fernández Martín, had become one of the largest companies in southeastern Mexico, vertically inte-grating all aspects of the production process, from the production of chicken food and packaging to reproduction, incubation, chicken raising, and egg laying. The company produced eighty tons of eggs daily, operated seventy-three ranches, satisfied about 80 percent of the regional market demand for eggs, and employed 570 workers, 320 of them as agricultural laborers.

The epicenter of Fernández's operations was in western Yucatán, an area that offered abundant, inexpensive land and labor, the workforce being com-posed primarily of male Maya speakers. Twelve farms were established near the town of Hunucmá, and forty-five more were based in the municipality of Tetiz, whose four thousand residents suffered from the acute poverty and unemployment characteristic of the henequen zone. With the expansion of the farms near Tetiz, Avícolas was poised to become a mainstay of the local economy, employing about two hundred residents of Tetiz under the supervision of Spanish-speaking managers and veterinarians from Mérida and other parts of Mexico. While finding regular employment with Avícolas, the workers on the ranches faced a level of exploitation far greater than they had experienced in the ejido system as well as abusive practices, including excessive working hours (ten to twelve hours a day, seven days a week), child labor, threats, beatings, arbitrary firings, and unhealthy working conditions. The workers labored in large puddles of chicken excrement, rotten eggs, and mud without any protective gear or boots.

The expansion of commercial poultry raising in Hunucmá coincided with the emergence of a movement to establish unions independent of the CTM in Yucatán. By 1973 the Despacho de Asesoría a los Sindicatos Independi-entes (independent union advisory office), under the leadership of the labor leader Efraín Calderón Lara, began several organizing drives. The movement was blocked, however, through the intimidation of labor organizers and the kidnapping, torture, and murder of Calderón Lara by order of Yuca-tán's director of public security. In addition, companies circumvented the movement through the formation of unions affiliated with the CTM—so-called phantom unions that either existed only on paper or were controlled by company owners and CTM bosses. Despite these setbacks, by the late 1970s the Despacho reemerged, now led by Julio Ruy Macossay Vallado, his wife, Isela Rodríguez, and his brother Mauricio Macossay Vallado, all of whom had worked in organizing campaigns in Campeche. All were self-declared libertarian socialists who drew inspiration from Karl Marx and the revolutionary-era Mexican anarchist Ricardo Flores Magón as well as from the martyred student leader Calderón Lara.[2]

From 1977 on, the renascent Despacho launched organizing campaigns in a diverse range of industries, from Coca-Cola bottling plants to the steel, beer, and salt industries, Yucatán's public university, and Textil Maya, a Maidenform affiliate. Some of these campaigns succumbed to intimidation and repression. Yet by the early 1980s the Despacho had secured the democratization of an avicultural workers' union and the establishment of an independent union of commercial poultry workers: the Sindicato Independiente de Trabajadores de la Industria Avícola (SITIA), based in the farms of the Campi company. In 1990, the Macossays set their sights on unionizing workers on the granjas near Tetiz and Hunucmá, the most ambitious organizing effort they had as yet attempted.

The workers on Fernández's farms had attempted to organize an independent union at various times in the 1980s, only to face dismissal and blacklisting. In 1987, however, Tetiz elected as mayor Timoteo Canché Tinal, an Avícolas worker, unionist, and activist in the rightist opposition party, the Partido de Acción Nacional (PAN). As Tetiz was the first municipality in Yucatán to break with the PRI, the issue of unionization became politically charged, as the PRI, the PAN, and the leftist opposition party, the Partido de la Revolución Democrática (PRD), all attempted to capitalize on events in that small pueblo. The stage was set for the unionization drive to be transformed from a workplace struggle into a statewide political conflict.

The campaign to organize an independent union began in Tetiz on 10 January 1990. After several clandestine meetings with advisors, the workers filed a petition for official recognition before Yucatán's Junta Local de Conciliación y Arbitraje, the state agency charged with certifying unions and labor contracts. In response, Fernández fired unionist workers, leading two hundred workers in Tetiz and fifty in Hunucmá to declare a strike on 24 January. The next day one hundred state police and armed strikebreakers arrived in Tetiz. As the police descended from their vehicles and confronted Canché, supporters of the strikers used church bells to ring an alarm. Hundreds of pueblo residents armed with rocks and clubs answered the call, routing the police and the strikebreakers. Over the next twelve days, large numbers of pueblo residents constructed barricades on the roads to the egg farms to prevent the return of the intruders.[3]

On 4 February Fernández conceded the workers' right to form a union and bargain collectively, and the next day production of eggs resumed. According to the terms of the new contract, conditions were improved, most notably through the elimination of child labor and the reduction of the daily individual work quota from twenty-five to fifteen crates of eggs. On the advice of the Despacho, the workers formed a union governing structure and held frequent mass meetings. Despite these arrangements, tensions soon began to increase as the company began a campaign to rescind its recognition of the union. Fernández and his representatives accused the workers of engaging in deliberate slowdowns and blamed them for the increasing scarcity of eggs in local markets. The workers responded by accusing the owner of surreptitiously stockpiling large quantities of eggs in order to drive up prices illegally and discredit the union. In mid-March, Fernández fired seventy-two workers, and the CTM leader José Pacheco Durán submitted to the Junta a list of workers who, he claimed, had affiliated with a CTM union two months before. While members of the independent union immediately denounced the list as a falsified and backdated document, the Junta declared the new contract illegal and rescinded recognition of the independent union. In response, unionists in Tetiz took control of the farms, maintaining the production of eggs while preventing all nonessential personnel and supervisors from entering the worksites. They requested mediation of the conflict by Governor Manzanilla, but none was forthcoming.

On 5 April a group of 300 armed strikebreakers assaulted the farms in Tetiz, while another 250 targeted Hunucmá. The workers at Hunucmá's farms were overwhelmed and fled to escape the assailants. In Tetiz, however, the call went out to inhabitants of the pueblo to fight off the intruders. Unionists and pueblo residents seized nine company trucks and detained more than a dozen supervisors and strikebreakers, whom they stripped naked and marched off to the pueblo jail. In Mérida, the Despacho advisor Julio Macossay filed a complaint with the state attorney general, only to find himself surrounded by strikebreakers, who detained him while the attorney general prepared formal charges to justify his imprisonment. Macossay began a hunger strike in jail, as numerous human rights and political organizations at the state and national level declared him to be a political prisoner.

Hundreds of heavily armed state police enter Tetiz. Sequestered vehicles are visible in the background. Courtesy *Diario de Yucatán*.

His fellow Despacho advisor Mauricio Macossay set off for Tetiz, where the unionists maintained their control of the granjas, refusing entry to company supervisors and blocking Fernández's trucks from picking up eggs until they were paid back wages. On 26 April hundreds of police armed with machine guns and tear gas briefly occupied Tetiz in order to recover the confiscated vehicles, eventually retreating under a hail of epithets and stones. Amid calls by some pueblo residents to burn the farms, the union advisors convinced them to remain calm, in the words of Mauricio Macossay keeping their "hearts hot, but heads cool."[4]

The battle in Tetiz gave rise to an escalating conflict in newspapers and other media. Yucatecan radio and television stations and the newspaper *Diario del Sureste*, all of them overtly allied with the PRI and the state government, denounced the unionists for embarking on a class war that could have far-reaching and nefarious consequences. Editorialists accused the Macossays of syndicalist terrorism, calling them "subversive agents" who were devoted to the "destruction of social harmony" and unionist "rats" who threatened the company and society in general. They blamed Canché Tinal for lending his support to the strikers and the PAN for supporting Canché and the strikers, and for transforming Tetiz into what they labeled a "lawless pueblo."[5]

For their part, the strikers, the Despacho, and their supporters in the PAN and in the media—notably the *Diario de Yucatán*, which was overtly allied with the PAN, and the national newspaper, *La Jornada*, which favored the PRD—

Residents of Tetiz, holding signs, protest opposite the Palacio de Gobierno in Mérida in mid-April 1990. One of the signs reads, "The bourgeoisie is slitting the throat of the dove of peace." Courtesy *Diario de Yucatán*.

also represented the conflict in Tetiz as a class war. In their view, however, the conflict was not a war waged *by* workers, but one waged *against* workers by the owners, the CTM, the PRI, and the state and federal governments. The SITIA and the Despacho issued regular press releases documenting the attacks by strikebreakers and police and publicizing the status of Macossay as a political prisoner. Such acts of repression, they argued, demonstrated the determination of the owners to preserve their dominion at the cost of the elementary rights and well-being of workers. At the same time, the unionists represented the situation not just as a labor conflict, but also as a struggle of the popular classes in Yucatán against a united repressive front composed of management, the government, and the leaders of the PRI and the CTM. Protesters assembled outside the seat of the state government in Mérida and taunted the governor: "Manzanilla, you thief! Fernández is your chief!"[6]

By mid-May, the situation had reached the breaking point. On 16 May pueblo residents again battled police, and nine strike leaders were detained and taken to the office of the attorney general, where they were forced to sign confessions to various criminal charges. The same day, the state congress introduced a measure to depose Mayor Canché for purported misconduct. In Mexico City, President Carlos Salinas de Gortari met with representatives of regional chambers of commerce, who urged him to order the use of federal troops against Tetiz. Soon a representative of the federal government arrived in Mérida to make clear the federal government's opposition to the unionists and negotiate an end to the conflict. On 25 May, in return for the freedom of those detained and compensation for the strikers, union members voted to disband the union and quit their jobs en masse. While some workers, with encouragement from the Despacho, planned to form agricultural and artisanal cooperatives, they faced an uncertain future.[7]

Several days later Carlos Caamal Couoh, general secretary of the defunct union, ruefully remarked that the constitutional rights the workers thought they enjoyed—rights to form unions and to strike—had proven to be nonexistent. In an archival letter addressed to "public opinion of the entire country," he declared that the unionists of Tetiz and Hunucmá had struggled as "truly responsible men and women: upright, with their heads held high, facing the sun." While not "bowing or kneeling before anyone," he declared, they had been defeated by "brute force and cowardice," as an "entire pueblo . . . was crushed viciously in order to impose the whims of a handful of powerful men." The history of their battle remained to be written, but for Caamal its message would be clear: "Let this remain for history," he concluded, "as a story of infamy."[8]

INCARNATIONS OF EL PUEBLO

As much as the conflict reflected Yucatán's contemporary situation, for many residents of the Hunucmá region the struggle touched upon a deeper history. Even now, despite the extensive improvements in working conditions that have been made over the decade following the unionization conflict, workers sometimes draw analogies between Porfirian indebted servitude and their own condition. When a shift ends and a worker leaves, he may shout, jokingly, to another who is still working, *Maare! Esclavoech!* ("Wow! What a slave you are!"). Such associations are common when workers are fired, denied bonuses, or face intensified labor discipline, from the use of a bell to sound the beginning of shifts, to penalties for lateness, to requirements that workers shower at the gates of the farm before beginning work. At such moments, references to slavery reflect a more serious and morally charged critique of exploitation and mistreatment.[9]

In the 1980s, when exploitation was more intense, such perceptions were sharper. For while the expansion of the commercial poultry business in Yucatán was part of a new, post-henequen economy based on the provision of cheap labor to national and multinational companies, the social world of henequen seemed to reemerge on the granjas. They were physically located on or near the old haciendas; moreover, Fernández named them after his patron saint and those of his wife and children—San Jorge, Santa Cecilia, and the like—thus mimicking practices followed by hacendados of old. On the granjas, dark-skinned Maya speakers once again labored under the supervision of light-skinned, Spanish-speaking supervisors, that is, ts'uls; supervisors subjected workers to a daily regime of abuse, frequently referring to them, according to one union leader, as "shitty Indians." Fernández also had a penchant for making racially charged public statements, such as one in which he referred to the workers of Tetiz as "bumpkins [huiros] who only know how to make babies."[10]

Soon after the conflict erupted, commentators in Mérida who were sympathetic to the unionists, especially those affiliated with the PRD, conveyed such associations to a wider public. One specifically evoked Barbarous Mexico, John Kenneth Turner's exposé from 1910 of alleged Porfirian slavery in Yucatán, finding parallels with the Porfirian system in the unhealthy and exploitative working conditions, meager pay, beatings, and insults and abuse of workers in Tetiz's granjas. This made the situation in the facilities, in his view, "seem to be part of a story from the pages of [that] book." Others blamed Yucatecan businessmen like Fernández for maintaining conditions tantamount to slavery and feudalism in Yucatán. One declaration, attributed to a group that called itself the Popular Independent Workers' Unity Party, compared the demands of the workers of Tetiz to goals achieved by workers' struggles of the seventeenth century in other countries. "We must say goodbye," the statement concluded, "to 'modernity' in Yucatán; we must laugh at capital's intentions to invest in a state marked by feudalism and semislavery."[11]

In leaflets and communications, representatives of the independent union made the most of such associations. Union leaflets decried the "slavemaster mentality" of Fernández and the government and demanded workers' liberation from the so-called state of "slavery" imposed by that alliance. In a more sardonic vein, union advisors and organizers created several bogus press releases mocking the racism and classism of owners and government officials. The putative author of one such letter—identified as Protocola Burgois Manzanita, surely a play on Manzanilla's name—declared that the "ferocious, unsibilized Mayan Indians must be pacified" in Tetiz. Calling the owner of the farms "Fernández of the House of Fernandería, great Ts'ul, King of Kings, Lord of Lords," the author reviled workers. They were "things . . . like talking Machines . . . or Robots," powered by two kinds of fuel, "hungerol" and "ignorasoline," which made them work "tirelessly without complaining . . . better than beasts of burden, how wonderful! Just yell at them once and hit them a few times, and they get right to work. It's a marvel of cybernetics!" The author expressed horror at the notion that such "things" would claim rights and urged his audience to set matters to rights with a "good lesson of repression." A similar letter, addressed to newscasters by several bogus authors, one of them identified as Porfirio Díaz Ordaz (a play on the name of Porfirio Díaz as well as on that of Gustavo Díaz Ordaz, who was president of Mexico in 1968, at the time of the massacre of student demonstrators at Tlatelolco, in Mexico City), attacked the union advisor Julio Macossay as the Antichrist and associated him with historical figures who similarly "preached against people of quality," from Jesus to independence-era heroes to Efraín Calderón Lara. The authors called on the government to quell the "disorder caused by the Antichrist in horrible conspiracy with the cannibal Indians of Tetiz."[12]

The tone of such letters is indicative of the sharpening rhetoric of both owners and labor organizers. Even as unionists denounced Fernández and others as throwbacks to the times of slavery and feudalism, owners, government officials, and Yucatecan business leaders associated the unionists with insurgents and socialists of the revolutionary period. Fernández and other business leaders considered the conflict in Tetiz to have been instigated by alien agitators, "deracinated" people who wound up in Yucatán, "as if Yucatán were the sewer of the Mexican Republic." Fernández argued that the union organizers not only were striking against a business that was "authentically Yucatecan and Mexican," but also threatened to undermine the "productive development of the State and the country." While initially Fernández and his representatives distinguished hardworking "boys" who worked on the farms from the advisors who had supposedly disoriented them, after events took a more violent turn in April, they considered the workers to have been lost to subversion by radical labor leaders. Even if the conflict were resolved, according to a columnist for the *Diario del Sureste*, it would be impossible to employ the people of Tetiz in the future: "It is clear," he wrote, "that [the agitators] have spoiled the worker, they have turned him into a liar, they have taught him to hate the businessman." Similarly, Fernández declared in outrage, "My employees in Tetiz don't obey me, they eject me from my own business. . . . These independent unionists want me to be their slave." In the end, businessmen and company officials greeted the arrest and imprisonment of the union leaders with satisfaction. Statements of renewed "investor confidence" in Yucatán were immediately forthcoming.[13]

Like Yucatecan Socialists and Liberals seventy years earlier, the unionists and their opponents shared a tendency to cast the dispute in broader terms, as one not only over workplace rights, but over the rights and responsibilities of el pueblo. Company representatives and state officials described Tetiz as a "lawless pueblo" and as a "jungle" where "anarchy" reigned; if rational and civilized means of settling the conflict were not found, according to Fernández's lawyer, a man of Lebanese descent named Ali Charruf, the pueblo surely would become a ghost town (pueblo fantasma). News commentators decried both the "messianic syndicalism" of labor organizers and the fanaticism of pueblo residents who followed them toward perdition—notably Canché, whom they derisively referred to as a "Batman in sandals." One commentator went so far as to suggest that heavy rains that caused damage in Tetiz in late April were divine retribution against the pueblo for its support of the unionists.[14]

On the opposing side, strike supporters from the PAN also represented the conflict in overtly religious terms. In an essay condemning the "inhumane primacy of eggs over men," a PAN leader argued that the conflict had become a battle between the "forces of good and of evil. . . . In the latter power conspires with lies, and in the former sacrifice and humility are joined." The Yucatecan federal congressional deputy Ana Rosa Payán Cervera went so far as to proclaim the voice of el pueblo, in Tetiz, to be the "voice of God." "As far as I know," she opined, "God is never wrong."[15] From Tetiz to Mérida, the union movement took on an explicitly religious cast, as pueblo residents and protesters lit candles and prayed to the Virgin for her intercession. Church officials in the Hunucmá region were sympathetic and helped to collect money, food, and clothing for the strikers and their families. Hunucmá's priest, Alvaro Carrillo Lugo, condemned the police crackdown as a demonstration of the government's recourse to the "power of arms and money" rather than to that of "reason, justice and truth" in its dealings with el pueblo.[16]

For supporters of the strike movement, however, it was in general appeals for liberation that el pueblo figured most prominently as a subject of collective material, political, and spiritual emancipation. At an assembly following the then apparently victorious January strike, a poet read an ode entitled "To the heroic pueblo of Tetiz." He urged workers to continue the fight for their constitutional rights and to "recover your dignity and the respect for you that those arrogant, powerful people have forgotten." After commending Tetiz for remaining united "like one single man," he concluded his poem by saluting that masculine entity's struggle for liberty:

El pueblo is united and alert
Facing the iron fist
That squelches every attempt at liberty,
With the support of cowardly laws.

To you, heroic pueblo of Tetiz,
To you, brother and friend:
Struggle ever harder,
Do not allow them to crush you,
And defend your liberty.[17]

Similarly, strikers circulated leaflets demanding their liberation from a state of slavery imposed by the alliance of company and government. In one they compared their enemies to a Goliath and themselves to David, as if that biblical figure offered the perfect incarnation of el pueblo. Demanding "justice and equality for our children," they declared their refusal to continue "bequeathing our misery [and] handing our children over to the voracity of the owner, so that he can continue appropriating everything that belongs to el pueblo."[18]

Through press releases, speeches, slogans, poetry, and pamphlets, union supporters and detractors alike represented the battle as a conflict not simply over the union, but also over the nature of el pueblo. In so doing, the unionists, in particular, did not limit themselves to a diagnosis of el pueblo's condition and possibilities in contemporary terms. Rather, they situated contemporary developments in a much longer history of possession and dispossession. As much as in the conflict over egg work and union rights, it was in a struggle over history—over slavery and liberation and over capitalism, socialism, and community—that the unionists incarnated el pueblo and evoked the prospect of its repossession.

LOS HUEVOS DE TETIZ

For residents of Tetiz, it was not in newspaper coverage or speeches that el pueblo found its most dramatic expression, but in the episodes of violence that punctuated the five-month conflict. The colloquial meaning of egg, or *huevo*, in Mexican Spanish, as a slang term for testicle made those confrontations highly sexualized and favorable both to the burlesque symbolic emasculation of the owner and to the workers' assertion of claims to masculine valor. Thus workers ridiculed Fernández's declarations that they would be forced to affiliate with the CTM union, literally "by their balls" (al huevo). When strike organizers urged the workers, once they had gained control of the egg farms, to maintain the level of egg production, some in the audience proclaimed, "We will demonstrate that in Tetiz we produce more eggs than Fernández, with all of his chickens!" When the owner's son came to the farms to castigate the workers for the decline in production, the strikers challenged the owner and his lawyer: "If Fernández and Charruf have no 'eggs,' let them come to Tetiz. Here there are many!"[19]

Such sexual invective accompanied outbreaks of violence between pueblo residents, strikebreakers, and police in ways that projected el pueblo as a rebellious, masculinized subject and characterized outsiders as effeminate. As the workers themselves generally remained inside the farms to prevent them from being retaken, it was largely the women of Tetiz who built and occupied barricades, blocked and guarded roads, and confronted strikebreakers and police, even using their shawls, as one union advisor told me, as "deadly weapons" to disarm police. During the strike in January, women captured eight company supervisors, whom they beat, stripped naked, and then punished under the "law of popox," that is, by whipping with prickly brush. On 5 April women captured sixteen strikebreakers and again stripped, whipped, and jailed them. On another occasion, upon hearing that state antiriot police were coming to Tetiz, some women reportedly declared, "If those maricones [a highly pejorative term for homosexuals] want to come here, they will face first the children, then us, and finally the workers. Let's see if they are so manly!"

When police did arrive, women confronted them, shouting, "This is our pueblo and here we give orders!" One agent attempted to strike a man, and a woman interceded, challenging him: "Let's go, maricón. Hit me if you are so valiant! I don't have any weapons . . . Go ahead! Hit me! Hit me!" An officer shouted, "The women here are screwed up!" to which a woman responded, "And your whoring mother? Isn't she screwed [up]?" A chorus of shouts of "maricón" was raised, as young boys used slingshots to pelt the officers, who hurriedly abandoned Tetiz. Enraged by the incursions, some women of Tetiz reportedly shouted, "Let's burn down the granjas, so Fernández sees that in Tetiz we have huevos!" It was no wonder the workers reportedly took to threatening police by warning, "If you insist on trying to interfere in our pueblo, we'll call the women, and then we won't be responsible for what might happen to you." In framing the conflict as one of a pueblo with "eggs" against incursions and betrayals by maricones—a term that, along

Women holding signs, accompanied by children with slingshots, protest outside a chicken ranch in Hunucmá occupied by CTM-affiliated strikebreakers. One of the signs reads, "Manzanilla . . . Don't Be Against the 'Pueblo.' " Courtesy *Diario de Yucatán*.

with *culeros*, also was used to refer to strikebreakers and to workers who opposed the union—both women and men seem to have placed the issue of heterosexual masculine honor and feminine valor at the center of the conflict with company and state. It was spectacles such as these and the public and carnivalesque inversion of the hierarchies of gender, ethnicity, and class that led hostile observers to declare that the conflict had become a carnival and that residents of Tetiz had succumbed to the "kiss of the devil."[20]

Similar dynamics characterized confrontations between union organizers and management. When representatives of the workers complained to Fernández about the constant insults directed at them by the supervisors of the farms, the owner responded mockingly, "Well, you bunch of bastards, what are you complaining about? If you are slackers they have to yell at you to get you to work, you bunch of idiots. You get annoyed if they swear at you, as if you don't know those words. But are you going to stop being so manly [*machitos*] if they say something? Do your ears hurt?" In response, Carlos Caamal responded, "Fine. So that you understand better I will speak to you just like you and your people speak to us. No, you bastard, the words don't hurt us. They are words we already know, but there is no reason to yell at us or insult us, you sons of whores." As Fernández's jaw dropped, Caamal concluded, "It bothers you too, doesn't it?" After the union initially seemed to

Advertisement for performance of Los huevos de Tetiz in Hunucmá. Photo by Paul Eiss.

have won recognition, the owner called the union's chief advisor and yelled, "You fucked me, Julio! You fucked me! I've dropped my pants!" Despite Macossay's assurances that "this is not about fucking anybody" Fernández continued his asseverations.[21]

Such performances did not remain confined to the theatrics of confrontation but took a literally theatrical form when the well-known Yucatecan regional theater artist Héctor Herrera wrote a short play based on events in Tetiz, entitled Los huevos de Tetiz. Performances opened in Mérida and in Hunucmá as the conflict was unfolding and contributed to the ongoing public debate surrounding the unionization drive and its suppression. Set in a small luncheonette in Tetiz, the play featured a series of characters that would have been recognizable to audiences: the owner Fernández and his lawyer Charruf, speaking in Arabic-accented Spanish; a male leader of the workers named Satahol Caamal, perhaps based on Carlos Caamal; a female protest leader, Romualda Tinal, who shared the surname of a prominent female protest leader from Tetiz; and several undercover police, a clergyman, and a few other pueblo residents, including the elderly luncheonette owner, Doña Candita.[22]

Los huevos de Tetiz depicts sexualized confrontations similar to those playing on the streets of the pueblo. Immediately after the main character, Satahol Caamal, opens the play by indicating its subject to be a "theatrical soap opera" set in "my pueblo," Doña Candita declares, "Everything began with huevos, and with the independent union. Or rather, with the union's huevos." The greatest bravado, however, is demonstrated by the female protester, Romualda Tinal. Near the beginning of the play, Tinal avows the determination of Tetiz's women to support the strike, states her intention to organize a ten-year protest in Mérida's central plaza, and then rises and shouts, ¡Arriba Tetiz! Thereafter, the play dramatizes the emasculation of police and the company owner. When two policemen ask to use a bathroom and then enter it, one character opines, "Those guys didn't go there to *huixar* [a Hispanicized Mayan term for urination] but to do . . . something else." It is in the owner Jorge Fernández, however, that the play finds its prime target for emasculation. While Fernández cries petulantly about the death of his chickens, Candita suggests that his "cock" is dying too. The owner's mounting distress comes to a culmination when he begins clucking, squats down, and, to the amazement of all present, lays a large egg: a symbol now not of the union's masculinity (as having huevos), but of the owner's emasculation (as laying them).

The Herrera troupe clearly intended *Los huevos de Tetiz* as a gesture of sympathy with the workers and also, as the actor Mario Herrera explained to me, as one of "support for el pueblo."[23] The play spares no derision of the owner and the police and gives voice to the workers' demand for fair wages and working conditions. At the same time, it offers no easy solution to the conflict. After a religious pueblo resident, named Doña Beata, pleads for divine intercession to "save this pueblo from perdition," a clergyman named Eulogio Poc Chuc appears on the scene. When not engaged in fondling Beata, the clergyman presents a cogent diagnosis of the conflict in Tetiz (as one in which labor, penal, and political questions had been confused) and offers a strategy for defusing and settling each aspect of the conflict in turn. He admits, however, that the "brothers of Tetiz" refused to accept the plan. By the end of the play, the police appear to be on the verge of imposing their own solution, as they arrest both Jorge Fernández, "for stealing and laying eggs," and Doña Candita, for possession of "high-caliber arms," namely, a small slingshot she uses to chase lizards out of her kitchen. Just at that moment, however, Satahol and Romualda return from Mérida, bringing what Satahol describes as "what we need, to end the conflict in Tetiz." At that moment, an actor dressed as Víctor Cervera, the all-powerful populist Yucatecan PRI leader and soon to be governor of Yucatán, appears onstage carrying two bags full of eggs. Seeing him, all shout, "Huevos!" and the curtain falls. After dramatizing the failed efforts of all parties to resolve the conflict, *Los huevos de Tetiz* offers a deus ex machina, suggesting that only through mediation by a traditional populist statesman—a man with true huevos—might the conflict be resolved.

Theater plays aside, in the end it was the owner and the state government that would have their way, as the workers resolved to quit en masse. At the assembly where they made this decision, some reportedly declared their determination to resign with dignity rather than "to drop their pants" before Fernández. While signaling the defeat of the movement, the announcement was greeted as a victory in Tetiz. To welcome the prisoners on their release several all-night fiestas were organized, at which some residents, perhaps inspired by the theatrical performance of Los huevos de Tetiz, performed corridas, or songs, chronicling the victories, villanies, and debacles of the conflict: "Fernández the tyrant"; "The son of el pueblo"; "Ballad for a scab"; "The Macossay lambada"; and the like. While in terms of labor rights, the conflict was a dramatic failure, as a set of carnivalesque performances—acted on the streets, on the farms, in confrontational negotiating sessions with the company, in a theater play, and in victory celebrations—workers, pueblo residents, and union organizers opened the war of the eggs to other readings.[24]

FROM ARCHIVE TO HISTORY

In the closing days of the conflict, several contributors to the official state government periodical, Diario del Sureste, expressed a desire to commit the events of the preceding months to the archive, as a place of interment and forgetting. One, declaring that a carnival for opposition politicians had finished as a tragedy for Tetiz, exclaimed that "those of us who feel respect and affection for Yucatán would give anything to archive this sad and painful case." Another blamed the PAN for turning Tetiz into a "Frankenstein's laboratory" and also called for the conflict to be consigned to oblivion: "Let us forget what is irreparable. Let us leave the past to history and the archive. Let us all accept this painful experience."[25]

In opposition to such pleas for forgetting, union advisors turned to history with a vengeance. They gathered and organized newspaper clippings, documents, and photographs, forming an unofficial archive of the union movement, one that might become a vehicle for remembering, rather than forgetting. They took testimony from participants, setting down those anecdotes as well their own recollections in writing. Then, as noted, they drew on those materials to compile a history of anonymous, or rather collective, authorship, La batalla de Tetiz y Hunucmá, composed of one hundred pages of narrative, anecdotes, and reflections.[26] The work was intended to be more than a chronology of discrete episodes; it was meant to represent the many happenings as parts of a single, comprehensible event of class struggle. Moreover, it was meant to remove that event from the particular history of Tetiz or even of partisan political conflict in Yucatán and to resituate it in a much broader history: that of the battle between labor and capital in Mexico.[27]

In *La batalla de Tetiz y Hunucmá* the years of conflict in the area of Hunucmá and Tetiz are constructed as a unified event in two ways. First, the account documents the existence of two distinct sides to the dispute and sets out in great detail the different groups and interests that made up the "forces of the bosses" and the "popular forces." Second, having established the two blocs that constitute its protagonists, the account proceeds as a detailed, chronological account of the conflict as a sequence of military engagements. In the first two phases of that war, the union and its allies win a series of victories, in large part through the bravery and mobilization of the "heroic pueblo of Tetiz." In the third, the "owners, blinded by greed and arrogance, and encouraged by the neoliberal and opportunistic politics of the present regime," determine to make an example of Tetiz by destroying the independent union. Thereafter, a series of "waves of repression" are detailed in chapters and sections entitled "The Strike," "The Calm before the Storm," "The Storm Is Unleashed," "The First Assault on el Pueblo," "The Legal Farce," "The New Wave of Repression, "The Second Assault on el Pueblo," etc.[28]

The identification of two sides to the conflict and the narration of the conflict as a series of military engagements support the representation of the conflict as a war of the classes. At particularly violent moments of the conflict, the upsurge of class consciousness is vividly dramatized. In an aside on female supporters of the strike, for instance, the authors write, "Their class instincts are clearly apparent in the way they expressed themselves, the way they speak." After the presentation of numerous such incidents, the authors conclude that the intransigence of the owners led the unionization movement to become a "complete class conflict." Owners "spared no effort" at repression, even as they saw that "the workers and el pueblo, which supported them, would not give up, but continued the struggle, growing stronger the more they were punished." Through the description of episodes of conflict, and commentary on them, the authors aim to reveal the essence of the conflict to have been an unmitigated struggle between polar opposites: capital and labor.[29]

Given the defeat of the unionization drive, however, the authors faced the challenge of relating its history as something other than a failure. Thus they incorporated Tetiz's story into a larger one: the history of independent unionization in Yucatán, which since the 1930s "has passed through stages of struggle as in the seventies, and through stages of stagnation and waning, as in recent years." The authors cast the conflict as a rekindling of earlier movements, as organizers worked at "reviving the rich, working-class and unionist historical memory" in the region. They wrote that before the conflict Yucatán "seemed not to awake from this long dream of prostration, on its knees"; Tetiz, however, and with it the labor movement in general, "awoke," after decades of "dormancy" and humiliation. Here the spectral figure of Efraín Calderón Lara makes his appearance in the narrative, beginning with the renaming of the independent union in his honor in the heat of the conflict. As the authors argued, Calderón Lara played an inspirational role, both in the "consciousness of el pueblo" and in the "collective unconscious of the owners and the government," who saw the specter of Cálderon Lara in every mobilization. "It seems," the authors wrote, "that conscience, that tyrant, does not allow them to rest."[30]

Even as La batalla de Tetiz y Hunucmá presents the conflict in Tetiz in such a way as to link that present to a historical past, it also made it a link to the future. While seen in "purely syndical terms," the authors admitted, the movement was a defeat; in the longer term it would be what they called a "spark": the "first outbreak of a movement of workers and peasants that will continue to grow, as long as the workers remain united." The conflict was a "moral and ideological victory" for working people in the region, who acquired collective awareness, experience, class consciousness, and "social energy" that would lead them toward the "construction of their future with the strength that the battle has given them." "Whoever today thinks that what happened in TETIZ and HUNUCMA was a defeat," they declared, "SIMPLY DO NOT UNDERSTAND THE DIALECTIC OF HISTORY."[31]

In this spirit, even as La batalla de Tetiz y Hunucmá tells a story of class struggle framed as tragedy, the account is shot through with competing story lines that are anything but tragic. The narrative, for instance, includes accounts of confrontations between workers and company officials and especially between female pueblo residents and police, exuberantly depicting sexual jibes and insults. A tone of comedy—and of the carnivalesque—pervades the document. Such episodes multiply as the account progresses, dramatizing the inversion of power relations characteristic of so-called slavery and of the hierarchies of class, race, and gender. Even more than as a tragedy or comedy, however, it was as a story of redemption that La batalla de Tetiz y Hunucmá offered a way to transcend the independent union's defeat. The authors stressed that throughout the conflict in Tetiz, the Catholic church stood "with great dignity and Christian spirit . . . on the side of justice and the oppressed, as never before in the recent history of Yucatán, where traditionally it has been disconnected from popular struggles or openly pro-business." Some sections apply metaphors of religious faith to unionization:

one devoted to women's protests in Mérida is entitled "The Calvary of faith of the women of Hunucmá and Tetiz," and another is entitled "Passion and Faith." Workers who were opposed to the union are called Judases. Above all, the Virgin of Tetiz is a constant presence in the narrative, as women and men pray to her and ask for her intercession on behalf of Macossay and the imprisoned workers. As the authors explained, "Symbolically, for el pueblo, it was a woman who won the liberation of those who were unjustly imprisoned. In the soul of those valiant women and of the pueblo of TETIZ and HUNUCMA, there is a firm conviction that liberty was won—not due to their heroic struggle—but because it was so desired by the Virgin of Tetiz."[32]

The authors argued that the defeat became a victory for "the creation of hope, through their blood, their sweat, their faith in the Virgin, and the tears generously spilled, that watered the roads of liberty, . . . [Thus] Tetiz learned how to dream after those 140 days of insurgency and liberty." After the dissolution of the union, two thanksgiving Masses were celebrated, the first following the release of seven imprisoned workers and the second to give thanks when the conflict ended. An extensive quotation of the sermon that concluded the Mass is featured in the account, including praise from Hunucmá's priest for workers' "Christian dignity" as they "liberated [them]selves" by choosing "hunger over humiliation, and blows and insults over the ignominious submission of beasts."[33] In *La batalla de Tetiz y Hunucmá* that victory is consummated in fiestas after the Masses, in which pueblo residents, unionists as well as so-called Judases, celebrated "the victory of the dignity, unity and liberty of an entire pueblo that, like a single man, knew how to struggle and to fall with its head held high, to rise again once more." "DZOCU YAHA U CAJI TETIZ," the account continues, translating those Maya words as "El pueblo, which was cornered, has awakened." As the sun rose the fiesta was still going strong, and the people of Tetiz turned to face its light, "ready to continue the epic of the emancipation of the poor, the tireless struggle for dignity, justice, and liberty." In a section entitled "Rebirth," *La batalla de Tetiz y Hunucmá* portrays the workers completing their collective rite of passage, as they prepare to organize agricultural and artisanal cooperatives after losing their jobs. A worker named Candelario declares that "now we will continue to be poor like before, pariahs who have to earn their living on the hardest roads, whether of god or the devil. Now, however, we are our own masters."[34]

It is in the final chapter of the historical account, in a section entitled "The Auguries of the Future," that the authors linked el pueblo's redemption most explicitly to their critique of "savage neoliberalism." The challenge that Hunucmá and Tetiz faced was "titanic"—as difficult as trying to "jump into the sky and hunt the stars." Their task was to realize a "workers' utopia . . . without owners, economic exploitation, social discrimination, misery, ignorance, or malnutrition." Here, the account turns once more to the Virgin as a source of hope: "Yes, it is a utopia, but these two pueblos with their faith in the Virgin and in their dignity, which for them are the same thing, have already moved mountains, and have already achieved miracles." It was in the prospect of the miraculous creation of that utopian community, under the Virgin's benevolent gaze, that the infamy of the present might be redeemed.[35] Thus La batalla de Tetiz y Hunucmá ends, after a concluding plea to readers not to allow events in the two pueblos to "sink into forgetting or indifference," but rather to profit, like the authors, from "so many rich experiences and lessons, which must never be forgotten." By providing an "unforgettable testimony" to those days, they offered La batalla de Tetiz y Hunucmá as the "first part of this history of the struggle of the working classes of Tetiz and Hunucmá." The second part of that history was just beginning and soon would be written as well, as what they called an "impassioned bid for dignity, justice, and liberty."[36]

La batalla de Tetiz y Hunucmá was completed just a few weeks after the dissolution of the independent union; Despacho advisors and independent union leaders hoped its dissemination might facilitate the continuation of their struggle for justice in Tetiz and elsewhere. Although it was never published, it circulated among unionists and their supporters, and for several years was posted on a web site. Moreover, the text, in abridged form, was circulated widely as a pamphlet by Despertar Obrero ("Workers' Awakening"), a monthly newsletter of Yucatán's independent unions that previously, in January 1990, had published a "Chronicle of the Workers' Victory in Tetiz and Hunucmá." This version of La batalla de Tetiz y Hunucmá was an illustrated text, with cartoon-style drawings dramatizing critical moments of the conflict and the repression of workers by the company, the state, and the CTM. Its cover presented a drawing, in outlined silhouettes, of a group of people in protest, a single gigantic, mallet-bearing figure rising in their midst, as if symbolizing the people as a single subject, united in rebellion. Most of the illustrations, however, were humorous in tone, mocking and satirizing the opponents of the union and playing upon comical associations with eggs, even as they highlighted the seriousness of the tale. The pamphlet begins with a drawing of a bearded narrator offering to tell readers a "history of huevos—of a great

Cover of *Despertar Obrero* with a version of *La batalla de Tetiz y Hunucmá*.

workers' and popular struggle . . . in a little pueblo, not far from here." In the same frame, a large fist holding a gun and labeled "state government-PRI-business leaders" points at the narrator, as a voice declares, "STOP, that [the telling of history] is also illegal." At the conclusion, there is a drawing of Governor Manzanilla sweating copiously and declaring, "Now let this pass into history (as a history of infamy)"; immediately adjacent to that defensive appeal for closure, the authors declare their hope that "this pamphlet contributes not only to the remembering of the conflict, but also to recover the teachings of those events, in a way that helps us in future struggles."[37]

Subsequent events seemed to frustrate rather than fulfill such hopes. In the wake of the conflict, Timoteo Canché was removed from power in Tetiz, bringing new municipal elections in which PRI activists, supported by strongmen from Yucatán's CTM taxi and bus driver's union, clashed with PAN supporters. The municipal government returned to the PRI's control. In elections in 1991, the PAN's candidate was defeated as well, amid allegations of fraud and accusations by some that the state-level PAN had abandoned its supporters in Tetiz. At the same time, even local PAN officials distanced themselves from the remnants of the union movement, and when they gained power behaved in ways almost undistinguishable from their *priísta* opponents. In ensuing years, local politics remained fractured, as partisan factions contended for the spoils of power, without attempting another broad popular movement under the banner of emancipation.

Many of those who had resigned their jobs in the granjas searched for employment elsewhere, in Mérida, Cancún, and the United States. Some found work, along with other pueblo residents (many of them female), in a cooperative that took its name and inspiration from the independent union movement: Dzocu Yaha u Caji Tetiz. With guidance from the advisors of the defunct union, they used a portion of the money from their settlement with Fernández to purchase a property, where they installed a shop dedicated to artisanal production, principally the decorative painting of crafts for sale in tourist markets. Union advisors were frustrated, though, that the movement that reached its climax during the war of the eggs now seemed unable to "lift up its head," as even members of the cooperative focused on the economics of running the operation rather than on broaching broader social and political issues. In any event, faced with the economic crisis and the precipitous devaluation of the Mexican peso in 1995 the cooperative went out of business.[38]

Even as political factionalism and economic crisis dimmed the prospects of popular mobilization in Tetiz, developments elsewhere in Mexico attracted the attention of the advisors of the Despacho. On 1 January 1994 the Zapatista insurgency broke out in the southern state of Chiapas. The Zapatistas denounced Mexico's neoliberal reformers both for their abandonment of agrarian reform and for their assaults on the welfare of Mexico's working poor. They gave voice to the special conditions and concerns of indigenous Mayan populations and claimed to "lead while obeying" (*mandar obedeciendo*)—a term they used to refer to a communitarian style of organizing in which leaders obeyed the mandates of their communities. The advisors of the Despacho declared their solidarity with the Zapatistas, joining a cultural wing of the movement based in Yucatán and providing legal advice on human rights issues to Tzotzil communities in Chiapas.[39]

Within a few years, however, the Zapatista movement, despite attracting great international attention and support, began to ebb both in Chiapas and nationally, and the activists of the Despacho moved on to other places and forms of political action. In the mid-1990s, the Despacho leader Julio Macossay provided legal counsel to several campesino cooperatives in northern Campeche as well as to taxi and truck drivers in Mérida. Then he moved

to Playa del Carmen on the Caribbean coast, where he collaborated with artisanal cooperatives and counseled groups of fishermen, workers, and envi-
ronmentalists. Mauricio Macossay, for his part, completed a doctoral dissertation, largely based on his analysis of the conflict in Tetiz. Then, as a faculty
member of Mexico's preeminent agricultural university, the Universidad de
Chapingo near Mexico City, he became involved in several projects relating
to labor rights, sustainable agriculture, and fair trade in Yucatán. He collaborated in the creation of an ecological agriculture school called U Yits Ka'an
in the town of Maní, intended to educate indigenous and working people
in autonomous communal and ecological agriculture and encourage them
to present "active resistance, with the force of rebellion, against neoliberal
policies."[40]

It was in the wake of the disappointments in Tetiz, by the economic crisis,
and by the hopes raised, if not entirely fulfilled, by the Zapatistas, that the
former Despacho advisors Isela Rodríguez and Mauricio Macossay revisted
the history of the war of the eggs more than a decade later. Although much
of the substance of the later narratives hewed closely to *La batalla de Tetiz y
Hunucmá*, in several ways their perspectives changed from those expressed
in the original text. If *La batalla de Tetiz y Hunucmá* had contextualized the
conflict in the history of the class struggle in Mexico, one decade after the
events Macossay and Rodríguez framed it instead in terms of the advent of
globalization: in Macossay's words, "a true earthquake, that has shaken everything." They linked developments in Tetiz more extensively to the policies
of the United States, the International Monetary Fund, and the World Bank
and to the replacement of traditional, state-mediated mechanisms of political control with a regime of direct domination by national and transnational
companies.

In these post-Zapatista accounts of the war of the eggs, ethnic identity,
specifically indigeneity, was privileged over class. In a reflection on the
movement in Tetiz, Rodríguez now opined that what distinguished it from
other workers' movements was the involvement of the entire pueblo of Tetiz,
with "indigenous forms of resistance." In recounting an initial secret meeting, hidden under the cover of trees, in which the decision to form an independent union was taken, Rodríguez declared that the union movement had
an "organizational dynamic that had more to do with ancestral indigenous
traditions than with those of workers." Such democratic assemblies, along
with strategies of collective physical defense, were "autonomous and atavistic ways that el pueblo maya organizes resistance." Similarly, in several

analyses, including his doctoral dissertation, Mauricio Macossay emphasized the Mayan nature of the workers and pueblo residents, noting how
"speaking, thinking and seeing themselves as Mayas is at the same time their
strength, and their weakness." While that shared identity gave them pride in
heritage, it also, in Macossay's view, brought predilections for conformism
and resignation, the legacy of "centuries of domination and subordination,"
which made indigenous heritage a "source of shame, due to the racism and
discrimination of which they are the object in Yucatecan society, a racist and
urban world that denigrates the Indian, and the rural, in equal measure."[41]

Reread in this way, the war of the eggs seemed to offer an alternative perspective on the unionization struggle as a political movement. In her retro-
spective account, Rodríguez drew attention—as the title of her essay indicates—to "What We Didn't Know" at the time of the strike: namely, that the
entire pueblo of Tetiz stood united behind the unionists. Similarly, Macossay
makes frequent references to "the solitary pueblo" ("el pueblo solidario") in
his account; for him, the collective and democratic nature of decision making in union meetings was an example, four years before the Zapatista uprising, of "leading while obeying." While this "direct, communitarian democracy" in Tetiz seemed to "come out of nothing" during the movement, it had
deep roots in the "hidden discourse of resistance" in indigenous history and
society. If such "vestiges" could be glimpsed but hadn't built into a sustained
movement, as in Chiapas, that was simply because of the movement's swift
collapse. Nonetheless, according to Macossay, for a time union and pueblo
"were united into a single actor, with a new social identity that included the
entire pueblo, based on the principle of autonomy and tending toward the
construction of a new state relation based on the participation of citizens,
rather than subjects." Out of the corrosive effects of globalization, there had
emerged, in Tetiz, a "new politics, and kind of citizenship" based on the
principle of "direct action."[42]

Both Rodríguez and Macossay now credit Tetiz for transforming their
consciousness as political organizers. Rodríguez recalls that "this Mayan
pueblo taught us—with all of our years of experience in union struggles—
their knowledge, intuition, creativity, wisdom, the organizational forms inherited from their ancestors, and, above all, the deepest meaning of dignity."
According to Macossay, in Tetiz the advisors learned to apply the "Indian and
communitarian principle of leading while obeying." Through their "intellectual commitment to el pueblo," in his view, the advisors distinguished
themselves from state and partisan political actors, who manipulated con-
sensus in conformity with their personal ambitions. The union advisors thus

became part of a "new way of making and exercising politics, of taking public spaces and using them openly, in an inclusive way, embracing diverse social and individual forces, to the benefit of social interests, rather than groups in power." Indeed, for both Rodríguez and Macossay, the outcome of the struggle was their own recognition as part of el pueblo; according to Macossay, "By the end of the conflict, many people said that the union advisors had become Teticeños—and that is certainly how the advisors felt."[43] In perhaps the most vivid demonstration of this sentiment, upon the death of Julio Macossay in February 2006 executors of his will learned that he had requested that half of his ashes be scattered in the pueblo of Tetiz (the other half were to be scattered in his native Campeche).[44]

Taken together, later accounts of the conflict recast the war of the eggs as a kind of retroactive Zapatismo. Despite the disappointing outcome of the so-called war, the tale, retold, seemed to some to demonstrate the possibilities of el pueblo as an insurgent subject and as the focus of a new politics, one in which intellectuals and organizers might join workers and pueblo residents in forming a common front of resistance to neoliberalism. Although the movement in Tetiz had dissolved, Macossay reflected, "Perhaps it is only in recess, awaiting a new, more favorable moment to return to its history and its path, with new energies and experience." In the meantime, though, Tetiz's conflict had become a metaphor and a charter for other things: the first chapter of a tale whose subsequent installments would be written elsewhere, whether by Zapatistas in Chiapas, by cooperative agriculturalists elsewhere in Yucatán, or by direct action activists far beyond the state's borders.[45]

When I began fieldwork in Tetiz in 1994, the aftermath of the war of the eggs was everywhere present, but rarely discussed—at least with me. The conflict was still fresh, as were the wounds it had left: jobs lost, men who had to leave the pueblo in search of work, families riven by their members' choice of allegiances during the conflict or by the ensuing years of partisan political rivalry. Over the years to follow, in the wake of economic crisis and the failure of the cooperative, I heard stories about the war of the eggs in bits and pieces that reflected the profoundly divergent ways those events are remembered. La batalla de Tetiz y Hunucmá was not circulated in Tetiz, but some pueblo residents recall the conflict in ways that accord with the perspective of the activists of the Despacho. Others, though, blame the advisors, the unionists, and the PAN for inciting a damaging conflict, one that caused the Fernández company to curtail plans for expansion that might have brought jobs and opportunities to el pueblo.

Residents of the ex-hacienda Nohuayum, who have constituted the vast majority of workers ever since the resignation and blacklisting of most workers from Tetiz, have their own perspectives on the matter. Many of them joined the union movement in its initial stages only to withdraw in the middle of the struggle, leading them into conflict with pueblo residents, who accused them of being scabs. A few were even stripped and beaten when they tried to return to work. Residents of the ex-hacienda also suffered from the strikers' blockade of the only road to Nohuayum during the conflict. Moreover, those who continued working at the farms after the conflict benefited from increased pay and improved working conditions after the introduction of the CTM union. Some younger men even prefer agricultural work to traditional milpa or henequen work: "There is shade there [in the granjas]," one once explained to me. Yet those who returned to the granjas continue to face intense exploitation and complain of arbitrary firings—typically just before end-of-year bonuses are due to be paid—unfair punitive measures, and other demeaning measures. From time to time, workers still talk of slavery, whether in jest or frustration, as during a bout of drinking or a "little strike" (huelguita) organized outside the granja's gates. Such events loosen tongues and offer opportunities to recall the war in a variety of ways, from pride to resentment to condemnation. Indeed, the only shared perspective on the war of the eggs, if one can be said to exist, is one of deep ambivalence—an ambivalence that finds a place neither in La batalla de Tetiz y Hunucmá nor in subsequent accounts that represent Tetiz as a "solidary pueblo."

Unionists were not the only ones to continue documenting and pondering the meaning of the war of the eggs. Avícolas Fernéndez kept its own archives, composed of press reports, videos, and lists of strikers and union members. That archive was not made available to me, despite my requests, though it was mentioned to me both by a supervisor and by workers. For supervisors, the events of 1990 are object lessons that informed changes in the company's strategies and labor relations, such as technological improvements, the use of temporary workers, the recruitment of workers from pueblos outside Tetiz, and the improvement of baseline conditions of work and remuneration for permanent employees. Workers and pueblo residents describe the archives of the company, like those of the old hacendados of Nohuayum, as a comprehensive record of their behavior and their union activities. Ku archivarta'al tuláakal, one worker told me in Maya: "Everything is archived," including the blacklists of workers who had affiliated with the independent union years before.

Eventually, the residents of Tetiz and Nohuayum began to speak more openly with me about their recollections of the war of the eggs. Several people told me that audiotapes of the theater play *Los huevos de Tetiz* had circulated in the pueblo in preceding years. Someone I knew had one but had passed it along to his cousin, and so I went to the cousin's house. The cousin said he had had it once but had passed it on to someone else—he did not remember whom. We spoke, though, about his recollections of the conflict and about the play. Over several succeeding years I followed many such trails of taped versions of *Los huevos de Tetiz*, all of them leading to nothing, except to opportunities to talk with more people about the conflict. This happened often enough that it became something of a joke. "He is looking for Tetiz's 'eggs'! Where are its 'eggs'?" they would say, in Spanish or Maya, introducing me to the many comic associations of *huevo* for pueblo residents. In the end, even I came to view my futile search for los huevos to be merely a pretext for more conversation.

During one of these searches I spoke with Tiger, an ejidatario, milpero, and hunter who was a PRI supporter and had served briefly as mayor of Tetiz a few years after the strike. Tiger has always refused to work in the granjas ("I can't stand the smell," he says), but he still gets upset when he talks about the war of the eggs and is unsparing in his criticism of the strikers and of the Despacho. "They ruined el pueblo!" he fumes, contemplating how much work there would be and how much money, if only the unionists had not created problems with Fernández. Then he describes the violence: "It was terrible what they did. Have you heard? The women got the supervisors and then. . . ."—his expression changes as he smiles and then begins to chuckle, unable to maintain his indignation—"they stripped them naked! And then they hit them"—openly laughing now—"with popox, on the huevos!" It is here, not in struggles over class, race, and work, but on the huevos that the conflict seems to have found its deepest register, neither in tragedy nor redemption but in memories of pain and laughter.

BY THE VIRGIN'S GRACE

The Archival Landscapes of Miracle,
Money, and Memory

EVERY YEAR IN TETIZ, pilgrimages, fiestas, and
other acts of devotion are dedicated to the Virgin of
Tetiz, one of the most venerated religious figures in the
Yucatán peninsula. At the heart of the annual cycle of
religious events is not only a well-adorned icon of the
Virgin, but a story, circulated and recounted in religious
pamphlets, sermons, and by word of mouth. In the winter of 1730, according to a version recorded in the late
nineteenth century by the Yucatecan bishop Crescencio
Carrillo y Ancona, the Virgin of Tetiz took on a woman's form and journeyed to Seville, in Spain. Clad in a
mendicant's tattered garb, she sought out a Francis-
can friar, Francisco de San Buenaventura Martínez de
Tejada, and begged him to give her alms to rescue her
and her son from the torments of poverty. While Fray
Francisco, himself impoverished, searched for money,
the woman continued her entreaties. "One day you will

see with your own eyes the miserable state of my humble shanty," she declared. "Then you will know my entire history and do for me everything that the holy charity that burns in your heart inspires." Francisco could find only a single Spanish peso to give to the woman, who went on her way. For years to come he often dreamed of her and of the coin he had given her. It was "inscribed in his memory," seeming always to "lie before his eyes, with its bust and seal on both sides, marked by the date and place of its coining." Francisco was sure that if he ever saw the coin again he would recognize it, even if it were "mixed up with many others, apparently identical in form."[1]

Subsequently, Francisco rose through the church hierarchy and traveled to the new world, eventually becoming bishop of Yucatán. One day, during a pastoral tour, he stopped at Tetiz, a small indigenous village. Followed by a procession of Indians, Francisco entered a rustic building that, "less than a temple, less than a church, was a hut on the point of collapse." He was shocked to see before him the image of the woman who had visited him, carved in wood and dressed in tattered, stained silk. As he drew closer, Francisco recognized before him, hanging on the figure amid other gold and silver coins, the very peso he had given away in Seville fourteen years before. Astonished by the coin's miraculous reappearance, Fray Francisco fell to his knees, and the Virgin appeared before him once more. She declared that while the people of Yucatán had been "very dear" to her from the moment of their "discovery and conquest" by her "beloved sons, the Spaniards," shrines dedicated to her veneration had been allowed to fall into decrepitude. "The day the Yucatecans forget my love," she warned, "will be the day of their complete disappearance as well." The bishop immediately devoted himself to fulfilling his "sacred debt" with the mendicant Virgin. The church devoted its resources to rescuing the pueblo's failing system of confraternities and to the construction of a sanctuary, which was completed in 1751.[2]

Almost three centuries after the Virgin's journey to Spain, residents of contemporary Tetiz continue to honor her and to retell the story of her miracles, both inside the pueblo's church and beyond its walls. To attempt a reading of the story of the Virgin's miraculous travels from the perspective of pueblo residents, however, is to embark upon a far-flung journey. It is to follow hunters to woodlands where they hunt deer in the Virgin's name and to track the transformation of those deer first into venison, then into money, and finally into the festivities that the gremios, especially the hunters' gremio (gremio de cazadores), finance; it is to follow the presence of the Virgin as she travels from forest to pueblo to nearby towns and haciendas and even to the homes of migrant workers in Seattle and Los Angeles. Read against the backdrop of the circulation of commodities, money, and people, the story of Fray Francisco and the Virgin demonstrates how a coin may bear within it not only abstract value, but also the concrete history of individuals, groups of people, and even of el pueblo: a collective entity that through sacred money and through a miraculous way of telling history finds a way to transcend not only poverty, but time and space as well.

PROMISES, MIRACLES, AND THE HUNT

Whistling; the sound of breaking foliage; barking and the smell of human sweat: all these signal danger. The deer (keh) bounds off downwind in flight, racing past a peccary and another deer, also on the run. Leaving its pursuers behind, the deer bolts through a clearing and braces to jump a barbed wire fence. Then there is a gunshot and another one, and the deer falls, wounded. It rises, jumps sideways, and bolts in a staggering run, evading the dogs for a moment, but then the barking draws closer, as they follow the scent of blood. The wounded deer is cornered, falls before the dogs, and struggles to rise as they circle. There are shouts and the sound of men running nearby. There is one more shot, and the hunters close in.[3]

Deer and peccary are protected species in Yucatán, and forest rangers fine and imprison poachers and confiscate their guns. In the years following the outbreak of the Zapatista uprising, forests adjacent to the pueblo of Tetiz were subject to particularly intense supervision. Even the most experienced hunters exercised extreme caution or avoided the hunt altogether. Tetiz's priest and its mayor requested special permission from forestry officials to hunt deer for the summer festivals of the Virgin. The officials showed them a book of laws forbidding the hunting of deer and peccary and offered permission for the entire pueblo of several thousand people to kill a maximum of three adult male deer. Pueblo residents criticized the priest and the mayor for having requested something considered to be a right of el pueblo and ridiculed the forest rangers. "How can you tell the sex of a deer as it bounds past you in the brush?" Cat asked me in exasperation. Had the officials brandishing their books of laws ever ventured out into the woods at all? Such restrictions are seen as unfair by pueblo residents, given the importance of the hunt for subsistence. "With these restrictions they are harming us," Monkey explained to me, "but our poverty obliges us to continue—you have to eat, don't you?" Faced with the possibility of imprisonment and the confis-

The quarry: recently killed deer.
Photo by Paul Eiss.

cation of their weapons if captured, the hunters reacted in a way that indicated their familiarity with forest surveillance: they decreased their visibility. They reduced the size of the largest hunting parties, stayed to little-used paths and roads to evade detection, and avoided the public display of deer carcasses and the sale of venison tacos for the rest of the summer.[4]

Amid, and to some extent despite, such concerns, the members of the hunters' gremio agreed to meet outside Tiger's house on the outskirts of the pueblo, at around 4:00 A.M. I had asked to accompany them, and the men agreed. The men straggled in one by one, dressed in sandals, long-sleeved shirts, and patched and torn trousers; they carried old single-barreled, breech-loading shotguns and satchels to carry water bottles and balls of corn dough for making gruel. There were a few dogs, scrawny but seasoned in the hunt. When a rickety flatbed truck arrived, the men and the dogs and I leaped in and crowded together, making room for latecomers who ran up as the engine roared. We set off, two dozen of us, clinging to ropes as the truck lurched. Before long we left the main road, swerving onto a rocky path.

Thorny branches sharp enough to rip fabric and skin whipped the unfortunate ones standing on the sides of the truck bed, as the truck lurched and rolled. Tiger shouted at the driver, "Step on it, son of a bitch!" There was laughter and then silence.

Several hours later we arrived at the camp, Chen Sotzil, just a clearing by a small ranch. There was a well and a hunters' shelter: three walls of piled rocks, with a roof of huano. Dragon, an elder and once the head of the gremio, though now hobbled by arthritis, lit a fire. Every man produced something he carried in his bag—eggs, liver, some tortillas—and passed them around to the rest of us. We sat and ate. The sun was just rising as we set off silently, single file. We paused for a moment as a few men turned off the narrow trail to head downwind. They would lie in wait: the pa'atlil. The rest of us continued the quiet march into the woods to flush the deer: the p'uh. We walked awhile, and then Tiger turned and pointed at Rabbit, who moved into the woods to take his position, shouldering his gun. We continued, and soon Tiger pointed to the next man, who stepped off the path. Then Tiger pointed to Bug, who steered me into the woods, telling me with his eyes to wait. The rest were lost to sight. Listening attentively, Bug gripped his shotgun and scanned the trees and bramble. Then there was a low whistle: Tiger's whistle, followed by Bug's response, and more whistles ever fainter in the distance. Bug headed straight into the woods, threading his way through what seemed an impenetrable wall of brush. I marked his passage and followed, crashing clumsily through the thicket and fighting off thorny branches and cattle flies. Bug looked ahead to identify the flora: "This is called chukum. Watch out for its spines!" Every few minutes he stopped, whistling and listening for the others. He didn't want us to be too far ahead of or behind the others or else the deer might escape; and if too far to one side or the other, we risked being mistaken for game or hit by stray shot. Ever vigilant, Bug scanned the ground for spoor: deer feces, tracks, or mounds of earth that betrayed the rooting of peccaries.

There was a rustle nearby. Bug raised his gun, but it was only a dog, racing ahead. There were more whistles, and we moved faster, for the quarry was near, running before the advancing line of hunters. A shot rang out ahead and then one to the right, where the other group of men lay in wait. Then there was the sign that the first of the men on p'uh had made it to where the pahtal was: a five-note whistle that marked the syllables of ts'ok in k'uchul ("I have arrived"). In a moment we reached a barbed wire fence enclosing cattle pasturage, and we followed it until we met the others. Chicken Thief

Carrying the deer to camp.
Photo by Paul Eiss.

was binding the deer's feet while the dogs licked at its wounds. Armadillo had already hoisted a small peccary onto his shoulders, strapping it to his forehead with a rope. Chicken Thief followed suit, hoisting the heavy deer onto his shoulders.

Through forest and milpa, cattle land and old henequen fields, we continued on our way, keeping to trackless thickets and narrow paths. Returning to camp, we were laden with carcasses: four deer, two peccary, and a wild turkey. Dragon and Squirrel set their gnarled, skilled hands to dressing the animals. A swift cut from neck to belly, and the stomach and organs came out; Dragon hung them on a nearby branch. More cuts, and the flesh came away in chunks, thrown into a bucket of boiling water. Squirrel dangled a peccary over the fire, singeing the bloated carcass. Tiger hoisted some other deer onto the truck, concealing them under a layer of recently harvested maize. The rest of us poured hot water over our limbs and plucked out ticks we had picked up in the woods. The sun set, and we ate deer stew; a few pitched hammocks, while the rest of us settled onto palm leaves spread on the hard ground.

The next day, we continued hunting, and then returned to Tetiz. After dark we met by Corncob's house, where the carcasses lay hidden behind closed doors. Venison cooked in a roasting pit, while the men passed around a bucket filled with aguardiente and ice, along with a bowl of deer brains flavored with lime juice. Soon the meat was ready, and every man chose his portion according to the rules of the hunt.[5] One leg was for the driver of the truck that carried us to the forest. The stomach, liver, and skin were for the man who shot the deer; two men had fired, and now each challenged the other's right. Then equal shares were apportioned to every man who participated in the hunt, regardless of whether or not he had shot. There was laughter and joking, bickering over choice pieces of meat, and drinking. Finally, each man returned home with a bag of meat, which would be consumed in his house or passed along to relatives and friends.

Taking a deer is hard work. Considerable energy and material resources are dedicated to the hunt, and the venison brought back to the pueblo is a valued contribution to family subsistence. Most hunters, however, do not see hunting as a form of productive labor, or the forest as a resource to be exploited; rather, they understand the woodlands as an arena of reciprocal exchanges between humans, animals, spirits, and divinities. Such ideas have ancient roots. Mayan sculpture and glyphs, codices, and colonial-era texts depict the forest as a world inhabited and guarded by supernatural entities like Yum K'ax (the lord of the forest), Chac (lord of rain and wind), Yum Keh (lord of the deer), and a host of lesser beings charged with protecting the forest and its denizens. Those who dared to cut and burn the forest to make milpa performed sacrifices and rituals meant to appease the anger of the guardians of the forest and secure the right to clear and plant. The same was true of hunters, who formed large groups to hunt deer and other creatures of the forest with bows and arrows and traps. Large-scale ceremonies were held each year to appease the spirits of the forest and secure permission for future hunts through sacrifice, ritual, and entreaty.[6]

Even in the wake of the Spanish conquest and over the course of ensuing centuries, belief in and exchanges with a wide array of supernatural actors in the forest continued. While some of the largest public rituals were eliminated, Mayan populations continued to honor a large array of supernatural entities: *balamob* or *yuntzilob*, the protectors of human settlements, milpas, and beehives; *kuilob k'axob* or *yumil k'axob*, the guardians of the forest; the *chaako'b* as spirits of the rain; and a large number of Christian saints. Ritualized exchanges link the presence and disposition of such entities to the fate of the milpa, to the arrival or absence of rains, to the maturation of maize and its protection from animals, and to the protection of beehives. Such syncretic public ceremonies as the ch'a chaak (a rain ceremony) and the u janli kol (giving thanks for the maize harvest) combine practices of Christian and Mayan origin and often involve sacrifices of chickens and offerings of corn gruel or other foods.[7]

The hunt is governed by other supernatural entities, the metan lu'um, which, along with saints like San Gabriel, San Cecilio, and San Marcelino, are custodians of flora and fauna. Beneath these figures are the laj kajob or sepob, stones that guard particular areas of the forest and the creatures that reside there. Traditionally, hunters pay their respects to the forest guardians by burning incense or making other offerings. Upon killing a deer, it is customary to put the animal's head, liver, and stomach on a tree for one hour, as a symbolic offering. Other sacrifices and offerings are made to the lords of the forest in ceremonies like the loh ts'on and the k'ex, and entreaties are made for their assistance during the ch'a chaak ceremony as well.[8] The most feared entity, however, is the sip, a creature that looks like a small deer with large horns, from which a nest of wasps often hangs suspended. To protect the deer the sip deceives hunters into shooting instead at iguanas. If a hunter misses his target, the sip is often held responsible. The sip's appearance is taken as a warning sign that hunters are exceeding the acceptable number of prey. If shot at or if it decides to punish hunters, the sip afflicts them with a lethal illness or releases its wasps to punish the men with their stings.[9]

The deer play a crucial role in exchanges of flesh. This is most evident in the case of the venado de virtud (an enchanted deer), which is much more difficult to hunt and kill than an ordinary deer. In its stomach, the venado de virtud carries a tunich keh, or "deer stone," which reputedly brings its bearer great fortune in the hunt. With such a talisman, a hunter brings down deer every time he enters the forest, even while others return empty-handed. The stone works only as long as it is kept hidden. The moment the hunter reveals its existence to another man, the stone loses all its power. As one older hunter, Armadillo, explained to me, "The tunich gives you good fortune, but it is all counted. Like money, the tunich becomes devalued," finally bringing misfortune to its possessor.[10] In any case, the stone will only work for four years, after which time it must be shallowly buried in the forest, where another deer will recover and consume it, thereby becoming a venado de virtud in turn. As a magical talisman that derives from the deer's body, the tunich thereby configures the hunt as a relationship of exchange. By analogy with money, however, it is a token of exchange whose overuse, in violation of communal norms, brings peril.[11]

As a productive activity and form of exchange, the hunt is closely governed by custom, with punishments for those who violate norms. First, while women take part in some sylvan occupations like cutting wood and gathering oregano and other herbs, hunting is a male prerogative whose transgression by females brings peril. The gun is considered to be masculine in gender, and its effectiveness is linked to the moral character of its male possessor.[12] Some believe, as Doña Leonor told me, that if a woman so much as touches a shotgun she will take away the weapon's force forever; if the possessor of a tunich keh allows it to be seen or touched by a woman, he will go insane. The ritual and sacrificial exchanges realized between hunters and the lords of the forest are masculine affairs that women are not allowed to attend or view.[13]

Greater still is the peril to hunters who violate the spirit of restraint that structures the practice of hunting. Hunters recount stories about the yumil keh, a figure who cares for the deer as a rancher would tend his cattle and punishes offending hunters with fatal illnesses. As Armadillo told me, one man from Tetiz who hunted excessively began to have bad luck, missing most of his targets. When he finally wounded one animal and set off in pursuit of it, he found his way to a corral full of deer in the forest. A yumil keh approached, scolded him for killing so many of his deer, and then struck him with a whip. Fleeing the forest, the hunter fell deathly ill. Though cured of his malady by an herbalist, he never entered the forest again.[14] The most severe penalties, however, are reserved for the hunter who misuses the tunich keh, typically by not returning the stone to the earth. A group of deer, who keep count of the number of deer killed by each hunter, turns the tables by chasing him down and devouring him.[15] On Nohuayum, one man reported that a friend of his father had suffered such a fate. After excessive hunting for personal profit, one day he found himself surrounded by a voracious horde of deer. Terrified, he climbed up into a tree to save himself, only to die later that night from a mysterious illness.[16]

Tetiz is by no means a traditional Mayan pueblo. Many Mayan rituals and practices that have been documented in eastern Yucatán no longer exist in the pueblos located in the former henequen zone or are no longer practiced with frequency; communal hunts are now performed instead, in association with gremios' veneration of Christian saints. When men from Tetiz organize a hunt, however, they continue to do so in cognizance of the forest as a domain of exchanges, with norms, custodians, punishments for violators, and rewards for those respectful of its customs and authorities. If a hunter has poor luck it is said he may regain his fortune by making an offering to the lords, at crosses placed alongside a woodland road or path. He places three stones in a pile there and recites an *Ave María* and a *Padre Nuestro* ("Our Father"); if he brings down a deer that day, then he should return to light a candle as an offering to the same cross. Similarly, if excessive hunting has led the forest to become what some hunters describe as "exhausted" or "stale," an offering of food, sugar, or matches in the woods may regenerate it. When a rattlesnake bit the leader of Nohuayum's gremio de cazadores during a hunting trip, for instance, the absence of symptoms of poisoning evidenced the protection of San Antonio, the saint to whom the gremio is dedicated. Older residents of Tetiz sometimes even refer to Jesus as El Señor de los Venados (The Lord of the Deer).

The hunt's sacred reciprocities are especially evident in Tetiz's gremio de cazadores. All the gremio members obey a strict prohibition on the consumption of alcohol while in the woods on a hunt and describe their abstinence, like the hunt, as the fulfillment of *promesas* ("promises") they make to the Virgin.[17] The Virgin is present at every moment of the hunt, working her miracles. If a deer is missed by a shot at close quarters, it is because it was so decreed by the Virgin. If another falls, whether the shot is fired from a distance or close by, it is seen as evidence of the Virgin's intercession. Every deer that is killed is thought to bear a mark on one ear that indicates it had been chosen for that destiny by the Virgin. Hence every death is a miracle; even the tunich keh is seen, as Don Mauro told me, as a "great miracle." If hunters go unharmed by stray bullets, escape the fangs of poisonous serpents, or recover from serious sickness, these are, like the carcasses they carry home, all evidence of the Virgin's intercession. In so many ways, hunters perceive the presence of the Virgin whenever they enjoy the bounty of the hunt and emerge unscathed, having exchanged their promesas for miracles of the Virgin.

FROM VENISON TO FIESTA

Those promesas, however, contract a debt that is not discharged out in the woods. If hunters do not offer sacrifices to the Virgin in the forest, as some do to the traditional Mayan forest guardians, how do they compensate her beneficence? The answer resides in the deer's flesh and in its subsequent transubstantiation into other commodities, including money. One half of the venison of the hunt is distributed to the hunters, providing immediate sustenance to them and their families and friends, as the meat is carried from house to house in plastic bags or trays. The rest of the deer, however, is taken furtively to Mérida, where it is sold at the high prices offered on the black market for illegally hunted venison. At that moment, the deer's flesh is transformed into a sum of pesos, as "deer money" [tak'in keh] which returns to Tetiz to fill the coffers of the gremio de cazadores, merging with monies donated by nonhunting gremio members and beginning the liquidation of a sacred debt.[18]

Thus converted from venison into money, the deer embarks on a series of transformations, from money to commodity and back to money, and through alternating moments of exchange and use. Deer money finances the purchase of the food and drink that are publicly distributed and consumed at the fiestas of the gremio: maize, beans, onions, sugar, flour, rice, turkeys, and chickens. These commodities, along with other in-kind contributions to the gremio, are further transformed by the intensive labor of cooking and food preparation contributed by female members of the gremio de cazadores, as they prepare tamales, deer stew, and drinks of chocolate or corn gruel for devotees of the Virgin. The sale of deer meat also finances the purchase of beer, which is sold by the gremio to men and women at its fiestas, allowing the deer money to sprint back, with monetary increase, to the treasury of the gremio.

Among the most costly of gremio activities is the production of colorful and costly banners, or estandartes, that are commissioned by the gremio. The banners are fashioned by women at great cost in time and materials. After so many transformations—from living animal to venison to sequential transformations into commodities and money—the deer triumphantly, if momentarily, reappears in the banners, which typically depict the Virgin surrounded by flowers and kneeling deer. On the morning of the gremio's annual fiesta, gremio banners are carried in procession by hundreds of women and men as they walk toward the church. There, the gremio offers rosaries, decorations and lights for the altar, and candles to light the chapel, all financed largely with deer money. There are paid Masses dedicated to the Virgin and hired groups of mariachi musicians to sing in her honor. As the fiesta begins thereafter, there are groups of dancers hired to perform jaranas, sometimes accompanied by a man dancing with a pig's head held aloft or even a deer's head, as if to recall the animal whose presence, as money, animates the fiesta. As the fiesta continues into the evening, there are fireworks,

Women making tortillas for the fiesta of the *gremio de cazadores*, or hunters' guild, Tetiz. Photo by Paul Eiss.

whose precise cost seems to be a subject of endless public discussion and fascination, along with a "fire cow" [*wakax k'ak'*] or a "fire deer" [*keh k'ak'*], facsimile animals bearing fireworks that men carry on their backs while the fireworks explode in every direction, sending observers scattering and laughing excitedly.[19]

The diverse activities of the gremio de cazadores are not unique to it but characteristic of the fiesta system throughout the Yucatán peninsula. A money economy came to permeate religious practice in the pueblos. Thus, what might be considered the domain of the sacred enjoys little if any autonomy from the profane world of commodity exchange and money relations; both have been shaped by the increasing social and class division characteristic of contemporary Yucatán. The fiestas afford an opportunity for an expression of solidarity among poorer pueblo residents; at the same time, they offer wealthier residents the prospect of pecuniary gain and an opportunity for displays of status through public performance of supposedly traditional mestizo cultural practices and multifarious associated acts of conspicuous consumption.[20]

The Keh K'ak', or "Fire Deer" at
the fiesta of the gremio de cazadores, Tetiz. Photo by Paul Eiss.

The veneration of the Virgin of Tetiz, though centuries old, has been
transformed in similar ways. Though situated at the center of Tetiz's religious life, the Virgin is in constant motion, on procession through the streets
of the pueblo and carried to nearby haciendas, pueblos, and towns. The annual cycle of events culminates in a series of fiestas and bullfights attended
by thousands of people in mid-August in Tetiz. A diverse set of actors takes
part in organizing the August festivities, from priests and church officials
to *cargadores*, or carriers, who after making promesas to the Virgin assume
various ritual obligations, including bearing the Virgin during processions.
Well-to-do families conspicuously and competitively donate outside the gremio system, paying for their own Masses or for mariachis to serenade the
Virgin in their family's name or assuming the role of dressing the Virgin or
providing other services to her. The festivities fuel a local economy geared
to the celebrations, and many people and institutions profit from the purchase, sale, and consumption of a host of commodities, from foodstuffs to
firecrackers. The church raises a good deal of money through the sale of ta-

cos and through direct monetary donations. As in other pueblos in Yucatán, in Tetiz the fiestas partake of a commercial ethos that blurs any distinction between profane and sacred.

The gremios—the gremio de cazadores and many others besides—play a key role in the planning, elaboration, and financing of the fiestas, processions, Masses, and other activities involved in the celebrations. Both men and women participate, and many are members of multiple gremios. While gremios differ in membership and in style, they are organized in similar ways, channeling their members' contributions of cash, kind, and labor into the fiestas of the Virgin and facilitating the flow of prestations, most notably the distribution of large amounts of free tacos, tamales, and other food to gremio members and their friends and neighbors. Toward the climax and conclusion of the fiestas in mid-August, there are increasingly large processions, celebrations, and traditional dances as visitors from neighboring pueblos and from across Yucatán arrive to join in the celebrations. Among the gremios, the gremio de cazadores stands out as the most important. It is the largest and best financed; its processions are the largest and grandest; and it plays a leading role in organizing the fiestas as an occasion for symbolic display and public spectacle. In the past—before the crackdown on deer hunting—that role would be publicly recognized, with dozens of deer displayed in the church festooned with ribbons and awaiting their transformation, first into meat and then into money, to feed the faithful and honor the Virgin. Such displays are wistfully remembered by many residents (ku exhibirta'al ["they were exhibited"], one man told me) and are perhaps evoked in dances with deer heads, which are performed for the fiesta of the gremio de cazadores.

Only when the hunt is related to this sacred economy encompassing both forest and pueblo and involving the activities of other gremios can the full significance of the deer's miraculous sacrifice and the hunters' sacred debt be understood. To follow a deer from its life and death to its subsequent transformation into and consumption as various kinds of commodities is to survey the gifts and debts that link those human and divine actors through a series of transactions: from the moment the Virgin marks the ear of a deer that will fall in the hunt to the offerings made to the Virgin during the fiestas by those who venerate her. It is to find the story of the Virgin's miraculous journey to Seville resonating throughout the gremio's activities: from the promise, miracle, and debt that permeates the activity of hunting to the dramatic resolution of the fiestas, which echo Fray Francisco's miraculous

Dance with a deer's head at the fiesta of the gremio de cazadores, Tetiz. Photo by Paul Eiss.

reencounter with his coin and with the Virgin. Here, the story of the Virgin, enacted as much in readings of that story as in the activities of the gremios, reveals itself as a story of a sacred journey—from venison to fiesta and from Fray Francisco's money to the Virgin's grace.

TIME, MONEY, AND THE VIRGIN'S GRACE

In Tetiz, as in all places, time flows in multiple currents. There is the yearly passage between the cool, dry season and the season of intense heat and rains. There are cycles of labor as well. Milpa lands are cleared, burned, planted, and harvested; henequen is cut and processed, and new shoots are planted. Women and men travel to neighboring pueblos or to Mérida to sell produce or search for work; some set off for Los Angeles or return with their earnings. Labor in the chicken farms proceeds as a series of tasks, paychecks, raises, and occasional dismissals. Newspapers arrive daily and along with television and radio broadcasts advertise the passage of holidays, elections, and newsworthy events that link the time of Tetiz with the time of Mexico.

Time's deepest channel may be that of the Virgin. The very sense of time passing in Tetiz is strongly related to the yearly cycle of fiestas, processions, and other events associated with her veneration. Every week and every day

Procession from Hunucmá
to Tetiz during the fiesta of the
Virgin of Tetiz. Photo by
Paul Eiss.

are filled with her, both in the prayers of individuals and families, who en-
treat her for assistance in times of trouble, and in public events relating to
her veneration, which always seem to be either happening or on the verge of
happening. In addition to the quotidian cycle of Masses and church events
that take place under the Virgin's gaze, a series of processions and other
events extends through the year, typically occupying hundreds and sometimes thousands of people. These processions accompany the Virgin to
nearby pueblos like Hunucmá and Kinchil, to ex-haciendas like Nohuayum,
and farther afield, as for example in the Virgin's yearly boat journey from the
coastal pueblo of Celestún accompanied by dozens of fishing boats. While
the largest processions of the Virgin are her journeys to and from Hunucmá
in January, the cycle of activities reaches its climax in the August festivals
held in Tetiz. The fiestas have, in some sense, become transnational affairs
in that residents send videos of the processions and of the annual fiestas to
migrants in Los Angeles, whose cash remittances help to finance the fiesta
system. The Virgin thus repeats her far-flung journeys in digital form, as
the recorded performances of such acts of collective veneration, along with

shrines to the Virgin in migrants' homes, help to reconnect migrants with their pueblo of origin.[21]

Although there are large, commercial movements of money associated with the fiestas and processions in Tetiz, these monetary transactions neither dominate those events nor take on an important symbolic role in them. The gremios' money does, however, play a crucial material and symbolic role for devotees of the Virgin. A sizable proportion of the adult population of Tetiz, both male and female, participates in one or more gremios. While a gremio will sometimes tender an invitation to a particular individual to join its ranks, membership in the gremios generally is open to whomever elects to make a donation in cash or kind. Indeed, donation of cash is often equated with membership; one man indicated his membership in multiple gremios by explaining, "I put a little bit of money [dinerito] here, I put my dinerito there." The donation of even a "dinerito" places the new member on a par with all other participants, as all gifts, whether of one peso or one hundred, are said to be equal in the Virgin's eyes. People can remain members even after death by willing regular donations to be made in their names in ensuing years. Members aim at giving a respectable amount of money in line with the norms of the gremio, while not attempting to outdo the donations of other members through ostentatious giving. Nonmembership is generally ascribed either to extreme poverty or stinginess (ts'uutil).

The management of the gremios and their resources is sometimes entrusted to a formal junta composed of a president, secretary, treasurer, vice president, and officials, or vocales. The gremio de cazadores is led by a group of untitled "big or old men" (nohoch makob) who manage the affairs of the gremio. The treasurer collects and manages the funds, while the president hosts the fiesta of the gremio in his or her backyard and usually must spend up to three days preparing for the fiesta as well as donate several turkeys for the gremio lunch in gratitude for the privilege of hosting the fiesta. Some vagueness of responsibilities seems to be common in the gremios: as Don Mauro, the leader of the Fe y misericordia (Faith and mercy) gremio, related, "I'm part president, part treasurer, and part secretary." As the gremio leaders age, they are seen as less likely to be able to meet the arduous responsibilities of leadership, and the responsibilities and eventually the title of office are shifted to younger members, through either a vote or the uncontested offer of a volunteer.[22]

Leaders and participants now consider the gremios to be explicitly apolitical. The intensity of this sentiment is largely a product of the late 1980s and early 1990s, when partisan political conflict between the PRI and the PAN triggered conflicts within the gremios, leading to the departure of some panista gremio members. After the related sequestration of the Virgin by residents of Hunucmá during her visit to that town and a resulting dispute between the two pueblos, church officials and gremio leaders pledged to keep partisan politics out of the gremios. Ever since, delegations from Hunucmá have had to travel to Tetiz with hats in hand to formally request the Virgin's January visit and to hear lectures from Tetiz's church leaders regarding the proper care of the Virgin and the conditions of her return.

The gremios' management of funds structures the temporal extension and rhythm of their activities. In the first phase, from September to July, called (recaudo) collection, the gremio leaders collect money and other donations from members. Monies from male labor in fields and chicken facilities, from the sale of fruit and vegetables by market women, from migrant workers in Los Angeles, and from the sale of venison enter the gremio coffers. Recently, some gremios, including the hunters' gremio, have begun to receive large amounts of money from younger, migrant members in the form of remitted dollars, which are converted to pesos. While this makes the gremios, in a sense, transnational institutions, their functioning and spirit thus far have changed little. Whatever the source of the funds, collection requires particular skill, since the money arrives not all at once but in sporadic small quantities given by individuals to the gremio officials, for which they are held responsible.[23]

In the second phase of the fiestas, called junta ("assembly"), meetings are held in June and July to organize and account for the funds, plan for the fiestas, and make appropriate purchases, ensuring that the income of the gremio will cover its anticipated expenditures for the year. Gremio leaders often use metaphors derived from the world of business to describe the scope of their responsibilities, as both sacred and financial in nature. When funds fall short, additional hunts and sometimes the sale of tacos or beer are arranged to cover the short-term debt (p'ax). Although there are sometimes surpluses or debts of a few hundred pesos after the fiestas are concluded, the goal of the gremio is to finish the fiesta cycle even (nivelado), with neither surplus nor debt. Discussing his gremio, one leader told me that it was "for the Virgin . . . that is why we are in this business [negocio], more or less." Another leader of the gremio de cazadores said of smaller groups that made donations to the Virgin but didn't rise to the level of a gremio, "They have no music, no possibilities, no economy, no money . . . you have to spend more [to make a gremio]"

Collecting coins for the Virgin before a bull fight in Tetiz.
Photo by Paul Eiss.

(mina'an música, mina'an pósibilidad, mina'an économia, mina'an tak'in . . . yan a betik mas gastó).²⁴

The third phase is the fiesta itself. The fiestas center on a series of processions, Masses, and fireworks displays, but among their central moments are the fiestas of the gremios themselves, which are typically held in the backyard of the presidents or gremio founders. In every rocket exploded, every Mass conducted, every candle burned, in the large-scale gifts of food and drink made by the gremio to nonmember pueblo residents, and even in the music of the fiesta and the mariachis paid to sing to the Virgin, gremio members recognize their own investment in and contribution to the gremio, cease-lessly·reiterated as a share in every moment of the spectacle. Like Fray Francisco's coin, their modest contributions seem to return to them increased in value.

As in forms of circulation associated with commercial capitalism, the circulation of goods and commodities in the fiesta system begins and ends in the exchange of money and other forms of symbolic wealth. But while commercial capitalist circulation typically involves the purchase and sale of commodities for monies that are distinct in quantity but identical in quality, the hallmark of this remarkable circulatory process is the *qualitative* transformation of diverse means of exchange: the tunich keh; deer money; expenses of the gremios; the coins and valuables adorning the Virgin, when Francisco reencounters her.[25] This qualitative difference is reflected in contemporary perceptions of Francisco's coin. While some Teticeños identify the coin as a Spanish peso, others call it a Spanish *real*, while still others report even that it was a U.S. dollar. All are agreed, however, that it was not a Mexican peso. Reconsidered against the backdrop of the circulation of the Virgin's money in the gremios, the story of Francisco's coin takes on a different meaning, as a story not only about the recognition of a lost coin, but also about the Virgin's power to transform apparently identical currency into qualitatively and recognizably distinct forms, forms whose apparent similarity as currency masks their radical difference as coin. Deer money, like Francisco's peso, may appear identical to Mexico's secular currency, as the product of the articulation of an older form of communal production and exchange within a wider capitalist economy. Through circulation in the gremio system, however, monies are recoined in a sacred economy, becoming not only measures of time and quantities of money, but also tokens of the Virgin's grace.

THE MONEY OF HISTORY

Outside of the planning of the fiestas, the central activity of the juntas is the drafting of *libretas*, or ledgers, in which every income and expense of the gremio is scrupulously recorded; as one secretary explained to me, "They must be credited on the list [*Yan u abonarta'al ti u listá*]." Throughout the junta phase, gremio leaders render accounts, often by memory, of gifts given them in cash or kind, and the secretary records these in a draft ledger. The expenses of the gremio are divided into house expenses, for the purchase of corn, chickens, turkeys, beans, onions, sugar, banana leaves, and chocolate, and fiesta expenses, for music, fireworks, Masses, candles, and the like. All are carefully listed, with price and quantity noted. At the last junta before the fiesta, the final list of members, individual donations, and expenses is inscribed in the libreta, which extends back through years or decades of gremio fiestas. Typically dog-eared old school notebooks or sheaves of papers, the libretas are carefully guarded, because the members understand them as constituting archives whose formation and conservation are essential to the gremio.

The libretas of the gremio de cazadores record the contributions of each hunter as shares of the total cash derived from venison sales, from as little as one hundred pesos for Squirrel, a sporadic hunter, to one thousand for Tiger, who never missed a hunt. The origins of that money are masked, or laundered, as simple sums of pesos, erasing any trace of the deer's flesh and its commerce.[26] Indeed, in the libretas of all of the gremios the use of money as a measure of accounting implies a kind of money fetishism that, in classic fashion, effaces the origins of individual contributions to the gremios (that is, the money's origin in a particular kind of labor) and disassociates producers from the product of their labors.[27] Moreover, while all members are acknowledged, the extensive labor of food preparation for the fiestas, largely performed by females, is not quantified in the ledger. Nonetheless, female members of the gremio de cazadores are recognized by being named in the member lists, and they insist that their contributions to the gremio, whether in cash, kind, or labor, be given parity.[28]

The accounting of the gremio's resources is provisional, however, until its performative enactment in public readings of the libreta by the secretary during the fiestas of August. While members listen in rapt attention, the secretary recognizes their contributions as a series of quantities of money attached to the names of gremio members, in separate recitations of lists of male and female contributors. At this time, every member has the right to challenge publicly the amount attached to his or her name, a right seen as the guarantee of the legitimacy of the gremio and the honesty and competence of gremio leaders (although one leader found a question I raised about the possibility of the misappropriation of gremio funds absurd: "You would only be defrauding yourself if you did that!"). While the writing of the ledgers marks the individual contributions to the Virgin as quantities of cash and commodities rather than as wage labor performed or deers hunted, the public reading of the ledgers and the attendant display and consumption of collective wealth at the fiestas facilitate the broadest possible notions of ev-

Public reading of the *libreta*, or ledger, at the fiesta of the Fe y Misericordia (Faith and Mercy) guild. Photo by Paul Eiss.

ery individual's share. As participants in the gremios frequently emphasize, although one might have contributed only a single peso, one holds a stake in every aspect of the costly fiestas, processions, and gifts to the Virgin. Far from simply realizing the alienation of producers from their labor, money thus associates members with the gremio's material and symbolic wealth, as expressed in its works and festivities, precisely through the process of abstraction, which recognizes particular contributions in accountable form.

Most importantly, gremio money facilitates a long-term accounting of history, making the gremios into institutions of group memory. Each gremio is associated with a particular group of people, often connected by ties of family or friendship, and their lives shape the course of the gremio from its birth to its subsequent expansion and eventually—as members age and hunting and other fundraising activities become more difficult—to its contraction and eventual disappearance. The oldest existing gremios of Tetiz are about sixty years old.[29] It is through an explicit accounting of money, as a conveyance and a representation of value, that gremio members understand the decades-long careers of the gremios as corporations. One way they do so is through the production of costly estandartes, which become symbolic "banks" of surplus funds left after the fiesta expenses have been paid and also commemorate important dates, such as the founding of the gremio. In addition to being decorated with ornate depictions of the Virgin and, in the case of the gremio de cazadores, deer, the banners are marked with the date and year of the fiesta at which they were first exhibited in procession in the fiestas of the gremio and are displayed on the church altar flanking the Virgin on the day of the gremio fiesta. They are carefully guarded and maintained and constitute public documents of great importance as stored expressions of the gremio's bounty in previous years.

The central document of the gremio archives is the libreta itself. At junta meetings and at the public readings of the ledgers records from previous years or decades are often reviewed and discussed. The libretas are kept for their value in financial administration, but in addition they are read with interest, even marvel, as accounts of the contributions of members past and present to the gremio's material and symbolic wealth. In the libretas there is also evidence of the meteoric rise of commodity prices and of the dramatic devaluations of the Mexican peso over the decades. In them, one may read evidence of the changing fortunes and misfortunes of the gremio, of the political conflicts that disrupted meetings or reduced the numbers of the membership, and of the years when economic crisis or luckless hunts shrank the income of the gremio. As one gremio leader remarked on inspecting the ledger, "Wow! We had hard luck that year! [¡Mare! ¡Apretadó'on le añó'o!]." In comparing it with the present, he exclaimed, "Look at how much money we raised on those three hunts! The hunt was good this year."

Gremio leaders explicitly refer to the libreta as an archival document. When I asked Don Mauro why his gremio retained previous years' records, for instance, he responded simply, "It must be archived (Yan u archivarta'al)." Those charged with maintaining the documents think of themselves as archivists; one gremio leader said to me, "I record those who bring money. Year after year, I record. . . . Everything is recorded. I have everything, written down in the libreta—how much the men give, and how much the women give." He expressed distress about the lackluster record-keeping of the gremio in its first years, which frustrated his attempts to make an ordered libreta of scraps of undated and barely legible paper. In retaining and inspecting records of previous years and decades and through the storage and display of the estandartes, the gremio officials demonstrate an acute awareness of the historical trajectory of the gremio, from the times decades ago when, in Mauro's recollection, "just pennies were collected" and the entire fiesta cost fifty pesos, to the fiestas of the present day, which cost thousands of (devalued) pesos.[30]

Banners, or *estandartes*, of Tetiz's gremio de cazadores, depicting Virgin of Tetiz flanked by deer and henequen. Photo by Paul Eiss.

Members of the gremios perceive even the structure of Tetiz's church as a manifestation of the bounty and money of the gremios. In earlier years, the lack of restrictions on hunting and the sale of beer and deer tacos by the gremio de cazadores allowed it to amass surplus funds sufficient to make significant improvements to the church: fans, fluorescent lighting fixtures, and an organ were added.[31] The gremio is no longer in a position to donate sums of money sufficient to such purchases. The history of their successful efforts to do so, however, and the large amounts of money the church is able to earn through bazaars and food and beer stands attending to the thousands of procession goers lead many to continue to see their small contributions of meat and money as themselves miraculous, and as the means through which their church and their pueblo have been made.

Gremio members may join and contribute to the gremios as individuals, but they experience their place in it and look upon its works as Teticeños; they see the works of the gremio as evidence not only of dedication to the Virgin, but also of the autonomy and honor of their pueblo. In answering my questions about how they felt upon witnessing the fiesta and the reading of the libretas, gremio members avoided statements of individual pride or accomplishment, referring instead to their Virgin and their pueblo. As one man explained when referring to construction works financed by his gremio, "You feel pride . . . but pride for your pueblo [*orgullo ti a kahal*]. You feel happy, you feel satisfied . . . because you are focused on supporting the fiesta of the Virgin. You are dedicated to her . . . because all the money spent is an homage to the Virgin. . . . It is a pleasure to be able to collect the few pennies that the members give us." Similarly, when I asked Don Marcos, a former president of Tetiz's church, to recount the story of the Virgin's journey to Seville, he quickly switched to an account of the history of the chapel's expansion and improvement in recent years. For him, processions, the construction of new chapels, materials amassed to expand the altar, and funds raised to build a new church in the seaside pueblo of Celestún were all miracles of the Virgin.[32]

In so many ways, in a population divided by social position and political affiliation and by differences of class and gender, money makes possible the construction of a community united in worship. It does so, in part, through money's abstracting properties, properties that facilitate both amnesia and recollection, laundering and naming, alienation and recognition, as even poorer pueblo residents represent their labor, themselves, and their pueblo in monetary form. The Virgin's money is a means for the expression of personal honor and communal belonging despite the legacies of capitalist economic transformation. The Virgin thereby plays a significant role in the self-definition of Teticeños as members of a community in tense relation with wider polities and economies. The Virgin's money, like other kinds of money, conceals many aspects of its history in acts of production and exchange and separates persons from products, temporally and spatially. Yet for many Teticeños that sacred money is the purchase price of Tetiz itself. By collecting and counting coins, the people of Tetiz honor their sacred debt to the Virgin and bring value, honor, and grace to their pueblo. At the same time, they restore and reshape their connection to the woodlands of the Hunucmá region and, in so doing, to the histories—of kah, común, and pueblo—that have been inscribed so deeply in that landscape.

In 1885, Crescencio Carrillo y Ancona left Mérida for Tetiz, determined to follow in the footsteps of Fray Francisco. He walked along the road to Tetiz, passing the series of large wooden crosses Francisco had ordered erected along the route to the church long ago—"monuments" that inspired Carrillo to "remember the entire history and popular tradition [of Francisco and the Virgin] . . . that I was hearing recounted for the hundredth time." Arriving in the "historic sanctuary," the visitor fell to his knees as Fray Francisco had, long before him, and adored the "miraculous statue" of the Virgin of Tetiz. Searching for Francisco's coin, though, he could not find it and was told it had been lost years before. Like Francisco, Carrillo decried Tetiz's poverty and what he called its "decadence," as well as the decrepit state of the sanctuary, which he perceived to be in ruins. Carrillo y Ancona, who soon would become bishop of Yucatán, became an advocate for the restoration of the sanctuary, perhaps entertaining the idea of continuing Francisco's works in the present.[33]

During an interview I conducted with the church leader Don Marcos on one of my own trips to Tetiz, I asked the same question Carrillo y Ancona had asked more than a century earlier: "What about Francisco's peso? Whatever happened to it?" Don Marcos answered without hesitation, "Look! It is everywhere—all around you."[34] His answer identified the presence of the coin in the world that surrounded him, especially in the gremio system and in the church and its works. Francisco's miraculous coin for Marcos was not an object fixed in place and on display, but one that circulated constantly, appearing in varied forms and moments—perhaps even in the form of the Virgin's story.

This is the greatest miracle of the Virgin and her money—the power to transform her own history into the history of Tetiz. Thereby, Francisco's coin is transformed from a relic of the past into a miraculous force in the present, and the story of Francisco and the Virgin becomes a charter of Tetiz's origins. The coin conveys a history, as much by its movement as by its presence; its recognition and remembrance testify to the Virgin's miraculous powers. The residents of Tetiz have inherited the aftermath of a violent history of colonization, expropriation, enslavement, and impoverishment that have found their highest expression in monetary forms: the peon's debt; the falling price of henequen fiber; the devaluated peso. Through the Virgin and the deer and the coin that links the two, however, they recognize and relate themselves to a history of wealth, miracle, and grace—while not forgetting the other histories and other monies of which their poverty was made.

CHAPTER NINE

POET, PROPHET, AND POLITICIAN

Forgetting and Remembering Hunucmá

HUNUCMÁ'S COAT OF ARMS displays three boots, a fortified rampart fronting on ocean waves, and a dove flying over water. As adopted by that municipality in 1990, the emblem offers tribute, respectively, to its well-known shoemakers, the colonial-era fortified port of Sisal, and the etymology of Hunucmá, a word that, according to some scholars, derived from the Maya for "water that makes a sound like a dove's song." The coat of arms graces the cover of a book, which by that image as much as by its title—*Breves datos históricos y culturales del municipio de Hunucmá*—announces its nature as a compendium of local history and culture.

At first glance, *Breves datos históricos y culturales* might seem an antiquarian regional or local history, of a piece with similar local histories published in Mexico and elsewhere. Such a reading would, however, ignore aspects of the text, particularly its ambivalent cultural politics. While the book offers unrelenting criticism of the abuses of the then-dominant party, PRI, it alternates between praise for the conservative PAN party, for the left-wing Zapatistas of Chiapas, and even for classic heroes of the PRI like Lázaro Cárdenas. Moreover, the text includes frequent references to the ancient Maya and to the Quiché Mayan text *Popol Vuh*, seemingly in the mode of literature written by contemporary Mayan intellectuals in Guatemala and Chiapas as well as by indigenous intellectuals associated with other movements, in Mexico and beyond.[1] Unlike such works, however, the points of reference for *Breves datos históricos y culturales* are decidedly local—Hunucmá and its people, traditions, and history, whether of Mayan or non-Mayan origin—rather than Mexican, Mayan, or pan-Mayan in compass.

To understand the politics of *Breves datos históricos y culturales*, one must move beyond the borders and boundaries of the text and read it biographically, in two senses: first, in that the work is a document of its author, Anacleto Cetina Aguilar, and a register of the complexities, commitments, and contradictions of his life and work as a poet, activist, historian, and teacher; and second, in that the meaning of *Breves datos históricos y culturales* was not fixed at the moment of its writing or publication, but instead has evolved as circumstances and Cetina's reading of his text changed over time. Both the author and his writings, in other words, are works in progress and defy reduction to any one theme or issue. To read *Breves datos históricos y culturales* is to converse with Don Anacleto and to follow the thread that unifies the book and that ties together Cetina's work as a teacher, poet, *panista* (PAN activist), Mayanist, and admirer of the Zapatistas.[2] That thread is el pueblo, an entity Cetina has dedicated his life to defending, edifying, depicting, ennobling, preserving, liberating, and reclaiming. His efforts to do so—most notably through *Breves datos históricos y culturales*—have provided him a basis for engaging critically with indigeneity, nation, and history amid the challenges posed by what he calls modernity and neoliberalism. Both Cetina's life and *Breves datos históricos y culturales* are unfinished works. They conjure the possibility of liberation from impoverishment and subjection via a kind of cultural education which, Cetina hopes, might succeed where politics and revolution seem to have failed, thus forming, or reforming, el pueblo as a liberated subject.

EXODUS

I first encountered Anacleto Cetina Aguilar through a copy of *Breves datos históricos y culturales*, which a resident of Tetiz handed me during a walk through that pueblo. I was momentarily disconcerted, for in it were recounted in detail the stories of Feliciano Canul Reyes and José Pío Chuc, stories which I had until then taken to be entirely forgotten or ignored by historians and even, to a large extent, by residents of the area.[3] My consternation soon was replaced by intrigue, and I determined to find and speak with the school-teacher who had made such a thorough accounting of Hunucmá's past. Soon, I was sitting in Don Anacleto's living room, scrutinizing it for signs and traces of a varied intellectual, political, and personal life. There was a large bookcase holding encyclopedias, histories, school textbooks, and an enormous dictionary of ancient and modern Maya; display shelves were crowded with objects ranging from framed religious images to wedding souvenirs to a Don Quijote figurine. On one wall hung some painted wooden carvings in the neo-Mayan style of souvenirs typically sold at tourist sites; on another was a framed image of Che Guevara, browned with age. This struck me as odd since the exterior of Cetina's house was painted boldly in blue and white, colors that announced its occupant to be an activist in the conservative, right-of-center National Action, or PAN, party.

Cetina and his family clearly enjoyed a measure of privilege. He was a secondary school teacher in the pueblo, and all of his children were teachers as well, thus enjoying higher incomes than those of many of their neighbors. It was equally apparent, though, that Cetina was not wealthy. The cramped space of his house and the occupations of his daughters' spouses (a fisherman and a taxi driver) served to identify him as a member of what might be called Hunucmá's working middle class. Notwithstanding his relatively comfortable position today, when Cetina discussed his life history with me the struggle with poverty loomed large. Cetina referred to his grandfather as a onetime hacienda "slave" and considered his parents to have led a humble existence in town. His father was a fishmonger, and his mother worked as a washerwoman, while two brothers worked in the extraction and sale of salt from the pools near Sisal. Born in 1941 into a bilingual family, Anacleto was the first in his family to learn how to read and the first to complete primary school. While Anacleto's schoolmates continued on to secondary school, though, his parents could not afford to finance their son's continued education, and so he found work in a local bakery for a few years, indulging his passion for writing love poems in his spare time. Eventually, he returned to school to study accountancy.

On completion of his studies, Cetina found only low-paying work in Hunucmá, leading him to conclude that the town had no future to offer and to move to the state capital, where he found work in a bookstore in Mérida.

That job soon disappeared in the wake of a dispute between workers and the store owner that resulted in the dismissal of several workers, including Cetina. In the course of that yearlong struggle, Cetina gained an acquaintance with the writings of Karl Marx, an author whom he now credited with providing him with class consciousness and helping him achieve a different perspective on life. By reading Marx and witnessing the labor dispute at the bookstore, Cetina told me, he came to realize that the world was divided into what he called "two currents: the right and the left." The rightists were a reactionary group allied with owners and the government, and the leftists were a vanguard" that fought on behalf of the exploited. At the same time, as the conflict at the bookstore grew more entrenched, Cetina began to long to return to his homeland, which might offer escape from such class conflict. In a nostalgic poem he wrote at that time, entitled "Hunucmá" (1961), Cetina declared his "love and devotion" for the town and evoked the remembrance of "days past/Which return to my mind/Like the magical rush/Of distant melodies" and voices a desire, upon his death, to "make your insides my hearth/ [So you might] offer me the songs/Of your eternal spring."[4]

Notwithstanding such sentiments, Cetina did not return to Hunucmá. Instead, he abandoned both accountancy and poetry, finding work in 1965 as a secretary with the Instituto Nacional Indigenista on the basis of his fluency in Maya. After taking several years of classes at a federal normal school for teachers of literature, Cetina was ordered out into the countryside to work as a "cultural agent" (promotor cultural), charged with residing in small and distant Mayan settlements in southeastern Yucatán. His objective was to educate the inhabitants and secure the "Castilianization" of the children through instruction in Spanish. During his several years of postings in indigenous communities that suffered a degree of poverty he described to me as incomparable to Hunucmá's lesser deprivations, Cetina's political awakening continued. He read the poetry of Pablo Neruda and studied the history of Latin American revolutionary heroes like Emiliano Zapata, Simón Bolívar, and Che Guevara.

As Cetina's political awareness sharpened, he grew outraged over the repression of Mexican student leaders and guerrillas, from the slaughter at Tlatelolco in 1968 to the killings of the guerrilla Lucio Cabañas and the Yucatecan labor leader Efraín Calderón Lara in 1974. With an inspiration born of idealism and outrage in equal measure, Cetina returned to poetry after an eight-year hiatus, a moment he described as one of personal resurrection. In works from these years, Cetina decried the suffering of what he called the "valiant, hard-working," long-suffering urban and rural poor of Mexico, Nicaragua, and El Salvador, whom he often referred to collectively as el pueblo. At the same time, he denounced those he held responsible for the "rotten system" that oppressed them: wealthy capitalists and corrupt officials, whom he reviled as "beasts," "genocidal worms," "venomous serpents," and "viscous arachnids." In contrast, Cetina celebrated the guerrillas, insurgents, and revolutionaries who resisted such tyranny as "paladins" and "titans," whose causes were destined to triumph despite apparent defeats. In 1972, upon the death of the Mexican guerrilla leader Genaro Vázquez, Cetina wrote, "Your fall is an ill-fated event; That perhaps means a setback / But not that the enemy has won." In a similar vein, in 1979 he saluted Nicaraguans who "instead of crying . . . will intone hymns / And . . . will build new temples and altars / To the honor of Augusto César Sandino!"⁵

In such works, Cetina Aguilar enunciated an explicitly internationalist vision of Latin American revolutionary solidarity. This is most clearly expressed in "To Argentina," a poem Cetina wrote in the wake of the British retaking of the Falklands or Malvinas islands. After declaring that Argentina's volcanoes "course with blood / Shared with those of my own land," Cetina asks, "Why do we divide up with frontiers / This, our America / Exploited by unscrupulous people? Let us put away our rivers / And bring our seas together." Declaring the Americas a "wasteland" because "day and night / They have taken away its right / To choose its own road," Cetina ends the poem with the hope that the figure of Sandino might show the way for Argentina to win its liberation. "To Argentina" is perhaps the best measure of the distance Cetina Aguilar had traveled by the early 1980s, from his exodus from Hunucmá through his work as a teacher and political agent and his radicalizing encounters with politics, history, and poetry. El pueblo, for him, had come to mean something much larger than Hunucmá, embracing the tragic history of a whole continent of peoples and evoking a revolutionary and romantic desire for their collective exodus from bondage.⁶

HOMELAND AND HISTORY

Cetina Aguilar's career made another abrupt turn in the early 1980s, when he decided to make his return to Hunucmá. Since Hunucmá was located outside the areas of the Yucatán peninsula defined by the federal government as indigenous, Cetina ended a promising career in indigenous education to assume a much less prestigious position as a primary school teacher in Hunucmá. He told an incredulous supervisor, "I want to return to my pueblo, because my people are from there. I want to live in my pueblo." When we spoke, Cetina recalled this decision with some regret. On his return, he found that many of the friends of his youth had emigrated to Mérida, leaving him feeling like a stranger. Moreover, his political ideas found a cold reception in his hometown. When Cetina, inspired by the socialist experiment in Cuba, tried to found a communal cooperative milpa in Hunucmá, he was met with derision, as even friends and family members ridiculed him, questioning his sanity and calling him a Communist.

Homecoming brought not only loneliness, but also a crisis of political consciousness. Two decades later, when I met Cetina, he described how he came to question the nationalist, internationalist, and what he called "universal" perspectives he previously embraced. "After trying all of these levels," he explained, "I asked myself, what is closest to me? My pueblo. Here is where I have work to do, where I can really do something. All the rest is very nice, but it is practically unattainable: a chimera." Cetina recalled searching for a way to "begin once again in the community," as a poet, through a kind of poetry that abandoned complicated metaphors in favor of what he called the "language of el pueblo." Eventually, he found inspiration neither in history books nor in Neruda's poetry, but in reflections on daily life in Hunucmá that were almost ethnographic in quality. As he told me, "I began to focus more on the physical aspects of el pueblo, its material nature: the clock tower, the church, the bell-ringer, the smith. . . . The personalities of the inhabitants of the pueblo. Now I saw them from another perspective. . . . Not coexisting with them, but rather through their work, through what they represent for the community. After admiring the guerrillas—Che, Sandino, and all the rest—I arrived in el pueblo and my vision began to focus on the residents of el pueblo . . . those who ring the bells, make tools, make a machete."

Throughout the 1980s Cetina explored such themes in his poetry, which was published in 1983 in an illustrated collection entitled *Cahtal-K'ay: Canto a Mi Pueblo* (Song of the kah: Song for my pueblo), published on the occasion of the one hundred and thirty-third anniversary of the promotion of the pueblo of Hunucmá to the category of *villa*, or town. Those works portray el pueblo not so much as a political or even a social entity as one invested in material life and material objects.[7] The clock tower is a "venerable guardian, that my grandparents /placed at the heart; of my beautiful pueblo"; the church is the "vigilant sentinel of my pueblo," and its bells are "ripe fruit which Father Cronos has left in the furrow of his passage"; the town square is a "sleeping oasis / in which children are rocked; in infantile dreams / by the vigorous arms /of leafy laurels / your green heart"; the streets are the "arteries / through

The clock tower in Hunucmá.
Photo by Paul Eiss.

which the life of el pueblo courses." Cetina's material language of el pueblo permitted him to elide the problematic history of Hunucmá's built environment and specifically of the role of class and racial exploitation in producing it. Through such materialism, the poet could lay claim, in the name of el pueblo, to structures like the church, a product of Spanish colonialism, and the clock, an artifact erected not by Cetina's grandparents but by nineteenth-century gentry who ruled the haciendas where indigenous debt peons, like Cetina's grandparents, labored.[8]

Throughout his poetry, Cetina addresses Hunucmá and its features in the informal pronoun for "you," tú. In the Mayan dedication of *Cahtal-K'ay*, for instance, Cetina addresses Hunucmá as if it were a child: "Today I would like to tell you a story, like all children are told stories, because that is what you are: a child." Thus, he invests el pueblo with the status of an entity both corporeal and familiar and endows material objects with life, even personality. Addressing the church, Cetina credits "the embrace of your white dome," rather than religious ritual or the spiritual counsel of priests, with making "peace rise to the spirit." Gazing on the streets of el pueblo, Cetina declares, "you have contemplated / happy marriage processions; and you have endured the grief / of solemn funeral corteges." "You offer your carpet / of tender grass," he continues, "when the tired knees / of the wretched wayfarer / succumb to the implacable / assaults of Cronos." Similarly, addressing Hunucmá's clock tower, Cetina writes, "you show us with your arms / The inscrutable and fatal road / That your sure strokes mark for us. . . . You, who opened your arms in joy / When we came here to dream / At the moment we leave, devout / Bring your arms together in prayer." One illustration of a pueblo street exemplifies such personification, with a caption that reads, "My pueblo, *whom* I love so much" (emphasis added).

Even as Cetina's poetry personifies objects, it objectifies persons—shoe-makers, bell ringers, and the like—making them into representations of el pueblo and material icons of its qualities. In a poem entitled "The Smith" Cetina describes that figure as the "Synthesis of the pure soul / Of this, my pueblo, forged / In the hard daily / Struggle for the holy bread." Forging axes and plows for laborers and a "romantic hook" for a young girl's hammock, the smith emerges as a producer not only of physical objects, but of el pueblo itself, as a material, spiritual, and gendered entity. Addressing himself to "political leaders" (*gobernadores*) at the poem's conclusion, Cetina offers the smith as an example of working people of el pueblo who make no "cruel grenades" or "tools for destruction and death," but who "Create / With those agile hands / Work tools / For all of the brothers / Who today live without hope."[9]

Throughout such nostalgic stanzas, Hunucmá emerges as a homeland: a physical and spiritual place of return, not only for pueblo residents, but also for outsiders and for those who, like Cetina, feel themselves a little of both. This is conveyed in the poem "Fiesta of el Pueblo," in which Cetina urges a visitor, "come, foreigner, to enjoy my fiestas / . . . compendium of happiness, faith, and devotion / and you will feel your heart beat / to the sweet rhythm of the orchestra of el pueblo." Yet the poet is not without ambivalence, as expressed most poignantly in the work entitled "My pueblo." "Even if you were only / A Wasteland, desolate and cold," Cetina writes, "Even without the spirit / With which you sow your fields / I would love you just the same." After a series of similar stanzas, Cetina concludes by representing his affection for Hunucmá as a love unrequited: "Because in you there is wasteland and spring / Because you are laughter and you are weeping / My pueblo, whom I love so much / Even if you did not love me / I would love you just the same."[10]

Such aspects of Cetina Aguilar's work were lost on the Yucatecan man of letters Roldán Peniche Barrera, who in a preface to *Cahtal-K'ay* introduces the poet by declaring his most important virtue to be that of "simplicity." According to Peniche, Anacleto Cetina lived "surrounded by tranquility" in Hunucmá, a "serene population" that had only witnessed two "secular events" in which the pueblo had become a stage for outsiders: the first an invasion by pirates in the eighteenth century, and the second a visit by Empress Carlota, wife of Emperor Maximilian, who stopped for a bath on her way to Mérida in 1865. For this Hunucmá, Peniche announced, Cetina had become "the voice of el pueblo, for el pueblo."[11] Peniche's preface—a classically paternalistic gesture from an upper-class capital city intellectual—was followed immediately, however, by a prologue by Cetina depicting the conquest of Hunucmá by the Spanish, an account that featured both the brutality of conquest and the entrenched resistance of indigenous populations. Peniche ignored as well Cetina's deliberately Mayan framing of his collection, both in its titling and in its initial dedication and address. By framing Hunucmá's culture as indigenous and its history as bracketed by the violence of conquest, Cetina suggested that far from being tranquil, the region had shared the violent and tumultuous history characteristic of other indigenous populations in the wake of conquest.

Moreover, an explicit politics in *Cahtal-K'ay* further undercuts Peniche's image of a serene Hunucmá. In a poem entitled "Fire," Cetina addresses a field of henequen plants scorched by a fire through the "criminal negligence" of ejidal and governmental officials who were charged with their care. The charred plants are "specters" of a "defeated battalion / that returns with heads hung low and arms slack / and hearts broken." "One day," he declares, "may your arms girded with sharp spines / pierce the opprobrious breasts; of so many Cains / who have brutally assaulted / the peaceful life / of so many brothers!" In another work, "Rubble," Cetina again draws on religious metaphors, mourning the agony and death of an henequen plant that vainly dreamed of future growth only to be betrayed: "Its sharp, green leaves / that point to infinity, seemed to voice a cry / against all of those Judases / a cry of its first fruits. Thus they destroyed its dreams / it had rapacious owners / who have turned it to ashes." Other poems bring the theme of material destruction and the resulting loss of heritage and cultural integrity to the heart of el pueblo. In "Town Square," Cetina laments, "I do not know who destroyed / your old architecture / destroying, out of pure / ignorance, the past, and throwing you to the ground / unintentionally, made of you / a layer cake." Then he voices hopes that Hunucmá's old bandstand might be reborn like a "Phoenix of legend." In another work dedicated to the port of Sisal,

Colonial-era figure holding
a fish, atop a house in Sisal.
Photo by Paul Eiss.

which Cetina calls the "ancestral port of my Mayan forefathers," the poet laments the ruined condition of colonial-era structures. "Why let yourself / die,
forgotten / and ignorant of your past?" he admonishes the ruins: "Arise, and
reclaim destiny / may it yield you a better road / less hostile and spiny / than
the one you have walked until now." Such poems suggest that Cetina's romantic celebrations of el pueblo were meant, in part, to pose the virtues of
el pueblo in opposition to the failings and corruption of the collective ejidos
and of the exploitative political system to which they were subject.[12]

Cetina did not limit himself to expressing such views in his poetry, but
brought them to the terrain of politics as well. By the time of Cetina's birth
in 1941, the Cárdenas reforms already had been contained, if not rolled back,
by local elites and dominant political cliques. Over the course of his lifetime
Cetina had witnessed the evolution of the collective ejidos as they seemed
to become a means not of the promised emancipation, but of subjection,
exploitation, and incorporation within the networks of state power and political patronage. While initially Cetina viewed such issues through the lens

of his Marxist sympathies, eventually he came to address them through the only viable oppositional movement in Hunucmá: the right-of-center PAN party, the indirect descendant of the Yucatecan Liberal Party. Established in Yucatán in 1940, one year after the formation of the party at the national level, the PAN began to organize an opposition movement in Yucatán as in other areas in Mexico, lodging a critique of state socialism, agrarian reform, and official anticlericalism and advocating for the restoration of the power of the church and for free-market liberalism as the only ways to secure Mexico's progress. The PAN took the collective henequen ejido as one of its principal targets, perceiving it both as a cog in the PRI's corporatist political machine and as a socialistic impediment to the operations of the market. Whereas the PRI had always represented itself as ruling on behalf of and working for the benefit and redemption of el pueblo, at the local, state, and national levels PAN activists represented themselves as advocating for the true interests of el pueblo against the corrosive effects of state corruption and one-party rule.[13]

Determined to bring about what he described to me as a "minimal transformation" in a town resistant to left-wing politics, Cetina Aguilar joined the PAN after his return to Hunucmá and quickly rose in its ranks. By the mid-1980s Hunucmá's panistas were garnering increasing support in their attempts to overthrow single-party rule in the municipality but met repeated electoral defeat by the PRI, which the panistas would ascribe to fraud, ranging from bribery to the falsification of electoral returns. In 1987, the victory of the panista Timoteo Canché Tinal in Tetiz's mayoral elections triggered political upheaval throughout the region. In Hunucmá in 1991, in the wake of a closely contested municipal election, some three thousand PAN sympathizers took to the streets, surrounding and occupying the town hall. State police cracked down in response and even broke into and vandalized Hunucmá's church, where, they said, priests were sheltering and supporting the panistas. In 1993 Anacleto Cetina, in what would represent the climax of his career in politics, stood as mayoral candidate for the PAN in Hunucmá, only to lose in elections the opposition once again denounced as fraudulent.[14]

Even as his political career intensified and then reached its denouement, Cetina began to move in a new direction as a writer, taking on a project that would occupy him for the next eight years: the writing of a history of Hunucmá. Although Cetina felt ill-equipped for such an endeavor, he read regional histories of other towns and municipalities in the region, the structure and organization of which he applied to the composition of *Breves datos históricos y culturales*.[15] On his days off, Cetina traveled to Mérida to do research in its libraries, where he lost himself in nineteenth- and early twentieth-century newspapers, searching for details of the exploits of figures like Canul Reyes and Pío Chuc. He read histories of colonial Yucatán, collecting bits of information that related to Hunucmá. He questioned elderly town residents on the town's history and collected testimony on local beliefs, traditions, festivities, and stories about the remnants of ancient Mayan structures, always taking care, he later explained to me—a university-trained anthropological historian—to distinguish what he regarded as credible recollections from those he dismissed as "fantastical," "romantic," or "superstitious." In the wake of his electoral defeat, Cetina redoubled his efforts to complete the project, which he published in 1996 with the assistance of a competitive federal grant.[16]

Breves datos históricos y culturales begins with an account of the origins of Hunucmá's name, an account that frames its history and culture as Mayan in foundation, originating well before the Spanish conquest. Rejecting what he calls its official etymology, as provided by Yucatecan men of letters who conjectured that it might derive from "water that makes sounds like a dove's song," Cetina locates the origins of the name in the Pleistocene epoch, as the sea level gradually receded and the northern coast of Yucatán emerged from the waters. "Hunucmá," according to Cetina, reflects a moment in that epoch when the waters had not yet receded completely, making Hunucmá the northernmost tip of the peninsula and one of the oldest settlements in the peninsula, aptly named in Maya, "U NAC HA'" (the limits of the water). In response to those who might doubt his hypothesis regarding the ancient pedigree of "Hunucmá," Cetina responds, "Now, the skeptics may ask, 'Did the Mayas witness this so long ago, or did they learn it afterward? If the latter was true, how could they have discovered that?' These are questions that must remain in the deepest mystery, and perhaps may never be answered. That is the nature of the mysterious *Mayab* [land of the Maya]."[17]

After thus evoking the region's indigeneity and antiquity, the rest of the volume is a comprehensive survey of Hunucmá, past and present. A chapter entitled "Antecedents" offers descriptions of Hunucmá's geography, followed by a chapter entitled "Demography," which provides information on the pre-Hispanic, colonial, and contemporary population sites. A third chapter is divided into three sections. The first section, "History," stretches from before the conquest to the present, including substantial sections discussing an invasion by pirates in the eighteenth century and the visit by Empress Carlota. The second section, "Public Figures," identifies prominent local leaders, educators, musicians, and the church bell ringer, while the third, "Edifices and Monuments," describes built structures, like Hunucmá's church, clock tower, town hall, and central plaza. Chapter 4, entitled "Culture," presents information on education, public health, and roads and communications as well as traditions like the processions of the Virgin of Tetiz, Corpus Christi celebrations, and the Day of the Dead. Chapter 5, "Production," surveys activities from henequen agriculture to gardening to artisanal work, and a final chapter presents a chronology of events in the history of Hunucmá.[18]

Breves datos históricos y culturales bears the mark of the political struggle between the PRI and the PAN in the 1980s and early 1990s. A description of the impoverished inhabitants of ex-haciendas near Hunucmá provides occasion for a denunciation of their exploitation by "little caciques" of the dominant party who use them as a source of "immoral and illicit enrichment." For Cetina, that such poverty and ignorance still plagued the "majority of the Mexican pueblo" reflected badly on a revolution that had been in power for more than sixty years and demonstrated what Cetina refers to as the "immorality" of attempting to maintain that government in power. The section of the book dedicated to Hunucmá's history offers an extensive critique of one-party rule, and descriptions of the electoral campaigns of local panistas; in it, Cetina denounces the tactics of electoral fraud employed by the PRI, which, in the service of a "system that unjustly strives to perpetuate itself in power by any means," facilitates the continued exploitation of workers in order to "produce the immense fortunes seized by the politicians of the official empire." Even Cetina's descriptions of local traditions are punctuated with occasional slaps at local caudillos and at the failed revolution in Yucatán and Mexico.[19]

The politics of *Breves datos históricos y culturales* are not limited to a justification of the PAN. Alongside his critique of the PRI, Cetina reveals a degree of unease with the PAN. At the state and national level the PAN, committed to the dismantlement of Mexico's corporatist institutions and beholden to neoliberalism, seemed to him to offer no viable alternative leading to the survival and prosperity of henequen agriculture and hence to the welfare of rural workers. At the municipal level, the performance of the PAN government that took power in Hunucmá the year before the publication of *Breves datos históricos y culturales* was disappointing. The difference between the new panista municipal government and its predecessor, according to Cetina, had become unnoticeable; like the priístas, the new leaders hadn't demonstrated any "interest in solving the true and deepest problems of the most abandoned social classes." Concluding the section on politics, Cetina admits that some opposition leaders might have become part of the system, noting, "We have not advanced much in political questions, because a dictatorial system that has lasted for more than sixty years in power continues to hang on against wind and surf to the helm of a ship that is on the point of sinking."[20]

It would be a mistake, however, to read the cultural politics of Breves datos históricos y culturales as being limited to its ambivalent forays into partisan critique. Like Cahtal-K'ay, the book is laden with expressions of local patriotism and love for the municipality of Hunucmá, effusive celebrations of park benches, public buildings, and local traditions and even a selection of poetry and songs composed in Hunucmá's honor. But more than in his earlier work, in Breves datos históricos y culturales the physical destruction and loss of the material features of el pueblo emerge as a dominant theme. This process of deterioration is no longer a simple indication of the passage of time or of the incapacity of local authorities, but a product of the systematic and pernicious assaults of what Cetina alternately terms modernization or civilization on el pueblo. In addition to an extensive denunciation of the destruction of Hunucmá's old bandstand, accompanied by a photograph of the prior structure, Cetina describes the removal and destruction of an old baroque altarpiece in the town's church as the loss of "one of our great artistic treasures." Describing the remains of an old Mayan road, or sak'be, in the center of town, he writes, "Let us hope that the advance of 'civilization' will never destroy this evidence of our remote pre-Hispanic past." Cetina also decries the loss of the images that traditionally identified particular corners in the town, like a rock carved in the form of an arm that was dynamited during the paving of a street. "One of the things that leads to the loss of a pueblo's image," he writes, "is the forgetting of the names of the traditional corners, which is happening in our pueblo." Perhaps the most evocative example is that of Hunucmá's "ancient guardian," the public clock. "Today," he writes, "with the passage of time, our old clock has lost the sonority with which it announces the passage of the hours. Despite all the recent scientific advances, this old artifact—our pride and the pride of future generations, if they learn how to preserve our values—has not been able to be repaired satisfactorily." Portrayed in Cahtal-K'ay as material icons of el pueblo and its enduring virtues, these objects in Breves datos históricos y culturales figure as icons of forgetting, loss, and degradation.[21]

The sense of dispossession or loss that pervades Breves datos históricos y culturales is notably acute in Cetina's description of the effects on young people of what he terms modernization: the decline of traditional occupations, labor migration, increased access to mass media, the disuse of Maya language,

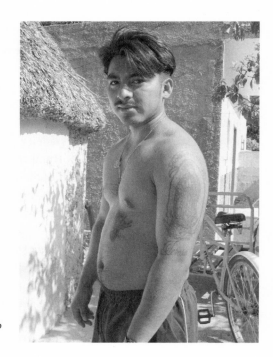

Young man of Tetiz, recently
returned from Los Angeles, where
he had traveled to find work. Photo
by Paul Eiss.

and the disappearance of popular customs and traditions. Cetina describes
the practice of crossing oneself on hearing church bells and the tradition of
constructing a simulated *monte* (woods) where the crucifixion is reenacted
near the church on Good Friday as "beautiful customs that have disappeared
from our community, as it gives way to 'modernization.'" A description of
Corpus Christi festivities concludes, "Young generations: Do not allow the
phantasm of modernity to devour these cultural forms. Struggle to preserve
them, so that they endure for as many centuries into the future as they have
endured to the present!" In his discussion of el pueblo's traditions, Cetina
Aguilar calls on his readers to "maintain and preserve our rich traditions for
future generations, instead of imitating other customs that are foreign to
us." He charges youth above all to "investigate what is ours, such beautiful
traditions that are so old, perhaps thousands of years old. . . . The day that we
lose them, we will lose part of ourselves."[22]

Cetina's critique of Hunucmá's cultural dispossession is sharpest in the
matter of clothing, particularly as it relates to younger men and women.
Boys and young men, especially those who migrated to Los Angeles and
then returned, have abandoned traditional Yucatecan garb for baseball caps,
T-shirts, shorts, and even, to Cetina's horror, tattoos and earrings. For Cetina,

this threatening attenuation of regional identity, whether among working-class migrants or middle-class residents adopting more cosmopolitan or more characteristically Mexican forms of self-presentation, seemed to represent the replacement of "our ancestors' way of dressing" by "ways of dressing that are foreign to our idiosyncrasies." In similar terms, he faults young women who dedicate themselves to "copying the latest fashions" and dress in loud colors like their "idols on television." Alongside the reclamation and remembrance of traditional culture, the use of traditional clothing, notably mestizo *traje*, stood for Cetina as an urgent task, a way of arresting el pueblo's continuing degradation and loss of authenticity.

The politics of *Breves datos históricos y culturales*, therefore, was limited neither to a romantic evocation of traditional regional identity nor to the partisan politics of the PAN. Rather, the work was intended, like Cetina's earlier, poetic works, as a call to reclaim el pueblo against the threat of economic, political, and cultural dispossession. If the authoritarian politics of the PRI continued to subject and degrade Hunucmá's working inhabitants, if the oppositional politics of the PAN seemed to be going astray, and if the assaults of modernity threatened the very foundations of popular identity and virtue, then it was only in a repossession—of homeland and history—that the path to reclaiming el pueblo might be found.

CROSS AND CALVARY

Hunucmá's history, as presented in *Breves datos históricos y culturales*, is no seamless narrative. At the heart of Cetina's chapter on history are several sections dedicated to the years of the Revolution that in substance and tone break sharply with the apocrypha of town history that precede and the details regarding town notables and edifices to follow. They represent the history of el pueblo not merely as a series of quaint episodes like the visit of Empress Carlota, but according to a narrative of martyrdom and redemption that is equally secular and sacred, Christian and Mayan. In it, Cetina discloses his intention to be that of "reclaiming the names of the great men of our pueblo whose names, despite having struggled and given their lives for the benefit of future generations, have remained in the dark complicity of anonymity."[23]

Cetina Aguilar proceeds to reclaim those names through an emancipationist narrative that divides history into times of slavery and times of liberty in which the exploited rise to break their chains. His account, like that of the unionist authors of *La batalla de Tetiz y Hunucmá*, draws upon a reading of John Kenneth Turner's *Barbarous Mexico* to depict the era of so-called slavery during the Porfiriato, in which, according to Cetina, "tyrants sank their claws into the flesh of el pueblo," and rural workers in places like Hunucmá suffered a "violent death, dying slowly with each passing day, crucified on the spines of the henequen fields, on land that once was [their] own." Cetina recounts the experiences of townspeople in that period, including those of Canul Reyes's mother, Isabel Reyes, who was brutally beaten by a landlord for poaching wood on hacienda lands. Such experiences were what Cetina calls the "prime material" of revolution: "Our pueblo," he writes, "though traditionally peaceful, knows how to react when faced with injustice—as an implacable judge, ready to punish tyrants." Thus men like Canul Reyes and Pío Chuc emerged, ready to exercise what Cetina—explicitly inspired by the Mexican anarchist Ricardo Flores Magón—calls "el pueblo's sacred right of rebellion." An account of the attack on Progreso, including the tragic death of Canul Reyes, follows; Cetina goes on to describe the killing of Pío Chuc six years later at the hands of "false socialists" who later would engineer the killing of the Socialist leader Felipe Carrillo Puerto and eventually would seize control over and corrupt the PRI as well.[24]

In narrating the history of slavery and liberation in Hunucmá, however, Cetina casts Hunucmá's past not only into an emancipationist paradigm, but also into a much older tradition: that of Mayan prophecy and millennial revolt. Thus he explicates Canul's experiences by reference to the Chilam Balam manuscripts, Mayan prophetic texts dating to the eighteenth century or earlier. "Feliciano," Cetina writes, "had to flee to the countryside in order to fulfill the prophecy of Nahua Pech, one of the five prophets of ancient times, who says: 'The whites will be content neither with what is theirs, nor with what they won in war. They will also desire the poverty of our food, and the poverty of our houses. They will raise their hate towards us, and they will oblige us to seek refuge in the woods and in distant places. Then we will go like ants, beneath the vermin, and we will eat bad things: roots, smelly things, crows, rats and locusts. And the poverty of this food will fill our hearts with resentment, and the war will come.'" Similarly, Cetina portrays Pío Chuc as a millenarian Mayan leader on a par with the leaders of colonial resistance movements and the Caste War, who rose to "punish el pueblo's executioners." This calling earned Pío Chuc, like the great leaders who preceded him, only vilification, which Cetina decries: "Some call them murderers. That does not surprise us, because it has always been that way. When the Spanish came, to despoil, attack and humiliate the native Indian, nobody—with a few honorable exceptions—raised their voices in protest.

Anacleto Cetina Aguilar
standing beside the
"clandestine" grave of
Feliciano Canul Reyes in
Hunucmá cemetery. Photo
by Paul Eiss.

But when, after enduring more than three hundred years of slavery el pueblo
rises up to punish its executioners, then the world is shocked, and condemns
Jacinto Canek, Cecilio Chí, Jacinto Pat, and Manuel Antonio Ay, calling them
savages and butchers." According to Cetina, Pío Chuc's life, like that of
Canul Reyes, fulfilled the Chilam Balam prophecies, exposing him to "the
same persecution, the same attacks, and the same necessity . . . to flee like
a game animal, hunted by predators, to seek refuge in the woods—the only
place that offers him protection, and lovingly opens its thick arms to protect
him with its green fronds."[25]

If Cetina understood the struggles of insurgents like Canul and Chuc as
expressions of indigenous resistance, he viewed their deaths in battle and
the denouement of their struggles through a different lens: that of Christian
martyrdom. Canul Reyes, for Cetina, was an "immortal warrior" who "generously offered his life" for his ideals; Pío Chuc's sacrifice placed him on a
par with the most notable spiritual and political martyrs, who "throughout
humanity's history" "emerged to offer their lives for the sake of the freedom

of their pueblos." Such figures included Spartacus, Mahatma Gandhi, Jesus, Miguel Hidalgo y Costilla, José Martí, and Che Guevara, "all of them, in their moment," Cetina writes, "heaped with the most degrading epithets by the tyrants they fought."[26]

The honor of martyrdom corresponded not only to Hunucmá's fallen leaders, but also to those who had followed them as foot soldiers. Thus Cetina Aguilar includes the stories of a few commoners like Donato Chacón, a man who had fought alongside Canul Reyes. While Chacón was off in the woods at that time, his knee was punctured by the thorn of a ch'imay tree; symbolically, the wound was a stigmatum. Although he survived the liberation war, many years later the injury returned to haunt him, leaving him crippled and unable to work and eventually leading indirectly to his death. Similarly, Guillermo Chuc Pat never received a response from the government to his request for a pension on behalf of his deceased father, a onetime insurgent. Decades later, the poor, elderly man continued "gazing at the horizon, awaiting a new, luminous dawn, that might announce the definitive liberation of the campesinos." Cetina presents the stories of Chacón and Chuc as sad tales of how Hunucmá's unsung heroes had offered their lives to the struggle for liberation, only to die in anonymity, their sacrifice ignored by "present-day 'revolutionaries' who shut themselves up in their glass palaces, elaborating absurd programs and engaging in Byzantine discussions that do nothing to provide relief to the campesinos who made the Revolution."[27]

Here, the martyrdom of Hunucmá's heroes and their followers sets the stage for the collective martyrdom of el pueblo in the postrevolutionary period, in which the "same old enemies of el pueblo continued in power, encrusting themselves once again in the governmental apparatus . . . and not receiving the just punishment for the crimes they had committed against el pueblo." Despite what Cetina sees as Cárdenas's laudable attempt to better the situation of the campesinos through the "truest and deepest reform" attempted, the "bourgeoisie—the eternal enemy of the campesino," sabotaged such efforts, "fabricating laws" aimed at "protecting the owners." The creation of Henequeneros de Yucatán and the Agrarian Bank served merely to prevent workers from ever becoming true landowners and to buy off their leaders. These leaders, in Cetina's eyes, were what he called "Judases" who betrayed their brethren: "Not for thirty coins, exactly, but for large sums of money, translated into the cattle ranches and other properties that are shown off by those who long have sucked the blood and sweat of their brothers." As Cetina relates, the privatization of Cordemex in 1991 and the liquidation of the remaining ejidatarios consummated the final theft of the state's riches from the "sacred hands of el pueblo, which generated that wealth." The scale of el pueblo's continuing collective martyrdom could be conveyed only by comparison with—indeed, as a reiteration of—that of Emiliano Zapata himself. As Cetina notes, "Cordemex's declaration of bankruptcy, and the resulting liquidation of the workers, paradoxically occurred on 10 April 1991, the tragic anniversary of the death of the campesino leader Emiliano Zapata. For me, that represented the second murder of the southern leader, at the hands of the bourgeoisie."[28]

This symbolic reiteration of Zapata's killing lends a dark cast to *Breves datos históricos y culturales*, as if el pueblo were doomed to suffer an endlessly repeated martyrdom. Indeed, the story of Hunucmá's martyrdom, repeated from the Spanish conquest to the present, leads Cetina to conclude that el pueblo suffered the burden of a past that prevented it from having a history of its own. "History is written by the winners," he writes, "and the history that we know is what serves the present system. The definitive history of the campesinos and workers has not yet been written, because today, they are as unredeemed as they were before the armed struggle of 1910." When I asked Don Anacleto what he meant by those words, he answered that true history could not yet be written because, in his words, "much remains to be done." True history could be said to exist only when the liberation had come, in fulfillment of prophecy, to redeem el pueblo.[29]

Despite the gloominess of *Breves datos históricos y culturales*, it was precisely Cetina's religiously charged fusion of emancipationism and millenarianism that allowed him to rescue hope from the tale of el pueblo's many martyrdoms. In the aftermath of the outbreak of the Zapatista uprising in Chiapas in early 1994, it seemed to Cetina that an era of true history might be drawing near, evoking the fulfillment of ancient prophecy and the redemption of el pueblo's martyrs in Hunucmá and elsewhere. Even as he continued to work for the PAN, Cetina's imagination was captured by this movement that seemed to capture the spirit of so many of his own preoccupations. Along with other activists from Yucatán and elsewhere in Mexico—including those of the Despacho, whom he had met during the war of the eggs—Cetina traveled to Chiapas in 1995 to take part in a large meeting with the Zapatistas in their jungle stronghold. As Cetina now recalls, he was powerfully impressed by the indigenous Zapatistas he met and by their leader, Subcomandante Marcos, whom he met and presented with a poem he had composed in his honor.

That visit was fresh in Cetina's memory as he finished the *Breves datos históricos y culturales* and may have influenced his millenarian interpretation of Hunucmá's insurgent struggles. Moreover, Cetina made explicit reference to the contemporary Zapatista movement in his book in the context of a discussion of state corruption and the decline of henequen. He states that insurgency, like that of the "campesino guerrillas in Chiapas," was the "only road that bad governments and the executioners of el pueblo have left to el pueblo." Toward the conclusion of his text, Cetina again evokes the Zapatistas, noting that if the injustices perpetuated by Mexico's government were not remedied, they would trigger a new era of popular insurgency. That future liberation movement would learn from history and would not allow those he termed enemies of el pueblo to "encyst themselves in power" once again. In 1994, Cetina concludes, the "first step toward that campesino uprising was taken in the brother state of Chiapas."[30]

Thus in *Breves datos históricos y culturales* Cetina gestured to the possibility that not just Hunucmá and not just Yucatán but all of Mexico might return at last to its interrupted march toward liberation. Cetina's critique of Mexico's national government and of its oppression and abandonment of working-class, rural, and indigenous populations was unrelenting. Yet, like the Despacho advisers who wrote *La batalla de Tetiz y Hunucmá*, he ended up restoring, in a spiritual register, the faith in Mexico that had been so thoroughly betrayed in the secular realm. He glimpsed, in the recovery of the historical memory of martyrdom and liberation, the possibility of a reconciliation of pueblo and patria. It is in this spirit that Cetina concluded *Breves datos históricos y culturales* with a brief quotation from "Credo" ("Creed"), a song made famous by the singer Ricardo López Méndez on the occasion of Cárdenas's nationalization of Mexico's oil industry in 1939. Celebrating Mexico's newfound independence from foreign capitalists, López Méndez had drawn upon tropes of martyrdom and crucifixion to evoke the tragic history of the patria and its longing for redemption. Quoting that famous song, Cetina concluded: "Mexico, I believe in you, because you write your name with an 'X' that is both cross and calvary."[31]

THE WIDE ROAD OF FREEDOM

The years after the publication of *Breves datos históricos y culturales* were no kinder to Don Anacleto's hopes than they were to those of Tetiz's independent unionists. Shortly after the book appeared, the Zapatistas sent representatives to Yucatán as well as to other states to explain their cause. Cetina welcomed several of the masked visitors, offering them lodgings in his home, where they showed videos to groups of town residents and explained the Zapatista movement to them. But deadlocked negotiations with the government and the military occupation of the highlands of Chiapas by federal troops would contain the movement. Don Anacleto has found the rebels' seeming immobilization as a national movement profoundly disheartening, as it has seemed for him to call into question the status of Zapatismo as the "first step" toward a new revolution.

The PAN, by contrast, enjoyed a striking series of successes from the 1990s forward. In 2000, the party overthrew the PRI's long legacy of one-party rule when Vicente Fox was victorious in his campaign for the presidency; the next year, another PAN candidate, Patricio Patrón Laviada, was elected governor of Yucatán. In the ensuing years, however, perceptions of the PAN would change, as it made the transition from an opposition party campaigning under the promise of a sweeping but undefined change to a governing party stymied by misdirection and inexperience, blocked by the opposition of the PRI, and riven by factionalism at every level. When Cetina and I spoke in 2004, a few years after our initial conversations, he expressed consternation with the arrival of politicians he called rightists to power in the wake of the PAN's victories. The national government, in his view, continued to favor the interests of capital and the wealthy classes, while leaving el pueblo to the mercies of what he ironically termed "blessed globalization."

By 2007, when I interviewed Cetina again, he evinced increased skepticism about the PAN. While in 2004 he had told me that his "highest aspiration" still was to work toward the victory of the PAN in mayoral elections in Hunucmá, his hopes were dashed when the PRI won by a wide margin, leading some local panistas to question Cetina's loyalties and to call publicly for his "head to roll." Cetina remained active in the party thereafter, but by 2007 he decried the emergence of familiar patterns of patronage and corruption in the state government of Patrón Laviada, especially in an attempt by state officials to seize a portion of Hunucmá's ejidos for an expansion of Mérida's airport. The victory of the PRI in Yucatán's gubernatorial and legislative elections shortly thereafter seemed to confirm what Cetina described as a state of profound disillusionment regarding the PAN and its promises of change. "Right now I feel very, very disoriented," he told me. "The change we wanted did not come."[32]

Beyond the waning of Zapatismo and changed perceptions of the PAN, another event has profoundly affected Don Anacleto's attitude toward the history of Hunucmá: the terrorist attacks of 11 September 2001 and the militaristic response of the United States over the years to follow. When I first interviewed Don Anacleto a few months before the attacks, we spent much of the time discussing Pío Chuc as a forgotten and nameless martyr of liberation. When I mentioned stories I had heard about Pío Chuc's involvement in the mass killings in Hunucmá in 1920, Cetina dismissed them, suggesting that such rumors were a product of the defamation that tyrants always visited on liberation heroes. By 2004, however, when I next asked about Pío Chuc, Cetina's views had changed. When I asked him why Pío Chuc had been consigned to oblivion, while Canul Reyes had a tomb and a school named after him in Hunucmá, Cetina responded that Canul Reyes had died a hero, while Pío Chuc's "very cruel vengeance" had "reaped the hate of el pueblo." Pío Chuc's struggle was "well directed, in the beginning," he explained, but by the end of his life he had become corrupted. While in *Breves datos históricos y culturales* Cetina had compared Pío Chuc to Gandhi and Jesus, now he drew other, more contemporary comparisons, no doubt careful to respect what he thought my sensitivities might be, as a native New Yorker. "I believe," he told me, "that Pío Chuc resorted to a version of what we are seeing today: terrorism." Such indefensible actions of terrorism, as Cetina now saw it, had left a traumatic memory in the town, a residual terror Cetina described to me for the first time in the years of our acquaintance. He noted that during his youth in Hunucmá residents often were afraid to answer knocks at their doors. "I don't know if they remembered the events of those times," he explained, "or if it was just the fear that stayed with them, without any understanding of where it came from."

Now, when I asked Don Anacleto what the meaning of "liberty" had been for the insurgents of the revolutionary years, he distanced himself from Hunucmá's insurgents and their cause. "Liberty, for them, was not how you and I understand it," he told me; their understanding of liberty's meaning was, he said, "more restricted." Canul Reyes, Pío Chuc, and their followers toppled walls and attacked haciendas and other symbols of private property as a way of declaring what Cetina called the "freedom of the land" from private ownership and to reestablish "free use of the land." Their actions, however, had nothing to do with political freedom or economic freedom, and ultimately they became vulnerable to political manipulation and the resulting exploitation. While Cetina rejected the measures the United States took in response to the attacks of 11 September as violent and imperialistic, it is clear that Al Qaeda's actions had tarnished the earlier struggles of Hunucmá's insurgents by calling into question their vision of liberty and, perhaps more profoundly, by discrediting martyrdom as a paradigm for remembering and writing the history of el pueblo. The disorientation Cetina described feeling in the political realm found echoes in his disorientation from his earlier idealizations of liberty, insurgency, and history. Events, it seemed, had wrested from him his attachments to various strains of left- and right-wing activism, Zapatismo and PANismo. They seemed to leave him clinging to a conventional liberalism, effacing his earlier recognition of the expansive political dimension of the struggle Hunucmá's insurgents had waged in el pueblo's name. It seemed as if he—like Pío Chuc, the old communalist insurgents, ejidal leaders, or even some of the independent unionists—had followed the road of liberation to its end, to a place of cynicism and disenchantment.

As Cetina's romantic hopes for an imminent true history of liberation as expressed so forcefully in *Breves datos históricos y culturales* seemed to fade, it might have seemed that tragedy would become the only genre available for relating Hunucmá's history.[33] Yet Cetina did not draw this conclusion. Instead, he began to focus on other aspects of Hunucmá's history and culture and the possibility of a different kind of liberation, one that might be pursued in the schoolhouse. With his students, he told me, he began working to redress the dual effects of the "trauma of the conquest" and of Yucatán's modernization under neoliberal auspices. The combination of the two, he felt, had led Hunucmá's youth to "discard their history, their language [and] their past." Their cultural mimicry, shame, and will to forget, when added to the supposedly disorienting effects of contemporary life, had led to the most distressing development of all. Hunucmá's youth, Cetina explained to me in 2004, no longer possessed either an interest in imagining or projecting the future or the capacity to do so. "It seems," he mused, "that they don't believe in the future, perhaps due to the economic and political situation that they are experiencing, the chaos that the country and the world are now experiencing. This, I think, has made them into skeptics."[34]

After the publication of *Breves datos históricos y culturales* and in the wake of the different kinds of denouement those years brought, Cetina has redoubled his efforts to advance a program of what he calls cultural education that might counter such jaundiced skepticism by recuperating traditional and Mayan culture and consciously restoring a connection to a forgotten historical past. Cetina wrote and published several stories in Maya, using them as an opportunity to speak with earring-wearing *cholos* in his classroom about what he calls their loss of roots through their disuse of Maya language and what he sees as their mimicry of foreign customs. He began to revive disused Mayan customs, for instance, by learning about the traditional Mayan *hetsmek'* ceremony (in which infants are presented with the kinds of work tools they will use upon becoming adult men or women) and then publicly performing it—before camera-wielding newspaper reporters—with one of his grand-children. He encouraged his students to "keep a little something from the past"—a cultural repertoire that, like a book, allows them to "flip back to earlier pages, to remember what you have read." Here Cetina emphasized—in ways that evoke traditional performances by Hunucmá's landed gentry, as much as its indigenous or mestizo heritage—the importance of performing traditional dances in mestizo garb. The vaquería is, for Cetina, a "seedbed" that maintains a connection with "our root, Mayan culture" while providing for its growth and reproduction among younger generations. This was also the pedagogical role of history: a means of "remembering our origins, our past, and what we are, as descendants of a great culture."

Considered in this context, *Breves datos históricos y culturales* becomes a catalogue or compendium of material and cultural properties of el pueblo: of its Mayan heritage, as expressed in language, dress, and tradition; of its customs and religious practices, whether Mayan or Christian in origin; of its historical struggles, martyrdom, and frustrated but ennobling attempts at liberation; of its built structures, from church bells to streets and band-stands. The book is also an indictment of dispossession: of the corrosive legacies of colonialism; of the assaults of modernity and globalization; of the dangers of forgetting and the difficulties of remembering. Cetina offers his work as a resource for the reconstruction of a viable sense of pueblo iden-tity through a conscious repossession of el pueblo, by collecting the disag-gregated fragments of its culture and its past. His project is traditionalist in spirit yet multicultural in style; one alternately conservative and progressive in means and ends; one severely critical of neoliberalism, while favorable to the individualistic ethic of responsibility and self-empowerment that are hallmarks of that ideology.[35] Against the tragedy and disillusionment of past and present, education, for Cetina, offered the possibility of "transforming this world full of injustice and selfishness" into a better place. In that spirit, despite all of the disappointments, he stood by his dedication of *Breves datos históricos y culturales* to "all the teachers of Mexico, so that they remember that they should be the torch that illuminates minds; so that they do not con-spire with the darkness and so that they allow the blindfold to fall from the underprivileged so that they might learn, and might find the wide road of freedom."[36]

In the years following the publication of *Breves datos históricos y culturales*, Don Anacleto consciously put it to use, distributing copies to town residents and donating copies to libraries and primary and secondary schools in the area. The result, according to Cetina, was dramatic: "It was as if el pueblo awakened, encountered its past, and became interested in it." Teachers gave schoolchildren assignments relating to the history of the town, directing them to read Cetina's book. To this day, Don Anacleto proudly describes firing the imagination of apathetic adolescent students in town with his tales of Canul Reyes and Pío Chuc and through his attempts to preserve and to revive Hunucmá's indigenous culture, traditions, and history.

The positive reception of his book led Don Anacleto to consider publishing a new edition, which he did in 2006. In our conversations about Hunucmá and its history at that time, he emphasized that he still considered history to be an "open book," despite its tragic lessons. It was a source of "inspiration, so that we can find the strength to continue forward—not stagnate, and not be conformists, resigned to accepting what we have." Notwithstanding the outcome of events in the decade that followed the publication of *Breves datos históricos y culturales*, Cetina continued to express his determination to use history as a means to "project the future"—a future in which Hunucmá, despite all of the forces arrayed against it, might become "a harmonious, prosperous, and cultured society."

In short, the "wide road of liberation," for Don Anacleto, would always lead back whence it came: to el pueblo. *Breves datos históricos y culturales* is of a piece with the rest of Cetina Aguilar's poetry and writings, with his work in indigenous education in southern Yucatán and as a schoolteacher in Hunucmá, and with his work and the ideals he held as a PAN activist, a Zapatista sympathizer, and an admirer of Che Guevara. All of these are expressions of the unsettled intellect of a man whose life has been spent in search of el pueblo, ceaselessly moved by desires both frustrated—to become its savior or guardian, guide or redeemer—and fulfilled—to become its teacher. At the most fundamental level, however, Don Anacleto's work, from his poetry to his activism and teaching and historical scholarship, may arise from his own troubled search for a place within el pueblo. He has found, if nothing else, a refuge in el pueblo, in the spirit of a poem he wrote under that title. The poem, "Refuge," first traces connections between a house and the landscape of materials out of which it has been built and then offers that house as a metaphor for a pueblo able to receive and to heal wayfaring outsiders and perhaps a few troubled insiders as well. Don Anacleto Cetina Aguilar, like so many others, continues to seek and to find a way, in the words of that poem, to make of el pueblo's "constellations of rocks and stars" the "sweet prison" of his "tears and afflictions."

"NO"-PLACE

ONCE UPON A TIME, the story goes, a peaceful Mayan people lived at the foot of a stone temple, offering
incense to the gods to the accompaniment of priestly
chanting. One day, on the coast nearby, strange beings
arrived, mounted on ferocious beasts and vomiting fire
and death. They imprisoned the leaders of the little
pueblo and subjected them to horrible tortures, searing
their feet with hot coals. The Spanish had Mayan translators with them and ordered them to ask the leaders
of el pueblo, "Do you know where we can find gold?"
But the translators, betraying their overlords, simply
told the prisoners in Maya, "Nuc ma ti!" ("answer no to
them!"). As the interrogation and torments intensified,
the valiant leaders refused to give over their gold and
silver. They refused even to speak, maintaining a "stony
silence, like the stones of their majestic temples," until
death took them. Inhabitants of the pueblo would re-

member how the heroes had sacrificed themselves rather than allow sacrilege against the "mysteries of their race" by invaders who "only recognized the material value of minerals, but not the greatness of el pueblo's spirit." For ages to come they told and retold the story: "U NUC MA!"—"their answer was no!" they would recall, eventually adopting those words as the name of their pueblo.

In 1983 Anacleto Cetina Aguilar published this story about the conquestera origins of the name Hunucmá as the preface to his poetry collection Cahtal-K'ay. When I traveled to Hunucmá in 2001 to interview Don Anacleto, he explained to me that he had heard the story many years before, from an elderly man named Rufino Uc. According to Cetina, even through his old age Uc spent much of his time out in the woods making milpa. One day, while walking back to town, the old man met Cetina and shared the "Nuc ma ti" story with him.

Though Uc was long dead by the time I interviewed Don Anacleto, this was not my first encounter with him. I knew him, even if only slightly, as a name on a list of so-called soldiers of José Pío Chuc and as a suspect in a penal file, both documents dating from 1920. Uc had been arrested, along with a group of other young men, including several from the Canul and Chuc families, under suspicion of involvement in an arson attack against henequen fields of San Joaquín, a finca owned by the hacendado Manuel Castilla and his brothers. Those fields were just a few of the dozens targeted at that time, as arson attacks scorched haciendas throughout the district. Confounded by the spectacle of the destruction, the Castillas claimed ignorance of any quarrel, ill will, or political motive for the attack, noting only that "what has happened to us, and what has happened to others, makes it seem that this is all about destroying the wealth of the State. Doubtless, it will bring us nothing but misery."[1]

Those were prescient words. On 26 April, after an initial investigation went nowhere, Uc and his fellows were released, just in time for the worst of the violence. On 29 April Hunucmá's chief of police would make his ill-fated decision to search the house of Pío Chuc, setting off a fatal chain of events: the killing of the chief; the flight of Pío Chuc and his men—Uc may have been one of them—to the woods; the violent reprisals of soldiers, against Chuc's family and friends; kidnappings, including the seizure of two of Manuel Castilla's sons from one of San Joaquín's rail cars; the gruesome killings and interments at Cacab Dzul; and finally, Chuc's killing and dismemberment. It seems likely Uc witnessed or took part in these events in some way, though it is unclear to me exactly how, for I have found no other trace of him or of his life in the archives. What is certain is that Uc survived those hard times to live into old age, until one day he met the schoolteacher Anacleto Cetina and told him a story.

One might be tempted to read Uc's story about the name of Hunucmá as a collective myth of origins. At the same time, one must recognize the limited constituency of this tale. Perhaps the "Nuc ma ti" story had some degree of currency among residents of Hunucmá half a century ago or more; perhaps, once upon a time, it circulated among a smaller group of communalists—Feliciano Canul Reyes, Isabel Reyes, José Pío Chuc, María Dolores Chuil, or even El Rey de los Bosques—as inspiration for their struggles. Perhaps Uc invented the story later on, to make sense of some of the events he had witnessed by relating them to an older, imagined history. In contemporary Hunucmá, however, despite its publication by Cetina, the "Nuc ma ti" story seems to be known by only a handful of residents, and even Cetina himself now regards the story as implausible.

Nor does the story seem to have much validity as a historical account of the origins or making of el pueblo in Hunucmá. The "Nuc ma ti" story is strikingly anachronistic, seeming to project el pueblo back to the moment of conquest. In contrast, this book—in exploring el pueblo historically and genealogically—has revealed the making of el pueblo to be a complicated process, one taking place over the course of centuries, and still ongoing. It has demonstrated the importance of prior, alternative, communal frameworks and histories, like those of kah and común, and has shown how African- and Spanish-descended mestizo populations joined with Hunucmá's indigenous residents in shaping the terms of community, both before and after the consolidation of el pueblo. Moreover, this book suggests that as much as it was shaped by insiders, el pueblo was also shaped and structured by outsiders, of various ethnicities and classes, who claimed possession through, and over el pueblo—notably, the landowning elites, and government officials, who played roles in vesting, disinvesting, and reinvesting kah, común, and pueblo as collective entities. Finally, in distinction from the "Nuc ma ti" story, close study of the historical and contemporary experience of the Hunucmá region makes clear the central role of internal, rather than merely external, conflict and violence, in shaping communal and collective identity both before and after el pueblo took on the appearance of a unified social and political subject.

How, then, is one to judge the significance of such a story—one that is, on one hand, so partial as a historical account, and on the other, so lacking in the generality that scholars normally consider to be characteristic of collective or group memory? My response to that question has been to seek to understand this story and others like it, not as reflections of prior events, or even products of shared imaginings of the past, but rather as expressions of shared *ways* of telling stories about the past, and shared ways of using those stories to lay claim to el pueblo. In this book I have asked: What might the "Nuc ma ti" story, and others like it, convey about the nature of el pueblo, and about the varied ways in which history is rendered in its name?

In the "Nuc ma ti" story, place, community, and collectivity emerge into being simultaneously, a union of origin and essence symbolized by the assumption of a shared name, as el pueblo. As such, the story—like so many other stories of el pueblo—manifests a conception of pueblo that cannot be translated as referring *either* to place (the town of Hunucmá), *or* to people (the community that inhabits that place), *or* to political collectivity (the people, projected against a common oppressor). This account of el pueblo's origins demands that the reader begin by transcending such schematic distinctions. Moreover, in the "Nuc ma ti" story, el pueblo figures as a collective entity that belongs and that has belongings—something that possesses, and is possessed. Thus, physical features mentioned in the story, from the geography to the temples, evoke a presence and possession antedating the Spanish conquest. The gold, moreover, stands as a general signifier of possessions at once material and spiritual in nature, with a value far greater, the story reminds us, than that of mere minerals. The story, however, is not only about possession, but also about dispossession. Gold does not make its appearance solely in terms of its value for its Mayan possessors, but also in terms of its potential seizure by the Spanish. Indigenous leaders, after being tortured, are dispossessed of their lives, as martyrs for a pueblo that is as yet nameless. It is only through the conquest, in fact, that Hunucmá becomes a pueblo, entering history as an object of dispossession and as a martyred subject. Yet by its end, the "Nuc ma ti" story reveals itself to be neither a tale of possession, nor of dispossession, but rather one of repossession. Dispossessed of gold, land, and lives following the conquest, the people of Hunucmá come to recognize themselves as el pueblo through the recognition of a shared history, and with it, the repossession of a collective name—a treasure of greater value than any hoard of gold.

Inspired by this, and other, stories of el pueblo, I have sought to explore the making of el pueblo as place, people, and collectivity. I have done so by conducting an anthropological and historical exploration of the many manifestations of el pueblo as a subject claimed, invoked and evoked in Hunucmá, a region where the meanings of that term have been contested with great intensity from the eighteenth century to the present. Even before the advent of el pueblo as a unifying framework for communal identity, kah, común, and pueblo existed as place-based expressions of communal and political sovereignty. Though apparently local, those entities also provided points of transaction with wider political structures as nexuses of political control and incorporation within far-flung structures of state, nation, and empire. The same is true of el pueblo, from the revolutionary period on, as it became at one and the same time an emblem of emancipatory struggle, a framework for state formation and communal incorporation, and a place of social and spiritual habitation. As I have attempted to demonstrate through this historical and ethnographic study, this grounded, yet transcendent, quality is one of el pueblo's constitutive features in the Hunucmá region, and perhaps beyond.

The structuring of the "Nuc ma ti" story, like so many of el pueblo's stories, as a tale of collective dispossession and repossession, has led me to ask two questions, above all: What and how did el pueblo come to possess, and to be possessed?[2] This book represents an attempt to answer these questions through a historical and ethnographic study of how el pueblo came to have its hold not only over people, but also over a host of different kinds of possessions: over land and wood, salt pools, and deer; over abstractions, like rights, liberty, and patria; over dances, language, and dress; over religious icons, sacred money, and the Virgin's grace; and over archives and historical documents. At the same time, I have searched out the things whose dispossession, or loss, seems so critical to pueblo consciousness: from lands seized by hacendados and ranchers; to the lost freedoms and dignity of workers enslaved; to pueblo buildings and bell towers, destroyed or falling into ruin; to the lives lost by martyrs. Above all, in seeking to understand the consolidation of el pueblo as a social, political, and religious subject, I have sought out the places and moments of its repossession: whether as an insurgent subject reclaiming lands and liberty, or as a subordinate entreating the state for assistance; whether through redemption by the Virgin's grace, or by the performance of el pueblo in genres poetic, historical, or carnivalesque.

In light of this complex historical and ethnographic genealogy, what kind of a history might the "Nuc ma ti" story be? Should it even be dignified with the name of history? I would argue that it should be, although the history it represents is history of a particular kind. Along with other texts like the land petition from 1915 signed by Pío Chuc, the story of the Virgin of Tetiz, La batalla de Tetiz y Hunucmá, and Anacleto Cetina's Breves datos históricos y culturales del municipio de Hunucmá, the "Nuc ma ti" story demonstrates the operations not of a reduplicative kind of historical memory—one that conserves and transmits discrete facts about the past—but of allegory. That term literally means "other stories," and these are all, indeed, other stories.[3] Their deepest significance arises not from their specific content as representations of prior happenings, but rather from their evocation of another, more encompassing story. Despite the radical difference in the content of these "stories" of el pueblo, all are allegories of repossession, whose plot and structure incorporates a common sequence, from possession to dispossession to repossession. The story of el pueblo, in other words, is a story of collective repossession, one that in some respects resonates with the stories of Eden and of Exodus.

When considered in this way, it becomes clear that even if historical accounts like the "Nuc ma ti" story are partial or selective, they do not thereby constitute acts of silencing those pasts unrepresented or even misrepresented in them.[4] As I have tried to demonstrate, there is content to the form.[5] The allegorical construction of el pueblo in historical narrative bears the traces of concrete historical experiences that lend power to the allegory of repossession. These have included conquest, forced labor, the commodification of land and labor, and recent social, economic, and cultural dislocations; they have also included processes of state formation, as well as mobilizations in past and present in which pueblo residents rose up, in the name of el pueblo, to demand their repossession. The presence of these histories, even if occluded, makes el pueblo at once abstract and concrete, both generic and particular, as a collective body embedded in material and cultural resources and one shaped by the allegory making, or allegoresis, through which these relationships have been "storied" as histories of el pueblo written and read from within and without. In short, in Hunucmá and perhaps beyond, el pueblo is both inherently allegorical, and inherently historical. Its continuing power to possess peoples and places, things and politics, ultimately derives from the allegory of repossession that underwrites its history, undergirds its communal and collective life, and articulates its past, present, and future.

Here, the "Nuc ma ti" story, and this book, may offer an interesting counterpoint to philosophical discussions of popular politics in which el pueblo, or "the people," is described either as a timeless and originary entity, or as a purely political or oppositional concept—one abstract, empty, rhetorical, or fictive in nature. What such analyses miss is what a close study of Hunucmá—indeed, of any place where el pueblo is deeply rooted and deeply felt—provides: an understanding that el pueblo is also possession, community, and place of habitation. El pueblo, in other words, may have its part and possession not in the domain of politics, but in other registers of communal life, from which el pueblo comes before the moment of politics and to which it returns afterward. Its apparent abstraction may be materiality ignored; its emptiness, depth misperceived. From those depths arises its extraordinary capacity to accommodate so many places, possessions, and histories—so much loss and yet so much improbable but unextinguished hope for the repossession of things, people, and even names.

Finally, the "Nuc ma ti'" story evokes one additional feature of el pueblo I have left unexplored to this point: that of negation. Anthropological analyses of historical narrative have stressed the uses of history, and one can imagine that the "Nuc ma ti" story, in some contexts, might be a useful one to tell. In itself, however, this is a story about the refusal of use. It is about a pueblo that refuses to be made into an object of exploitation by others. To stress the dimension of negation in the making of el pueblo is to suggest that el pueblo is a relational rather than an insular construct. It is one whose claims are dialectical rather than foundational—one often objectified in instrumental ways, but whose deepest history may reside in its refusal to be used. Within the Hunucmá region and far beyond its boundaries, it is that history of refusal and contestation that charges el pueblo with historical significance even as it leaves it open to appropriation. The power of el pueblo may derive from the fact that once, or now, or at some point, el pueblo did, does, and will say "No!"—and in that moment names itself and claims a history that may not be fully known but that cannot be denied.

In short, the hold Hunucmá has on el pueblo and the hold el pueblo has over Hunucmá may relate as much to what el pueblo denies as to what it asserts. Here, perhaps, resides its power and its promise, as a collective way to reclaim the past, challenge the present, and imagine the future differently. In this sense, Hunucmá, el pueblo, the people that answered no is, like "U-topia," quite literally no place but also every place. This is the last of el pueblo's possessions: a possession of, by, and for its spirit. "Nuc ma ti" may serve, in the last instance, as a reminder of the ghostly presence of el pueblo in Hunucmá and beyond, as a spirit that ever returns to possess those who are grouped under its name and a specter that ever returns to haunt those who are not.

POPULATION CHANGE IN THE HUNUCMÁ REGION, 1900–1940

THE GRAPHS that appear below represent a summary of population statistics from 143 population sites (towns, pueblos, haciendas, and ranches) in the Hunucmá region from 1900 to 1940. Population totals for haciendas are tabulated separately from those for pueblos and towns in order to demonstrate the differences between population change in the vicinity of the town of Hunucmá and the pueblos of Kinchil and Tetiz (where hacienda populations plummeted during the revolutionary years, never to recover) and that in the vicinity of the pueblo of Samahil and especially the town of Umán (where hacienda populations initially decreased in the revolutionary years but then stabilized and, in Umán's case, returned almost to prerevolutionary levels by 1930).

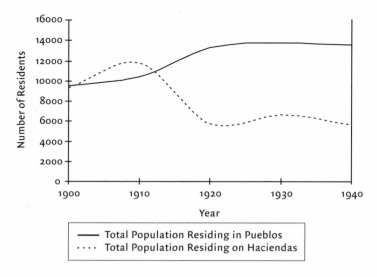

Resident population of pueblos and haciendas in the entire Hunucmá district, 1900–1940.

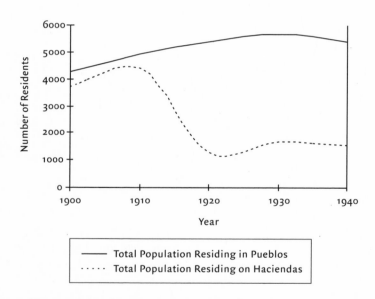

Resident population of pueblos and haciendas in Hunucmá municipality, 1900–1940.

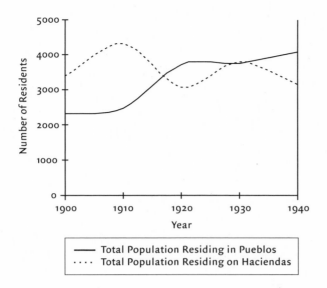

Resident population of pueblos and haciendas in Umán municipality, 1900–1940.

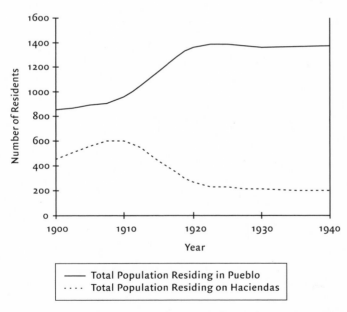

Resident population of the pueblo of Tetiz, and of haciendas in Tetiz municipality, 1900–1940.

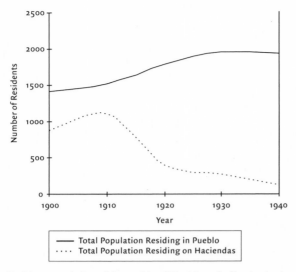

Resident population of the pueblo of Kinchil, and of haciendas in
Kinchil municipality, 1900–1940.

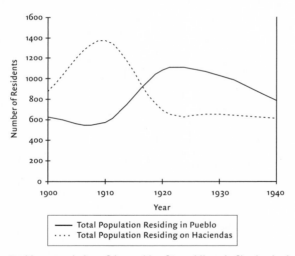

Resident population of the pueblo of Samahil, and of haciendas in
Samahil municipality, 1900–1940.

Sources for the figures: México, Dirección General de Estadística, Censo general de la República Mexicana verificado el
28 de octubre de 1900 (Mexico City: Oficina Tip. de la Secretaría de Fomento, 1901–7); Enrique Cantillo M. de
Oca, Censo de 1910: Cuadros estadísticos formados con autorización del Gobierno del Estado (Mérida: Imp. de la Escuela
Correccional de Artes y Oficios del Estado, 1912); México, Dirección General de Estadística, Censo general de
habitantes 30 de noviembre de 1921 (Mexico City: Talleres gráficos de la nación, 1925–28); México, Dirección
General de Estadística, Quinto censo de población, 15 de mayo de 1930 (Mexico City: Talleres gráficos de la nación,
1934); México, Dirección General de Estadística, 6 censo de población, 1940 (Mexico City: México, Dirección
General de Estadística,1943–48).

NOTES

INTRODUCTION

1 See Velasco, "Signos y sentidos"; Gorman, *Inventing the People*.

2 Malinowski, *Argonauts*, 25.

3 Burke, "An Appeal from the New to the Old Whigs," 84; Gorman, *Inventing the People*; Hardt and Negri, *Empire*, xiv, 79; Laclau, *On Populist Reason*; Rancière, *Disagreement*; Dussel, *Twenty Theses on Politics*, 73.

4 Cf. Latour, *We Were Never Modern*.

5 Cf. Smith, *Livelihood and Resistance*; Mallon, *Peasant and Nation*; Thurner, *From Two Republics*; Nugent, *Modernity at the Edge of Empire*; Gould, *To Die in This Way*; Grandin, *Blood of Guatemala*; Wade, *Blackness and Race Mixture*; Appelbaum, *Muddied Waters*; Appelbaum, Macpherson, and Roseblatt, *Race and Nation*; and Larson, *Trials of Nation Making*.

6 Cf. Alonso, *Thread of Blood*; Rubin, *Decentering the Regime*; Nugent, *Spent Cartridges*; Joseph and Nugent, *Everyday Forms of State Formation*; Beezley, Martin, and French, *Rituals of Rule*; Becker, *Setting the Virgin on Fire*; Vaughan, *Cultural Politics*; Bantjes, *As If Jesus Walked on Earth*; Kourí, *A Pueblo Divided*; Purnell, *Popular Movements*; and Lomnitz Adler, *Exits and Deep Mexico*.

7 For scholarship on Yucatán, see references in relevant chapters of this book.

8 See, for instance, Redfield, *Tepoztlan, Folk Culture*; Redfield and Villa Rojas, *Chan Kom*; and Lewis, *Tepoztlan*.

9 González y González, *Pueblo* and *Invitación*, 12.

10 See Brooks et al., eds., *Small Worlds*; and Ginzburg, "Microhistory."

11 Redfield "The Folk Society," 293. Cf. Anderson's opposition between "face-to-face" and "imagined" communities, in *Imagined Communities*; and Appadurai's references to communities before globalization, in *Modernity at Large*.

12 Wolf, "Types of Latin American Peasantry," 454; and Smith, *Livelihood and Resistance*, 26. See also Mallon, *In Defense of Community*; Thompson, *Whigs and Hunters*; and Creed, *Seductions of Community*.

13 Scott, *Weapons*, xvi. Cf. De la Cadena, *Indigenous Mestizos*.

14 Kantorowicz, *King's Two Bodies*; Halbwachs, *Collective Memory*. Cf. Connerton, *How Societies Remember*.

15 Young, *Texture*; Geary, *Phantoms*; Dening, *Death*; Price, *Convict and the Colonel*.

16 Rappaport, *Cumbe Reborn*, 177–78. Cf. John Comaroff and Jean Comaroff, *Ethnography*; Trouillot, *Silencing the Past*; Blouin and Rosenberg, *Archives*; Stoler, *Along the Archival Grain*.

17 Cf. Fogelson, "Ethnohistory."

18 Foucault, *Discipline and Punish*, 30–31.

19 Benjamin, *Illuminations*, 262.

20 Cf. Reyes Domínguez, *Carnaval en Mérida*; and Mintz, *Carnival Song*.

21 Cf. Taylor, *The Archive and the Repertoire*; Roach, *Cities of the Dead*.

CHAPTER ONE   THE LAST CACIQUE

1 "1856. Causa por acusación de Doña Juana Peña contra el casique Pascual Chac," AGEY, JUS, PEN, 78, 20. See also "1857. Causa seguida al cacique de Hunucmá Pascual Chac . . . ," AGEY, JUS, PEN, 80, 50.

2 Patch, *Maya and Spaniard*, 19; Bracamonte y Sosa, *Los mayas*, 35; Roys, *Political Geography*, 11–13, 26–37.

3 Farriss, *Maya Society*; Restall, *Maya Conquistador*, 46–48.

4 "1664. Confirmación de encomienda de Tetiz," AGI, Mexico, 244:41, 243:61, and 245:5; "1682. Encomienda de Cauquel, Ucú y Yabucú," Mexico, 248:4; and "1660. Confirmación de encomienda de Umán," Mexico, 244:8 and 247:8. See also Patch, *Maya and Spaniard*, 23, 48–51, 75, 79; Restall, *Maya World*, 24–25, 49; Roys, *Political Geography*, 29; Solís Robleda, *Bajo el signo*, 47; Bracamonte y Sosa, *Los mayas*, 51; García Bernal, *Población y encomienda*; and Rubio Mañé, *Casa de Montejo*, 36–37.

5 Patch, *Maya and Spaniard*, 71–73; Restall, *Maya World*, 120, 172–75; Bracamonte y Sosa, *Los mayas*, 9, 65–70, 103–5.

6 Rugeley, *Yucatán's Maya Peasantry*; Restall, *Maya World*, 53–83, 151–52; Farriss, *Maya Society*.

7 "1781. Cuentas presentadas por D. Gregorio José de la Cámara . . . ," CA, 1779:007. See also Farriss, *Maya Society*; Patch, *Maya and Spaniard*, 29–35, 84–89, 101, 105, 121, 132; Restall, *Maya World*; and Solís Robleda, *Bajo el signo*.

8 Solís Robleda, *Bajo el signo*, 234–36; and Solís Robleda, *Contra viento*, 215–18, 241–46.

9 See Patch, *Maya and Spaniard*, 116, 182, 183; Bracamonte y Sosa, *Los mayas*, 82, 106; and Restall, *Maya World*, 196.

10 Restall, *Maya World*, 5, 54–56, 189–200, 235–66, 276–92; Restall 1995; and Bracamonte y Sosa, *Los mayas*, 39–40, 45, 50–53.

11 Farriss, *Maya Society*, 359–60; Patch, *Maya and Spaniard*, 138–47, 151, 153, 187, 201–8; Restall, *Maya World*, 35, 250; Bracamonte y Sosa, *Los mayas*, 75–81, 83, 156–60; Rugeley, *Yucatán's Maya Peasantry*, 14, 34; Contreras Sánchez *Historia de una tintorea* and *Capital comercial*.

12 Patch, *Maya and Spaniard*, 233, 234, 260; Restall, *Maya World*, 18; Gabbert, *Becoming Maya*, 32–36, 74–77.

13 "Alegato de los indígenas del pueblo de Hunucmá. . . ." AGI, Audiencia de México, leg. 3066; "Petición de justicia de los naturales . . . ," AGN, BN, 26, 55, f. 19 and 20. My thanks to Matthew Restall for sharing the latter document with me.

14 "Transunto de un convenio de uso común de tierras . . . ," AGN, Tierras, 1419, 2, f. 56r–v. See also "Informe que hace el procurador de los naturales Agustín Crespo . . . ," AGEY, COL, Tierras, 31, 1, 20, 1815, ff. 14r–17v; Restall, *Maya World*, 219, 256–57; Bracamonte y Sosa, *La memoria enclaustrada*, 171–74; Bracamonte y Sosa, *Los mayas*, 177–82, 199–202.

15 See license transcribed in "1871. Autos de mensura . . . San Eduardo," AGEY, JUS, CIV, 173, 3.

16 "1818. Venta de tierras . . . Julian del Castillo y Cámara," AGN, Tierras, 1421:13: 335–3684.

17 "1821. Expediente formado por el Ayuntamiento de Hunucmá . . . ," AGEY, COL, Ayuntamientos, 1, 33A. See also "1814. Copiador de la correspondencia del Gobernador Artazo y Torre de Mer, . . . ," AGEY, COL, Correspondencia de los gobernadores, 5, 2, 8; Melchor Menéndez, 28 June 1821, CA, VII-1821, 032; Rubio Mañé, "Los sanjuanistas," 1226; Rugeley, *Yucatáns Maya Peasantry*, 38–39, 48–49, 61–63; Güémez, *Liberalismo*, 51–64; Bracamonte, *Amos y sirvientes*, 217; Bracamonte, *Los mayas*, 176.

18 "1820. Copiador de la correspondencia de los gobernadores . . . ," AGEY, COL, COG, 6, 4, 2; "Copia legal . . . Cumpich . . . ," 1 July 1823, AGEY, PE, Tierras, 1, 10; Rugeley, *Yucatán's Maya Peasantry*, 61–68; Bracamonte, *Amos y sirvientes*, 32, 35, 189, and *Los mayas*, 179–82; and Güémez, *Liberalismo*, 70, 175.

19 Valera, "Discurso." See also Suárez, *Estado de la industria*, 95–96.

20 Güémez, *Liberalismo*, 163. See also "1820. Copiador de la correspondencia de los gobernadores . . . ," AGEY, COL, COG, 6, 4, 2; "1831. Expediente promovido por milperos . . . ," AGEY, PE, GOB, Tierras, 38, 1, 20; "Representación de Magdalena Mendicuti . . . ," 4 April 1837, AGEY, PE, Tierras, 9, 11; Güémez, *Liberalismo*, 41, 51–64, 68, 92–95, 135–36, 217–18, 220–23, 228, 230–31, 235–37; Bracamonte, *Los mayas*, 134, 156, 160–76; Restall, *Maya World*, 218–23; Patch, *Maya and Spaniard*, 226–29; Rugeley, *Yucatán's Maya Peasantry*, 39–44, 93–94; and Bracamonte, *Amos y sirvientes*, 46.

21 Rugeley, *Yucatán's Maya Peasantry*, 93–96; Bracamonte, *Los mayas*, 184; and Gabbert, *Becoming Maya*, 62.

22 "Repúblicas de indígenas. Los alcaldes y justicias de la república de indios de Hunucmá . . . ," 16 December 1831, AGEY, PE, GOB, 16, 3, 47; "1834. Causa seguida contra Andrés Uitz . . . ," AGEY, JUS, 11, 28; "Representación de varios vecinos del pueblo de Kinchil . . . ," 9 November 1840, AGEY, PE, GOB, 21, 14, 1; and "1843. Causa instruída contra la indígena Paula Canché . . . ," AGEY, JUS, 32, 34. See also Rugeley, *Yucatán's Maya Peasantry*, 105.

23 "Padrón general . . . pueblo de Hunucmá . . . ," AGEY, Censos y Padrones 1841, 48, 2, 22; and "Padrón general . . . pueblo de Tetiz . . . ," AGEY, Censos y Padrones 1841, 41, 5, 62; and "1845. Causa seguida á Don Joaquín Barros . . . ," AGEY, JUS, 40, 47.

24 "Expediente instruído . . . Antonio Anguas . . . ," 3 June 1831, AGEY, PE, Justicia, 24, 3, 11; "1838. Queja de José Dolores Zetina . . . ," AGEY, JUS, 19, 14. "1838. Causa promovida por José Agustín Manzanilla . . . ," AGEY, JUS, PEN, 18, 18; AGEY, Congreso (CON), Correspondencia, 1832–34, vol. 4, 2 April 1832; "1835. Testamentaria de José Eduardo Peña . . . ," AGEY, JUS, CIV, 21, 1.

25 "1838. Causa promovida por José Agustín Manzanilla . . . ," AGEY, JUS, PEN, 18, 18.

26 "1838. Causa promovida por José Agustín Manzanilla . . . ," AGEY, JUS, PEN, 18, 18.

27 "1856. Testamentaria de Juana Peña . . . ," AGEY, JUS, CIV, 72, 11.

28 "1824. Causa criminal contra Juan Navarro . . . ," AGEY, JUS, PEN, 2, 18; "1855. Causa de Norberto Chuil . . . ," AGEY, JUS, 70, 8. See also Gabbert, *Becoming Maya*, 72–73; and Dumond, *Machete*.

29 Document cited in Bracamonte, *Los mayas*, 199–200.

30 Juan P. Ríos to gobernador, 7 August 1857, AGEY, PE, GOB, 125, 75, 27.

31 "1820. Copiador de la correspondencia . . . ," AGEY, COL, Correspondencia de los gobernadores, 6, 4, 2.

32 Document cited in Güémez, *Liberalismo*, 254–55.

33 "Representación de Felipe Gil . . . ," 11 July 1837, AGEY, PE, Tierras, 7, 30; "Información de la república de indígenas del pueblo de Kinchil . . . ," 1 November 1837, AGEY, PE, Tierras, 38, 1, 32.

34 José Cosgaya, JP Mérida, to Sec. Gral. de Gob., 9 July 1844, AGEY, PE, Tierras, 212, 162, 07.

35 Rugeley, *Yucatán's Maya Peasantry*, 115–51, 183; and Bracamonte, *La memoria enclaustrada*, 113–14; Reed, *Caste War*; and Dumond, *Machete*. See especially Rugeley, *Rebellion*.

36 J. Jesus Castro to Srio. Gral. de Gob., 1 April 1847, AGEY, PE, JUST, 144, 94, 49.

37 Manuel Correa, 14 October 1847, CA, XLIII–1847, 014. See also EC 13 February 1883; 17 May 1892, RDM; Baqueiro, *Ensayo histórico*, 21–25; Aurelio Castillo to Señor prefecto superior del Departamento de Mérida, 11 October 1866, AGEY, PE, GOB; Eduardo López, 15 October 1866, AGEY, PE, GOB, AM, 154. On the different forms of hidalguía during and after the Caste War, see Rugeley, *Rebellion*.

38 "1865. Intestado de José Tzuc . . . ," AGEY, JUS, CIV, 117, 05; and "1852, Testamentaria del indígena Crisanto Chan . . . ," AGEY, JUS, CIV, 51, 26.

39 Bruno Correa, to Sor. Prefecto superior del depto., 15 October 1866, AGEY, PE, AM, 155. See also Eduardo López to gobernador, 18 June 1864, AGEY, PE, GOB, AYUN, 139; Manuel Correa to Exmo. Sr. Gob. y Comandante Gral. de las tropas del Estado, 16 June 1859, AGEY, PE, Juzgado de paz Umán, 122; Bruno Correa to Sor. Prefecto pco. del Depto., 31 October 1866, AGEY, PE, GOB, AM; Juan Molina to gobernador, 4 November 1867, AGEY, PE, Tesorería del estado, 168; "1856. Sumaria instruída a José Domingo Chablé . . . ," AGEY, JUS, 77, 19.

40 Joaquín Barros, 17 March 1852, AGEY, PE, JUST, 145, 95, 27.

41 "1853. Queja de George Uc . . . ," AGEY, JUS, 56, 41. See also "1854. Causa de Vicente Puerto . . . ," AGEY, JUS, 66, 26; "1856. Queja contra el juez de paz 1 de Hunucmá Don Deciderio . . . ," AGEY, JUS, 77, 14; "1861. Diligencias contra el juez de paz de Kinchil . . . ," AGEY, JUS, 95, 62; Eduardo López, Alcalde municipal de Hunucmá, 3 May 1866, AGEY, PE, GOB, AM, 154.

42 "1858. Acusación contra el juez de paz de Umán, José María Paredes . . . ," AGEY, JUS, PEN, 99, 26; "1866. Queja de José Benito Chan contra el Cacique de Hunucmá por haberle azotado sin razón," 15 May 1866, AGEY, PE, GOB, 161.

43 Desiderio Escalante to gobernador, 19 November 1864, AGEY, PE, GOB, Ayuntamientos, 169.

44 "1862. Causa contra José María Naranjo . . . ," AGEY, JUS, 98, 15. Cf. De la Cadena, *Indigenous Mestizos*.

45 Joaquín Castillo Peraza to gobernador, 2 August 1861, AGEY, PE, 97, 47, 01; Tranquilino Puerto to gobernador, 23 March 1857, AGEY, PE, GOB, 124, 74, 52; Leandro Ancona to gobernador, 12 January 1861, AGEY, PE, Tierras, 212, 162, 93.

46 Tranquilino Puerto to gobernador, 23 March 1857, AGEY, PE, GOB, 124, 74, 52.

47 José María Fernández to gobernador, 11 April 1853, AGEY, PE, GOB, 118, 68, 18. See also Desiderio Escalante, 6 July 1852, to gobierno, AGEY, PE, GOB, 117, 67, 33.

48 José Cosgaya, JP Mérida, to Sec. Gral. de Gob., 9 July 1844, AGEY, PE, Tierras, 212, 162, 07; "1853. Queja de George Uc. . . ."; "1855. Expediente de mensura . . . Santa Rosa de Komat . . . ," AGEY, JUS, CIV, 65, 8.

49 Juan Flores to gobernador, 7 October 1856, AGEY, PE, Tierras, 212, 162, 68.

50 "1856. Testamentaria de Juana Peña. . . ."

51 "1856. Causa por acusación de Doña Juana Peña contra el casique Pascual Chac," AGEY, JUS, PEN, 78, 20.

52 "1845. Artículo promovido por Don Felipe Peña reclamando a sus dos hijas . . . ," AGEY, JUS, CIV, 38, 13; "1835. Testamentaria de José Eduardo Peña. . . ."

53 "1871. Demanda de Don Pilar Canto Zozaya . . . ," AGEY, JUS, CIV, 170, 27; "1871. Intestado de Doña Juana Peña," AGEY, JUS, CIV, 172, 6.

CHAPTER TWO KING OF THE FOREST

1 17 May 1892, *RDM*.

2 "Reglamento de policía . . . ," 20 July 1871, AGEY, CON, CGPC, 51, 1, 66 and 22 September 1871, AGEY, CON, CGPC, 51, 1, 82. See coverage in *RDP*, *EC*,

and *RDM*, 1870s–90s, and other district-related documentation in AGEY, CON (COM, CIAA).

3   Wells, *Gilded Age*; Joseph, *Revolution from Without*, and *Rediscovering the Past*; Wells and Joseph, *Summer of Discontent*; Batt, "Rise and Fall"; and Evans, *Bound in Twine*.

4   Wells, *Gilded Age*, 78–87; "1894. Interdicto de apeo . . . Yaxché . . . ," AGEY, JUS, CIV, 89, 1; 9 March 1886, 22 and 24 July 1886, *RDM*; 14 July 1890, *RDP*.

5   José María Vargas to gobernador, 24 October 1877, AGEY, PE, 197. See also "1879. Testamentario del C. Eduardo López . . . ," AGEY, JUS, CIV, 121-A, reel 139; Saturnino Solís to gobernador, 18 October 1878, AGEY, PE, 202A; Angel Rosado to gobernador, 24 August 1884, AGEY, PE, 229; "1891. Indice de escrituras del notario Eligio Guzmán," AGEY, JUS, 15, 32; and Rugeley, *Rebellion*.

6   Juan Cervera to gobernador, 15 October 1880, AGEY, PE, 211; "1871. Autos . . . Hacienda San Eduardo . . . ," AGEY, JUS, CIV, 173, 3.

7   "1892. Acusación de Isidro Quijano . . . ," AGEY, JUS, PEN, 20, 57; "Averiguaciones . . . Facundo Magaña," 14 March 1893, AGEY, JUS, PEN, 25, 16; 2 and 28 January 1880, *RDP*. See also Joseph, *Rediscovering*, 56–58, and *Revolution from Without*, 27–32; and Wells, *Gilded Age*, 83.

8   "1898. Diligencias de consignacion . . . Luciano Tuyub . . . ," AGEY, JUS, CIV, 197, 20; "1898. Causa a Juan Maldonado . . . ," AGEY, JUS, PEN, 95, 25; "1900. Acusación de Marcos Che . . . ," AGEY, JUS, PEN, 143, 32; Máximo Uc to Calixto Maldonado, 17 September 1915, AGEY, PE, GUE, 476; and "1891. Causa seguida a Lorenzo Baas . . . ," AGEY, JUS, PEN, 8, 58; 2 and 28 January 1880, *RDP*. See also Katz, "Labor Conditions"; and Joseph, *Rediscovering*, 62.

9   "1898. Causa a Carlos Perez . . . lesiones," AGEY, JUS, PEN, 105, 29. See also "1892. Causa seguida a Federico Mata . . . ," AGEY, JUS, PEN, 18, 28.

10   "1871. Expediente . . . prisión de la hija de Julian Mukul . . . ," AGEY, JUS, PEN, 153, 8. See also 18 May 1876, *RDM*; 28 February 1883, *UY*; Wells, *Gilded Age*, 157–62; and Wells and Joseph, *Summer of Discontent*, 156–60.

11   "1891. Diligencias . . . Juliana y Feliciano Uc, . . . ," AGEY, JUS, CIV, 4, 27. See also "1894. Juicio ordinario . . . Atanasia Canché . . . ," AGEY, JUS, CIV, 76, 16; Wells, *Gilded Age*, 158–59, 161–74; Joseph, *Rediscovering*, 60–69; Wells and Joseph, *Summer of Discontent*, 160–65; and Gill, "Intimate Life."

12   Abelardo Ponce, JP Hunucmá, AGEY, PE, Ayuntamientos, 267; 1892 survey in AGEY, PE, Ayuntamientos, 273; and 4 March 1881, *RDP*; Joseph, *Rediscovering*, 55–56.

13   5 May 1880 and 19 September 1881, *RDP*. Cf. Vaughan, "Patriotic Festival."

14   7 January 1876 and 4 March 1881, *RDP*.

15   4 April 1883, *UY*; 8 June 1983, *EC*.

16   8 January 1883 *EC*. See also 10 and 14 November 1883, *La Voz del Partido*.

17   See "1900. Causa instruída contra Alfonso Barrera . . . ," AGEY, JUS, PEN, 159, 50; and Eduardo López et al., 8 October 1878, AGEY, PE, 205. Cf. Hobsbawm and Ranger, eds., *Invention of Tradition*, and Maddox, *El Castillo*.

18   Montero, *El rábano*.

19   9 June 1884, *EC*.

20 5 January 1886, *RDM*. See also "1856. Causa seguida á José Hoy . . . ," AGEY, JUS, PEN, 75, 34; "La comisión de hacienda . . . Sinkeuel y Chunchucmil," 28 February 1883, AGEY, CON, CH, Dictámenes, 6, 77; "1894. Diligencias practicadas con motivo del robo de palo de tinte . . . Rafael Peón," AGEY, JUS, PEN, 39, 10.

21 "1889. Diligencias . . . Ricardo Aguilar Brito," AGEY, JUS, PEN, 170-C, reel 244; "1893. Causa seguida a Florentino Poot . . . ," AGEY, JUS, PEN, 23, 13; and "1895. Causa a José Chuc . . . ," AGEY, JUS, PEN, 54, 49. Cf. Rugeley, *Wonders*.

22 Francisco Manzanilla to Liborio Yrigoyen, 26 April 1859, AGEY, PE, MIL, 202, 152, III. See also Manuel Yturrarran to gobernador, 29 April 1859, AGEY, PE, MIL, 203, 153, 5; Joaquín Castillo Peraza to gobernador, 1 August 1861, AGEY, PE, Tierras, 212, 162, 95.

23 Eduardo López to gobernador, 18 June 1864, AGEY, PE, GOB, Ayuntamientos, 139.

24 Saturnino Solís to gobernador, 18 October 1878, AGEY, PE, 202-A; "1871. Autos . . . Hacienda San Eduardo . . . ," AGEY, JUS, CIV, 173, 3.

25 4 June 1876, *RDM*. Cf. Rugeley, *Rebellion*.

26 Palomino to gobernador, 28 May 1876, AGEY, PE, 195; 25 May 1876, *RDM*. See also "1876. Causa seguida a Juan Pablo Pech . . . rebelión . . . ," AGEY, PE, 195.

27 M. Pérez Sandoval to gobernador, 19 July 1880, AGEY, PE, 212-A. See also "1891. Expediente . . . José D. Rivero Figueroa," AGEY, JUS, PEN, 7, 26; Máximo Ancona to gobernador, 20 March 1881, AGEY, PE, 217; "1880. Causa seguida a Lino Tzuc . . . ," AGEY, JUS, PEN, 124.

28 Wells and Joseph, *Summer of Discontent*, 177–79.

29 "1889. Diligencias muerte de Ricardo Aguilar Brito," AGEY, JUS, PEN, 170-C, 244.

30 Ibid. See also "1890. Diligencias . . . homicidio . . . Ricardo Aguilar Brito," AGEY, JUS, PEN, 179, 251.

31 Angel R. Rosado to gobernador, 15 and 19 October 1882, AGEY, PE, 222; Angel R. Rosado to gobernador, 31 October 1882, AGEY, PE, 220.

32 3 July 1876, *RDP*; AGEY, CON, CJIP, 21 August 1889, 37, 6, 31.

33 "1876. Causa seguida a Juan Pablo Pech . . . rebelión . . . ," AGEY, PE, 195; "1889. Diligencias muerte . . . Ricardo Aguilar Brito," AGEY, JUS, PEN, 179, 251.

34 4 January 1892, *RDP*. See also 14 September 1891, *RDP*.

35 24 and 28 April 1892, *RDM*; 26 April 1892, *EC*.

36 7 and 21 May 1892, *EC*. See also "1892. Diligencias . . . muerte violenta de Jorge Castillo . . . ," AGEY, JUS, 15, 1.

37 "1893. Causa seguida a Florentino Poot . . . ," AGEY, JUS, PEN, 23, 13. See also "1892. Causa seguida a Isidro Tzuc y socios . . . ," AGEY, JUS, PEN, 16, 29.

38 "1893. Causa seguida a Florentino Poot. . . ." See also "Dictámen . . . corte de palo de tinte, en la población Cuyo . . . ," 11 September 1879, AGEY, CON, CH, Dictámenes, 5, 73; and "1896. Juicio promovido por Ramon Ancona Bolio . . . ," AGEY, JUS, PEN, 77, 30. Tzuc's pueblo of origin is unreadable in the transcription of his testimony.

39 "1894. Diligencias . . . robo de palo de tinte . . . Rafael Peón," AGEY, JUS, PEN, 39, 10.

40 "1891. Expediente relativo a la visita practicada en el juzgado de primera instancia de Hunucmá . . . ," AGEY, JUS, PEN, 9, 68. See also "1891. El C. José Dolores Figueroa, se queja . . . ," AGEY, JUS, PEN, 10, 25.

41 11 May 1892, RDY; 22 May 1892, SC.

42 3 May 1892, RDM. On the rivalries between factions led by Cantón and Olegario Molina, see Wells and Joseph, Summer of Discontent.

43 8 May 1892, SC.

44 17 May 1892, RDM.

45 "1892. Causa seguida a Isidro Tzuc. . . ."

46 "Acusación . . . Saturnino Solís," AGEY, PE, GOB, 280; "1894. Diligencias practicadas con motivo del robo de palo de tinte . . . Rafael Peón." See also Alfredo Tamayo to gobernador, 5 December 1892, AGEY, PE, GOB, 277; "1895. Causa a José Chuc y socios . . . ," AGEY, JUS, PEN, 54, 49; "1895. Juicio de intestado de Alfredo Tamayo," AGEY, JUS, CIV, 125, 8.

47 15 March 1893, RDP.

48 2 January 1893, RDP; Pérez Peniche, Reseña histórica, 83–84.

49 "Acusación . . . Saturnino Solís"; "1893. Causa a Florentino Poot. . . ."

50 Ibid.

51 Ibid.

52 Carlos Peón, Gobernador, 6 March 1894, AGEY, CON, CIPH, 36, 7, 65; 1 July 1895, RDP.

53 2 July 1895 EC; "1895. Causa a José Chuc . . . ," AGEY, JUS, PEN, 54, 49. Cf. Menéndez Rodríguez, Iglesia y poder.

54 11 July 1895, RDM.

55 "1896. Causa a Pedro Choch . . . ," AGEY, JUS, PEN, 68, 58; "1900. Expediente relativo a la solicitud de varios vecinos del pueblo de Bolon . . . ," AGEY, JUS, CIV, 260, 38; documents related to construction in AGEY, CON, CIAA, Dictámenes, 1899–1907; 17 September 1895, EC; 29 June, 26–31 October 1894, RDP; Wells, Gilded Age, 82–87.

56 30 October and 18 November 1895, RDP.

57 6 January 1899, DO.

58 21 September 1895, EC.

59 6 May 1899, DO; 17 December 1898, RDM.

60 See: "1899. Solicitud de Isidro Tzuc . . . ," AGEY, JUS, PEN, 135, 27.

61 3 May 1920, RDY.

CHAPTER THREE   HUNUCMÁ'S ZAPATA

1 "May 4, 1913. an fabricado el gran mauser de Yucatán y su gran espada de acero. Por motivo de la libertad que viva la libertad muchachos que viva que viva los balientes que viva. Juramos que no rendimos. Juramos hasta que no la libertad." "1913. Causa seguida á Fabian Caamal . . . ," AGEY, JUS, PEN, 928.

2 Knight, *Mexican Revolution*; Wells and Joseph, *Summer of Discontent*.

3 6 May 1913, RDY.

4 José Juanes G. Gutiérrez et al. to Enrique Muñóz Aristeguí, 17 November 1910, AGEY, PE, FOM, 629. Joseph and Wells, "Corporate Control"; Joseph, *Revolution from Without*, 41–65; Wells, *Yucatán's Gilded Age*, 29–59; and Wells, "Henequen," 110–14.

5 Wells and Joseph, *Summer of Discontent*, 66–69, 75–82, 142; "1908. Falsedad," AGEY, JUS, PEN, 676; "1909. Diligencias por Timoteo Alvarez," AGEY, JUS, PEN, 727; and "1912. Flagelación a Julio Pérez," AGEY, JUS, PEN, 897. See also Turner, *Barbarous Mexico*.

6 "1911. Causa seguida contra Pedro Crespo. . . . ," AGEY, JUS, PEN, 843.

7 19 April 1911, DY.

8 11 April; and 16–30 May 1911, DY.

9 Luis C. Curiel to JP Hunucmá, 17 April 1911, AGEY, PE, GUE, 752; Petrona Cardós to gobernador interino, 10 June 1911, AGEY, PE, GOB, 805. See also Santiago Chi to gobernador, 6 May 1911, AGEY, PE, GUE, 752; and 2 June 1911, DY.

10 15 June and 17 August 1911, DY. See also Wells and Joseph, *Summer of Discontent*, 218–20.

11 "1911. Causa seguida á Antonio Puc . . . ," AGEY, Justicia, 837. See also R. A. Manzanilla to gobernador, 2 June 1911, AGEY, PE, GOB, 725; "1911. Diligencias en averiguación . . . Miguel Santos," AGEY, JUS, PEN, 837; "1911. Diligencias contra Miguel Leyva . . . ," AGEY, JUS, PEN, 817; Juan Vázquez to gobierno, 12 June 1911, AGEY, PE, GOB, 725; "1911. Causa á Nabor Cumí . . . ," AGEY, JUS, PEN, 894; "1912. Toca a la causa seguida a Antonio Ku . . . ," AGEY, JUS, PEN, 876; "1911. Diligencias contra Magdaleno Pech . . . ," AGEY, JUS, PEN, 849; JP Ticul to gobernador, 14 September 1911, AGEY, PE, MIL, 742; and "1911. Diligencias practicadas á solicitud del señor Osvaldo González . . . ," AGEY, JUS, PEN, 838; and 17 February; 6 March; 21, 23, and 27 May; 11 and 14 June; 1 July; and 16 August 1911, DY.

12 "1911. Diligencias, la muerte de Anastasio Dzul," AGEY, JUS, PEN, 817. See also DY, 30 May 1911; and RDM, 16 July 1911.

13 23 May 1911, DY. See also Alfredo Ayala to gobernador, 14 June 1911, AGEY, PE, GOB, 725; "1911. Diligencias practicadas . . . Alfredo Ayala," AGEY, JUS, PEN, 848; and 11 and 28 June 1911, DY.

14 José María Vargas, 24 May 1911, AGEY, PE, GOB, 735; 12 July 1911, DY.

15 "1913. Toca á la causa seguida á Herminio Balam . . . ," AGEY, JUS, PEN, 928; José María Vargas to gobernador, 13 August 1911, AGEY, PE, GUE, 752; 8 and 15 August 1911, DY; 8 August 1911, RDM.

16 15 and 16 August 1911, DY. See also 8–14 August 1911, DY; and 8–23 August 1911, RDM.

17 16 August 1911, RDM.

18 23 and 27 August 1911, RDM.

19 16 August 1911, RDM.

20 18 August 1911, RDM.

21 18 August 1911, *RDM*. See also 15 August 1911, *DY*.

22 6 September 1911, *DY*.

23 5 and 6 September 1911, *RDM*.

24 15 September 1911, *DY*.

25 "1911. Testimonio de la causa seguida á Herminio Balam . . . ," AGEY, JUS, PEN, 837.

26 28 November 1911, *RDM*.

27 8 October 1911, *DY*.

28 5 December 1911, *DY*.

29 10 October 1911, *RDM*.

30 12 October 1911, *RDM*.

31 "1912. Causa seguida á Guillermo Canul Angulo . . . ," AGEY, JUS, PEN, 897.

32 17 and 19 May 1911, *DY*.

33 "1911. Testimonio de la causa seguida á Herminio Balam. . . ."

34 "Causa . . . Fabian Caamal y socios."

35 "1912. Causa seguida á Guillermo Canul Angulo. . . ."

36 See 8 August 1911, *DY*. See also José María Vargas to gobernador, 13 August 1911, AGEY, PE, Guerra y Marina, 752; 15 August 1911, *RDM*.

37 Tomás Pérez Ponce et al. to Gobierno, 14 March 1911, AGEY, PE, GOB, 725. See also "Bases del Círculo Libertario"; and 19 August 1914, *RDY*.

38 "1911. Diligencias practicadas . . . finca 'San Gerónimo' . . . ," AGEY, JUS, PEN, 854. See also "1911. Causa seguida a José Justo Canul . . . ," AGEY, JUS, PEN, 819; "1912. Toca á la apelación interpuesta por Francisco Chac . . . ," AGEY, JUS, PEN, 896; and 15 August 1911, *DY*.

39 "1912. Causa seguida á Guillermo Canul Angulo. . . ."

40 "1911. Testimonio de la causa seguida á Herminio Balam. . . ."

41 *RDM*, 21 November 1911; Nicolás Cámara Vales to Congreso, 19 January 1912, AGEY, CON, CJIP, 47, 16, 32.

42 "Libro de Sesiones," 19 January 1912, AGEY, CON, 84, 1. See also Nicolás Cámara Vales, gobernador, Decree to XXIV Congreso, 18 April 1912, AGEY, PE, GOB, 801.

43 Adolfo Montero to governor, 16 January 1912, AGEY, PE, GOB, 851; "1913. Toca a las diligencias . . . queja de Julio Pech . . . ," AGEY, JUS, PEN, 921. See also 19 May 1912, *RDY*.

44 "1912. Causa seguida á Guillermo Canul Angulo. . . ."

45 Ibid.

46 Ibid. See also "1912. Toca á la apelación interpuesta por Francisco Chac . . . ," AGEY, JUS, PEN, 896; and "1913. Toca á la causa seguida á Herminio Balam. . . ."

47 "1912. Causa seguida á Guillermo Canul Angulo. . . ." See also "1911. Testimonio de la causa seguida á Herminio Balam. . . ."; "1913. Cuaderno de prueba testimonial . . . Herminio Balam . . . ," AGEY, JUS, PEN, 922; and "1913. Toca á la causa seguida á Herminio Balam. . . ."

48 "1911. Testimonio de la causa seguida á Herminio Balam. . . ."

49 10 April 1912, *RDY*. See also "1912. Toca á la apelación interpuesta por Andrés Rodríguez . . . ," AGEY, JUS, PEN, 884; "1912. Toca á la apelación interpuesta

por Emigdio y Alejandro Puc . . . ," AGEY, JUS, PEN, 884; and "1913. Toca a la causa seguida a Bernabé Medina . . . ," AGEY, JUS, PEN, 909.

50 16 April 1912, *RDY*.

51 5 October 1912, *RDY*. See also "1912. Causa seguida á Agustín Caamal y Martino . . . ," AGEY, JUS, PEN, 889; 27 August 1912, *RDY*.

52 "1912. Testimonio de las constancias de la causa seguida a Federico Solis . . . ," AGEY, JUS, PEN, 880. See also "1912. Causa seguida á Federico Solis . . . ," AGEY, JUS, PEN, 896; and 12 July 1912, *RDY*.

53 "1911. Testimonio de la causa seguida á Herminio Balam. . . ."

54 "1913. Toca á la causa seguida á Bernabé Medina. . . ."

55 "1912. Testimonio de las constancias de la causa seguida a Federico Solis. . . ."

56 "Informe de Gobierno del Dr. Cámara Vales," AGEY, PE, GOB, 1 January 1913, 851. See also *La Revista Peninsular*, 3 January 1913.

57 Wells and Joseph, *Summer of Discontent*, 241–51.

58 "1912. Hilario Poot Euan. Amenazas . . . ," AGEY, Jus, 884; "1914. Diligencias practicadas contra Francisco Matú . . . ," AGEY, JUS, PEN, 941; and "1914. Lesiones a Cirilo Méndez . . . ," AGEY, JUS, PEN, 936; 16 January, 8, 9, 12, 21, and 26 February, 4 March, 5 and 26 April 1913, *RDY*.

59 "Causa . . . Fabian Caamal. . . ."

60 *RDY*, 27–29 April 1913. In the Yucatecan press in this period, outside of coverage of the Zapatistas of the state of Morelos, only indigenous insurgents in Maxcanú and Hunucmá were referred to as *Zapatistas*. 8 May 1913, *RDY*.

61 1 May 1913, *RDY*. See also José M. Rosado Almeida to Governor, 27 June 1914, AGEY, PE, MIL, 465; and 12 July 1914.

62 "1913. Causa seguida á Fabian Caamal. . . ."

63 The flag was embroidered with an inscription that is not recorded in any source I have located. Guillermo Mangas to gobernador, 23 January 1917, AGEY, PE, GOB, 577.

64 *RDY*, 7 and 13 May, and 8 June 1913; and "1913. Diligencias practicadas en averiguación de los sucesos ocurridos en Hunucmá el cinco del actual," AGEY, JUS, PEN, 929.

65 "1913. Causa seguida a Fabian Caamal y socios. . . ."

66 7 May 1913, *RDY*.

67 6 May 1913, *RDY*.

68 6 and 11 May 1913, *RDY*.

69 "Causa . . . Fabian Caamal y socios"; "1913. Diligencias . . . descargas hechas en Hunucmá," AGEY, JUS, PEN, 928; 7–15 May and 2 June 1913, *RDY*.

70 "Causa . . . Fabian Caamal y socios," and "1913. Diligencias practicadas en averiguación de los sucesos ocurridos. . . ."

71 "Relación de los individuos del Partido de Mérida . . . para cubrir las bajas del ejército . . . ," AGEY, PE, GUE, 719. Several other draftees were suspects in rebellion in the district of Maxcanú. José Loreto Baak to Juez de Distrito, 12 May 1913, AGEY, PE, Justicia, 721.

72 Juan Crisóstomo Dzib to Juez de Distrito, 1 July 1913, AGEY, PE, JUST, 721; and 21 November 1913, *RDY*.

73 2 February 1914, *RDY*. See also Wells and Joseph, *Summer of Discontent*, 241–51.

74 Bernabé Chan to gobernador, 4 April 1914, AGEY, PE, GOB, 462; Juana Canul Reyes to Juez de Distrito, 16 March 1914, AGEY, PE, GOB, 499.

75 Juana Canul Reyes to Juez de Distrito, 16 March 1914, AGEY, PE, GOB, 499.

76 26 November 1913, *RDY*.

77 Tomás Pérez Ponce to Juez de Distrito, 9 May 1913, AGEY, PE, JUST, 721.

78 13 and 19 May 1913, *RDY*.

79 Mario Marrufo to gobernador, 6 March 1914, AGEY, PE, FOM, 461; 15 March and 19 April 1914 *RDY*; Flores, "La vida rural"; and Wells and Joseph, *Summer of Discontent*, 256–58.

80 María Ana Mex and Nicolasa Pech to Governor, 5 February 1914, AGEY, PE, GOB, 464.

81 "1914. Causa seguida a María Isabel Reyes . . . ," AGEY, JUS, PEN, 962.

82 "1914. Juana Canul Reyes," AGEY, JUS, PEN, 961.

83 "1914. Denuncia del señor Manuel Rios . . . ," AGEY, JUS, PEN, 947; and 8 June 1913 and 29 April–1 May 1914, *RDY*.

84 "1914. Lesiones a Cirilo Méndez y socios," AGEY, JUS, PEN, 936. See also "1914. Diligencias practicadas contra Francisco Matú . . . ," AGEY, JUS, PEN, 941.

85 Tomás Pérez Ponce to gobernador, 13 January 1914, AGEY, PE, GOB, 462. Interview with Tomasa, Nohuayum, 2 March 2003.

86 Interview with Tiger, Tetiz, 31 January 2004.

87 28 April 1914, *RDY*.

88 J. W. Germon to Secretary of State, 20 August 1914, NA, RG 59, 812.00/13125. See also 24 June; 25–29 July; and 1 August 1914, *RDY*.

89 José M. Rosado Almeida to gobernador, 27 June 1914, AGEY, PE, MIL, 465; 12 and 16 and 24 July 1914, *RDY*.

90 6 August 1914, *RDY*.

91 Luis A. Sánchez to Prisciliano Cortés, 9 August 1914, AGEY. PE, GOB, 450.

92 J. W. Germon to Secretary of State, 20 August 1914, NA, RG 59, 812.00/13125; Wells and Joseph, *Summer of Discontent*, 267.

93 19 August 1914, *RDY*. See also 20–27 August 1914, *RDY*.

94 23 and 25 August 1914, *RDY*.

95 26 August 1914, *RDY*.

96 26 August 1914, *RDY*.

97 28 August 1914. See also 27 August 1914, *RDY*.

98 9 September 1914, *RDY*. See also 28 August 1914, *RDY*.

99 12 September 1914, *RDY*.

100 Ibid.

101 Acereto, "Historia política."

CHAPTER FOUR   THE REDEMPTION

1 José Pío Chuc et al. to Exmo. Señor Gobernador, 2 May 1915, AGEY, PE, GOB, 479.

2 21 December 1914, *RDY*.

3 Pacheco Cruz, *Recuerdos*, 37–48; Pacheco Cruz, *Traducción literal*; 15 September 1914, RDY; Eiss, "Redemption's Archive."

4 Vecinos of Hunucmá, Umán, Kinchil, and Samahil to gobernador, 21 September 1914, AGEY, PE, GOB, 465.

5 M. Ríos to J. D. Concepción y Ceballos, 31 October 1914, AGEY, PE, GOB, 493; J. Concepción to gobernador, 4 October 1914, AGEY, PE, MIL, 453.

6 Avila y Castillo, *Diario*, 3–15; Joseph, *Revolution from Without*, 7–8, 68–69, 113.

7 Salvador Alvarado, 30 April 1915, AGEY, PE, GOB, 471; Joseph, *Revolution from Without*, 53, 136–39; and Avila y Castillo, *Diario*, 6, 11.

8 Avila y Castillo, *Diario*, 5.

9 24 and 26 April 1915, VDR.

10 Avila y Castillo, *Diario*, 9.

11 Ibid., 10. See also March–April 1915, VDR.

12 Salvador Alvarado, 24 April 1915, AGEY, PE, GOB, 471 and 29 April 1915, AGEY, PE, GOB, 476.

13 Salvador Alvarado to presidentes municipales, 27 October 1915, AGEY, PE, GOB, 505.

14 Joseph, *Revolution from Without*, 123.

15 Salvador Alvarado, 6 April 1915, AGEY, PE, GOB, 471; and 8 April 1915, DO.

16 23 and 25 September 1914, RDY.

17 3 May 1915, VDR.

18 "Proyecto de Reglamento . . . ," 5 April 1915, AGEY, PE, JUST, 476. See also Joseph, *Revolution from Without*, 123–26.

19 14 April 1915, VDR.

20 Pedro A. Canul et al. to Toribio V. de los Santos, 5 February 1915, AGEY, PE, GOB, 488.

21 Pedro A. Canul to gobernador, 16 April 1915, AGEY, PE, GOB, 507.

22 Julian Garma to gobernador, 20 April 1915, AGEY, PE, GOB, 507.

23 Catarino Tinal et al., to gobernador provisional, 23 March 1915, AGEY, PE, GOB, 495.

24 Enrique Sánchez to gobernador, 24 April 1915, AGEY, PE, GOB, 499; Enrique Sánchez to gobernador, 6 April 1915, AGEY, PE, GUE, 496.

25 This description of Alvarado's visit is based on 4 May 1915, VDR.

26 José Pío Chuc et al. to Alvarado.

27 See also Alvarado, "Proyecto . . ."; Ramón García Núñez, 1 October 1915, AGEY, PE, GOB, 487.

28 OIPR report, 29 July 1915, AGEY, PE, GOB, 487; Ramón García Núñez to Alvarado, 29 July 1915, AGEY, PE, GOB, 487; Felipe Pérez Uribe to Ramón García Núñez, 7 August 1915, AGEY, PE, GOB, 487.

29 José Pío Chuc et al. to Alvarado.

30 CM Hunucmá to Agente de Fomento, 19 May 1915, AGEY, PE, GOB, 509-B. See also CM Hunucmá to gobierno, 29 May 1915, AGEY, PE, GOB, 488; Ramón García Núñez to Salvador Alvarado, 8 and 9 September 1915, in "Informes," AGEY, PE, GOB, 475; Patricio Sabido to Ramón García Núñez, 9 September 1915, AGEY, PE, GOB, 487.

31 Gonzalo Peniche to Florencio Avila Castillo, 9 October 1915, AGEY, PE, GOB, 472; Gonzalo Peniche, 25 September 1915, AGEY, PE, GOB, 475.

32 Atilano González to Salvador Alvarado, 3 July 1915, AGEY, PE, GOB, 478; Bartolomé García to Salvador Alvarado, 1 July 1915, AGEY, PE, GOB, 478.

33 Salvador Alvarado, 3 July 1915, AGEY, PE, GOB, 478; Atilano González to Salvador Alvarado, 20 July 1915, AGEY, PE, GOB, 478.

34 Oficial Mayor Int. to CM Hunucmá, 24 June 1915, AGEY, PE, GOB, 478; Enrique Sánchez to Secretario Gral. de Gobierno, 6 August, 1915, AGEY, PE, GOB, 478; Manuel Ríos to Ramon García Núñez, 9 August 1915, AGEY, PE, GOB, 487; Ramón García Núñez to José Polanco, 5 August 1915, AGEY, PE, GOB, 487; and Ramón García Núñez to Salvador Alvarado, 26 August 1915, AGEY, PE, GOB, 487.

35 Polanco transcribed in Ramón García Núñez, 24 August 1915, AGEY, PE, GOB, 487.

36 Ramón García Núñez to Salvador Alvarado, 1 September 1915, AGEY, PE, GOB, 475.

37 Ibid.

38 S. Alvarado to comandantes militares, 1 September 1915, AGEY, PE, GOB, 497; 23 November 1915, VDR.

39 Salvador Alvarado, 17 July 1915, AGEY, PE, GOB, 490.

40 Salvador Alvarado, "Cartilla revolucionaria," 3 September 1915, AGEY, PE, GOB, 473.

41 Pacheco Cruz, *Recuerdos*, 232.

42 Santiago Pacheco Cruz to Jefe de Información y Propaganda, 29 September 1915, AGEY, PE, GOB, 475.

43 Santiago Pacheco Cruz to Florencio Avila y Castillo, 27 September 1915, AGEY, PE, GOB, 475.

44 "1915. Diligencias asalto y robo . . . Nohuayun," AGEY, JUS, PEN, 981.

45 "1916. Donaciano Alcocer, homicidio," AGEY, JUS, PEN, 1019; Pacheco Cruz, *Recuerdos*, 255.

46 J. Isaac Centeno to gobernador, 21 October 1916, AGEY, PE, GOB, 517.

47 Nazario Ceballos H. to gobernador, 8 February 1916, AGEY, PE, GOB, 535.

48 Modesto Montero to gobernador, 9 May 1916, AGEY, PE, GOB, 524.

49 "1915. Diligencias practicadas en averiguación de varios delitos . . . Tetiz . . . ," AGEY, JUS, PEN, 969; "1915. Causa seguida a Manuel Poot . . . ," AGEY, JUS, PEN, 973.

50 A. Villanueva R. to Salvador Alvarado, 16 December 1915, AGEY, PE, GOB, 514.

51 2 November 1915, VDR.

52 Casiana Rodríguez et al. to gobernador, 5 October 1915, AGEY, PE, JUST, 503.

53 Raimunda Uicab to gobernador, 8 December 1915, AGEY, PE, JUST, 503.

54 José Inés Tec et al. to gobernador, 25 December 1915, AGEY, PE, JUST, 503. See also Antimo Rodriguez D. et al. to Salvador Alvarado, 14 December 1915, AGEY, PE, GOB, 503.

55 "1915. Diligencias . . . Julio Zapata . . . ," AGEY, JUS, PEN, 982.

56 Julio Correa to Of. May., 18 September 1915, AGEY, PE, JUST, 503. Pacheco Cruz, *Recuerdos*, 255.

57 Salvador Alvarado, "Adonde vamos," in *Obra*, 365–71.

58 Avila y Castillo, *Diario*, 147.

59 Jefe de la OIPR, 9 December 1915, AGEY, PE, GOB, 488.

60 Avila y Castillo, *Diario*, 148.

61 Alvarado cited in Chacón, "Yucatán and the Mexican Revolution," 384–89.

62 Miguel Noverola, 12 February 1916, AGEY, PE, GOB, 555. See also Joseph, *Revolution from Without*, 133.

63 Salvador Alvarado to comandantes militares, 9 May 1916, AGEY, PE, GOB, 522; Eiss, "Redemption's Archive."

64 J. Isaac Centeno to gobernador, 11 July 1916, AGEY, PE, GOB, 538; Laureano Franco Fuentes to gobernador, 19 October 1916, AGEY, PE, GOB, 533.

65 Abelardo de la Guerra to Jefe de la OIPR, 13 January 1916, AGEY, PE, GOB, 487.

66 A. Villanueva R. to Mario Calvino, 23 April 1916, AGEY, PE, GOB, 518. See also Plácido Lope to Salvador Alvarado, 22 December 1915, AGEY, PE, GOB, 475.

67 5 May 1916, *VDR*.

68 5 June 1916, *VDR*.

69 Ibid.

70 *Boletín municipal*.

71 J. Isaac Centeno to gobernador, 21 October 1916, AGEY, PE, GOB, 517.

72 Ibid.

73 Salvador Alvarado to Venustiano Carranza, 31 November 1916, AGEY, PE, GOB, 556.

74 Pacheco Cruz, *Recuerdos*, 251.

CHAPTER FIVE THE GENERAL AND THE BEAST

1 Untitled 1920, AGEY, JUS, PEN, 1183, 1119.

2 Cf. Coronil and Skurski, "Dismembering."

3 Mena Brito, *Bolshevismo*, 34–40; anonymous report to Salvador Alvarado, 17 February 1917, AGEY, PE, GOB, 569.

4 Mena Brito, *Bolshevismo*. See also Joseph, *Revolution from Without*, 117–20; Eiss, "Redemption's Archive," 409–21, 483–95.

5 7 January 1917, *VDR*.

6 Fediz Bolio, *Alvarado es el hombre*, 97. See also Alvarado, *Mi sueño*.

7 Felipe Carrillo Puerto to gobernador, 6 May 1919, AGEY, PE, GOB, 691. See also *Primer Congreso*.

8 Mena Brito, *Bolshevismo*, 170.

9 Ibid., 385–86, 389–91.

10 Ibid., 62–64, 117.

11 Carlos Castro Morales to CC. Representantes del pueblo, AGEY, PE, GOB, 631.

12 Mena Brito, *Bolshevismo*, 175; 7 January 1919, *RDY*.

13 16 February 1919, *VDR*; Salvador Alvarado to Carlos Castro Morales, 13 February 1919, AGEY, PE, GOB, 674.

14 Joseph, *Revolution from Without*, 169–70, 194–95.

15 Enrique López R. to gobernador, 8 June 1917, PE, GOB, 597.

16 Manuel Castellanos R. to gobernador, 8 January 1917, AGEY, PE, GOB, 572; E. Bojórquez to Sec. Gral., 12 October 1917, AGEY, PE, GOB, 601; Valentín Quintal to gobernador, 10 October 1917, AGEY, PE, GOB, 601.

17 Guillermo Mangas to gobernador, 15 December 1916, AGEY, PE, GOB, 538.

18 Gilberto Flores to gobernador, 20 November 1916, AGEY, PE, GOB, 528. See also 26 November 1916, AGEY, PE, JUST, 514B; and "1916. Diligencias contra Felipe Leal . . . ," AGEY, JUS, PEN, 995.

19 Guillermo Mangas to gobernador, 11 and 15 January 1917, AGEY, PE, GOB, 577.

20 Guillermo Mangas to Salvador Alvarado, 27 and 30 January 1917, AGEY, PE, GOB, 577.

21 A. Villanueva R. to gobernador, 3 December 1917, AGEY, PE, GOB, 587.

22 Simón Moreno Cetina to gobernador, 25 January 1917, AGEY, PE, GOB, 565.

23 Anonymous, undated 1917, AGEY, PE, GOB, 589.

24 Simón Moreno Cetina, to gobernador, 25 January 1917, AGEY, PE, GOB, 565.

25 Sec. de Gob. y Archivo, Gobierno del Edo. de Campeche, to Salvador Alvarado, AGEY, PE, GOB, 569.

26 Isidro Poot to gobernador, 11 June 1918, AGEY, PE, GOB, 652.

27 F. Rodríguez, V. de Ofs. Pubs., to gobernador, 21 May 1918, AGEY, PE, GOB, 660; Felipe Carrillo Puerto to gobernador, 8 July 1918, AGEY, PE, GOB, 656; Felipe Tzuc to Carlos Castro Morales, gobernador, 7 October 1918, AGEY, PE, GOB, 656; and 17 October 1918, RDY.

28 F. Rodríguez to Jefe de Visitadores de Oficinas Públicas del Estado, 9 March 1918, AGEY, PE, GOB, 645; Augusto Cámara to Jefe del DT, 28 October 1918, AGEY, PE, GOB, 631.

29 23 July 1919, La voz del indio.

30 E. Bojórquez to gobernador, 22 June 1917, AGEY, PE, GOB, 601. See also Virgilio Arce Méndez to gobernador, 11 July 1917, AGEY, PE, GOB, 558.

31 Guillermo Mangas to gobernador, 23 January 1917, AGEY, PE, GOB, 577.

32 August 1919, RDY. See also "1919. Diligencias practicadas contra Hiram O. García . . . ," AGEY, JUS, PEN, 1132:1085.

33 Gustavo Correa to gobernador, 31 October 1918, AGEY, PE, GOB, 634.

34 24 October 1918, RDY; Juan Bautista Pech B. to gobernador, 3 March 1919, SRA, HUN.

35 José Vadilla to Oficial Mayor, 20 July 1917, AGEY, PE, GOB, 558.

36 Ancona to Srio. Gral., 2 August 1917, AGEY, PE, GOB, 558.

37 Isidro Poot to Pres. Liga. Ctrl., 12 August 1917, AGEY, PE, GOB, 564.

38 Jefe DT to Isidro Poot 10 November 1917, AGEY, PE, GOB, 595.

39 José Palomeque to gobernador, 11 March 1918, AGEY, PE, GOB, 623; Gobernación to Comisión Permanente de Tierras, 16 April 1918, AGEY, PE, GOB, 623.

40 Miguel Laimon to gobernador, 20 February 1918, AGEY, PE, GOB, 644; Sec. Gral. to Alc. Mun. Hunucmá, 27 March 1918, AGEY, PE, GOB, 623.

41 Isidro Poot Q. to gobernador, 11 June 1918, SRA, HUN. See also Bartolomé García and Isidro Poot Q., Acta, 17 October 1918, SRA, HUN; E. Bojórquez to Jefe del DT, 13 December 1917, AGEY, PE, GOB, 601; Srio. Gral. to Pres. Liga Hunucmá,

14 December 1917, AGEY, PE, GOB, 668; Avelina A. Ceballos vda. de Puerto to gobernador, 30 November 1918, AGEY, PE, GOB, 691.

42 Andrés Lizama to gobernador, 1 September 1918, AGEY, PE, GOB, 607; 13 November 1918, *RDY*.

43 Felipe Carrillo Puerto to gobernador, 7 January 1919, AGEY, PE, GOB, 666; Felipe Carrillo Puerto to gobernador, 15 January 1919, AGEY, PE, GOB, 674. See also 17 January 1919, *RDY*.

44 21 January 1919, *RDY*.

45 Bartolomé García to gobernador, 14 February 1919, SRA, HUN. See also Juan Bautista Pech B. to gobernador, 3 March 1919, SRA, HUN; 14 August 1919, *RDY*.

46 19 November 1919, *RDY*. See also A. Canto to gobernador, 9 September 1919, AGEY, PE, GOB, 691; undated (1921) fragment of letter to gobernador, AGEY, PE, GOB, 739; 15 November 1919, *RDY*.

47 4 January 1920 and 25 November 1919, *RDY*. See also 20 February 1920, *RDY*.

48 "1920. Diligencias contra José Villafaña . . . ," AGEY, JUS, PEN, 1177; "1920. Diligencias practicadas . . . Petrona Gío . . . ," AGEY, JUS, PEN, 1190: 1124; 1 April 1920, *RDY*.

49 19 February 1920, *RDY*; "1920. Diligencias contra José Concepción Chablé . . . ," AGEY, JUS, PEN, 1169.

50 12 June 1920, *RDY*; Manzanilla Domínguez, *Bolchevismo criminal*, 65–69.

51 3, 9, and 17 May, *RDY*.

52 29 April 1920, *El Correo*; 29 April 1920, *RDY*.

53 2–9 May 1920, *RDY*.

54 Untitled 1920.

55 18–20 May 1920, *RDY*.

56 18 May 1920, *El Correo*; and 16–22 May 1920, *RDY*.

57 23 May 1920, *RDY*.

58 Untitled 1920; 8 June 1920, *RDY*.

59 21 May 1920, *El Correo*; 23 May 1920, *RDY*; Untitled 1920.

60 27 May 1920, *RDY*.

61 Untitled 1920.

62 24 June 1920, *RDY*.

63 28 September 1920, *RDY*; and Manzanilla Domínguez, *Bolchevismo criminal*, 62–69.

64 12 and 13 June 1920, *RDY*.

65 24 and 25 June 1920, *RDY*.

66 "1920. Denuncia a Manuel A. Torre . . . ," AGEY, JUS, PEN, 1180:1118.

67 15 August 1920, *RDY*.

68 24 September 1920, *RDY*.

69 Andrés Lizama to gobernador, 7 September 1920, AGEY, PE, GOB, 706; 25 September 1920, *RDY*; Miguel Cantón to gobernador, 1 October 1920, AGEY, PE, GOB, 706.

70 10 November 1920, *RDY*.

71 J. Zarate to gobernador, 4 November 1920, AGEY, PE, GOB, 701.

72 5 November 1920, El Correo.

73 15 November 1920, RDY.

74 Ibid.

75 J. Zarate to gobernador, 4 November 1920, AGEY, PE, GOB, 701; 10 May and 12 June 1921, RDY.

76 Cámara Agrícola de Yucatán to Alvaro Obregón, 9 March 1921, AGN, AO/PEC, 811-Y-2.

77 "1920. Causa contra Valerio Chuc . . . ," AGEY, JUS, PEN, 1202:1131. "1920. Diligencias . . . Tucichen . . . ," AGEY, JUS, PEN, 1196:1227.

78 1 January 1921, RDY. See also Subsec. Sec. de Gobernación to gobernador, 29 January 1921, AGEY, PE, GOB, 733.

79 17 April 1921, RDY. See also Manuel Torre to gobernador, 18 July 1921, AGEY, PE, GOB, 740; and Procurador General de Justicia to gobernador, 27 April 1921, AGEY, PE, GOB, 733.

80 16 August 1921, RDY; Adolfo Balam to Alvaro Obregón, 20 February 1921, SRA, HUN, RES.

81 4 May 1922 and 12 April 1923, RDY; Santiago Quintal to Felipe Carrillo Puerto, gobernador, 1 February 1922, AGEY, PE, GOB, 757.

82 Gustavo Molina Font, 26 April 1923, SRA, HUN.

83 A. Lizárraga H., 28 January 1922, SRA, UMAN.

84 Cámara Agrícola de Yucatán to Alvaro Obregón, 9 March 1921, AGN, AO/PEC, 811-Y-2; Cámara Agrícola de Yucatán, transcribed by Gral. Brig. Alejandro Mange, 13 March 1921, AGN, AO/PEC, 811-Y-2.

85 Subsec. de la Sec. de Gobernacion to gobernador, 30 May 1921, AGEY, PE, GOB, 733; 27 May 1921, RDY.

86 Rosado Vega, "¿Es posible un acercamiento . . . ?," 20, 41.

87 "1921. Causa contra Felipe Solís . . . ," AGEY, JUS, PEN, 1218:1141; "1921. Toca a la causa . . . Marcelino Villafaña . . . ," PJAH, 35A, 2083.

88 José B. Garma to Alvaro Obregón, 9 March 1922, AGN, AO/PEC, 408-Y-1.

89 9 November 1921, RDY; Felipe Carrillo Puerto to gobernador, 22 March 1922, AGEY, PE, GOB, 757. See also "1923. Diligencias . . . Manuel Contreras . . . ," AGEY, JUS, PEN, 1258:1165.

90 Cámara Agrícola de Yucatán to Alvaro Obregón, 4 July 1922, AGN, AO/PEC, 408-Y-3.

91 1 July 1922, RDY. See also "1923. Diligencias . . . Claudio Chuil . . . ," AGEY, JUS, PEN, 1259; "1923. Diligencias . . . Tito Puc . . . ," AGEY, JUS, PEN, 1257:1164; and Carmela Aragón et al. to Alvaro Obregón, 26 July 1922, AGN, AO/PEC, 408-Y-3.

92 14 August 1919, RDY.

93 1 June 1920, RDY; Juan Ventura to gobernador, 26 March 1922, AGEY, PE, GOB, 757.

94 16 May 1921, RDY.

95 Manzanilla Domínguez, Bolchevismo criminal, i.

96 Felipe Carrillo Puerto, 28 November 1923, AGEY, PE, GOB, 780; 8 December 1923, RDY.

97 Juan Ricardez Broca, 29 December 1923, AGEY, PE, GOB, 770; "1923. Diligencias . . . Jerónimo Poot," AGEY, JUS, PEN, 1252.

98 Juan Bautista Pech Balam to gobernador, 6 January 1924, AGEY, PE, GOB, 786.

99 Joseph, *Revolution from Without*, 281–87.

100 "1924. Causa a Dimas Novelo . . . ," AGEY, JUS, PEN, 1257:1164.

101 2 October 1920, RDY.

102 Various interviews, Hunucmá and Tetiz, 2001–4.

103 Interviews with Tiger, Tetiz, February 2004; and Corn Cob, Nohuayum, August 2001.

CHAPTER SIX THE PRESIDENT'S DEAD HAND

1 Edelmiro Conde et al., 21 October 1937, SRA, HUN.

2 For a study of the politics of contemporary ejidos, including a discussion of a "lost map," see Nuitjen, *Power*. See especially Gledhill, *Casi Nada*.

3 Sánchez Novelo, *La rebelión delahuertista*.

4 Fallaw, *Cárdenas Compromised*, 11; and Joseph, *Revolution from Without*.

5 C. R. Ricalde et al. to Procurador General de Pueblo y a la H. CNA, 15 May 1924, SRA, SAM.

6 Of. May. to Procurador General de Justicia, 4 December 1924, AGEY, PE, GOB, 785. See also "1924. Diligencias . . . Presidente Municipal de Tetiz . . . ," AGEY, JUS, PEN, 1272.

7 Ricardo Gil to Bartolomé García Correa, 11 July 1930, AGEY, PE, GOB, 889.

8 Mediz Bolio, *La agonía*, 8–9; Fallaw, "Bartolomé García Correa."

9 Fallaw, "Life and Deaths."

10 Javier M. Erosa, 28 January 1927, AGN, AO/PEC, 707-Y-3.

11 Manuel Prieto, "Informe," 12 March 1936, SRA, HUN. See also Enrique Gamboa Alonzo to Del. del Depto. Agr. en el Edo., 4 September 1935, SRA, SAM.

12 Isaac J. Bustamante to Rufino Lavín Jr., 4 July 1928, SRA, SAM.

13 Isaac J. Bustamante to Rufino Lavín Jr., 31 Jul 1928, SRA, UCU.

14 Rufino Lavín Jr., to Of. May. de la CNA, 31 July 1928, SRA, SAM; and Isaac J. Bustamante to Rufino Lavín Jr., 4 July 1928, SRA, SAM.

15 El Vocal Ponente to Del. de la C.N.A., 27 March 1926, SRA, KIN.

16 José Angel Sarmiento to Francisco Pérez Sierra, 6 November 1924, SRA, UCU.

17 Hiram O. García to Bartolomé García Correa, 1 March 1931, AGEY, PE, GOB, 930; Renán Alzama to Bartolomé García Correa, 1 March 1931, AGEY, PE, GOB, 930.

18 7–12 December 1931, DSE and DDY. See also Mediz Bolio, *La agonía*, 9.

19 12 December 1931, DDY.

20 Pres. of Coop. Agríola Ganadera de Hunucmá to Francisco Pérez Sierra, 28 March 1933, SRA, HUN; Quintín Rosas to Of. May. del Ramo, 30 August 1933, SRA, HUN.

21 Antonio Muñoz González to gobernador, 16 April 1934, AGEY, PE, GOB, 984.

22 Nicolás Poot et al. to gobernador, 17 July and 17 September 1934, AGEY, PE, GOB, 984; 17 August 1934, *DSE*.

23 Vicente Guanche P. to C. Del. del Depto. Autónomo Agrario en el Edo., 31 January 1934, SRA, TET; Vicente Guanche P. to C. Del del Depto. Autónomo Agr. en el Edo., 1 February 1934, SRA, SAM.

24 Vicente Guanche P. to Del. del Depto. Autónomo Agrario, 13 January 1934, SRA, HUN.

25 Fallaw, *Cárdenas*. Cf. Bantjes, *Jesus*; Becker, *Setting the Virgin*.

26 Fallaw, *Cárdenas*.

27 Enrique Gamboa Alonzo to Del. del Depto. Agr. en el Edo., 4 September 1935, SRA, SAM.

28 Manuel Prieto to Sec. de Agricultura y Fomento, 12 March 1936, SRA, HUN.

29 Cristóbal Uribe Gómez to gobernador, 17 March 1936, AGEY, PE, GOB, 1013.

30 Antonio P. García to Sec. Genl., Depto. Forestal y de Caza y Pesca, 28 April 1937, SRA, HUN.

31 José Isabel Molina to Lic. D. Gabino Vázquez, 9 September 1937, SRA, HUN.

32 Bartolomé Cervera Alcocer to Lázaro Cárdenas, 22 October 1935, SEP, KIN, IV/161(IV-14)/23066. See also Fallaw, "Life and Deaths."

33 Nazario Pisté et al. to Lic. Fernando López Cárdenas, 24 December 1935, SEP, KIN, IV/161(IV-14)/23066.

34 Bartolomé Cervera Alcocer to Jefe del Depto. Agr., 17 September 1936, SRA, KIN; Ramón Pech to Lázaro Cárdenas, 9 April 1937, SRA, KIN.

35 Bartolomé Cervera Alcocer to Lázaro Cárdenas, 11 July 1935, SEP, KIN, IV/161(IV-14)/23066; Fallaw, "Life and Deaths," 672.

36 Fallaw, *Cárdenas*.

37 "Memorial" to Lázaro Cárdenas, 10 December 1938, SEP, TED, IV/161(IV-14)/4825.

38 Guillermina Echeverría de Pérez, 5 July 1938, SEP, TIC, IV/161(IV-14)/4036; Ruth Ortegón Echeverría, 2 December 1938, SEP, NOH, IV/161(IV-14)/4874.

39 Fallaw, *Cárdenas*; and Brannon and Baklanoff, *Agrarian Reform*, 52.

40 Depto. Jurídico y Consultivo to Jefe de Depto. Agr., 11 August 1943, SRA, UCU, I; Fallaw, *Cárdenas*, 127; Baños Ramírez, *Yucatán*, 118–20.

41 Fallaw, *Cárdenas*, 135; Rufino Baas et al. to Gral. Lázaro Cárdenas, 4 September 1940, SRA, SAM.

42 See synarchist manifesto, at http://movimiento-sinarquista.blogspot.com; and Pedro Rodríguez to gobernador, 27 May 1940, SRA, KIN.

43 See assorted correspondence in SRA (HUN, TET, and KIN).

44 Ibid.

45 Adán Cárdenas Alonzo to Pres. del Consejo Directivo, Henequeneros de Yucatán, 15 November 1954, SRA, KIN.

46 See correspondence in SRA, HUN, TET, and KIN.

47 Alejandro Cool Euán et al. to Adolfo López Mateos, 18 January 1962, SRA, HUN.

48 Policarpo Tzuc et al. to Ezequiel Tec Chay, 27 November 1963, SRA, KIN; Anatolio May, 20 March 1962, SRA, TET.

49 See correspondence in SRA, HUN, and TET.

50 Francisco Ek Dzul to Ing. Adán Cárdenas, 19 June 1955, SRA, HUN; Acta, 21 January 1957, SRA, HUN.

51 Acta to Adán Cárdenas Alonzo, 27 July 1957, SRA, TET; and José Lucio Tinal to Adán Cárdenas Alonzo, 5 February 1958, SRA, TET.

52 Brannon and Baklanoff, *Agrarian Reform*; Baños, *Yucatán*.

53 Santiago Cetina et al. to Víctor Mena Palomo, 16 April 1956, SRA, HUN; J. Jesús Santana Gallo, to Del. del Depto. de Asuntos Agrarios y Colonización, 10 August 1960, SRA HUN.

54 Rafael Uc et al. to Roberto Barrios, 11 May 1961, SRA, HUN; Ejidatarios de Ucú to Gustavo Díaz Ordaz, 16 September 1967, SRA, UCU.

55 Marcelino Ek Canul et al., "Acta," 20 March 1966, SRA, HUN; Pascual Canché Cuxin to Jefe del Depto. de Asuntos Agrarios y Colonización, 19 March 1966, SRA, TET.

56 Villanueva, *Crisis henequenera*, 141–48; Brannon and Baklanoff, *Agrarian Reform*, 80.

57 Edilberto Canul Castro, Acta, 7 August 1967, SRA, HUN; El Comisionado to Del. del Depto de Asuntos Agrarios y Colonización, 31 July 1967, SRA, HUN; Pastor Vázquez to Del. del Depto. de Asuntos Agrarios y Colonización, 8 August 1967, SRA, HUN.

58 Rodolfo Kuhne Gutiérrez, Del. del Depto. de Asuntos Agrarios y Colnización, to Pres. del Com. Ejid., 25 September 1967, SRA, KIN.

59 Ing. Ermilo Guëmes Lara to Efrén F. Caraveo Caraveo, 3 October 1975, SRA, TET.

60 Ermilo Guëmes Lara to Efrén F. Caraveo Caraveo, 5 June and 11 July 1975, SRA, TET.

61 Pastor Vázquez Pérez to Efrén Caraveo Caraveo, 9 December 1971, SRA, HUN; Mariano Ku Cauich to Efrén Caraveo Caraveo, 11 June 1975, SRA, HUN.

62 Efrén F. Caraveo Caraveo, "Dictamen," 25 January 1974, SRA, KIN. See also Dir. Gen. de Gobernación, Armando Bolio Pasos, 17 January 1974, SRA, TET; and Félix May Maldonado to Armando Enrique Toraya Lara, 1 December 1981, SRA, KIN.

63 Com. Rodolfo Espadas I. to Agustín Franco Aguilar, 9 January 1979, SRA, KIN.

64 Com. Ejid. Kinchil, to Agustín Franco Aguilar, 13 July 1984, SRA, KIN. See also Pastor Vázquez Pérez to Prof. Efrén Caraveo Caraveo, 23 August and 11 November 1971, SRA, HUN.

65 Baños, *Neoliberalismo*; and Villanueva, *Crisis*.

66 Cervera, cited in Baños, *Neoliberalismo*, 135.

67 Salinas, cited ibid., 35.

68 Official cited ibid., 107, 135. See also Villanueva Mukul, *Crisis henequenera*, 50.

69 Baños, *Neoliberalismo*.

70 Ermilo Guëmes Lara to Rolando Ruiz Jiménez, 11 September 1990, SRA, HUN; Rolando Ruiz Jiménez to Ermilo Guëmes Lara, 15 November 1990, SRA, HUN.

71 Natalio Cervantes Yam to Efrén Caraveo Caraveo, 19 October 1992, SRA, KIN; Com. Ejid. Tetiz to Efrén F. Caraveo Caraveo, 12 May 1992, SRA, TET; Top. Félix May Maldonado to Efrén F. Caraveo Caraveo, 14 October 1992, SRA, TET.

72 Interview with Guillermo Chuc, cited in Cetina Aguilar, *Breves datos*, 150.

CHAPTER SEVEN   THE WAR OF THE EGGS

1 Baños, *Neoliberalismo*.

2 *La Batalla*; Macossay "Resortes," and 18 and 20 June 1990, *La Jornada*. Further information on the movement and the Despacho was provided in interviews with Julio Macossay, Isela Rodríguez, Mauricio Macossay, Timoteo Canché, one-time and current workers and unionists, and residents of Tetiz and Nohuayum, 1994–2008.

3 "Cronología del conflicto . . . ," Sección II del SITIA, 7 May 1990; petitions and collective agreement, archives of Despacho; Macossay, "Resortes"; and Rodríguez, "Lo que no sabíamos,"171–72.

4 Macossay, "Resistencia," 104.

5 For a few examples see 11 April 1990, *DDY*; 13 and 27 April 1990, and 3, 4, 21, and 26 May 1990, *DDS*.

6 Simón Romero Chan, Sec. Genl. SITIA, "Cronología de los hechos . . . ," 29 January 1990, Despacho; "Información de los hechos del 5 de abril de 1990 . . . ," Despacho; Mauricio Macossay to Queridos Hijos, 8 April 1990, Despacho; "Cronología del conflicto. . . ." Sección II del SITIA, 7 May 1990, Despacho; 12 April and 3 May 1990, *DDY*.

7 Macossay, "Resistencia."

8 Carlos Caamal Couoh, Srio. Genl. Sindicato Independiente de Obreros de Tetiz y Hunucmá, "A la opinión pública de todo el país," 30 May 1990, Despacho.

9 This characterization is based on my fieldwork, which I began to conduct on Nohuayum four years after the strike.

10 *La Batalla* (1:2); interview with an engineer of Avícolas, 7 July 1997, Mérida; and Rodríguez, "Lo que no sabíamos," 172–73.

11 1 and 8 February 1990, *Por Esto*; Pedro Echevarría V., "Gobierno sin ideas cava su tumba," 7 April 1990, Despacho; and Partido de la Unidad Obrera Popular Independiente, 14 May 1990, Despacho.

12 Rodríguez, "Lo que no sabíamos," 173; leaflet, 2 February 1990, Despacho; leaflet, April 1990, Despacho; "David contra Goliad," April 1990, Despacho; Jesús Solis Alpuche, por la comisión sindical del PRD to Director PRD, 6 April 1990, Despacho; "La honestidad y el valor de los pueblos no puede ser pisoteada por los explotadores," 20 April 1990, Despacho; Protocola Burgois Manzanita, April 1990, Despacho; Agustín Durazzo Negroe, Porfirio Díaz Ordaz, and Caro Noriega Pinochet to Muy honorable locutor del noticiero de la poderosa dobleu, 17 April 1990, Despacho.

13 2 February, and 8, 17 April, and 16, 18 May 1990, *DDY*; 27, 31 January, 3 February, 23 March, and 7, 13, 28, and 30 April 1990, and 3 May *DDS*.

14   27 January, and 27, 29 April, and 3, 18 May 1990, *DDS*; *La Batalla* (8:20).

15   3, 4 May 1990, *DDY*.

16   30 January, 24, 27, 29 April, and 4 May 1990, *DDY*.

17   Himer C. Díaz Ceballos, "Al heróico pueblo de Tetiz," 27 January 1990, Despacho.

18   Leaflet, 2 February 1990, Despacho; leaflet, April 1990, Despacho; "David contra Goliad," April 1990, Despacho; Jesús Solis Alpuche, por la comisión sindical del PRD to Director PRD, 6 April 1990, Despacho; "La honestidad y el valor de los pueblos no puede ser pisoteada por los explotadores," 20 April 1990, Despacho.

19   *La batalla* 8:2, 8:23. On "performative subversions," see Butler, *Gender Trouble*; on the sexual politics of carnivalesque inversions in Mexico, see Limón, "Carne, Carnales and the Carnivalesque."

20   See interviews with representative of Avícolas, 7 July 1997, Mérida, and Julio Macossay, July 1997. See also 6 April and 27 1990, *DDY*; *La batalla* 6:2, 7:2, 8:28–8:35; and Rodríguez, "Lo que no sabíamos," 17.

21   See *La batalla* 8:6, 9, and 11.

22   Herrera, *Los huevos*.

23   Interviews with Héctor Herrera Alvarez, July 2002, and Mario Herrera Alvarez, June 1997.

24   See Despacho archive and Rodríguez, "Lo que no sabíamos."

25   18 and 21 May 1990, *DDS*.

26   Mauricio Macossay describes "redacting" *La batalla*, out of conversations he had with unionists and union leaders over the course of the conflict and in its aftermath. María Eugenia Castillo Bravo collected and transcribed the anecdotes included in that text. Interview with Mauricio Macossay and María Eugenia Castillo Bravo, February 2009.

27   Cf. Amin, *Event, Metaphor, Memory*.

28   *La batalla* 2:3.

29   Ibid. 8:35.

30   Ibid. 1:4, 1:3, and 2:1. See also Orientación Proletaria, April 1990, Despacho; and 30 January 1990, *DDY*; Sindicato de Trabajadores Académicos de la Universidad Autónoma de Chapingo, 25 May 1990, Despacho; and Orientación Proletaria, "La heróica lucha de Tetiz," April 1990, Despacho. *La batalla* 1:1, 2:5.

31   *La batalla*, 6:2, 2:1.

32   Ibid. 5:12, 7:3, 7:6.

33   Ibid. 5:17, 5:18. See also 19 June 1990, *La Jornada*.

34   *La batalla* 5:16, 5:17, 5:19.

35   Ibid. 6:3.

36   Ibid. 6:4.

37   *Despertar obrero* 2:24 (January 1990); *La batalla de Tetiz y Hunucmá: 140 días de lucha*.

38   Vera Chablé, "Sociedad"; Macossay, "Arte de la resistencia," 78.

39   Cf. Harvey, *Chiapas*; and Stephen, *¡Zapata Lives!*

40   Macossay, "La escuela de agricultura."

41   Rodríguez, "Lo que no sabíamos," 171–72; Macossay, "Resistencia," 120.

42 Macossay, "Resistencia," 113, 115; "Resortes"; and "Arte de la resistencia."

43 Macossay, "Resortes" and "Resistencia," 126–27; Rodríguez, "Lo que no sabíamos," 172.

44 Interview with Mauricio Macossay, February 2009.

45 Macossay, "Resortes" and "Arte de la resistencia," 75.

CHAPTER EIGHT   BY THE VIRGIN'S GRACE

1 Carrillo y Ancona, El obispado de Yucatán, 765–78.

2 Ibid.

3 The discussion of hunting is based on my recollections of and field notes on hunting trips in pueblos and haciendas in northwestern Yucatán as well as on interviews conducted in Tetiz and Nohuayum in 1995, 1996, 1997, and 2001. Cf. Sobrino Campos, "El Pak-ppuh."

4 Interview with Don Míis (Cat), Tetiz, 4 July 1996; Interview with Monkey, Tetiz, 6 July 1997.

5 Cf. Sobrino Campos, "El Pak-ppuh"; Terán and Rasmussen, La milpa; and Redfield and Villa Rojas, Chan Kom.

6 Morley, Ancient Maya, 526; Ligorred Perramón, U mayathanoob, 163; and Terán and Rasmussen, La milpa, 275–83. Cf. Schele and Miller, Blood of Kings.

7 Villa Rojas, Los elegidos de Dios; Redfield and Villa Roja, Chan Kom; Terán and Rasmussen, Los mayas; Hanks, Referential Practice.

8 Hanks, Referential Practice.

9 Ibid; Peniche Barrera, Fantasmas; and Sobrino Campos, "El Pak-ppuh," and "Piedra de Virtud."

10 Interview with Huech (armadillo), Hacienda Nohuayum, 25 May 1996.

11 Sobrino Campos, "Piedra de Virtud." Cf. Parry and Bloch, Money.

12 Sobrino Campos, "Emchukil."

13 Interview with Doña Leonor, 19 November 1995. Cf. Terán and Rasmussen, Los mayas.

14 Ligorred Perramón, Consideraciones; Mediz Bolio, La tierra, 189; and Mimenza Castillo, "El Yumil Kaax." Cf. Burns, Epoch of Miracles.

15 Sobrino Campos, "Pak-ppuh" and "Piedra de Virtud"; Burns; Epoch of Miracles; Hanks, Referential Practice.

16 Don Pedro, Nohuayum, 3 July 1997.

17 Cf. Sklar, Dancing with the Virgin.

18 The following account of the gremio system and fiestas of the Virgin is based on my membership in two gremios and my observation of fiestas in 1995, 1996, 1997, and 2001. On a biographical approach to commodities, see Appadurai, Social Life; and Kopytoff, "Cultural Biography of Things."

19 For discussions of popular agency in the gremios and in cultural performances like the dance of the pig's head, or k'ub pol, see Fernández, "Fiesta System"; and Hervik, Mayan People.

20 By the 1940s, Robert Redfield argued that large-scale patron saint fiestas across the peninsula evidenced a process of transformation from "holy day to holiday"—

that is, from acts of communal homage to supernatural guardians to "commercial undertaking[s] for the profit of individuals." Redfield, *Folk Culture*, xix. For a discussion of the role of the gremios in fostering the aspirations of privileged residents of Maxcanú, see Loewe, "Ambiguity and Order."

21 Cf. Gálvez and Luque Brazán, *Traveling Virgins*.

22 Interviews of Tiger and Teresita, Tetiz, 6 July 1997; and Don Mauro, Tetiz, 21 June 1997.

23 Informants estimate that as many as half of the adult population may be involved in the gremios. Tiger and Doña Teresita, Tetiz, 6 July 1997; and Don Mauro, Tetiz, 21 June 1997.

24 Interviews of Don Mauro, Tetiz, 21 June 1997. Cf. Greenberg, "Capital, Ritual, and Boundaries"; and Taussig, *Devil and Commodity Fetishism*.

25 See Marx, *Grundrisse*, 201–4, and *Capital: Volume I* (New York: Vintage Books, 1977), 200–212, 247–57; Hutchinson, *Nuer Dilemmas*, and Zelizer, *Social Meaning of Money*.

26 Cf. Parry and Bloch, *Money*, 25.

27 Cf. Marx, *Capital, Volume I*.

28 Interview of Tiger and Doña Teresita, Tetiz, 6 July 1997.

29 The gremio Fe y misericordia was established in 1951, while the gremio de cazadores was established in 1974. I do not have exact information regarding the Gremio de Campesinos, the oldest gremio of Tetiz, which once included delegations from the towns of Hunucmá and Tixkokob.

30 Interview with Don Mauro, Tetiz, 21 June 1997.

31 Although they did not participate either in the gremio system or in the veneration of the Virgin, converts to Protestantism similarly formed hunting parties to raise money to buy building materials for an evangelical temple on Hacienda Nohuayum. Interview with Don Fredi, Nohuayum, 18 November 1995.

32 Interviews with Tiger, Tetiz, 6 July 1997, and with Don Marcos, Tetiz, 21 June 1997.

33 Carrillo y Ancona, *El obispado de Yucatán*, 774–75.

34 Interview with Don Marcos, Tetiz, 21 June 1997.

CHAPTER NINE   POET, PROPHET, AND POLITICIAN

1 Cf. Warren, *Indigenous Movements and Their Critics*; Montejo, *Maya Intellectual Renaissance*; Warren and Jackson, *Indigenous Movements, Self-Representation and the State*; Gutiérrez, *Nationalist Myths*; García, *Making Indigenous Citizens*; Rappaport, *Intercultural Utopias*; Postero, *Now We Are Citizens*.

2 This chapter is based in part on a series of interviews with Anacleto Cetina Aguilar at his home in Hunucmá in August 2001, February and March 2004, and February 2007. All reported conversation with him was recorded in the context of those interviews, whose dates I will specify when relevant.

3 Cf. Trouillot, *Silencing the Past*.

4 Cetina Aguilar, *Despertar*, 16. In the translation of this and other quotations from Cetina's poetry I make no attempt to reproduce rhyme and meter.

5   Ibid., 1, 21, 22, 32, 35, 40.

6   Ibid., 45.

7   Cf. Appadurai, *Social Life*; Miller, *Materiality*; and Keane, *Signs of Recognition*.

8   Cetina, *Cahtal-K'ay*, 11, 16.

9   Ibid., 17, 19–22.

10   Ibid., 9.

11   Ibid., 3.

12   Ibid., 16, 24–25, 29–30.

13   On the PAN in Yucatán, see Torres Ramírez, "The Mexican PAN"; and Ménendez Losa, *Chemax*, and "The PAN in Yucatán."

14   Cetina, *Breves datos*, 68–72.

15   Cf. Aranda González, *Ensayos monográficos*.

16   The Programa de Apoyo a las Culturas Municipales y Comunitarias (PACMYC; Program of Support for Municipal and Community Culture) financed the publication of Cetina's book. Established by the national government's Dirección General de Culturas Populares e Indígenas in 1989, PACMYC was created in the years leading up to the quincentennial commemoration of the conquest as a cultural program aimed, according to its directors, at furthering the "cultural development" of the "pueblos and indigenous and popular sectors" of Mexico.

17   Cetina, *Breves datos*, 9, 11–14, 142–44.

18   Ibid.

19   Ibid., 35–37, 68.

20   Ibid., 70, 72, 73.

21   Ibid., 44, 89, 92, 98, 101.

22   Ibid., 81, 136, 140, 142.

23   Ibid., 61.

24   Ibid., 49–61, 149.

25   Ibid., 60–63, 98. The Chilam Balam manuscripts are compilations of texts dating from before the conquest to several centuries afterward (Restall, *Maya Conquistador*). The actual name of one its ascribed authors was Na Hau Pech.

26   Cetina, *Breves datos*, 60–61, 66–67.

27   Ibid., 59–60, 149–51.

28   Ibid., 154–55.

29   Ibid., 59–60, 68.

30   Ibid., 59, 151.

31   Ibid., 167.

32   18 May 2004, *¡Por Esto!*; and 6 August 2004, *DDY*.

33   Cf. Scott, *Conscripts of Modernity*.

34   Interviews with Cetina in 2004. Cf. Price, *Convict and the Colonel*.

35   Cf. Postero, *Now We Are Citizens*.

36   Cetina Aguilar, *Breves datos*, 5.

CONCLUSION

1 Cetina, *Cahtal-K'ay*; Manzanilla Domínguez, *El bolchevismo criminal*, 68; "1920. Diligencias contra Gregorio Chan . . . ," AGEY, JUS, PEN, 1203:1132.

2 Cf. Appadurai, *Social Life of Things*; Ferry, *Not Ours Alone*; Weiner, *Inalienable Possessions*; Graeber, *Toward an Anthropological Theory of Value*.

3 Cf. Clifford, *Writing of Culture*. My reading of the "Nuc ma ti'" story is thus not as what Fogelson has called an "epitomizing event" ("narratives that condense, encapsulate, and dramatize longer-term historical processes"), but rather, in effect, as an epitomizing allegory. Fogelson, "Ethnohistory," 143.

4 Cf. Trouillot, *Silencing the Past*.

5 Cf. White, *Content of the Form*.

ᴄ᱘ GLOSSARY

SPANISH

acta: official document, or certificate

agrarismo: political movement or ideological stance in favor of agrarian reform

agrarista: one who favors agrarian reform and is dedicated to that cause (i.e., as agrarian engineer, politician, or activist)

aguardiente: cane liquor

albarrada: stone walls, typically used for enclosing lands

alcalde: mayor or chief judicial official of a town

Avícolas Fernández: Fernández Agricultural Company

ayuntamiento: town council

baldíos: uncultivated lands, or "wastelands"

cacique: indigenous leader, i.e., of an indigenous republic

campesino: peasant, small landholder

capitana: captain (feminine)

cazador: hunter

cofradía: confraternity

cohecho: incitement, or seduction of others; typically, to commit a crime

compañero: comrade

común: commons, or commune

deslinde: demarcation of property boundaries through a survey

Despacho de Asesoría a los Sindicatos Independientes: Independent Union Advisory Office

ejidatario: worker in an agricultural collective

ejido: in the nineteenth century, communal lands; from the 1930s on, also used to refer to agricultural collectives established on ejido lands

encomienda: colonial system of tributary labor

estandarte: banner, used by gremios in religious processions

fiesta: party or festivity

finca: a rural property, typically a large farm or ranch

fundo legal: town or pueblo limits

gobierno: government

granjas: farms, here used to refer to large-scale agricultural facilities as well

gremio: guild, league, or association, typically occupational or religious in nature

hacendado: plantation owner

hacienda: plantation

hidalgo: member of minor nobility; after Caste War, sometimes extended as a title of privilege to indigenous leaders and soldiers who fought against the rebels

huano: kind of palm, whose leaves are often used for roofing material

huevo: egg

indígena: indigenous person

indio: Indian (often pejorative in use)

jarana: folk dance and associated music, often performed at a vaquería

jefe: chief, or leader

jefe político: district prefect

junta: assembly or council

juntas municipales: municipal boards

libreta: notebook

Liga Central de Resistencia: Central Resistance League; an organization coordinating local Socialist groups

liga de resistencia: local Socialist resistance league

lindero: boundary

maquiladora: assembly plant, typically a foreign-owned manufacturing operation

maricón: homosexual (pejorative term)

mestizo: mixed race

milpa: subsistence plot

palo de tinte: dyewood

picado: breach, i.e., when clearing or surveying land

promesa: promise

recaudo: collection for safekeeping

regidor: town councilman

repartimiento de mercancías: forced purchase of goods (under colonial rule)

república de indígenas: indigenous republic, abolished 1868

Resolución Presidencial: Presidential Resolution, here ejidal grants by Lázero Cárdenas

sirviente: servant, often used to refer to indebted laborers on haciendas *soldado:* soldier

subdelegado: subdelegate; a government post with strong regional authority, in the
　late colonial and early national periods

terrenos nacionales: national lands

vaquería: traditional Yucatecan fiesta, with music and dancing

vecino: neighbor, or pueblo resident

venado: deer

YUCATEC MAYA

batab: indigenous leader of a kah (see cacique, above)

cenote: sinkhole

ch'a chaak: traditional Mayan ritual to summon rains

ch'ibal: noble families or clans

halach winic: "true man," or great lord

holche': breach, when clearing or surveying land

ik': wind, or spirit

kah: settlement, pueblo, or town

kahnal: kah dweller

k'ax: woodlands, or forest

keh: deer

kol: subsistence plot, or milpa

pa'atlil: waiting for or staking out prey

popox: thorny plant that causes irritation on contact with skin (known in
　Spanish as pica pica)

p'uh: flushing out of prey (as in the hunt)

sip: supernatural forest entity that takes the shape of a deer

ts'ul: non-indigenous person, typically one of privilege

tunich keh: deer stone; a talisman conferring power over deer in the hunt

tupil: indigenous police officer, of colonial and early national periods

vecinoil: pueblo or town residence, sometimes used to refer to non-indigenous
　residents

yum: lord

yumil keh: lord of the deer

BIBLIOGRAPHY

ARCHIVES

Seville, Spain
AGI   Archivo General de Indias (Mexico)

Washington, D.C.
NA   National Archives

Mexico City
AGN   Archivo General de la Nación
        BN   Bienes Nacionales
                 Tierras
AO/PEC   Archivo Alvaro Obregón/Plutarco Elías Calles
MOB   Mapoteca Manuel Orozco y Berra
SEP   Secretaría de Educación Pública
        HUN   Hunucmá
        TET   Tetiz
        KIN   Kinchil
        TED   Hacienda Tedzidz
        TIC   Hacienda Ticimul
        NOH   Hacienda Nohuayum

Mérida, Yucatán

AGEY   Archivo General del Estado de Yucatán
- COL   Colonial
  - Correspondencia de los gobernadores
  - Ayuntamientos
  - Tierras
- PE   Poder Ejecutivo
  - GOB   Gobernación
    - Tierras
    - Justicia
    - Alcaldías municipales (AM)
    - Ayuntamientos (AYUN)
  - GUE   Guerra
  - FOM   Fomento
  - MIL   Milicia
  - JUST   Justicia
  - Censos y padrones
  - Jefaturas Políticas
  - Tesorería del Estado
  - Tierras
- JUS   Justicia
  - PEN   Penal
  - CIV   Civil
- CON   Congreso
  - CGPC   Comisión de gobernación y puntos constitucionales
  - CH   Comisión de Hacienda
  - CJIP   Comisión de Justicia y de Instrucción Pública
  - CIAA   Comisión de Industria, Agricultura y Artes
  - CIPH   Comisión de instrucción pública y hacienda
  - Correspondencia

CA   Centro de Apoyo a la Investigación Histórica de Yucatán
- Manuscritos

SRA   Secretaría de la Reforma Agraria
- HUN   Hunucmá
- TET   Tetiz
- KIN   Kinchil
- UMAN   Umán
- SAM   Samahil
- BOL   Bolón
- UCU   Ucú

FOT   Fototeca Pedro Guerra, Mérida

NEWSPAPERS

Boletín municipal: órgano de los intereses del municipio libre de Hunucmá
El Correo
Despertar Obrero: voz de los sindicatos independientes
DDS   Diario del Sureste
DDY   Diario de Yucatán
DO   Diario Oficial
DY   Diario Yucateco
EC   Eco del Comercio
La Jornada
¡Por Esto!
RDM   Revista de Mérida
RDP   Razón del Pueblo
RDY   Revista de Yucatán
Revista Peninsular
SC   Sombra de Cepeda
UY   Unión Yucateca
VDR   La voz de la Revolución
La voz del indio: órgano de combate y de política del departamento de Hunucmá
La voz del partido: periódico noticioso de literatura y variedades
La voz del indio: órgano de combate y de política del departamento de Hunucmá
La voz del partido: periódico noticioso de literatura y variedades

PRINTED SOURCES

Acereto, Albino. "Historia política desde el descubrimiento europeo hasta 1920." Enciclopedia yucatanense, ed. Carlos A. Echánove Trujillo. Mexico City: Gobierno de Yucatán, 1946.

Alonso, Ana. Thread of Blood: Colonialism, Revolution, and Gender on Mexico's Northern Frontier. Tucson: University of Arizona Press, 1995.

Alvarado, Salvador. Mi sueño. Mérida: Maldonado Editores, 1988.

———. Obra. Mexico City: Liga de Economistas Revolucionarios de la República Mexicana, 1979.

Amin, Shahid. Event, Metaphor, Memory: Chauri Chaura, 1922–1992. Berkeley: University of California Press, 1995.

Anderson, Benedict. Imagined Communities: Reflections on the Origin and Spread of Nationalism. London: Verso, 1991.

Appadurai, Arjun. Modernity at Large: Cultural Dimensions of Globalization. Minneapolis: University of Minnesota Press, 1996.

Appadurai, Arjun, ed. The Social Life of Things: Commodities in Cultural Perspective. New York: Cambridge University Press, 1986.

Appelbaum, Nancy P. Muddied Waters: Race, Region, and Local History in Colombia, 1846–1948. Durham: Duke University Press, 2003.

Appelbaum, Nancy P., Anne S. Macpherson, and Karin Alejandra Roseblatt, eds. *Race and Nation in Modern Latin America*. Chapel Hill: University of North Carolina Press, 2003.

Aranda González, Mario H. *Ensayos monográficos campechanos: el municipio de Calkiní*. Campeche: CORACEC, 1981.

Avila y Castillo, Florencio. *Diario revolucionario*. Mérida: Imprenta La Voz de la Revolución, 1915.

Baños Ramírez, Othón. *Neoliberalismo, reorganización y subsistencia rural: el caso de la zona henequenera de Yucatán, 1980–1992*. Mérida: Universidad Autónoma de Yucatán, 1996.

———. *Yucatán: ejidos sin campesinos*. Mérida: Ediciones de la Universidad Autónoma de Yucatán, 1989.

Bantjes, Adrian. *As If Jesus Walked on Earth: Cardenismo, Sonora, and the Mexican Revolution*. Wilmington, Del.: Scholarly Resources Books, 1998.

Baqueiro, Serapio. *Reseña geográfica, histórica y estadística del Estado de Yucatán*. Mexico City: Francisco Díaz de León, 1881.

Batt, Rosemary L. "The Rise and Fall of the Planter Class in Espita, 1900–1924." *Land, Labor, and Capital in Modern Yucatán*, ed. Jeffery T. Brannon and Gilbert M. Joseph. Tuscaloosa: University of Alabama Press, 1991.

Becker, Marjorie. *Setting the Virgin on Fire: Lázaro Cárdenas, Michoacán Peasants, and the Redemption of the Mexican Revolution*. Berkeley: University of California Press, 1995.

Beezley, William H., Cheryl English Martin, and William E. French, eds. *Rituals of Rule, Rituals of Resistance: Public Celebrations and Popular Culture in Mexico*. Wilmington, Del.: Scholarly Resource Books, 1994.

Benjamin, Thomas. *La Revolución: Mexico's Great Revolution as Memory, Myth, and History*. Austin: University of Texas Press, 2000.

Benjamin, Walter. *Illuminations*. New York: Schocken, 1969.

Blouin, Francis Xavier, and William G. Rosenberg. *Archives, Documentation, and Institutions of Social Memory: Essays from the Sawyer Seminar*. Ann Arbor: University of Michigan Press, 2007.

Bracamonte y Sosa, Pedro. *Amos y Sirvientes: Las Haciendas de Yucatán, 1789–1860*. Mérida: Universidad Autónoma de Yucatán, 1993.

———. *Los mayas y la tierra: la propiedad indígena en el Yucatán colonial*. Mexico City, 2003.

———. *La memoria enclaustrada: historia indígena de Yucatán, 1750–1915*. Mexico City: CIESAS, 1994.

Brannon, Jeffrey, and Eric N. Baklanoff. *Agrarian Reform and Public Enterprise in Mexico*. Tuscaloosa: University of Alabama Press, 1987.

Brooks, James F., Christopher R. N. DeCorse, and John Walton, eds. *Small Worlds: Method, Meaning, and Narrative in Microhistory*. Santa Fe: School for Advanced Research Press, 2008.

Burke, Edmund. *An Appeal from the New to the Old Whigs, in Consequence of Some Late Discussions in Parliament, Relative to the Reflections on the French Revolution*. London, 1791.

Burns, Allan. *An Epoch of Miracles: Oral Literature of the Yucatec Maya*. Austin: University of Texas Press, 1983.

Butler, Judith. *Gender Trouble: Feminism and the Subversion of Identity*. New York: Routledge, 2000.

Carrillo y Ancona, Crescencio. *El obispado de Yucatán, historia de su fundación y de sus obispos desde el siglo XVI hasta el XIX, seguida de las constituciones sinodales de la diócesis y otros documentos relativos*. Tomo II. Mérida: Imp. y Lit. de Ricardo B. Caballero, 1895.

Cetina Aguilar, Anacleto. *Breves datos históricos y culturales del municipio de Hunucmá*. Mérida: Talleres Gráficos del Sudeste, S.A., 1996.

———. *Cahtal-K'ay: canto a mi pueblo*. Mérida: Talleres Gráficos del Sudeste, S.A., 1983.

———. *Despertar: Desarrollo poético del Profr. Anacleto Cetina Aguilar*. Hunucmá, Yucatán, 1982.

Chacón, R. "Yucatan and the Mexican Revolution: The Pre-Constitutional Years, 1910–1918." Ph.D. diss., Stanford University, 1983.

Clifford, James. *Writing Culture: The Poetics and Politics of Ethnography*. Santa Fe: School of American Research Press, 1986.

Comaroff, John, and Jean Comaroff. *Ethnography and the Historical Imagination*. Boulder: Westview Press, 1992.

Connerton, Paul. *How Societies Remember*. Cambridge: Cambridge University Press, 1989.

Contreras Sánchez, Alicia del C. *Capital comercial y colorantes en la Nueva España, segunda mitad del s. XVIII*. Zamora, Mich.: El Colegio de Michoacán, 1996.

———. *Historia de una tintorea olvidada: el proceso de explotación y circulación del palo de tinte, 1750–1807*. Mérida: Universidad Autónoma de Yucatán, 1990.

Coronil, Fernando. *The Magical State: Nature, Money, and Modernity in Venezuela*. Chicago: University of Chicago Press, 1997.

Coronil, Fernando, and Julie Skurski. "Dismembering and Remembering the Nation: The Semantics of Political Violence in Venezuela." *Comparative Studies in Society and History* 33:2 (April 1991), 288–337.

Craib, Raymond B. *Cartographic Mexico: A History of State Fixations and Fugitive Landscapes*. Durham: Duke University Press, 2004.

Creed, Gerald W., ed. *The Seductions of Community: Emancipations, Oppressions, Quandaries*. Santa Fe: School of American Research Press, 2006.

De la Cadena, Marisol. *Indigenous Mestizos: The Politics of Race and Culture in Cuzco, Peru, 1919–1991*. Durham: Duke University Press, 2000.

Dening, Greg. *The Death of William Gooch: A History's Anthropology*. Honolulu: University of Hawaii Press, 1995.

Dumond, Don E. *The Machete and the Cross: Campesino Rebellion in Yucatan*. Lincoln: University of Nebraska Press, 1997.

Dussel, Enrique. *Twenty Theses on Politics*. Durham: Duke University Press, 2008.

Eiss, Paul K. "Hunting for the Virgin: Meat, Money and Memory in Yucatán." *Cultural Anthropology* 17:3 (2002), 291–330.

———. "Redemption's Archive: Remembering the Future in a Revolutionary Past." *Comparative Studies in Society and History* 44:1 (January 2002), 106–36.

———. "Redemption's Archive: Revolutionary Figures and Indian Work in Yucatán." Ph.D. diss., University of Michigan, 2000.

Evans, Sterling. *Bound in Twine: The History and Ecology of the Henequen–Wheat Complex for Mexico and the American and Canadian Plains, 1880–1950.* College Station: Texas A&M University Press, 2007.

Fallaw, Ben. *Cárdenas Compromised: The Failure of Reform in Postrevolutionary Yucatán.* Durham: Duke University Press, 2001.

———. "The Life and Deaths of Felipa Poot: Women, Fiction and Cardenismo in Postrevolutionary Mexico." *Hispanic American Historical Review* 82:4 (2002), 645–83.

Farris, Nancy. *Maya Society under Colonial Rule.* Princeton: Princeton University Press, 1984.

Fernández, Francisco J. "Fiesta System in Yucatán: Popular Religion, Identity and Socioeconomic Organization." Ph.D. diss., University of Florida, 1994.

Ferry, Elizabeth Emma. *Not Ours Alone: Patrimony, Value, and Collectivity in Contemporary Mexico.* New York: Columbia University Press, 2005.

Flores D., Jorge. "La vida rural en Yucatán en 1914." *Historia Mexicana* 10 (January–March 1961), 470–83.

Fogelson, Raymond D. "The Ethnohistory of Events and Nonevents." *Ethnohistory* 36:2 (1989), 133–47.

Foucault, Michel. *Discipline and Punish: The Birth of the Prison.* New York: Pantheon, 1977.

Gabbert, Wolfgang. *Becoming Maya: Ethnicity and Social Inequality in Yucatán since 1500.* Tucson: University of Arizona Press, 2004.

Gálvez, Alyshia, and José Carlos Luque Brazán, eds. *Traveling Virgins.* Special issue of electronic journal *E-misférica* 5:1 (May 2008).

García, María Elena. *Making Indigenous Citizens: Identities, Education, and Multicultural Development in Peru.* Stanford: Stanford University Press, 2005.

García Bernal, María Cristina. *Población y encomienda en Yucatán bajo los Austrias.* Seville: Escuela de Estudios Hispano-Americanos, 1978.

García Montero, José. *El rábano por las hojas: una fiesta en Hunucmá.* Mérida: Imprenta Nueva de Cecilio Leal, 1901.

Geary, Patrick J. *Phantoms of Remembrance.* Princeton: Princeton University Press, 1994.

Gill, Christopher J. "The Intimate Life of the Family: Patriarchy and the Liberal Project in Yucatan, Mexico, 1860–1915." Ph.D. diss., Yale University, 2001.

Ginzburg, Carlo. "Microhistory: Two or Three Things That I Know About It." *Critical Inquiry* 20:1 (1993), 10–35.

Gledhill, John. *Casi Nada: A Study of Agrarian Reform in the Homeland of Cardenismo.* Albany: Institute for Mesoamerican Studies, 1991.

González y González, Luis. *Invitación a la microhistoria.* Mexico City: Clio, 1997.

———. *Pueblo en vilo: microhistoria de San José de Gracia.* Mexico City: El Colegio de México, 1968.

Gould, Jeffrey L. *To Die in This Way: Nicaraguan Indians and the Myth of Mestizaje, 1880–1965.* Durham: Duke University Press, 1998.

Graeber, David. *Toward an Anthropological Theory of Value: The False Coin of Our Own Dreams.* New York: Palgrave, 2001.

Grandin, Greg. *The Blood of Guatemala: A History of Race and Nation.* Durham: Duke University Press, 2000.

Greenberg, James B. "Capital, Ritual, and Boundaries of the Closed Corporate Community." *Articulating Hidden Histories: Exploring the Influence of Eric R. Wolf,* ed. Jane Schneider and Rayna Rapp. Berkeley: University of California Press, 1995.

Guardino, Peter. *The Time of Liberty: Popular Political Culture in Oaxaca, 1750–1850.* Durham: Duke University Press, 2005.

Güémez Pineda, Arturo. *Liberalismo en tierras del caminante: Yucatán, 1812–1840.* Zamora, Mich: El Colegio de Michoacán, 1994.

Gutiérrez, Natividad. *Nationalist Myths and Ethnic Identities: Indigenous Intellectuals and the Mexican State.* Lincoln: University of Nebraska Press, 1999.

Halbwachs, Maurice. *On Collective Memory.* Chicago: University of Chicago Press, 1992.

Hanks, William F. *Referential Practice: Language and Lived Space among the Maya.* Chicago: University of Chicago Press, 1990.

Hardt, Michael, and Antonio Negri. *Empire.* Cambridge: Harvard University Press, 2001.

Hervik, Peter. *Mayan People Within and Beyond Boundaries: Social Categories and Lived Identity in Yucatán.* Amsterdam: Harwood Academic Publishers, 1999.

Hobsbawm, Eric, and Terence Ranger, eds. *The Invention of Tradition.* Cambridge: Cambridge University Press, 1983.

Hutchinson, Sharon. *Nuer Dilemmas: Coping with Money, War, and the State.* Berkeley: University of California Press, 1996.

Instituto Nacional de Estadística, Geografía e Informática. *Conteo de población y vivienda 1995: estado de Yucatán.* Mexico City: INEGI, 1996.

Joseph, Gilbert. *Rediscovering the Past: Essays on the Modern History of Yucatán.* Tuscaloosa: University of Alabama Press, 1986.

———. *Revolution from Without: Yucatán, Mexico, and the United States, 1880–1924.* Durham: Duke University Press, 1988.

Joseph, Gilbert, and Daniel Nugent, eds. *Everyday Forms of State Formation: Revolution and the Negotiation of Rule in Modern Mexico.* Durham: Duke University Press, 1994.

Joseph, Gilbert, and Allen Wells. "Corporate Control of a Monocrop Economy: International Harvester and Yucatán's Henequen Industry during the Porfiriato." *Latin American Research Review* 17:1 (1982), 69–99.

Kantorowicz, Ernst H. *The King's Two Bodies: A Study in Medieval Political Theology.* Princeton: Princeton University Press, 1957.

Katz, Friedrich. "Labor Conditions on Haciendas in Porfirian Mexico: Some Trends and Tendencies." *Hispanic American Historical Review* 54:1 (1974), 1–47.

Keane, Webb. *Signs of Recognition: Powers and Hazards of Recognition in an Indonesian Society.* Berkeley: University of California Press, 1997.

Knight, Alan. *The Mexican Revolution*. Volume 1. Lincoln: University of Nebraska Press, 1986.

Kopytoff, Igor. "The Cultural Biography of Things: Commoditization as a Cultural Process." *The Social Life of Things: Commodities in Cultural Perspective*, ed. Arjun Appadurai. New York: Cambridge University Press, 1986.

Kourí, Emilio. *A Pueblo Divided: Business, Property, and Community in Papantla, Mexico*. Stanford: Stanford University Press, 2004.

Laclau, Ernesto. *On Populist Reason*. New York: Verso, 2007.

Larson, Brooke. *Trials of Nation Making: Liberalism, Race, and Ethnicity in the Andes, 1810–1910*. Cambridge: Cambridge University Press, 2004.

Lewis, Oscar. *Life in a Mexican Village: Tepoztlán Restudied*. Urbana: University of Illinois Press, 1951.

Ligorred Perramón, Francisco de Asís. *Consideraciones sobre la literatura oral de los mayas modernos*. Mexico City: Instituto Nacional de Antropología e Historia, 1990.

———. *U mayathanoob ti dzib: las voces de la escritura*. Mérida: Universidad Autónoma de Yucatán, 1997.

Limón, José E. "Carne, Carnales, and the Carnivalesque: Bakhtinian 'Batos,' Disorder, and Narrative Discourses." *American Ethnologist* 16:3 (August 1989), 471–86.

Loewe, Ronald B. "Ambiguity and Order in Yucatán: A Study of Identity and Statecraft at the Mexican Periphery." Ph.D. diss., University of Chicago, 1995.

Lomnitz Adler, Claudio. *Deep Mexico, Silent Mexico: An Anthropology of Nationalism*. Minneapolis: University of Minnesota Press, 2001.

———. *Exits from the Labyrinth: Culture and Ideology in the Mexican National Space*. Berkeley: University of California Press, 1992.

Macossay Vallado, Mauricio. "El arte de la resistencia popular: Yucatán, 1980–2004." *Revista de geografía agrícola* 36 (2006), 69–81.

———. "La batalla de Tetiz: Los resortes de la resistencia obrera y popular." June 2002.

———. "Resistencia popular en Yucatán, 1980–2004." Ph.D. diss., Universidad Autónoma de México, 2005.

Maddox, Richard. *El Castillo: The Politics of Tradition in an Andalusian Town*. Urbana: University of Illinois Press, 1993.

Malinowski, Bronislaw. *Argonauts of the Western Pacific: An Account of Native Enterprise and Adventure in the Archipelagoes of Melanesian New Guinea*. London: Routledge, 1922.

Mallon, Florencia E. *The Defense of Community in Peru's Central Highlands: Peasant Struggle and Capitalist Transition, 1860–1940*. Princeton: Princeton University Press, 1983.

———. *Peasant and Nation: The Making of Postcolonial Mexico and Peru*. Berkeley: University of California Press, 1995.

Manzanilla Domínguez, A. *El bolchevismo criminal de Yucatán: documentos y apuntes para la historia trágica del Estado peninsular*. Mexico City, 1921.

Marx, Karl. *Capital*. Volume 1. New York: Vintage Books, 1977.

———. *Grundrisse*. London: Penguin Books, 1973.

Mediz Bolio, Antonio, and José Castillo Torre. *La agonía de Yucatán: exposición de la actual situación política, social y económica del Estado*. Mexico City: Partido Socialista del Sureste, 1932.

———. *Alvarado es el hombre*. Culiacán, Sinaloa: Instituto de Investigaciones Económicas y Sociales, Universidad Autónoma de Sinaloa, 1985.

———. *La tierra del faisán y del venado*. Mexico City: Editorial México, 1934.

Mena Brito, Bernardino. *Bolshevismo y democracia en México: pugna entre dos partidos políticos en Yucatán durante la Revolución Constitucionalista*. Mexico City: M. A. Mena, 1933.

Ménendez Losa, Carlos R. "The PAN in Yucatán: An Ascendant Political Option." *Party Politics and the Struggle for Democracy in Mexico: National- and State-Level Analyses of the Partido Acción Nacional*, ed. Kevin J. Middlebrook. La Jolla: Center for U.S.–Mexican Studies, 2001.

Menéndez Rodríguez, Hernán. *Iglesia y poder: proyectos sociales, alianzas políticas y económicas en Yucatán (1857–1917)*. Mexico City: Editorial Nuestra América, 1995.

Miller, Daniel, ed. *Materiality*. Durham: Duke University Press, 2005.

Mimenza Castillo, Ricardo. "El Yumil Kaax." *Yikal than: revista de literatura maya* 2:11 (July 1940).

Mintz, Jerome R. *Carnival Song and Society: Gossip, Sexuality, and Creativity in Andalusia*. New York: Berg, 1997.

Montejo, Víctor. *Maya Intellectual Renaissance: Identity, Representation, and Leadership*. Austin: University of Texas Press, 2005.

Morgan, Edmund. *Inventing the People: The Rise of Popular Sovereignty in England and America*. New York: Norton, 1988.

Morley, Sylvanus. *The Ancient Maya*. Edited by Robert Sharer. Stanford: Stanford University Press, 1994.

Nugent, Daniel. *Spent Cartridges of Revolution: An Anthropological History of Namiquipa, Chihuahua*. Chicago: University of Chicago Press, 1993.

Nugent, David. *Modernity at the Edge of Empire: State, Individual, and Nation in the Northern Peruvian Andes, 1885–1935*. Stanford: Stanford University Press, 1997.

Nuijten, Monique. *Power, Community and the State: The Political Anthropology of Organisation in Mexico*. London: Pluto Press, 2003.

Pacheco Cruz, Santiago. *Recuerdos de la propaganda constitucionalista en Yucatan*. Mérida, 1953.

———. *Traducción literal al idioma yucateco del decreto expedido a favor de los jornaleros de campo y de las circulares que se relacionan con estos*. Mérida: Imprenta El Porvenir, 1914.

Parry, Jonathan, and Maurice Bloch, eds. *Money and the Morality of Exchange*. Cambridge: Cambridge University Press, 1989.

Partido Socialista del Sureste. *Primer Congreso Obrero Socialista celebrado en Motul, Estado de Yucatán*. Mexico City: Centro de Estudios Históricos del Movimiento Obrero Mexicano, 1977.

Patch, Robert. *Maya and Spaniard in Yucatan, 1648–1812*. Stanford: Stanford University Press, 1993.

Peniche Barrera, Roldán. *Fantasmas mayas*. Mexico City: Presencia latinoamericana, 1982.

Peniche Rivero, Piedad. "Gender, Bridewealth, and Marriage: Social Reproduction on Henequen Haciendas in Yucatán (1870–1901)." *Women of the Mexican Countryside, 1850–1990: Creating Spaces, Shaping Transitions*, ed. Heather Fowler-Salamini and Mary Kay Vaughn. Tucson: University of Arizona Press, 1994.

Pérez Peniche, Rodolfo S. *Reseña histórica de la administración del C. Coronel Daniel Traconis, Gobernador constitucional del estado de Yucatán, escrita por el Lic. Rodolfo S. Pérez Peniche. 1890 a 1892*. Mérida: Imprenta Gamboa Guzmán, 1893.

Postero, Nancy. *Now We Are Citizens: Indigenous Politics in Postmulticultural Bolivia*. Stanford: Stanford University Press, 2006.

Price, Richard. *The Convict and the Colonel*. Boston: Beacon Press, 1998.

Purnell, Jennie. *Popular Movements and State Formation in Revolutionary Mexico: The Agraristas and Cristeros of Michoacán*. Durham: Duke University Press, 1999.

Rancière, Jacques. *Disagreement: Politics and Philosophy*. Minneapolis: University of Minnesota Press, 1998.

Rappaport, Joanne. *Cumbe Reborn: An Andean Ethnography of History*. Chicago: University of Chicago, 1994.

———. *Intercultural Utopias: Public Intellectuals, Cultural Experimentation, and Ethnic Pluralism in Colombia*. Durham: Duke University Press, 2005.

Re Cruz, Alicia. *The Two Milpas of Chan Kom: Scenarios of a Village Life*. Albany: State University of New York Press, 1996.

Redfield, Robert. *The Folk Culture of Yucatan*. Chicago: University of Chicago Press, 1941.

Redfield, Robert, and Alfonso Villa Rojas. *Chan Kom: A Maya Village*. Chicago: University of Chicago Press, 1962.

Reed, Nelson. *The Caste War of Yucatán*. Stanford: Stanford University Press, 1964.

Restall, Matthew. *Maya Conquistador*. Boston: Beacon Press, 1998.

———. *The Maya World: Yucatec Culture and Society, 1550–1850*. Stanford: Stanford University Press, 1997.

Reyes Domínguez, Guadalupe. *Carnaval en Mérida: fiesta, espectáculo y ritual*. Mérida: Instituto Nacional de Antropología e Historia, 2003.

Roach, Joseph. *Cities of the Dead*. New York: Columbia University Press, 1996.

Rodríguez, Isabel Alonzo. "Lo que no sabíamos . . . El movimiento sindical de Tetiz, Yucatán." *Desacatos* 13 (winter 2003), 170–74.

Rouse, Roger. "Mexican Migration and the Social Space of Postmodernism." *Diaspora* 1 (spring 1991): 8–23.

Roys, Ralph. *The Political Geography of the Yucatan Maya*. Washington: Carnegie Institution, 1957.

Rubin, Jeffrey W. *Decentering the Regime: Ethnicity, Radicalism, and Democracy in Juchitán, Mexico*. Durham: Duke University Press, 1997.

Rubio Mañé, José Ignacio. *La Casa de Montejo en Mérida, Yucatán*. Mérida: Ediciones Díaz Rubio, 2000.

———. "Los sanjuanistas de Yucatán." *Boletín del Archivo General de la Nación* 12 (1971), 1226.

Rugeley, Terry. *Rebellion Now and Forever: Mayas, Hispanics, and Caste War Violence in Yucatán, 1800–1880*. Stanford: Stanford University Press, 2009.

————. *Of Wonders and Wise Men: Religion and Popular Cultures in Southeast Mexico, 1800–1876*. Austin: University of Texas Press, 2001.

————. *Yucatán's Maya Peasantry and the Origins of the Caste War*. Austin: University of Texas Press, 1996.

Sánchez Novelo, Faulo M. *La rebelión delahuertista en Yucatán*. Mérida: Talleres Gráficos del Sudeste, 1991.

Schele, Linda, and Mary Ellen Miller. *The Blood of Kings: Dynasty and Ritual in Maya Art*. New York: George Brazilier, 1986.

Scott, David. *Conscripts of Modernity: The Tragedy of Colonial Enlightenment*. Durham: Duke University Press, 2004.

Scott, James C. *Weapons of the Weak: Everyday Forms of Peasant Resistance*. New Haven: Yale University Press, 1987.

Sklar, Deidre. *Dancing with the Virgin: Body and Faith in the Fiesta of Tortugas, New Mexico*. Berkeley: University of California Press, 2001.

Smith, Gavin. *Livelihood and Resistance: Peasants and the Politics of Land in Peru*. Berkeley: University of California Press, 1991.

Smith, Stephanie J. *Gender and the Mexican Revolution: Yucatán Women and the Realities of Patriarchy*. Chapel Hill: University of North Carolina Press, 2008.

Sobrino Campos, Raul. "Emchukil o el Jordan Maya: El Celo de las Escopetas." *Yikal than: revista de literatura maya* 1:1 (19 September 1939).

————. "El Pak-ppuh el Venado Vengador o Ec-Bac." *Yikal than: revista de literatura maya* 1:6 (February 1940).

————. "La Piedra de Virtud: El Zip'Ceh o Venado del 'Mal Viento.'" *Yikal than: revista de literatura maya* 2:12 (August 1940).

Solís Robleda, Gabriela. *Bajo el signo de la compulsión: el trabajo forzoso indígena en el sistema colonial yucateco, 1540–1730*. Mexico City: Instituto de Cultura de Yucatán, 2003.

————. *Contra viento y marea: documentos sobre las reformas del obispo Juan Gómez de Parada al trabajo indígena*. Mexico City: Instituto de Cultura de Yucatán, 2003.

Stoler, Ann Laura. *Along the Archival Grain: Epistemic Anxieties and Colonial Common Sense*. Princeton: Princeton University Press, 2008.

Suárez, Victor M., ed. *Estado de la industria, comercio y educación de la provincia de Yucatán en 1802 y causas de la pobreza de Yucatán en 1821*. Mérida: Ediciones Suárez, 1955.

Sullivan, Paul. *Unfinished Conversations: Mayas and Foreigners between Two Wars*. Berkeley: University of California Press, 1991.

————. *Xuxub Must Die: The Lost Histories of a Murder on the Yucatan*. Pittsburgh: University of Pittsburgh Press, 2006.

Taussig, Michael. *The Devil and Commodity Fetishism in South America*. Chapel Hill: University of North Carolina Press, 1980.

Taylor, Diana. *The Archive and the Repertoire: Performing Cultural Memory in the Americas*. Durham: Duke University Press, 2003.

Terán, Silvia, and Christian H. Rasmussen. "La milpa de los mayas: la agricultura de los Mayas prehispánicos y actuales en el noreste de Yucatán." Mérida: n.p., 1994.

Thompson, E. P. *Whigs and Hunters*. London: Penguin, 1975.

Thomson, Sinclair. *We Alone Will Rule: Native Andean Politics in the Age of Insurgency*. Madison: University of Wisconsin Press, 2002.

Thurner, Mark. *From Two Republics to One Divided: Contradictions of Postcolonial Nation-making in Andean Peru*. Durham: Duke University Press, 1997.

Trouillot, Michel-Rolph. *Silencing the Past: Power and the Production of History*. Boston: Beacon Press, 1997.

Turner, John Kenneth. *Barbarous Mexico*. Chicago: C. H. Kerr, 1911.

Valera, Juan Antonio, and Francisco de Corres. "Discurso sobre la constitución de las provincias de Yucatán y Campeche (1766)." *Descripciones económicas regionales de Nueva España: Provincias del centro, sudeste y sur, 1766–1827*. Mexico City: SEP/INAH, 1976.

Vaughan, Mary Kay. "The Construction of the Patriotic Festival in Tecamachalco, Puebla, 1900–1946." *Rituals of Rule, Rituals of Resistance: Public Celebrations and Popular Culture in Mexico*, ed. William Beezley, Cheryl English Martin, and William E. French. Wilmington, Del.: Scholarly Resources Press, 1994.

———. *Cultural Politics in Revolution: Teachers, Peasants, and Schools in Mexico, 1930–1940*. Tucson: University of Arizona Press, 1997.

Velasco, Horacio. "Signos y sentidos de la identidad de los pueblos castellanos: el concepto de pueblo y la identidad." *Iberian Identity: Essays in the Nature of Identity in Portugal and Spain*, ed. Richard Herr and John H. R. Polt. Berkeley: University of California Press, 1989.

Vera Chablé, Domingo. "Sociedad de solidaridad social 'Dzocu Yahá u Cají Te-Tiz': una experiencia de organización económica y social colectiva (las empresas sociales de Tetiz y Hunucmá, Yucatán)." *La agricultura de Yucatán ante el tratado de libre comercio*, ed. Adolfo Rodríguez and Jorge Flores. Mérida: UACH/INI/Banco de Crédito Rural Peninsular/SARH, 1993.

Villa Rojas, Alfonso. *Los elegidos de Dios: etnografía de los mayas de Quintana Roo*. Mexico City: Instituto Nacional Indigenista, 1978.

Villanueva, Eric. *Crisis henequenera, reconversión económica y movimientos campesinos en Yucatán, 1983–1992*. Mérida: Maldonado Editores, 1993.

———. *Crisis henequenera y movimientos campesinos en Yucatán, 1966–1983*. Mexico City: Instituto Nacional de Antropología e Historia, 1985.

Villoro, Luis. *Estado plural, pluralidad de culturas*. Mexico City: Editorial Paidós, 1998.

Wade, Peter. *Blackness and Race Mixture: The Dynamics of Racial Identity in Colombia*. Baltimore: Johns Hopkins University Press, 1993.

Warren, Kay B. *Indigenous Movements and Their Critics*. Princeton: Princeton University Press, 1998.

Warren, Kay B., and Jean B. Jackson. *Indigenous Movements, Self-Representation, and the State in Latin America*. Austin: University of Texas Press, 2003.

Weiner, Annette. *Inalienable Possessions: The Paradox of Keeping While Giving*. Berkeley: University of California Press, 1992.

Wells, Allen. "Henequen." *The Second Conquest of Latin America: Coffee, Henequen, and Oil during the Export Boom, 1850–1930*, ed. Steven C. Topik and Allen Wells. Austin: University of Texas Press, 1998.

———. *Yucatán's Gilded Age: Haciendas, Henequen, and International Harvester,* 1860–1915. Albuquerque: University of New Mexico Press, 1985.

Wells, Allen, and Gilbert M. Joseph. *Summer of Discontent, Seasons of Upheaval.* Stanford: Stanford University Press, 1996.

White, Hayden. *The Content of the Form: Narrative Discourse and Historical Representation.* Baltimore: Johns Hopkins University Press, 1990.

Wolf, Eric R. "Types of Latin American Peasantry: A Preliminary Discussion." *American Anthropologist* 57:3 (June 1955), 452–71.

Young, James E. *The Texture of Memory: Holocaust Memorials and Meaning.* New Haven: Yale University Press, 1994.

Zelizer, Viviana A. *The Social Meaning of Money: Pin Money, Paychecks, Poor Relief, and Other Currencies.* Princeton: Princeton University Press, 1997.

INDEX

PAUL K. EISS is an associate professor of anthropology and history and also the director of the Center for the Arts in Society at Carnegie Mellon University.

Library of Congress Cataloging-in-Publication Data

Eiss, Paul K.
In the name of el Pueblo : place, community,
and the politics of history in Yucatán / Paul K. Eiss.
p. cm. — (Latin America otherwise)
Includes bibliographical references and index.
ISBN 978-0-8223-4711-8 (cloth : alk. paper)
ISBN 978-0-8223-4727-9 (pbk. : alk. paper)
1. Yucatán (Mexico : State)—History.
2. Yucatán (Mexico : State)—Social conditions.
I. Title. II. Series: Latin America otherwise.
F1376.E377 2010
972'.65—dc22   2009051108